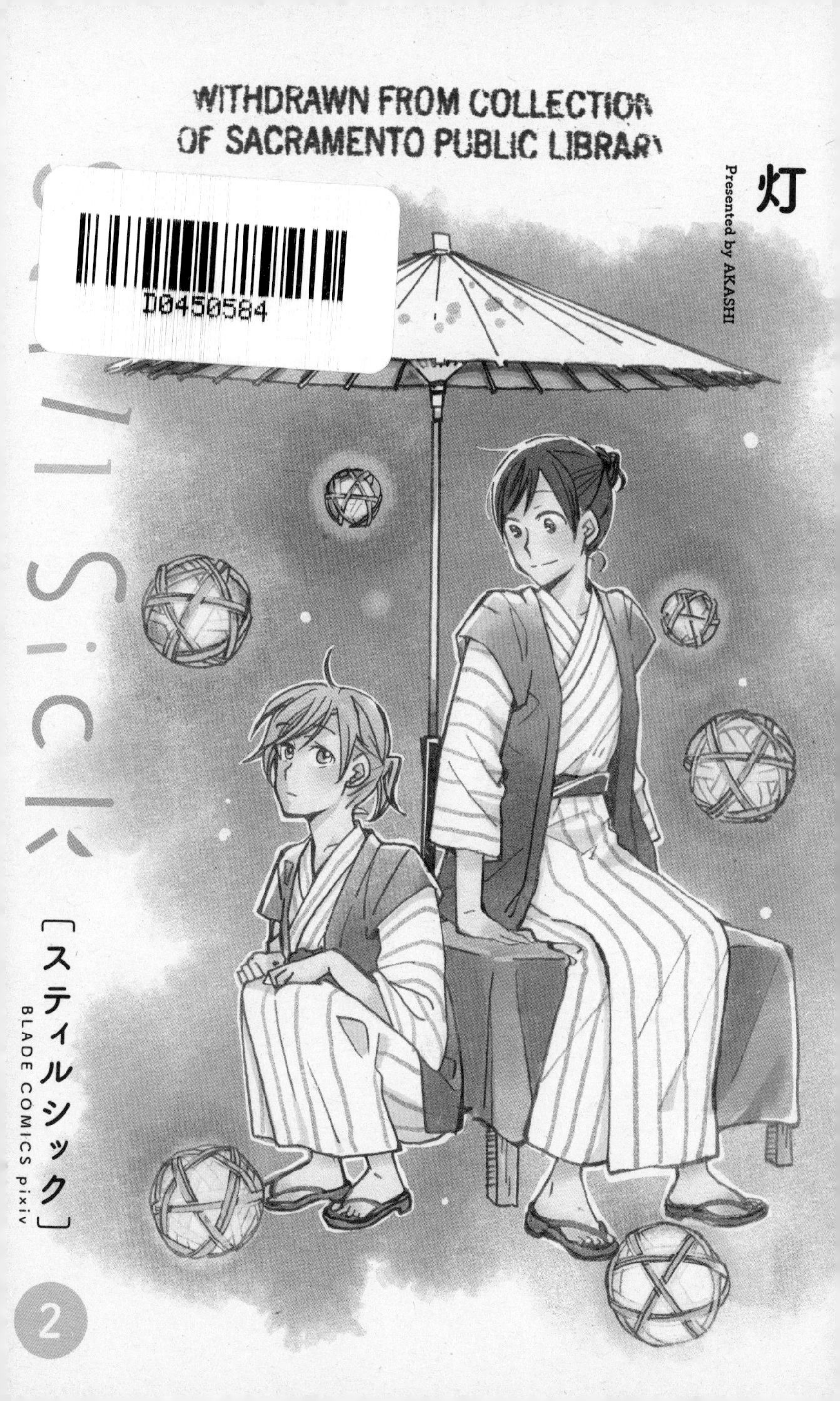
灯
Presented by AKASHI
Still Sick
[スティルシック]
BLADE COMICS pixiv
2

[CONTENTS]

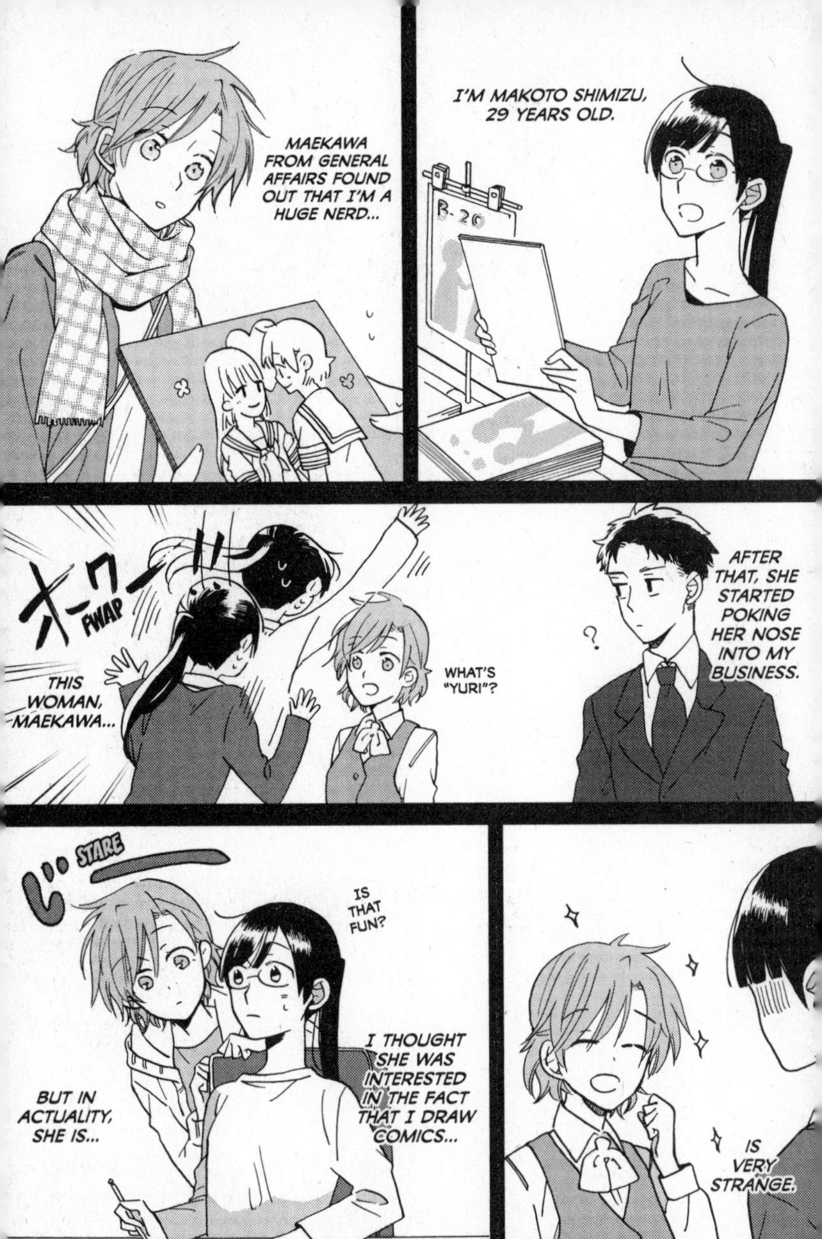
I'M MAKOTO SHIMIZU, 29 YEARS OLD.
B-20
MAEKAWA FROM GENERAL AFFAIRS FOUND OUT THAT I'M A HUGE NERD...
AFTER THAT, SHE STARTED POKING HER NOSE INTO MY BUSINESS.
WHAT'S "YURI"?
PWAP
THIS WOMAN, MAEKAWA...
IS VERY STRANGE.
IS THAT FUN?
STARE
I THOUGHT SHE WAS INTERESTED IN THE FACT THAT I DRAW COMICS...
BUT IN ACTUALITY, SHE IS...

*IN JAPAN, MANGA CREATO

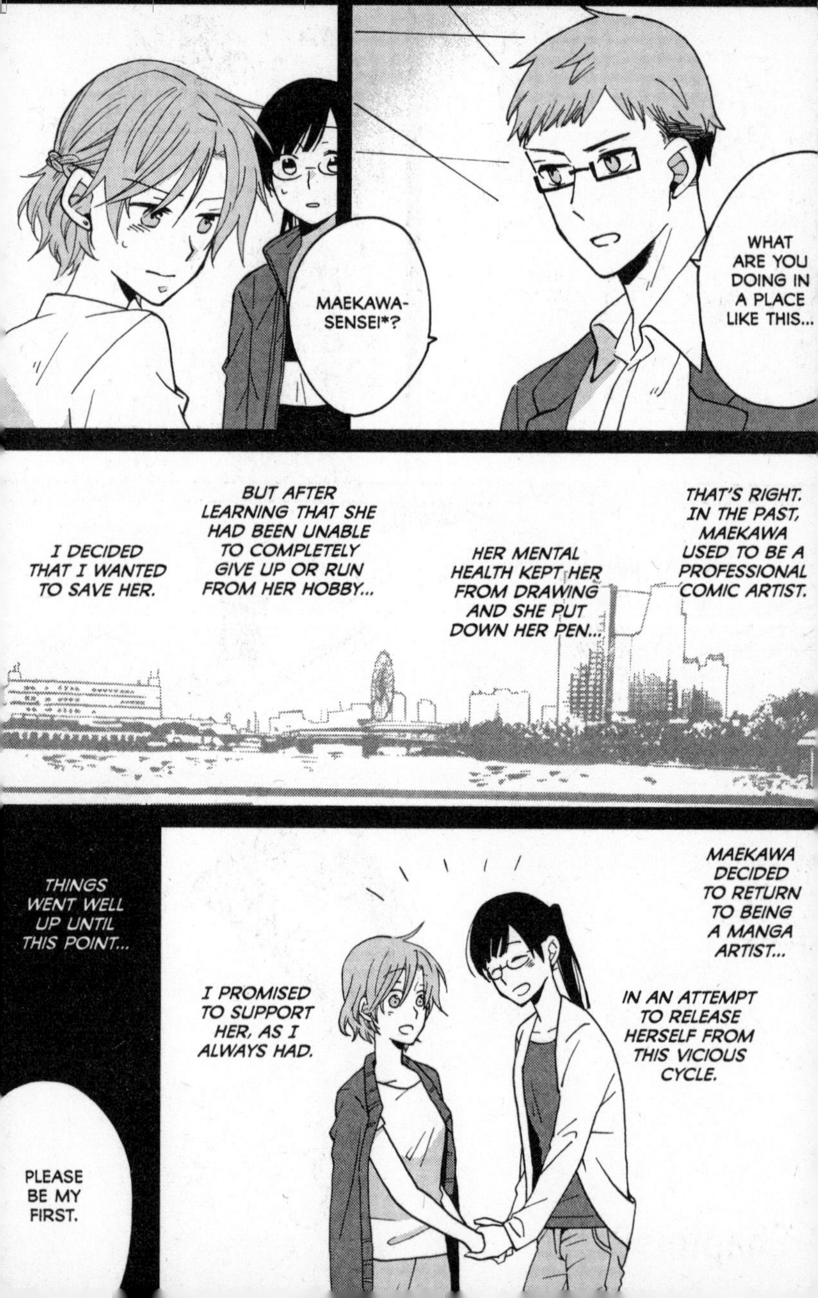
WHAT ARE YOU DOING IN A PLACE LIKE THIS...
MAEKAWA-SENSEI*?
THAT'S RIGHT. IN THE PAST, MAEKAWA USED TO BE A PROFESSIONAL COMIC ARTIST.
HER MENTAL HEALTH KEPT HER FROM DRAWING AND SHE PUT DOWN HER PEN...
BUT AFTER LEARNING THAT SHE HAD BEEN UNABLE TO COMPLETELY GIVE UP OR RUN FROM HER HOBBY...
I DECIDED THAT I WANTED TO SAVE HER.
MAEKAWA DECIDED TO RETURN TO BEING A MANGA ARTIST...
IN AN ATTEMPT TO RELEASE HERSELF FROM THIS VICIOUS CYCLE.
I PROMISED TO SUPPORT HER, AS I ALWAYS HAD.
THINGS WENT WELL UP UNTIL THIS POINT...
PLEASE BE MY FIRST.

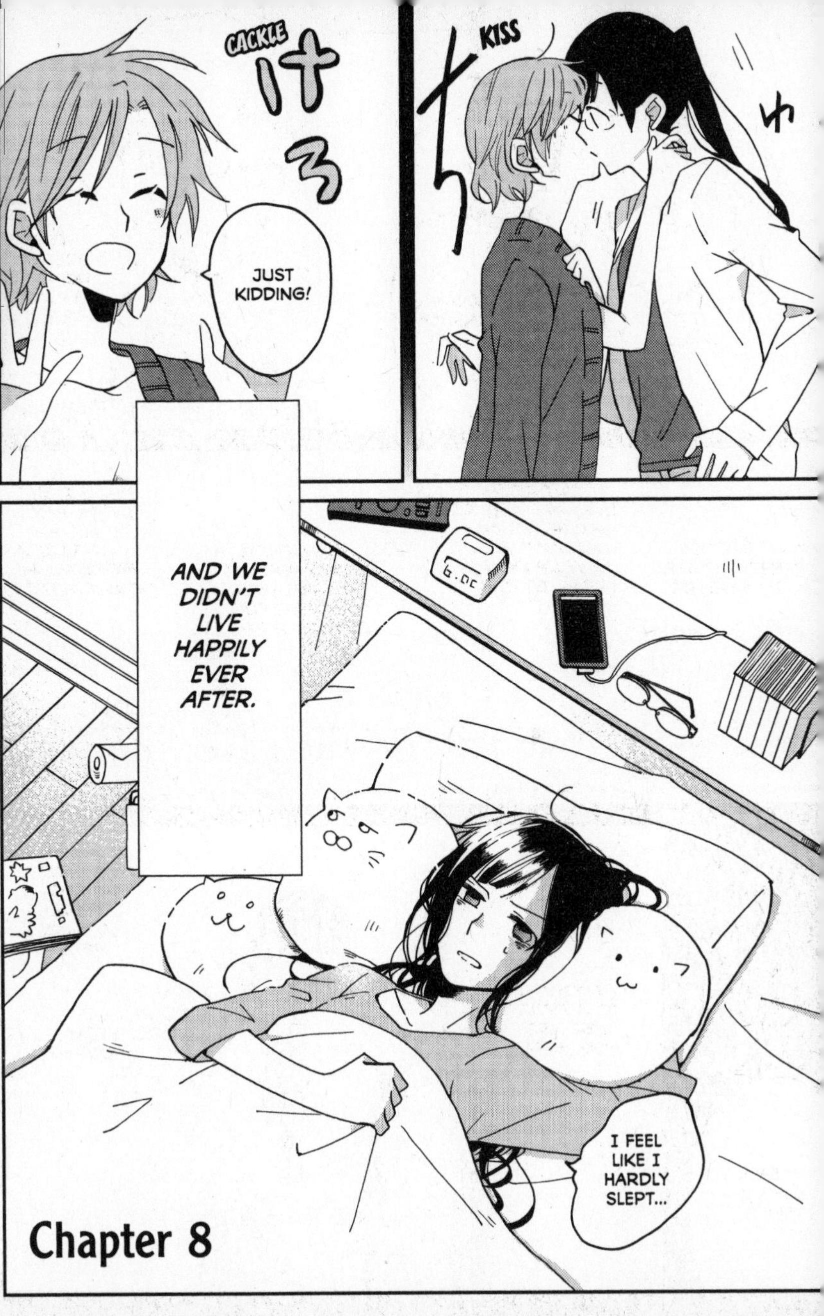
KISS
ちゅ
CACKLE
けろ
JUST KIDDING!
AND WE DIDN'T LIVE HAPPILY EVER AFTER.
I FEEL LIKE I HARDLY SLEPT...
Chapter 8

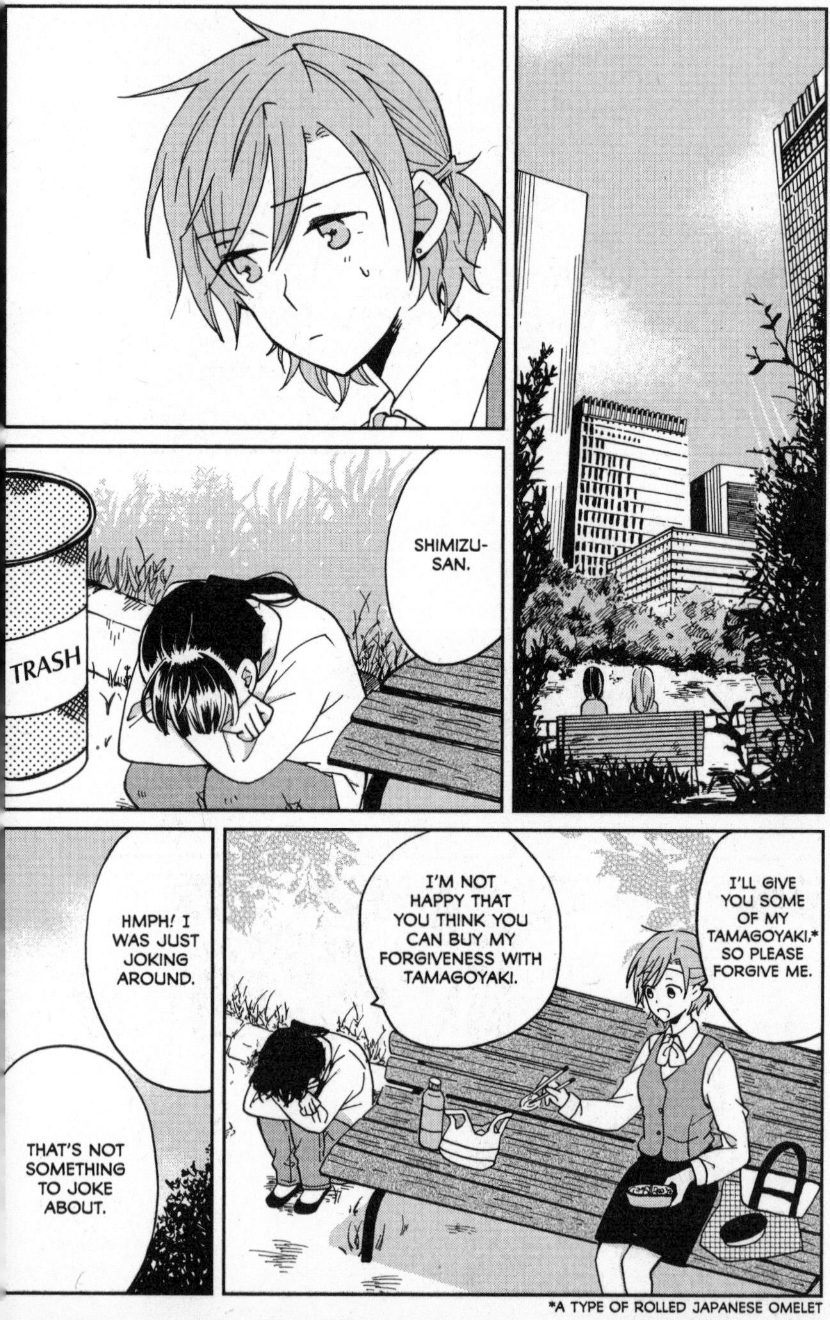
SHIMIZU-SAN.
TRASH
I'LL GIVE YOU SOME OF MY TAMAGOYAKI,* SO PLEASE FORGIVE ME.
I'M NOT HAPPY THAT YOU THINK YOU CAN BUY MY FORGIVENESS WITH TAMAGOYAKI.
HMPH! I WAS JUST JOKING AROUND.
THAT'S NOT SOMETHING TO JOKE ABOUT.

*A TYPE OF ROLLED JAPANESE OMELET

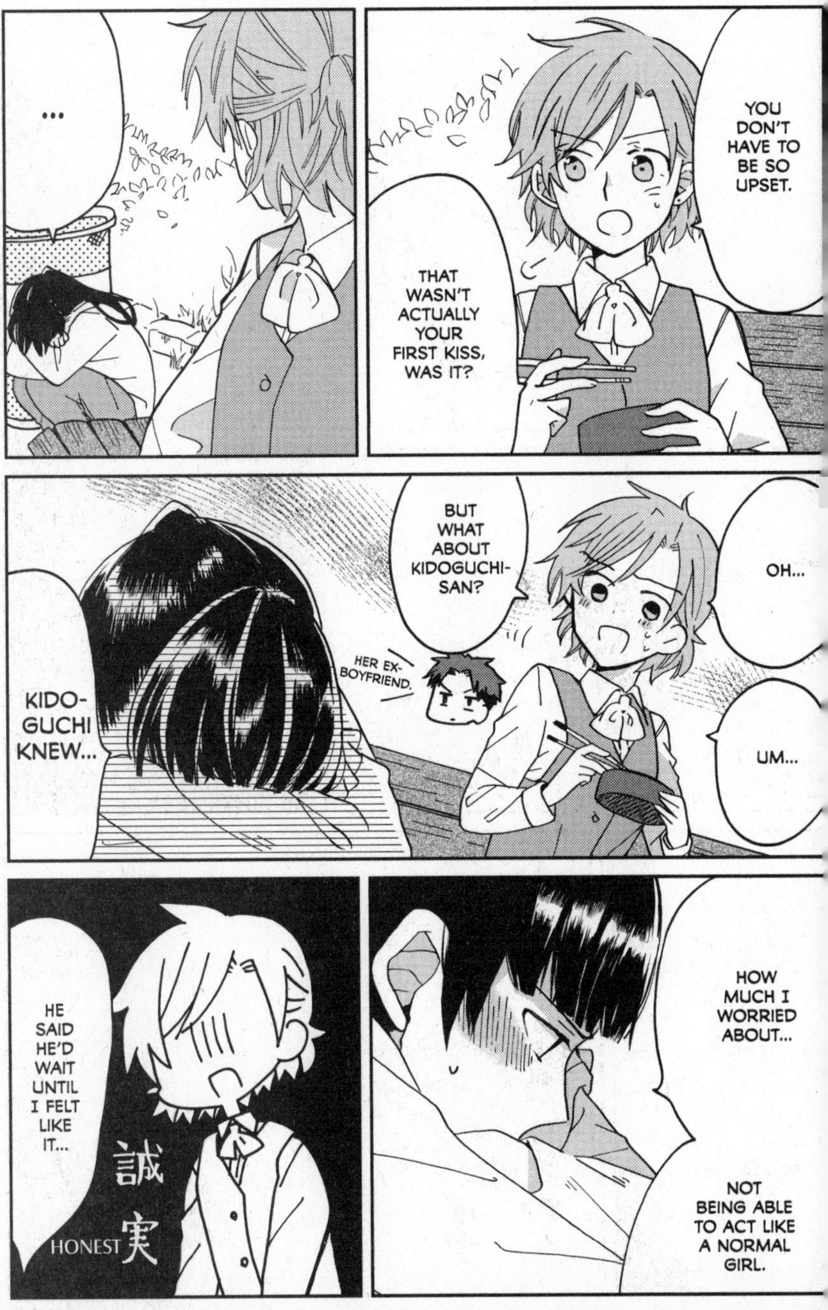
YOU DON'T HAVE TO BE SO UPSET.
THAT WASN'T ACTUALLY YOUR FIRST KISS, WAS IT?
...
OH...
BUT WHAT ABOUT KIDOGUCHI-SAN?
UM...
HER EX-BOYFRIEND.
KIDOGUCHI KNEW...
HOW MUCH I WORRIED ABOUT...
NOT BEING ABLE TO ACT LIKE A NORMAL GIRL.
HE SAID HE'D WAIT UNTIL I FELT LIKE IT...
誠実
HONEST

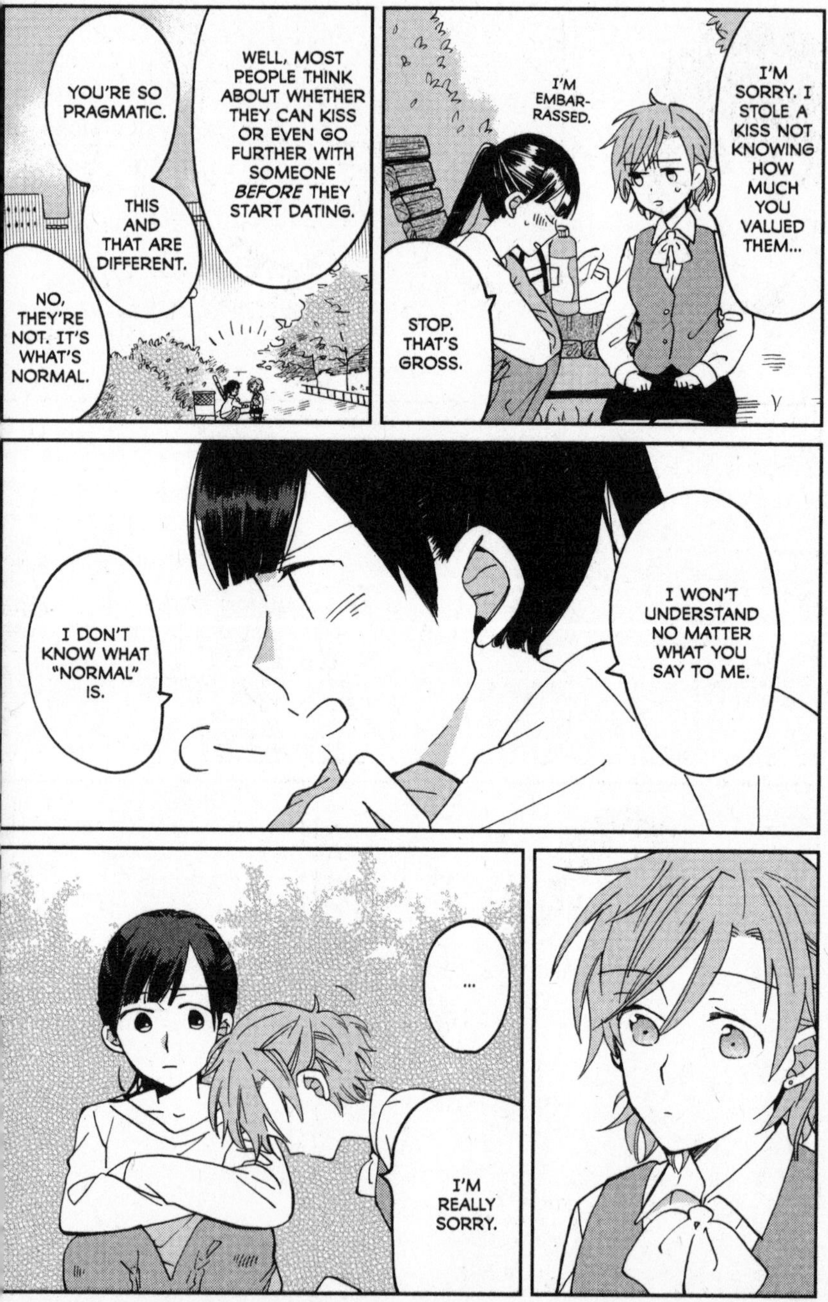
I'M SORRY. I STOLE A KISS NOT KNOWING HOW MUCH YOU VALUED THEM...
I'M EMBAR-RASSED.
STOP. THAT'S GROSS.
WELL, MOST PEOPLE THINK ABOUT WHETHER THEY CAN KISS OR EVEN GO FURTHER WITH SOMEONE *BEFORE* THEY START DATING.
YOU'RE SO PRAGMATIC.
THIS AND THAT ARE DIFFERENT.
NO, THEY'RE NOT. IT'S WHAT'S NORMAL.
I WON'T UNDERSTAND NO MATTER WHAT YOU SAY TO ME.
I DON'T KNOW WHAT "NORMAL" IS.
...
I'M REALLY SORRY.

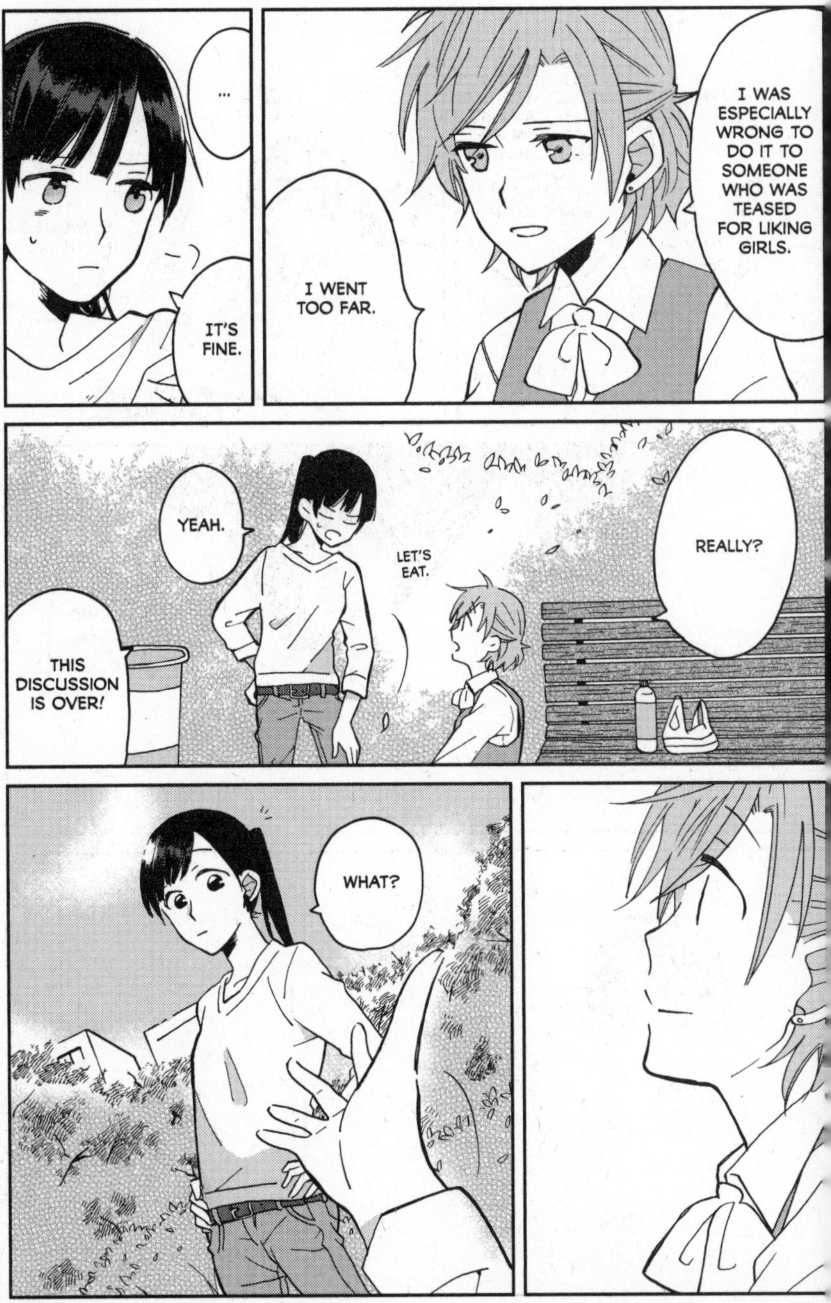

I WAS ESPECIALLY WRONG TO DO IT TO SOMEONE WHO WAS TEASED FOR LIKING GIRLS.
I WENT TOO FAR.
...
IT'S FINE.
REALLY?
LET'S EAT.
YEAH.
THIS DISCUSSION IS OVER!
WHAT?

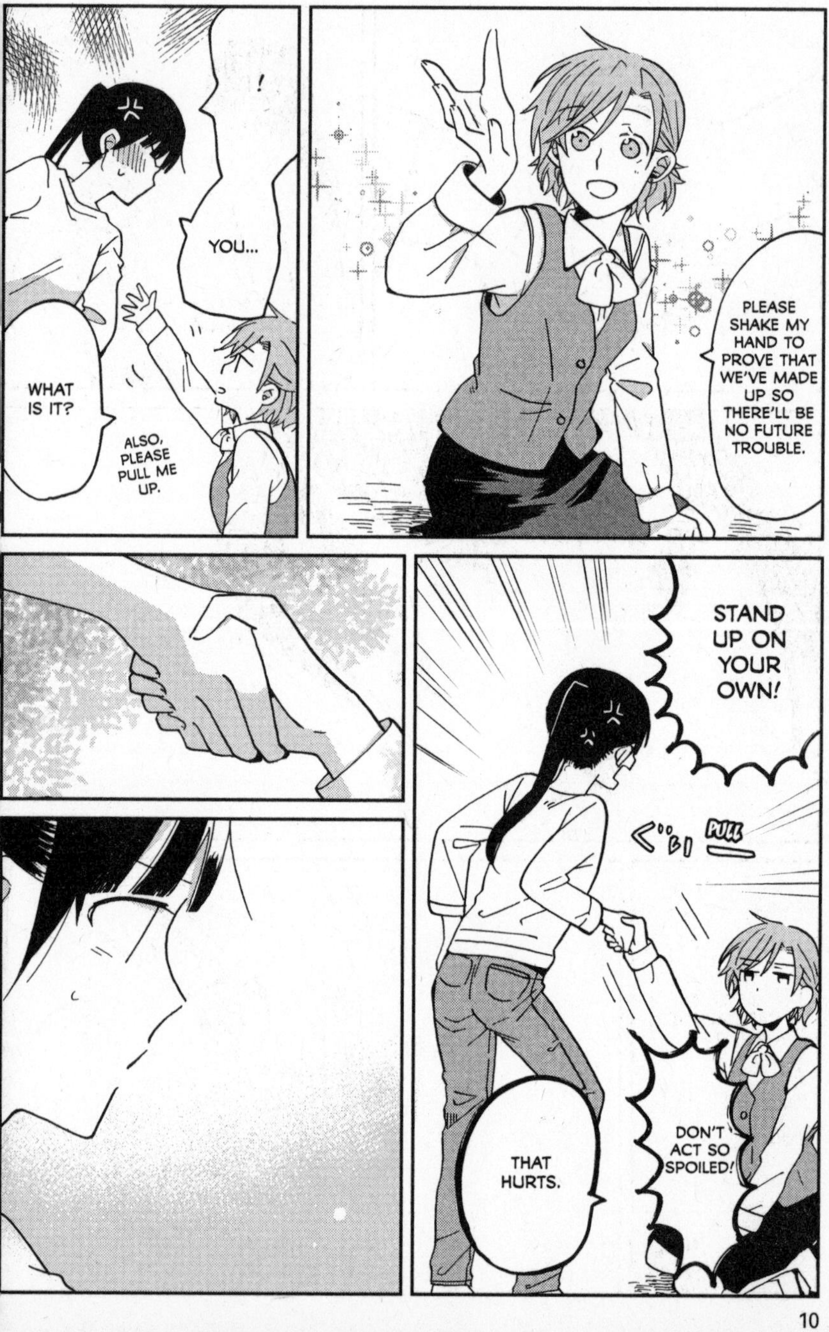
PLEASE SHAKE MY HAND TO PROVE THAT WE'VE MADE UP SO THERE'LL BE NO FUTURE TROUBLE.
!
YOU...
ALSO, PLEASE PULL ME UP.
WHAT IS IT?
STAND UP ON YOUR OWN!
PULL
DON'T ACT SO SPOILED!
THAT HURTS.

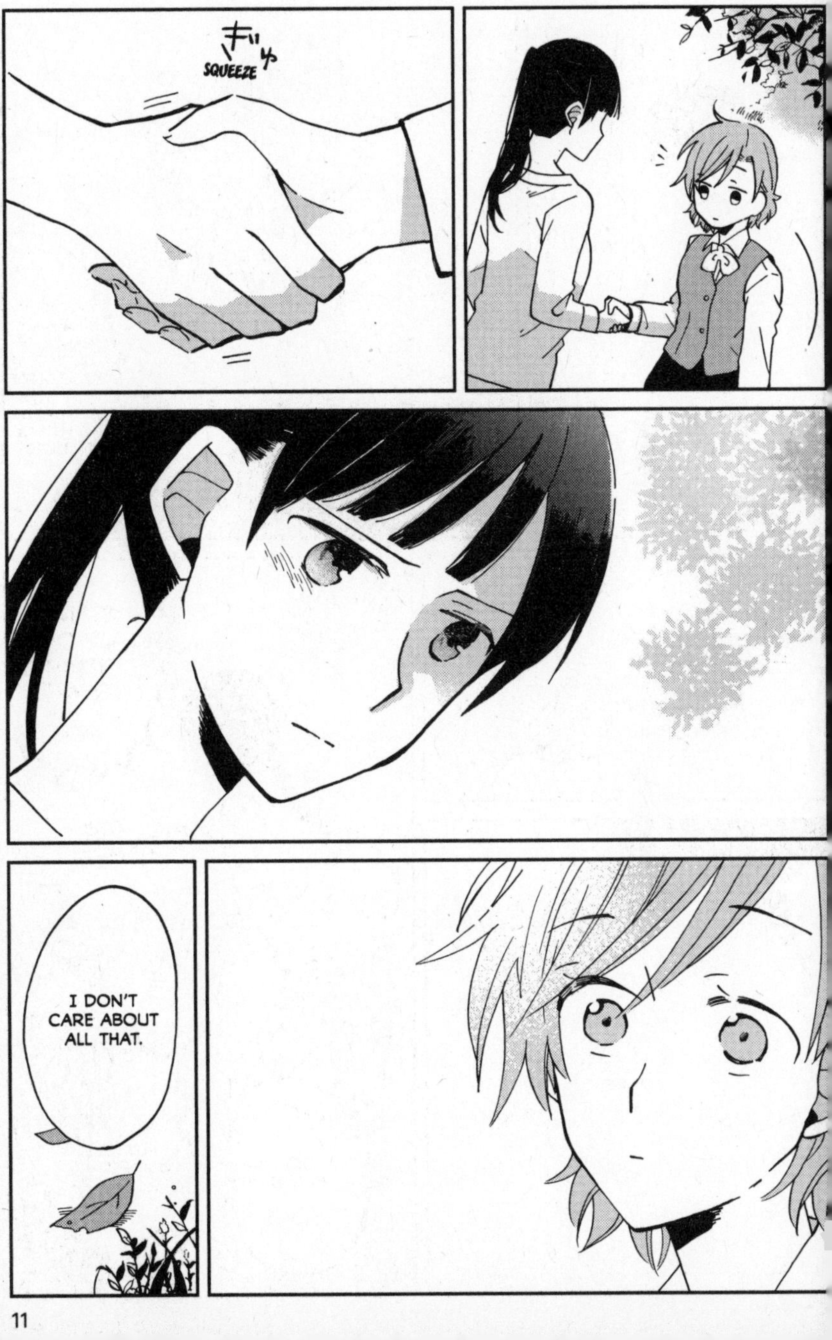
SQUEEZE
I DON'T CARE ABOUT ALL THAT.

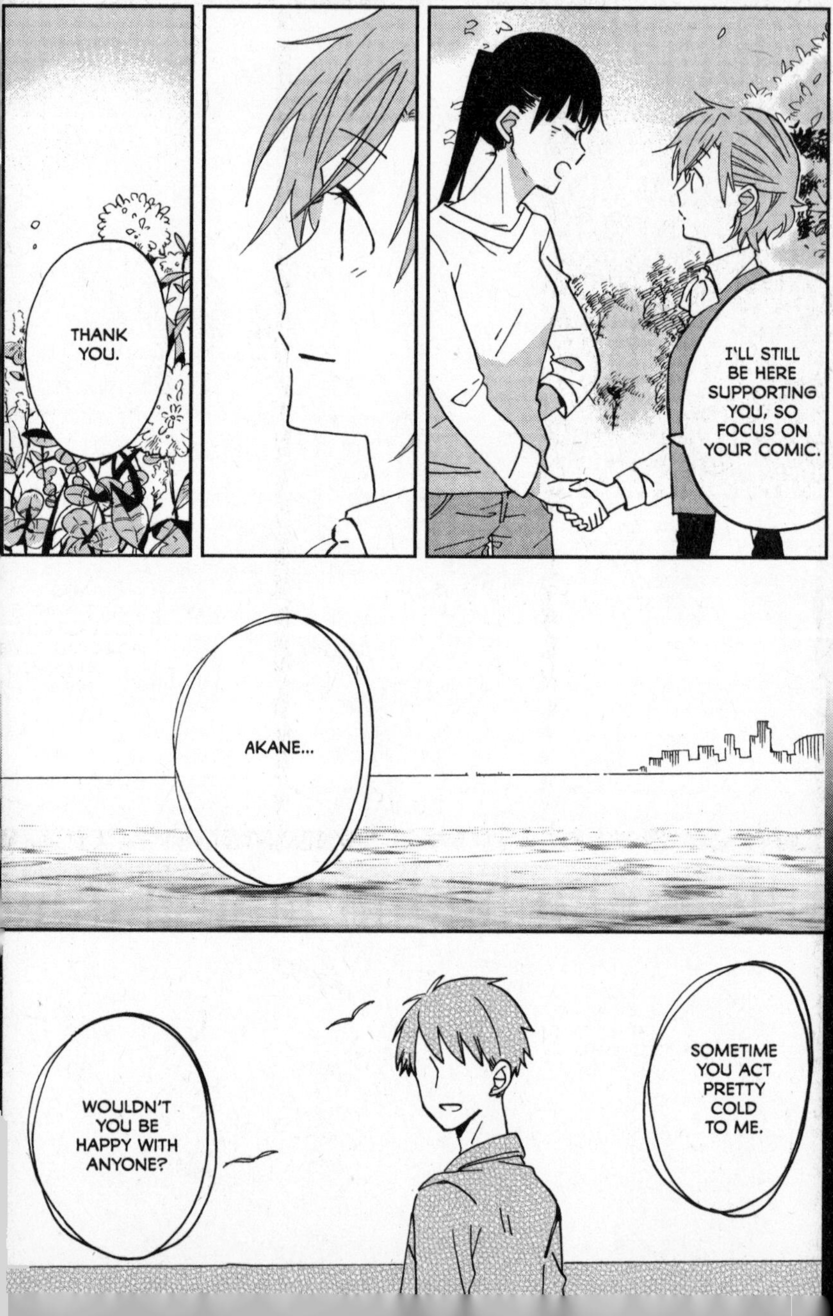
I'LL STILL BE HERE SUPPORTING YOU, SO FOCUS ON YOUR COMIC.
THANK YOU.
AKANE...
SOMETIME YOU ACT PRETTY COLD TO ME.
WOULDN'T YOU BE HAPPY WITH ANYONE?

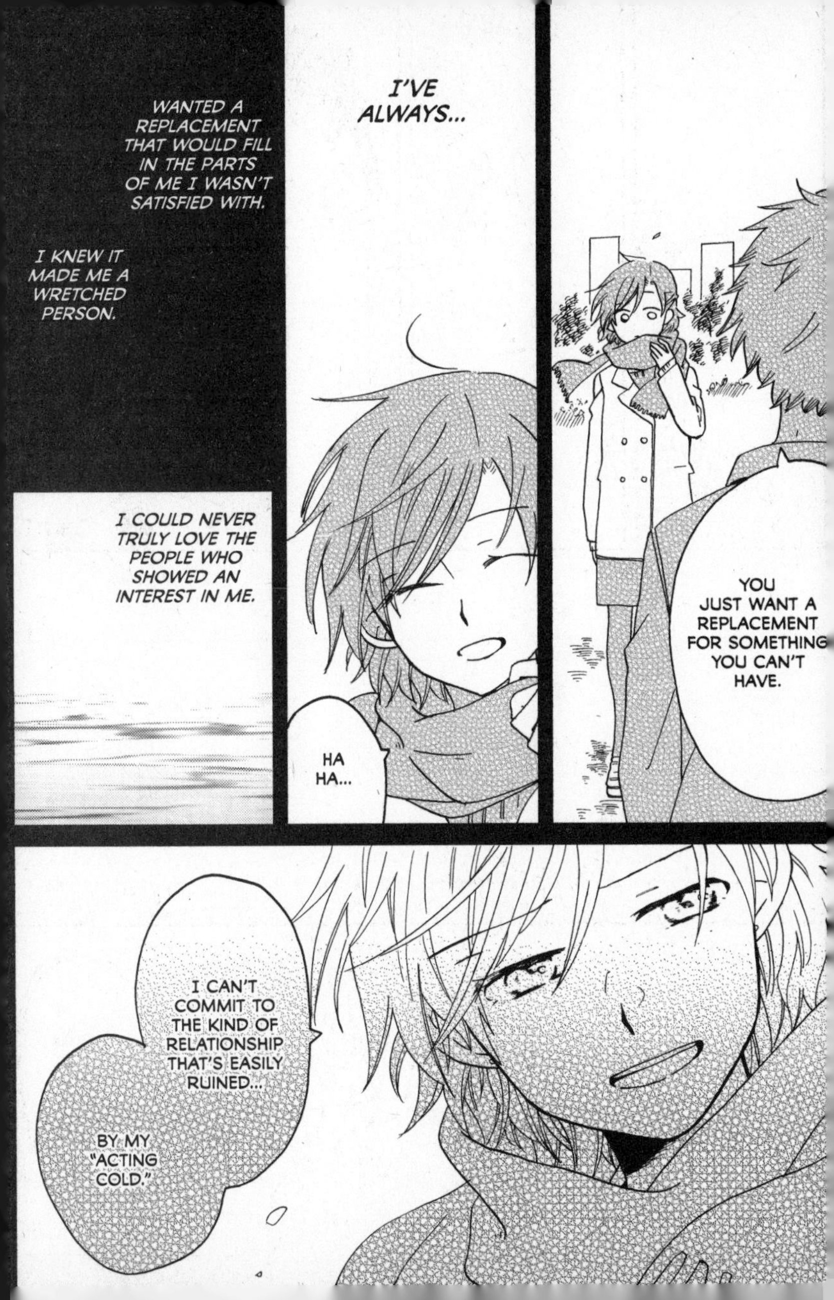
YOU JUST WANT A REPLACEMENT FOR SOMETHING YOU CAN'T HAVE.
I'VE ALWAYS...
HA HA...
WANTED A REPLACEMENT THAT WOULD FILL IN THE PARTS OF ME I WASN'T SATISFIED WITH.
I KNEW IT MADE ME A WRETCHED PERSON.
I COULD NEVER TRULY LOVE THE PEOPLE WHO SHOWED AN INTEREST IN ME.
I CAN'T COMMIT TO THE KIND OF RELATIONSHIP THAT'S EASILY RUINED...
BY MY "ACTING COLD."

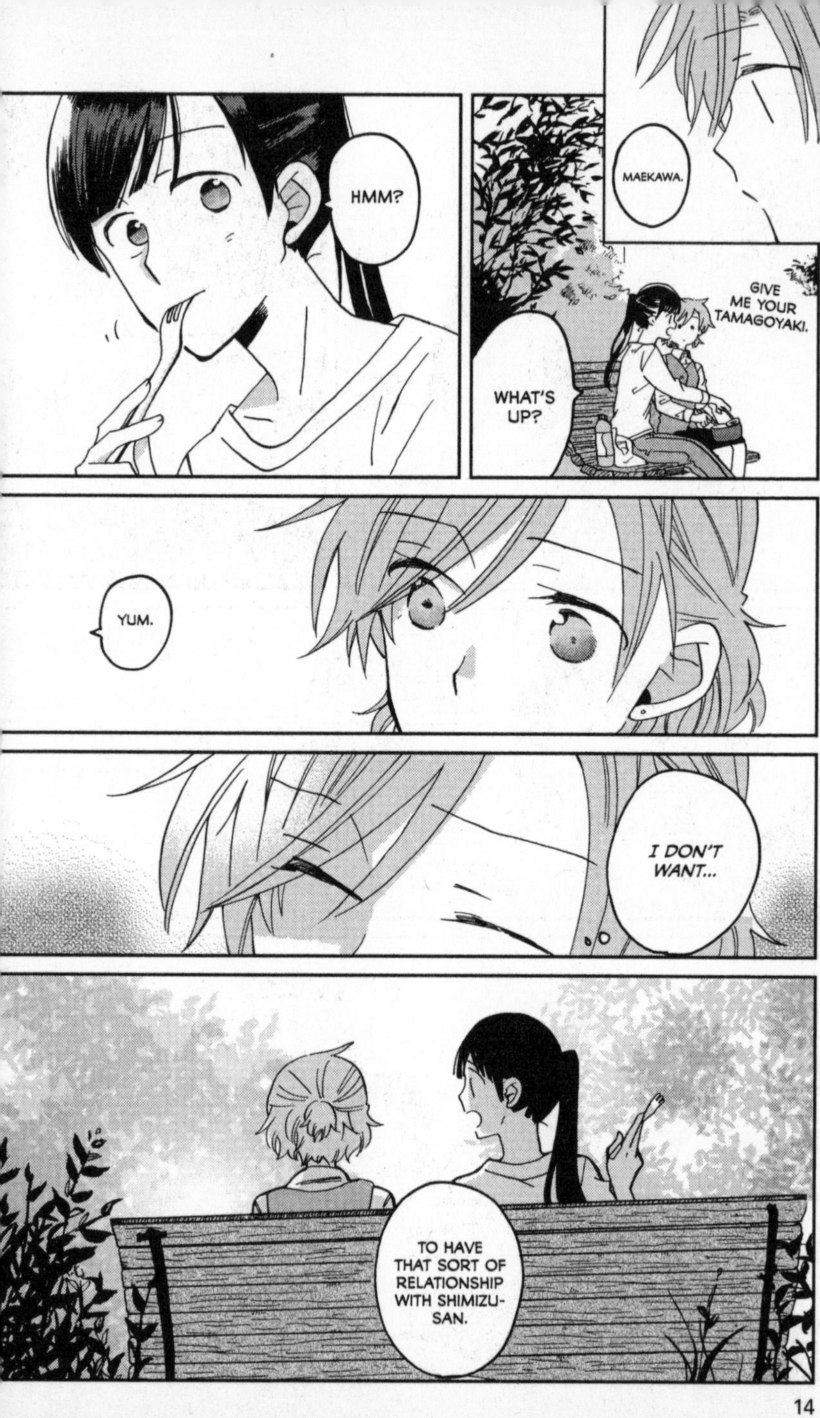

MAEKAWA.
GIVE ME YOUR TAMAGOYAKI.
WHAT'S UP?
HMM?
YUM.
I DON'T WANT...
TO HAVE THAT SORT OF RELATIONSHIP WITH SHIMIZU-SAN.

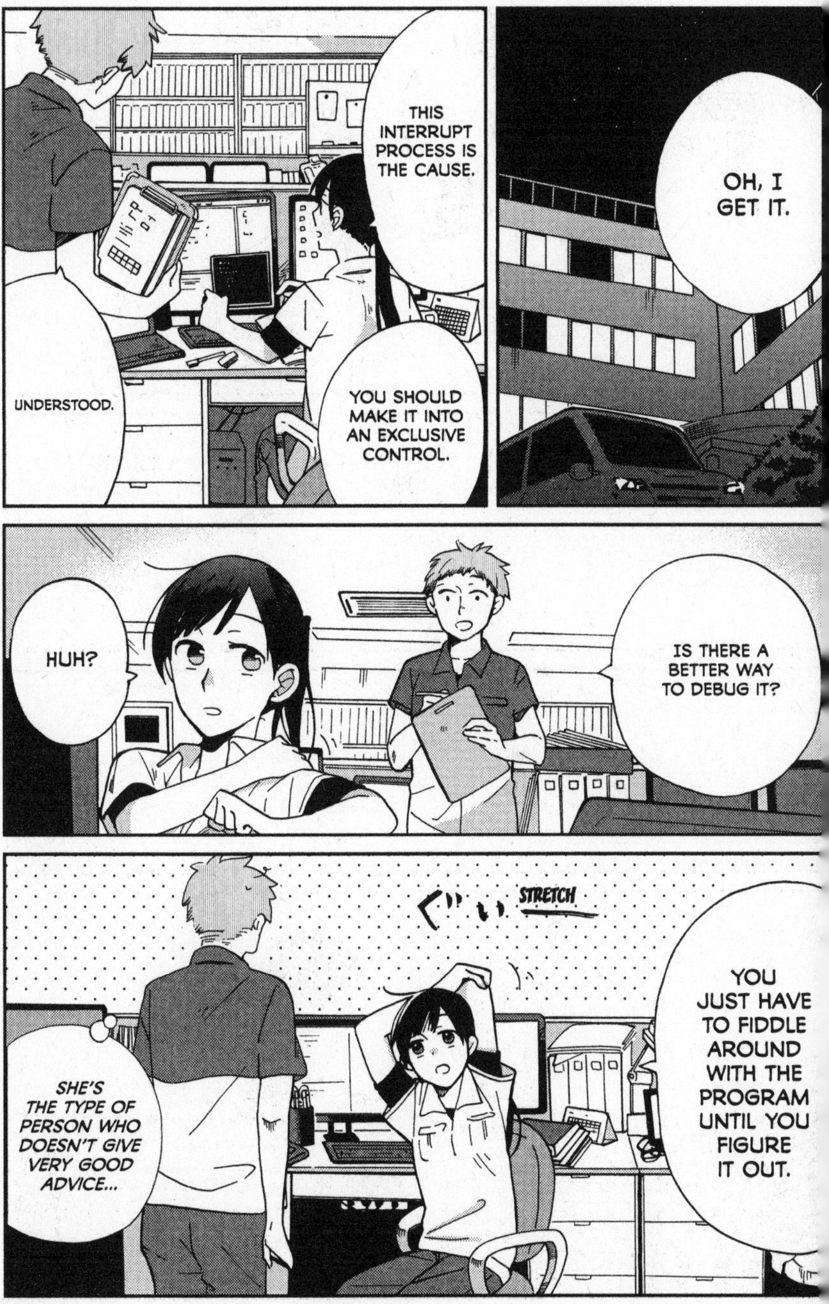
OH, I GET IT.
THIS INTERRUPT PROCESS IS THE CAUSE.
YOU SHOULD MAKE IT INTO AN EXCLUSIVE CONTROL.
UNDERSTOOD.
IS THERE A BETTER WAY TO DEBUG IT?
HUH?
YOU JUST HAVE TO FIDDLE AROUND WITH THE PROGRAM UNTIL YOU FIGURE IT OUT.
STRETCH
SHE'S THE TYPE OF PERSON WHO DOESN'T GIVE VERY GOOD ADVICE...

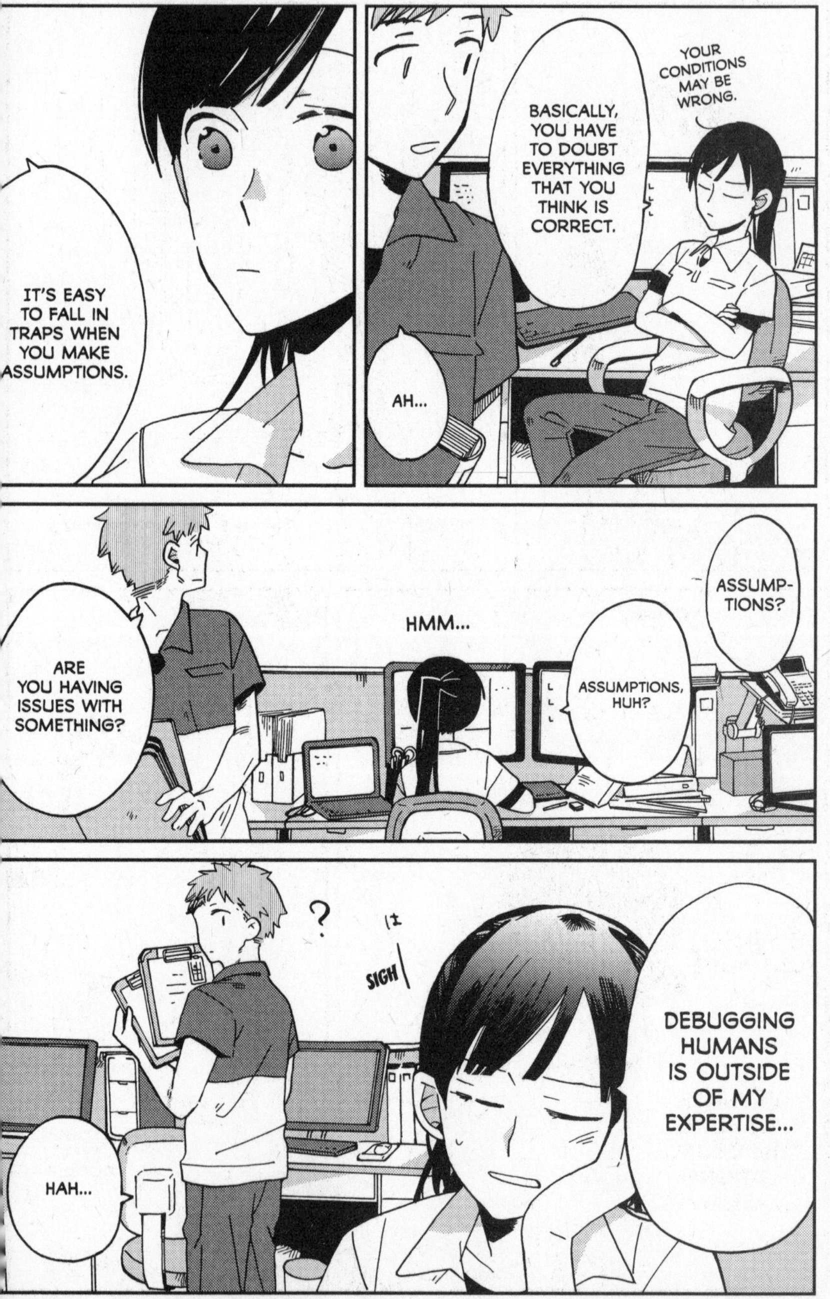
YOUR CONDITIONS MAY BE WRONG.
BASICALLY, YOU HAVE TO DOUBT EVERYTHING THAT YOU THINK IS CORRECT.
AH...
IT'S EASY TO FALL IN TRAPS WHEN YOU MAKE ASSUMPTIONS.
ASSUMP-TIONS?
ASSUMPTIONS, HUH?
HMM...
ARE YOU HAVING ISSUES WITH SOMETHING?
DEBUGGING HUMANS IS OUTSIDE OF MY EXPERTISE...
は
SIGH
?
HAH...

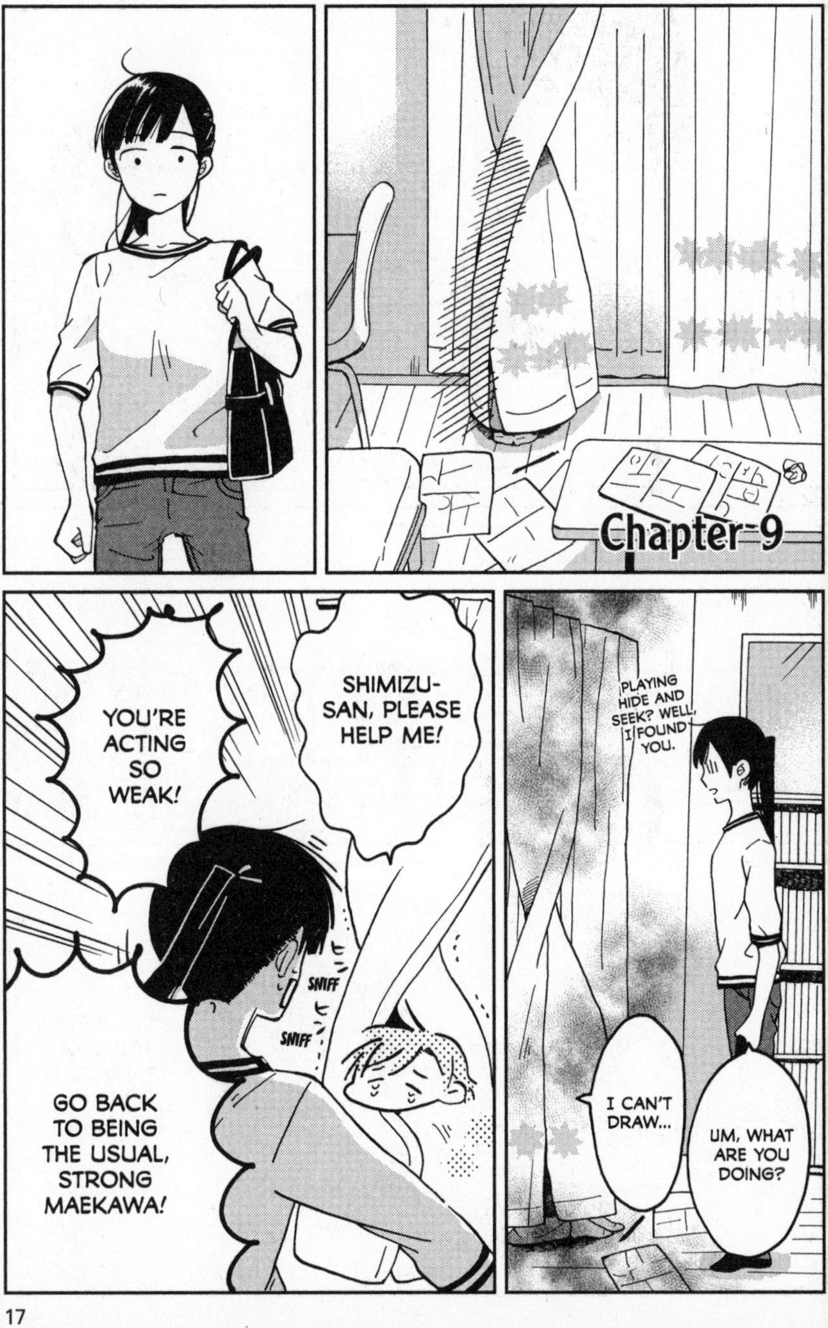
Chapter 9
PLAYING HIDE AND SEEK? WELL, I FOUND YOU.
UM, WHAT ARE YOU DOING?
I CAN'T DRAW...
SHIMIZU-SAN, PLEASE HELP ME!
YOU'RE ACTING SO WEAK!
SNIFF
SNIFF
GO BACK TO BEING THE USUAL, STRONG MAEKAWA!

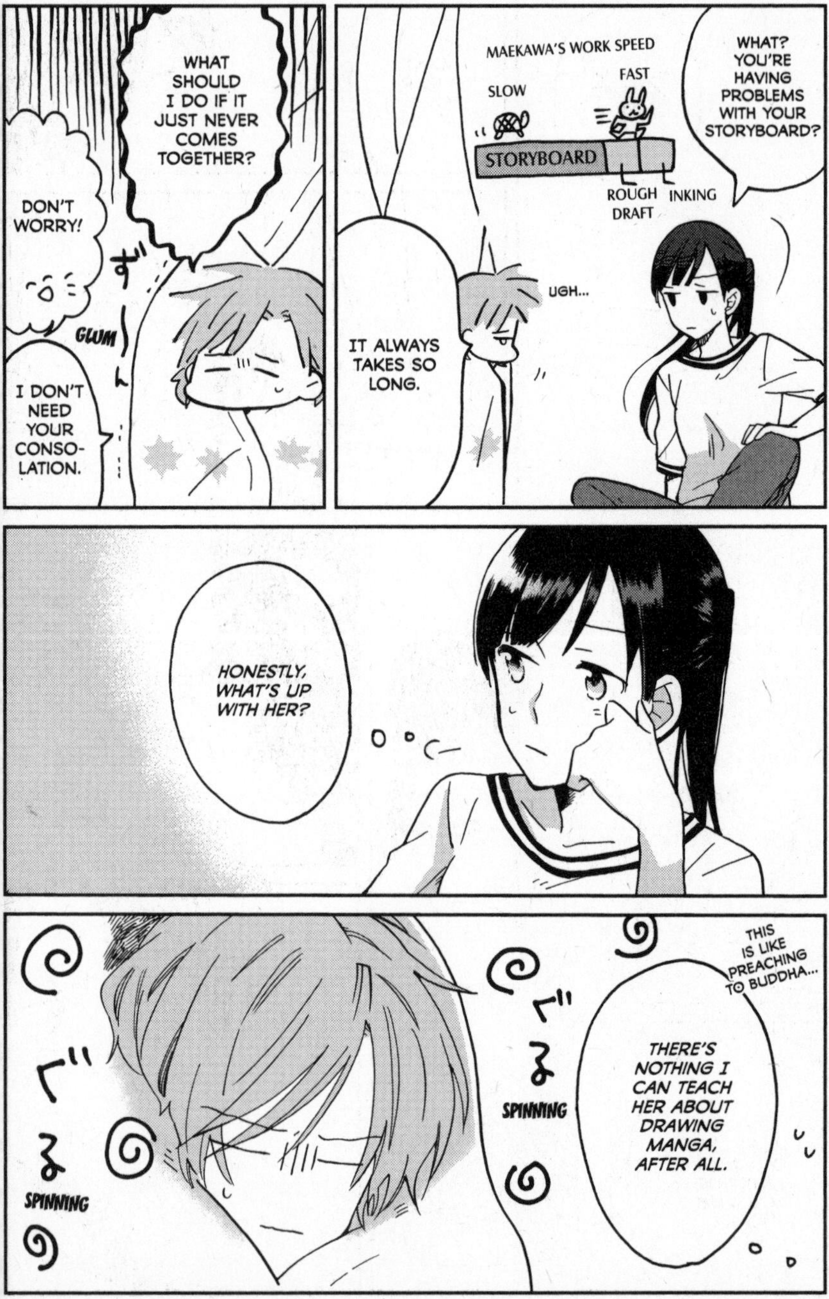
WHAT? YOU'RE HAVING PROBLEMS WITH YOUR STORYBOARD?
MAEKAWA'S WORK SPEED
SLOW
FAST
STORYBOARD
ROUGH DRAFT
INKING
UGH...
IT ALWAYS TAKES SO LONG.
WHAT SHOULD I DO IF IT JUST NEVER COMES TOGETHER?
DON'T WORRY!
GLUM
I DON'T NEED YOUR CONSOLATION.
HONESTLY, WHAT'S UP WITH HER?
THIS IS LIKE PREACHING TO BUDDHA...
THERE'S NOTHING I CAN TEACH HER ABOUT DRAWING MANGA, AFTER ALL.
SPINNING
SPINNING

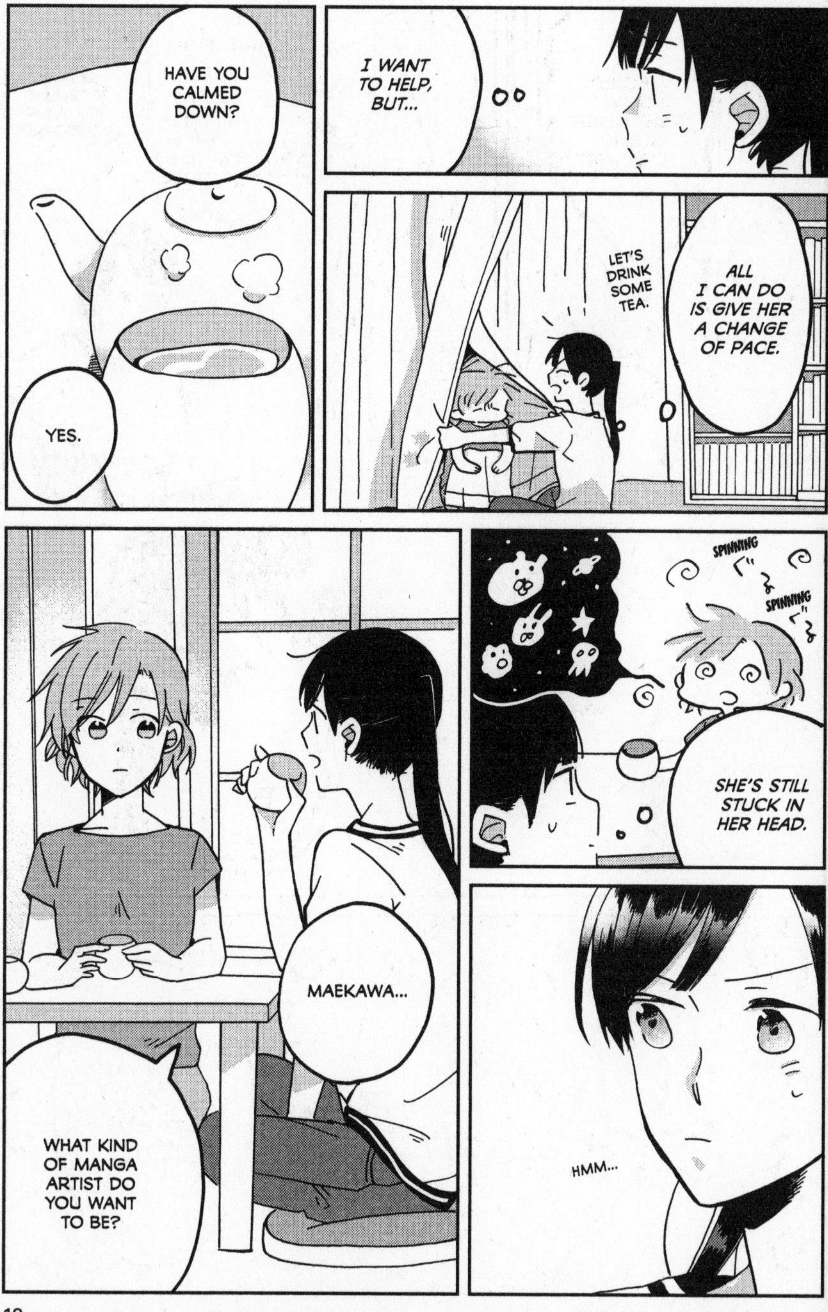

I WANT TO HELP, BUT...
ALL I CAN DO IS GIVE HER A CHANGE OF PACE.
LET'S DRINK SOME TEA.
HAVE YOU CALMED DOWN?
YES.
SPINNING
SPINNING
SHE'S STILL STUCK IN HER HEAD.
HMM...
MAEKAWA...
WHAT KIND OF MANGA ARTIST DO YOU WANT TO BE?

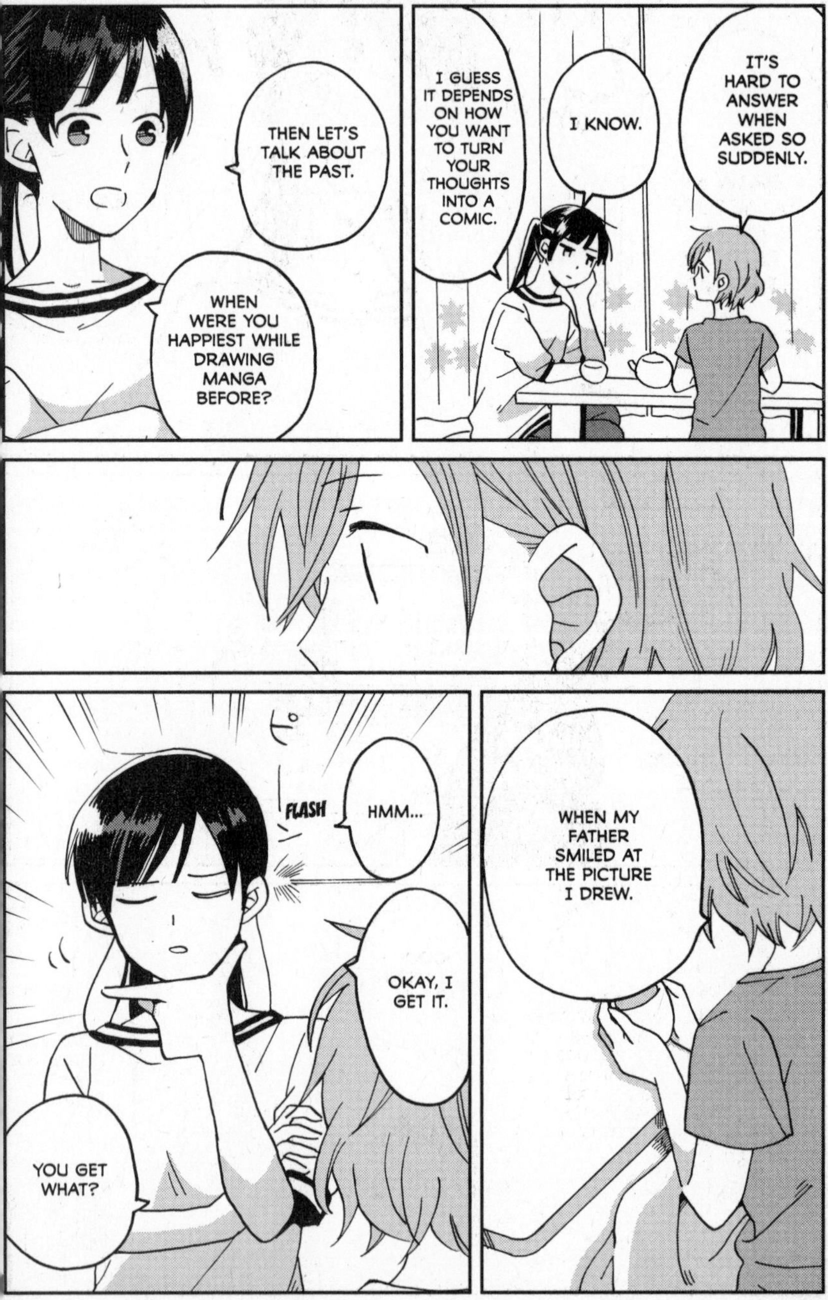
IT'S HARD TO ANSWER WHEN ASKED SO SUDDENLY.
I KNOW.
I GUESS IT DEPENDS ON HOW YOU WANT TO TURN YOUR THOUGHTS INTO A COMIC.
THEN LET'S TALK ABOUT THE PAST.
WHEN WERE YOU HAPPIEST WHILE DRAWING MANGA BEFORE?
WHEN MY FATHER SMILED AT THE PICTURE I DREW.
HMM...
FLASH
OKAY, I GET IT.
YOU GET WHAT?

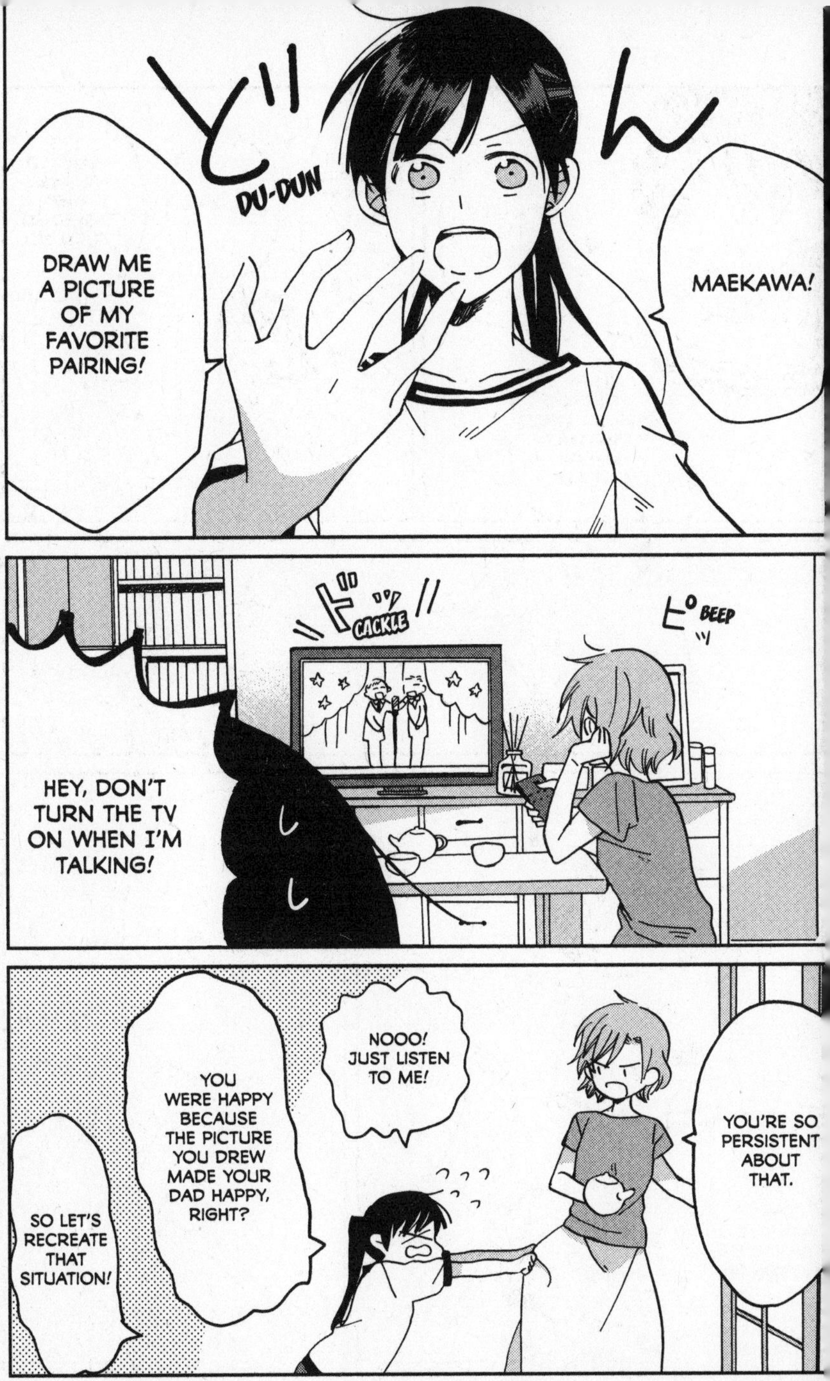
MAEKAWA!
DU-DUN
DRAW ME A PICTURE OF MY FAVORITE PAIRING!
BEEP
CACKLE
HEY, DON'T TURN THE TV ON WHEN I'M TALKING!
YOU'RE SO PERSISTENT ABOUT THAT.
NOOO! JUST LISTEN TO ME!
YOU WERE HAPPY BECAUSE THE PICTURE YOU DREW MADE YOUR DAD HAPPY, RIGHT?
SO LET'S RECREATE THAT SITUATION!

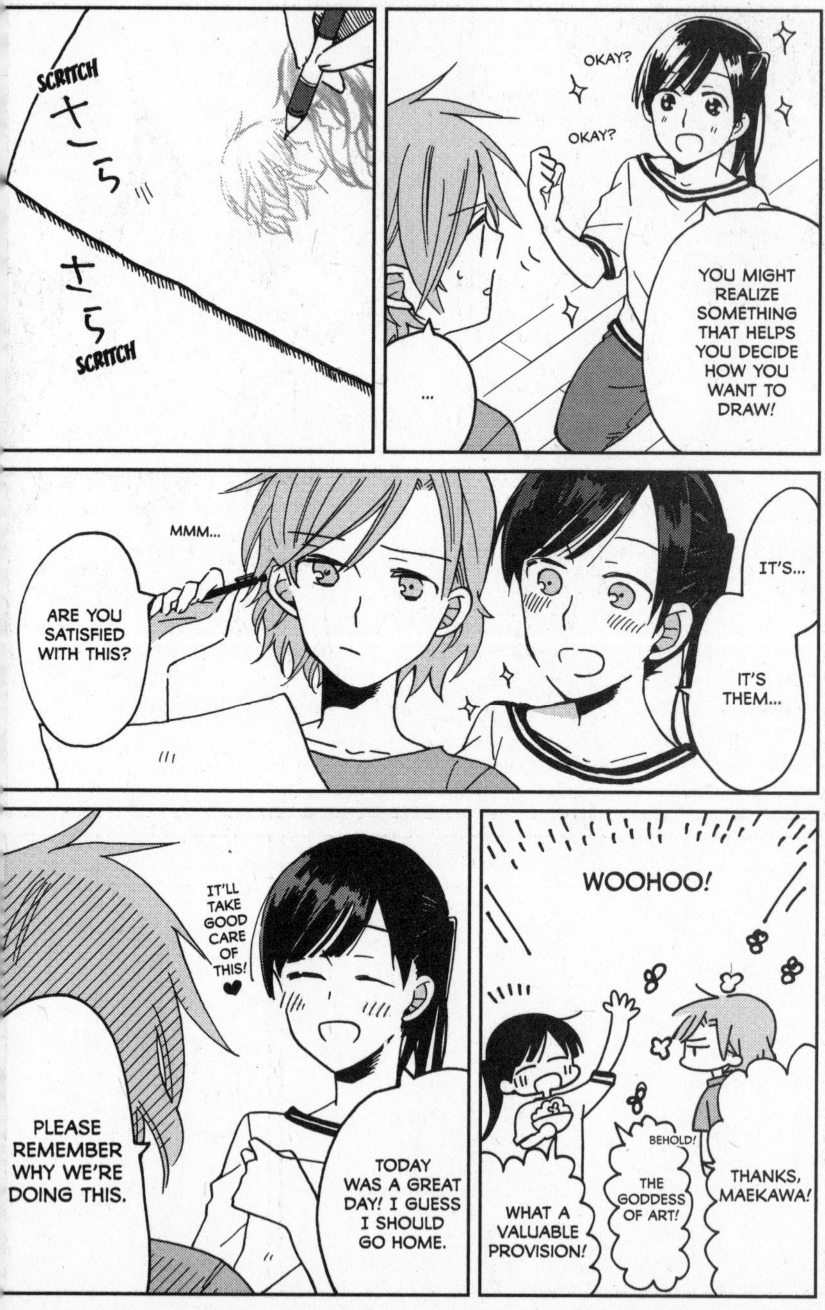
OKAY?
OKAY?
YOU MIGHT REALIZE SOMETHING THAT HELPS YOU DECIDE HOW YOU WANT TO DRAW!
...
SCRITCH
さら
さら
SCRITCH
IT'S...
IT'S THEM...
MMM...
ARE YOU SATISFIED WITH THIS?
WOOHOO!
THANKS, MAEKAWA!
BEHOLD!
THE GODDESS OF ART!
WHAT A VALUABLE PROVISION!
TODAY WAS A GREAT DAY! I GUESS I SHOULD GO HOME.
IT'LL TAKE GOOD CARE OF THIS! ♥
PLEASE REMEMBER WHY WE'RE DOING THIS.

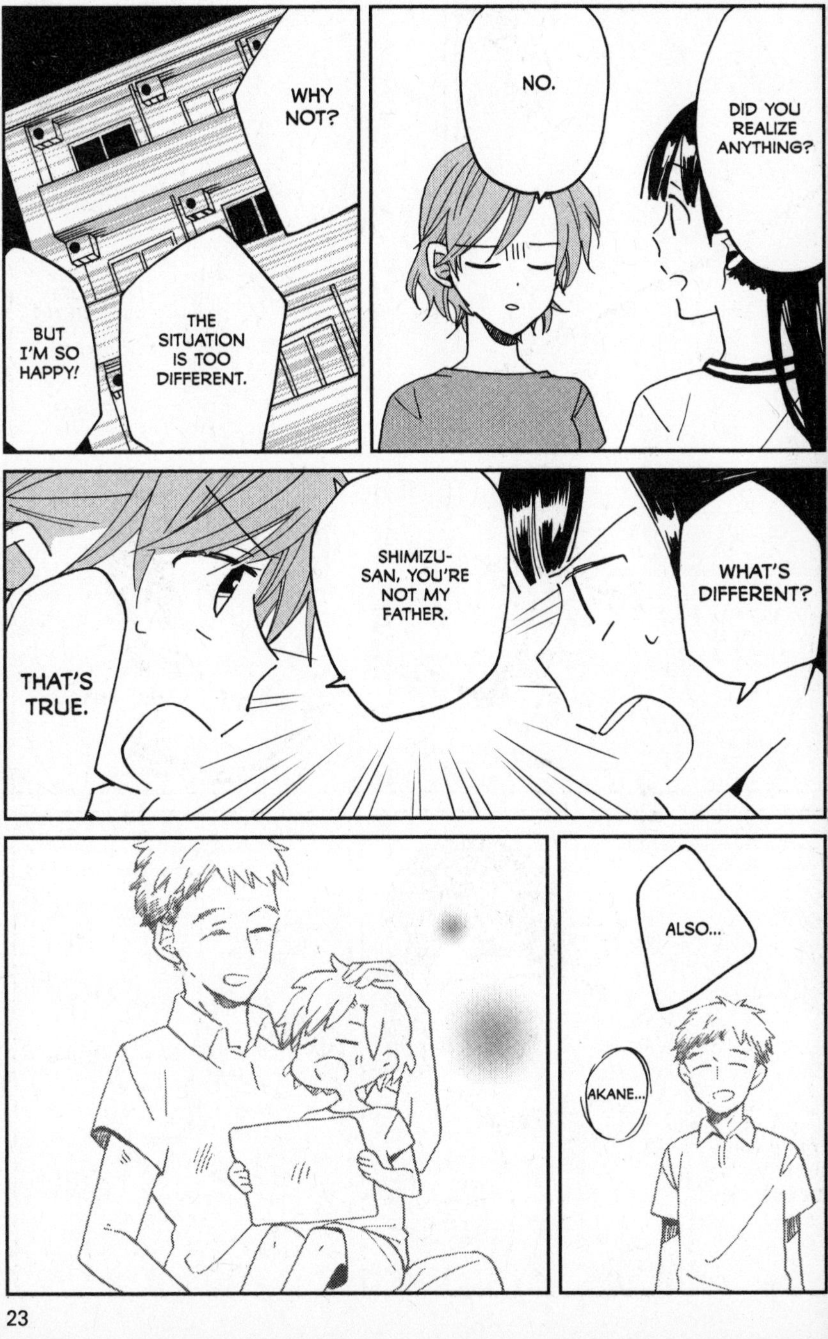
DID YOU REALIZE ANYTHING?
NO.
WHY NOT?
THE SITUATION IS TOO DIFFERENT.
BUT I'M SO HAPPY!
WHAT'S DIFFERENT?
SHIMIZU-SAN, YOU'RE NOT MY FATHER.
THAT'S TRUE.
ALSO...
AKANE...

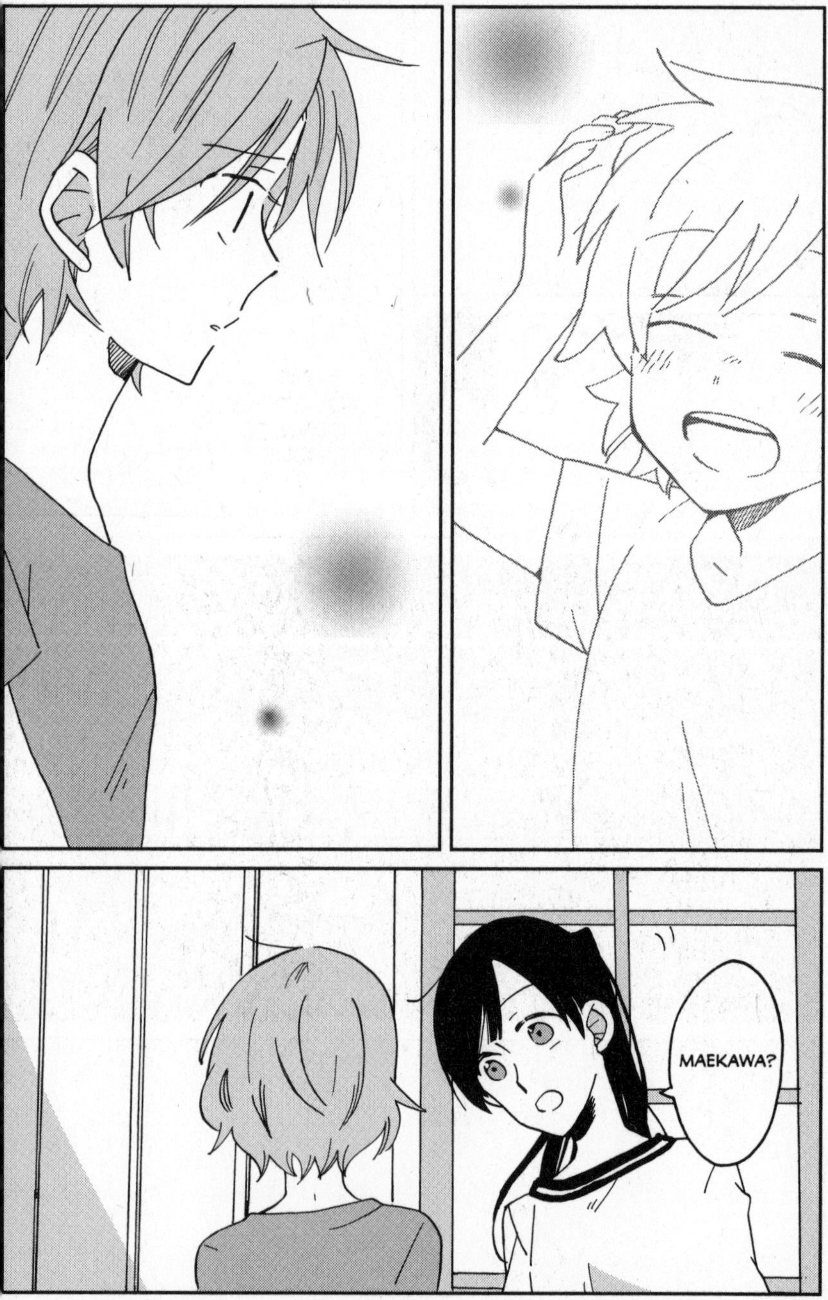
MAEKAWA?

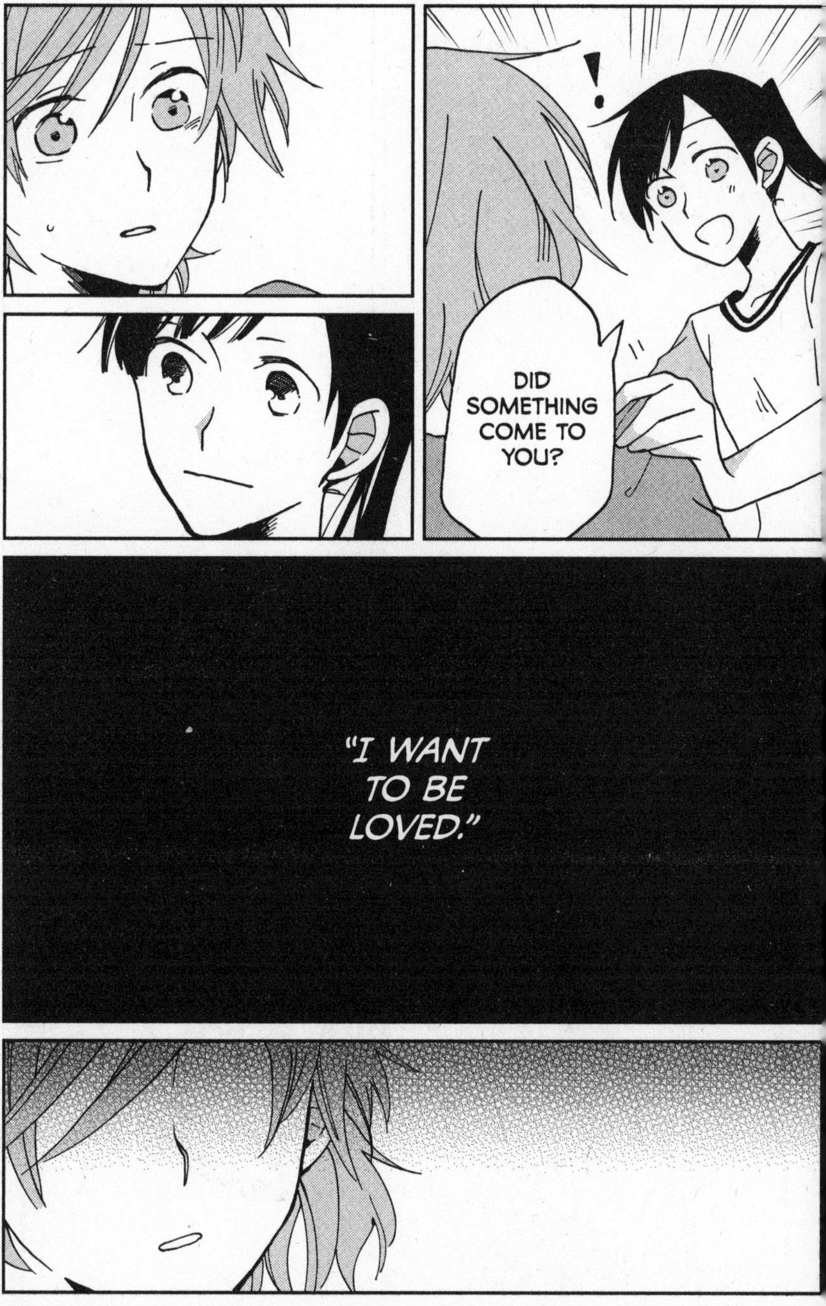
!
DID SOMETHING COME TO YOU?
"I WANT TO BE LOVED."

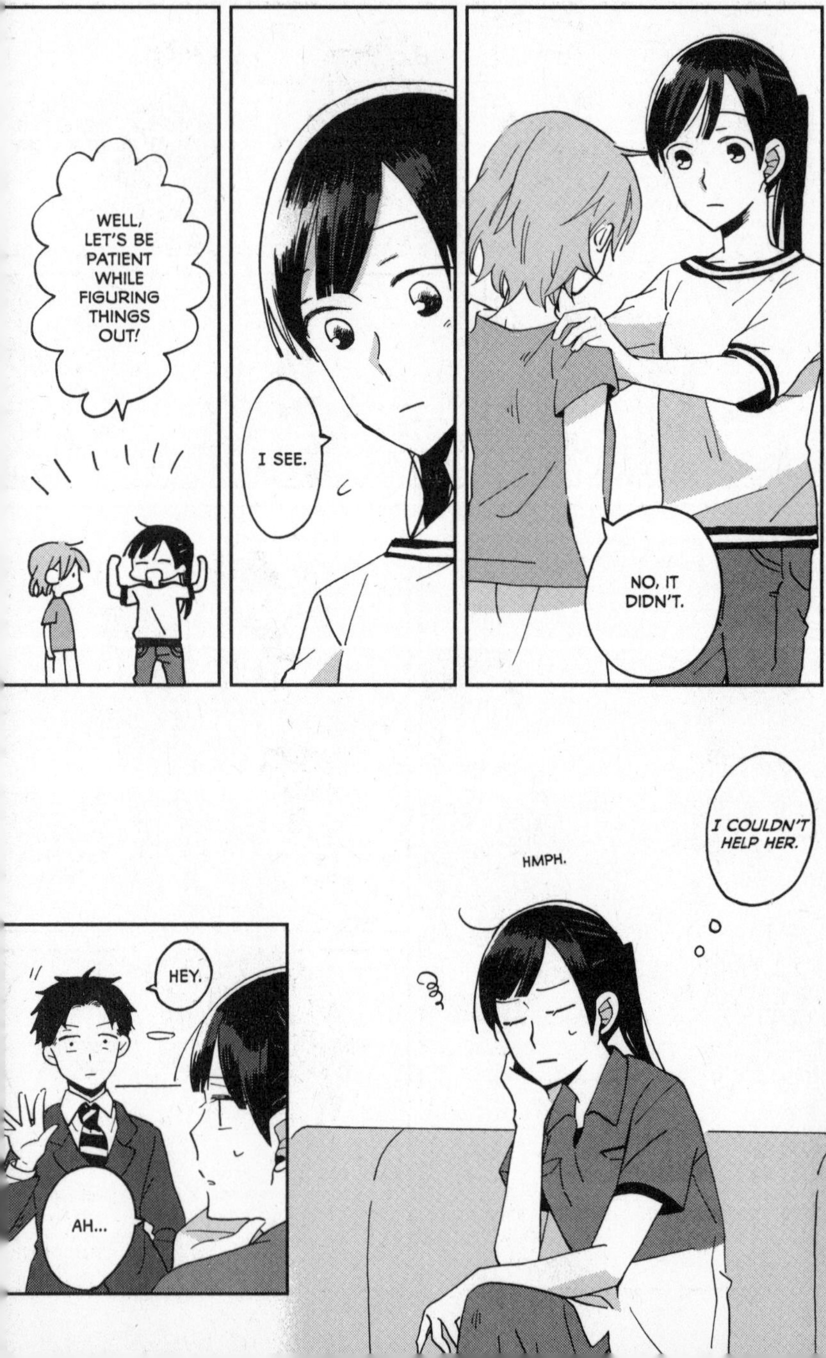
NO, IT DIDN'T.
I SEE.
WELL, LET'S BE PATIENT WHILE FIGURING THINGS OUT!
I COULDN'T HELP HER.
HMPH.
HEY.
AH...

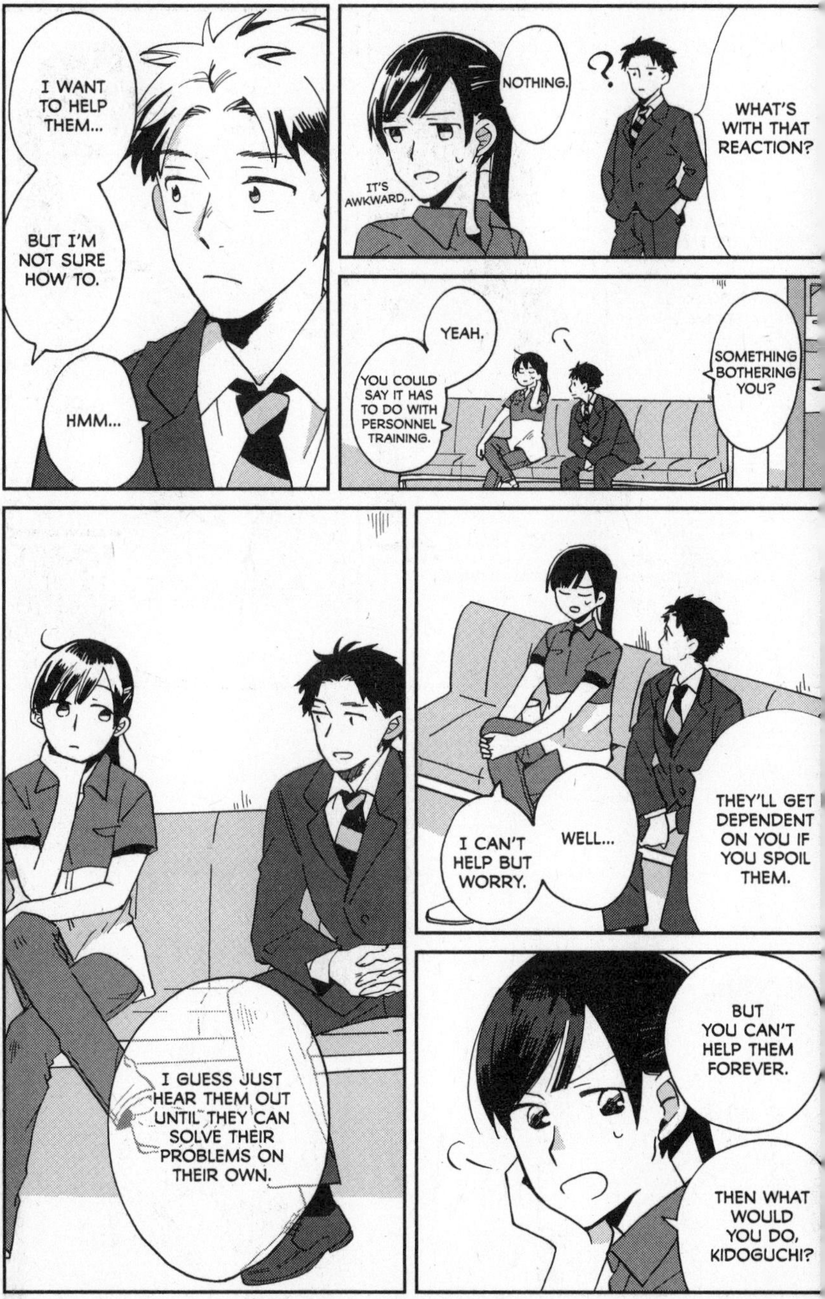
WHAT'S WITH THAT REACTION?
NOTHING.
IT'S AWKWARD...
SOMETHING BOTHERING YOU?
YEAH.
YOU COULD SAY IT HAS TO DO WITH PERSONNEL TRAINING.
I WANT TO HELP THEM...
BUT I'M NOT SURE HOW TO.
HMM...
THEY'LL GET DEPENDENT ON YOU IF YOU SPOIL THEM.
WELL...
I CAN'T HELP BUT WORRY.
BUT YOU CAN'T HELP THEM FOREVER.
THEN WHAT WOULD YOU DO, KIDOGUCHI?
I GUESS JUST HEAR THEM OUT UNTIL THEY CAN SOLVE THEIR PROBLEMS ON THEIR OWN.

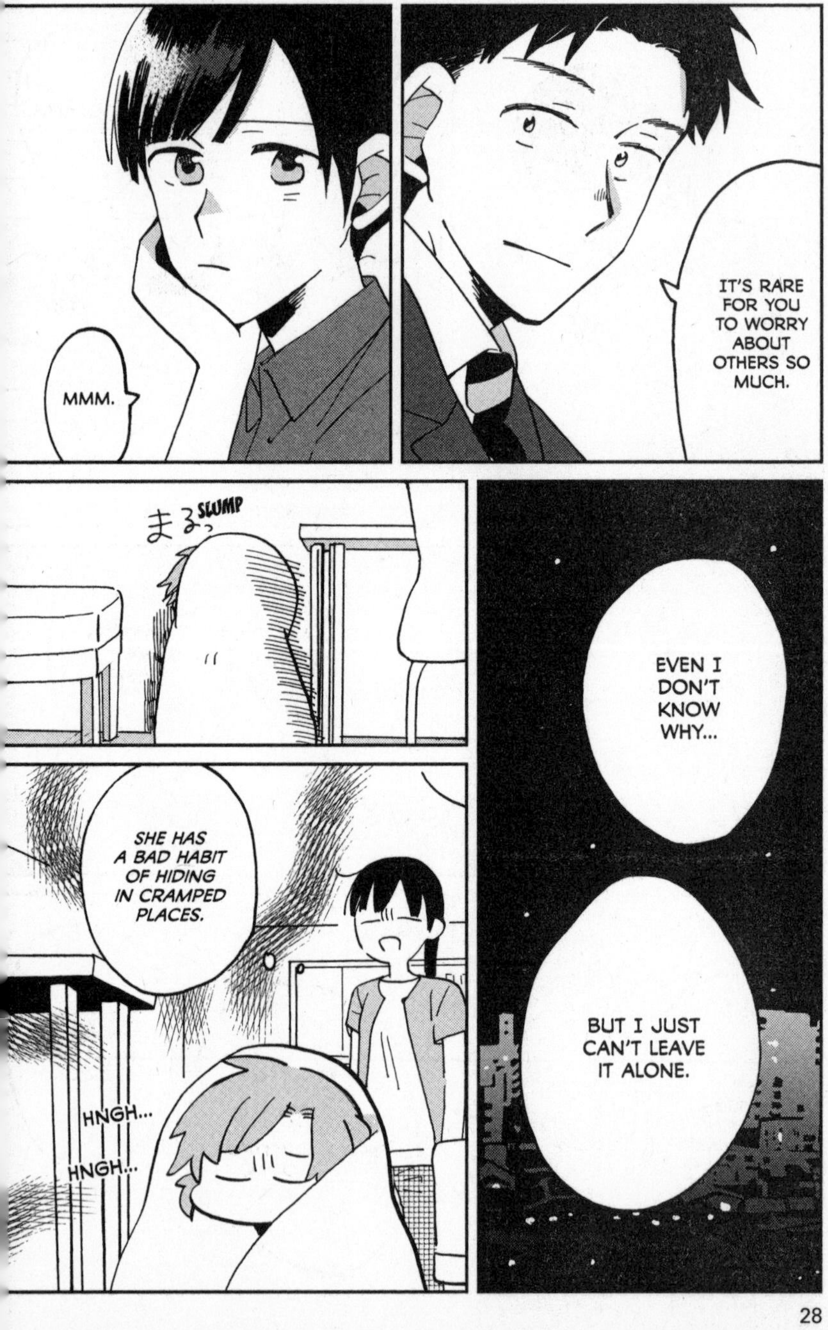
IT'S RARE FOR YOU TO WORRY ABOUT OTHERS SO MUCH.
MMM.
EVEN I DON'T KNOW WHY...
BUT I JUST CAN'T LEAVE IT ALONE.
まるっ
SLUMP
SHE HAS A BAD HABIT OF HIDING IN CRAMPED PLACES.
HNGH...
HNGH...

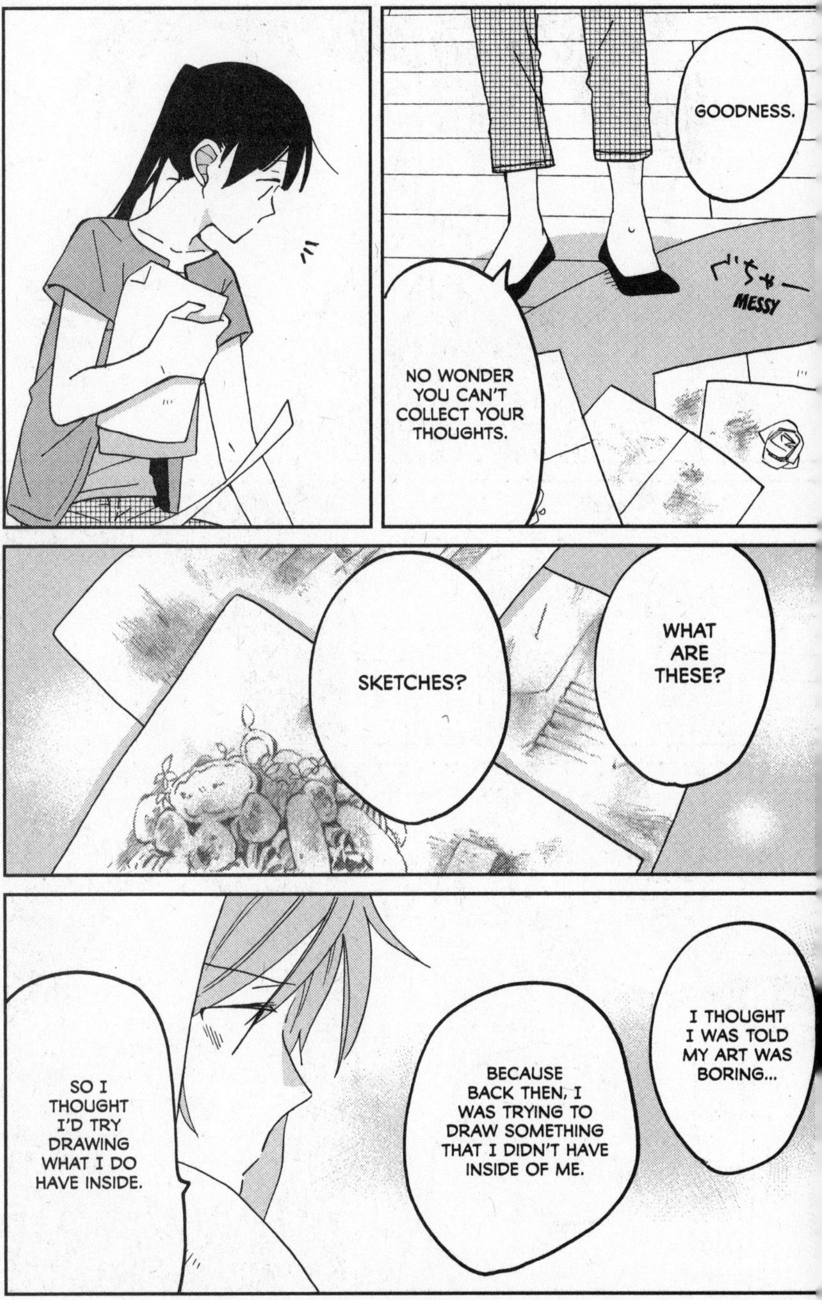
GOODNESS.
ぐちゃー
MESSY
NO WONDER YOU CAN'T COLLECT YOUR THOUGHTS.
WHAT ARE THESE?
SKETCHES?
I THOUGHT I WAS TOLD MY ART WAS BORING...
BECAUSE BACK THEN, I WAS TRYING TO DRAW SOMETHING THAT I DIDN'T HAVE INSIDE OF ME.
SO I THOUGHT I'D TRY DRAWING WHAT I DO HAVE INSIDE.

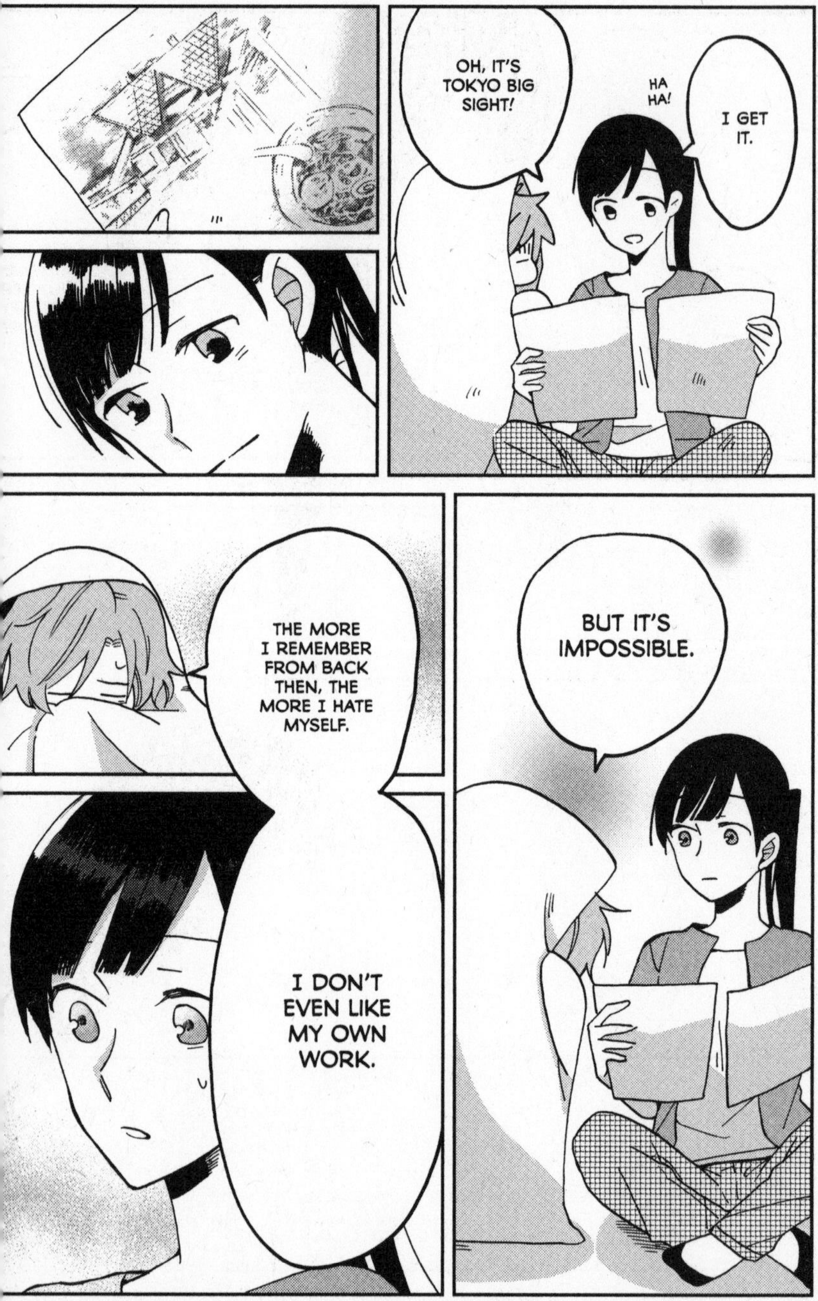
OH, IT'S TOKYO BIG SIGHT!
HA HA!
I GET IT.
BUT IT'S IMPOSSIBLE.
THE MORE I REMEMBER FROM BACK THEN, THE MORE I HATE MYSELF.
I DON'T EVEN LIKE MY OWN WORK.

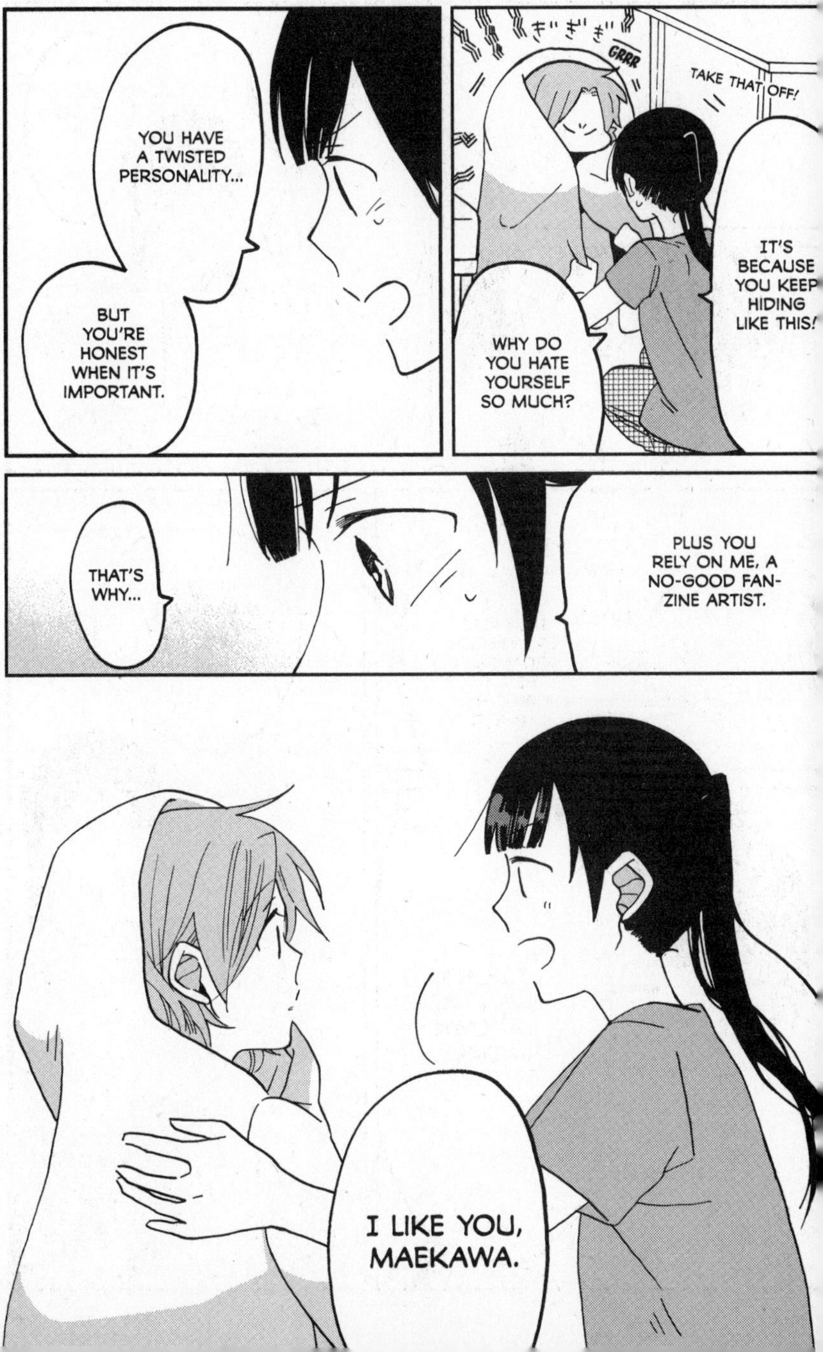
TAKE THAT OFF!
GRRR
IT'S BECAUSE YOU KEEP HIDING LIKE THIS!
WHY DO YOU HATE YOURSELF SO MUCH?
YOU HAVE A TWISTED PERSONALITY...
BUT YOU'RE HONEST WHEN IT'S IMPORTANT.
PLUS YOU RELY ON ME, A NO-GOOD FAN-ZINE ARTIST.
THAT'S WHY...
I LIKE YOU, MAEKAWA.

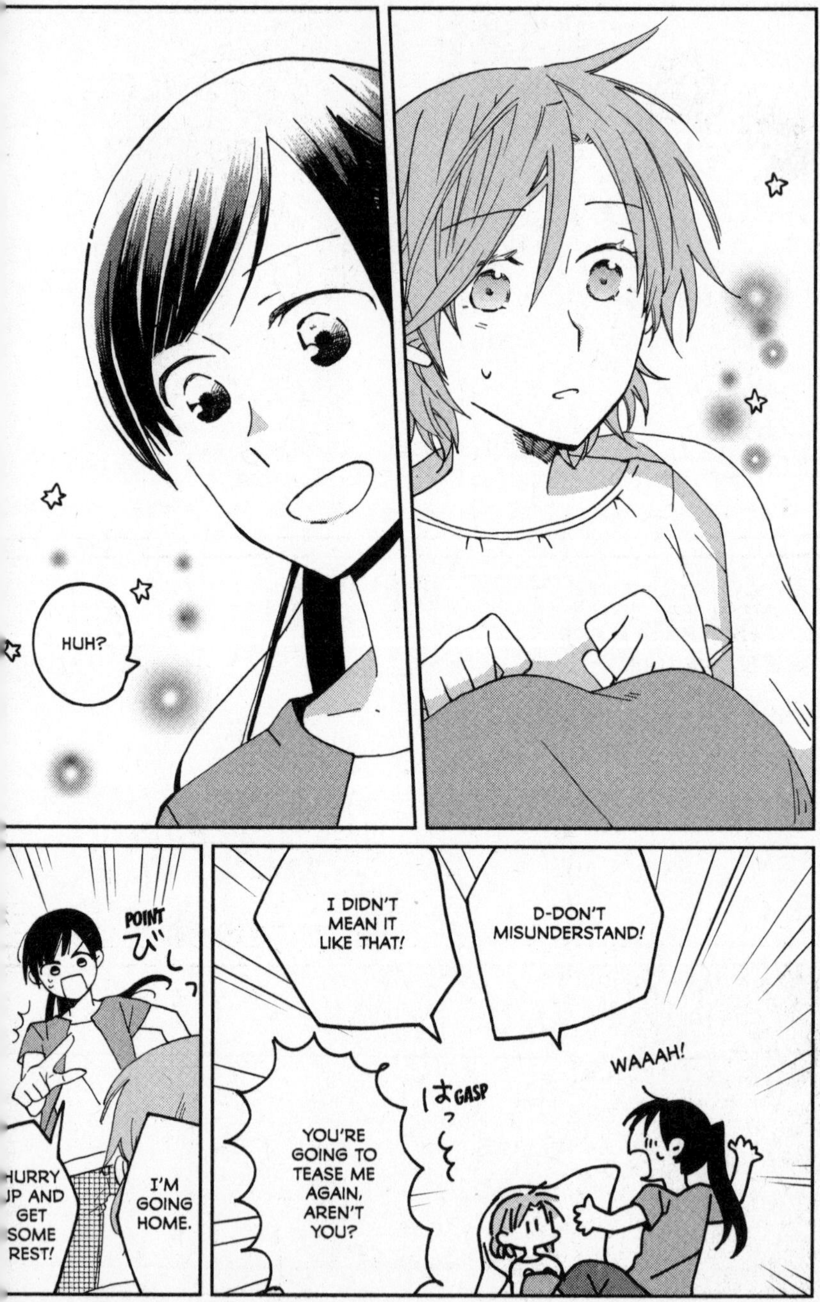

HUH?
D-DON'T MISUNDERSTAND!
I DIDN'T MEAN IT LIKE THAT!
WAAAH!
はっ GASP
YOU'RE GOING TO TEASE ME AGAIN, AREN'T YOU?
POINT びしっ
I'M GOING HOME.
HURRY UP AND GET SOME REST!

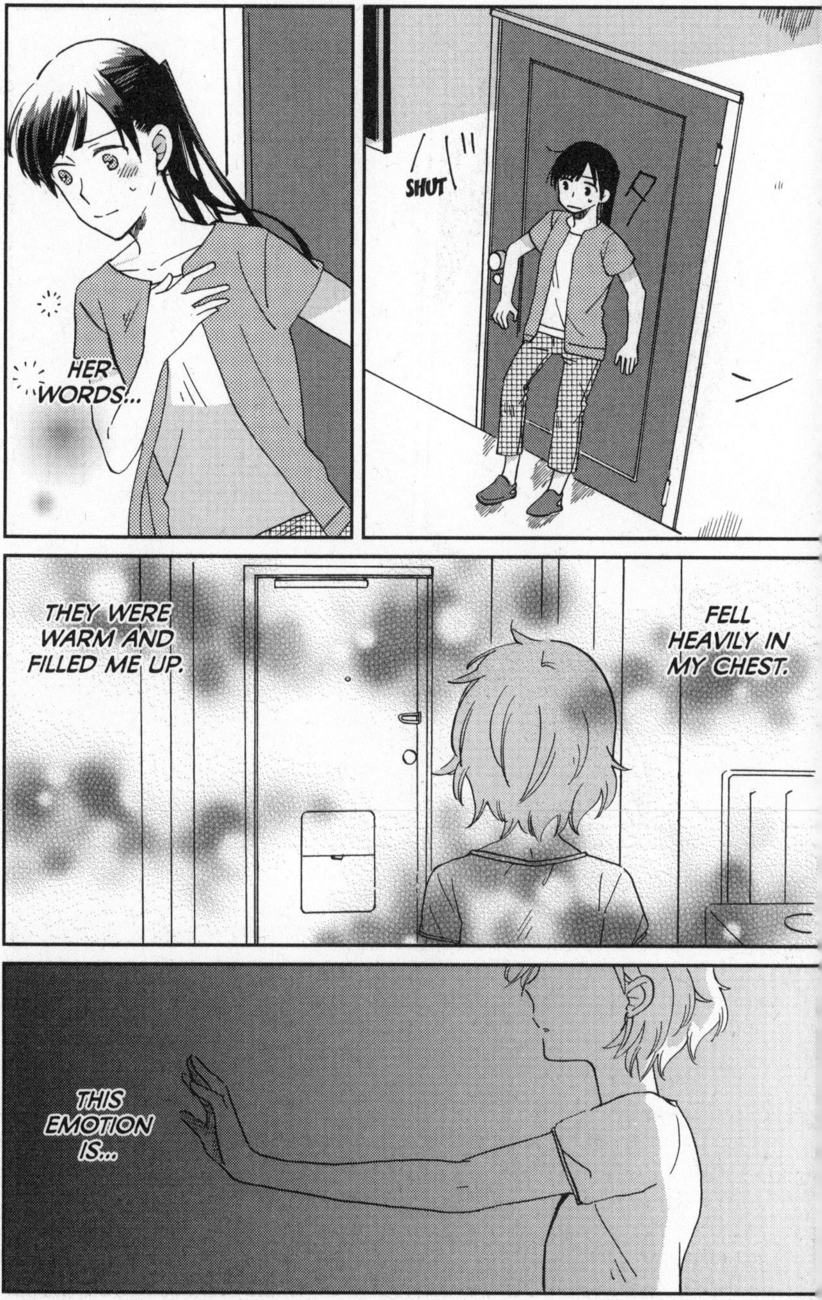
SHUT
HER WORDS...
FELL HEAVILY IN MY CHEST.
THEY WERE WARM AND FILLED ME UP.
THIS EMOTION IS...

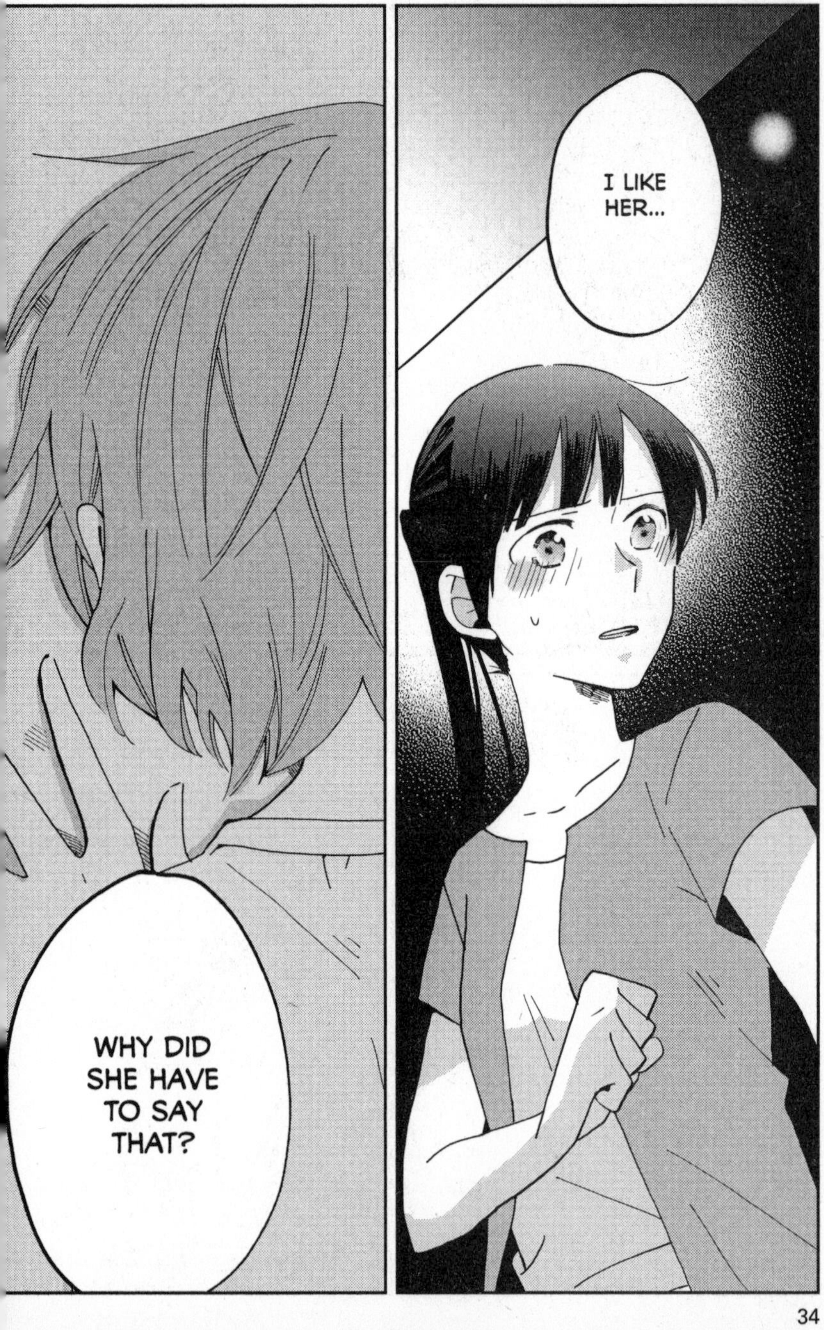
I LIKE HER...
WHY DID SHE HAVE TO SAY THAT?

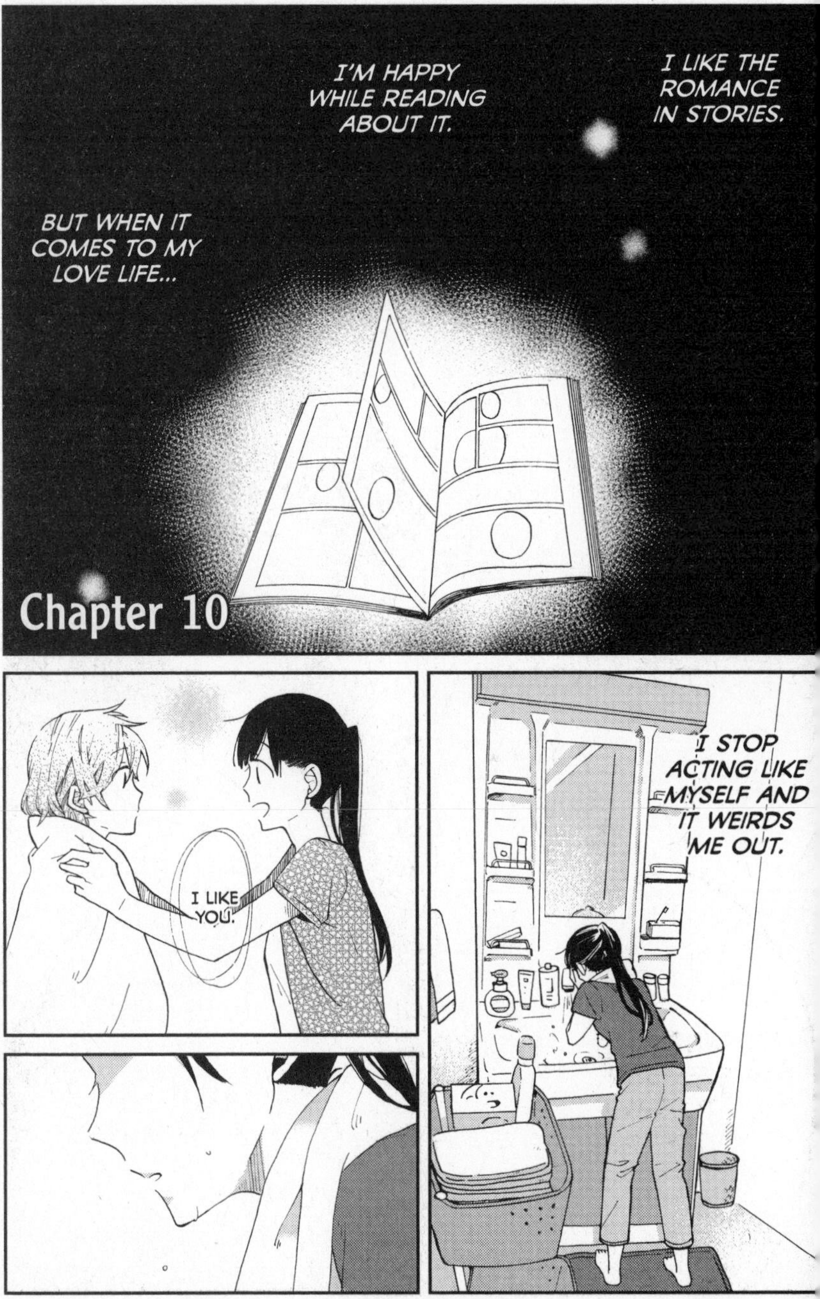
I LIKE THE ROMANCE IN STORIES.
I'M HAPPY WHILE READING ABOUT IT.
BUT WHEN IT COMES TO MY LOVE LIFE...
Chapter 10
I STOP ACTING LIKE MYSELF AND IT WEIRDS ME OUT.
I LIKE YOU.

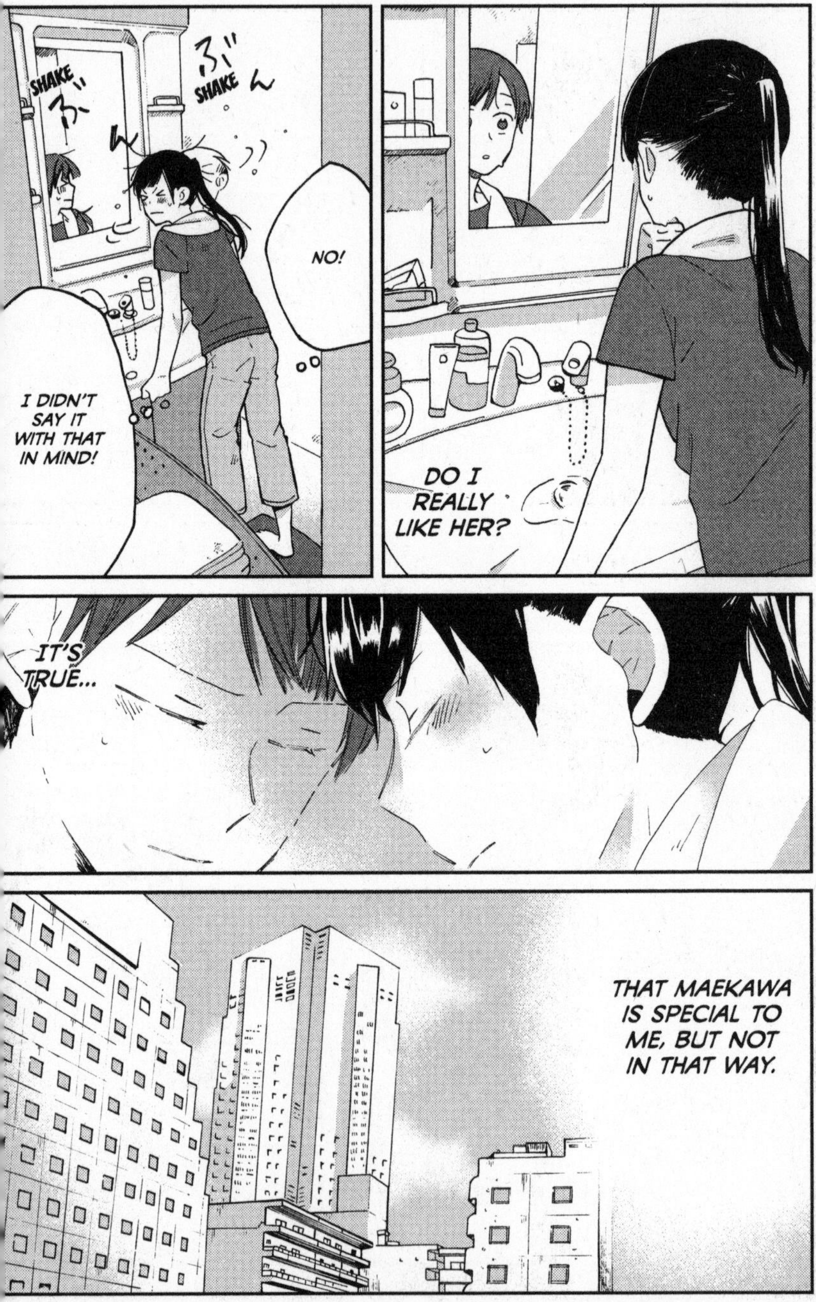
DO I REALLY LIKE HER?
ぶん SHAKE
NO!
SHAKE ぶん
I DIDN'T SAY IT WITH THAT IN MIND!
IT'S TRUE...
THAT MAEKAWA IS SPECIAL TO ME, BUT NOT IN THAT WAY.

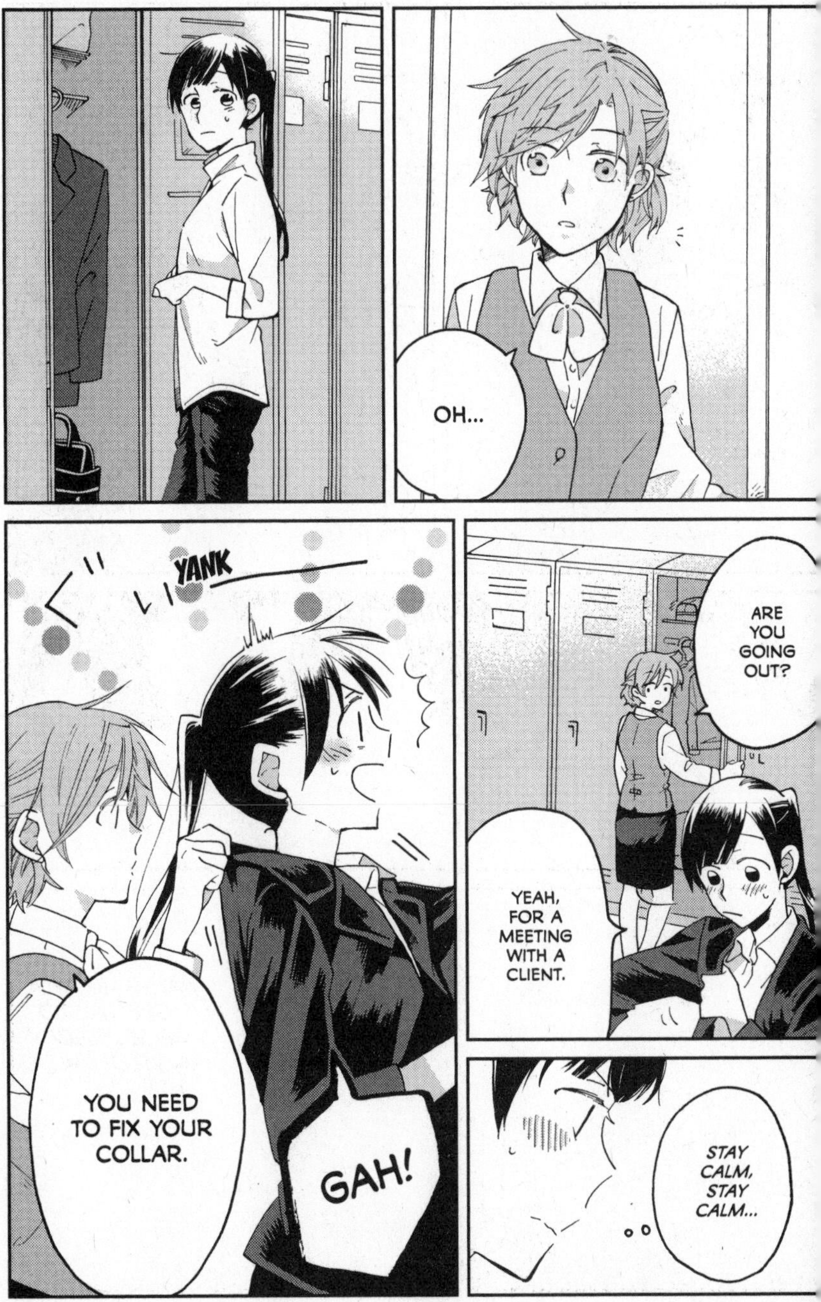
OH...
ARE YOU GOING OUT?
YEAH, FOR A MEETING WITH A CLIENT.
STAY CALM, STAY CALM...
YANK
GAH!
YOU NEED TO FIX YOUR COLLAR.

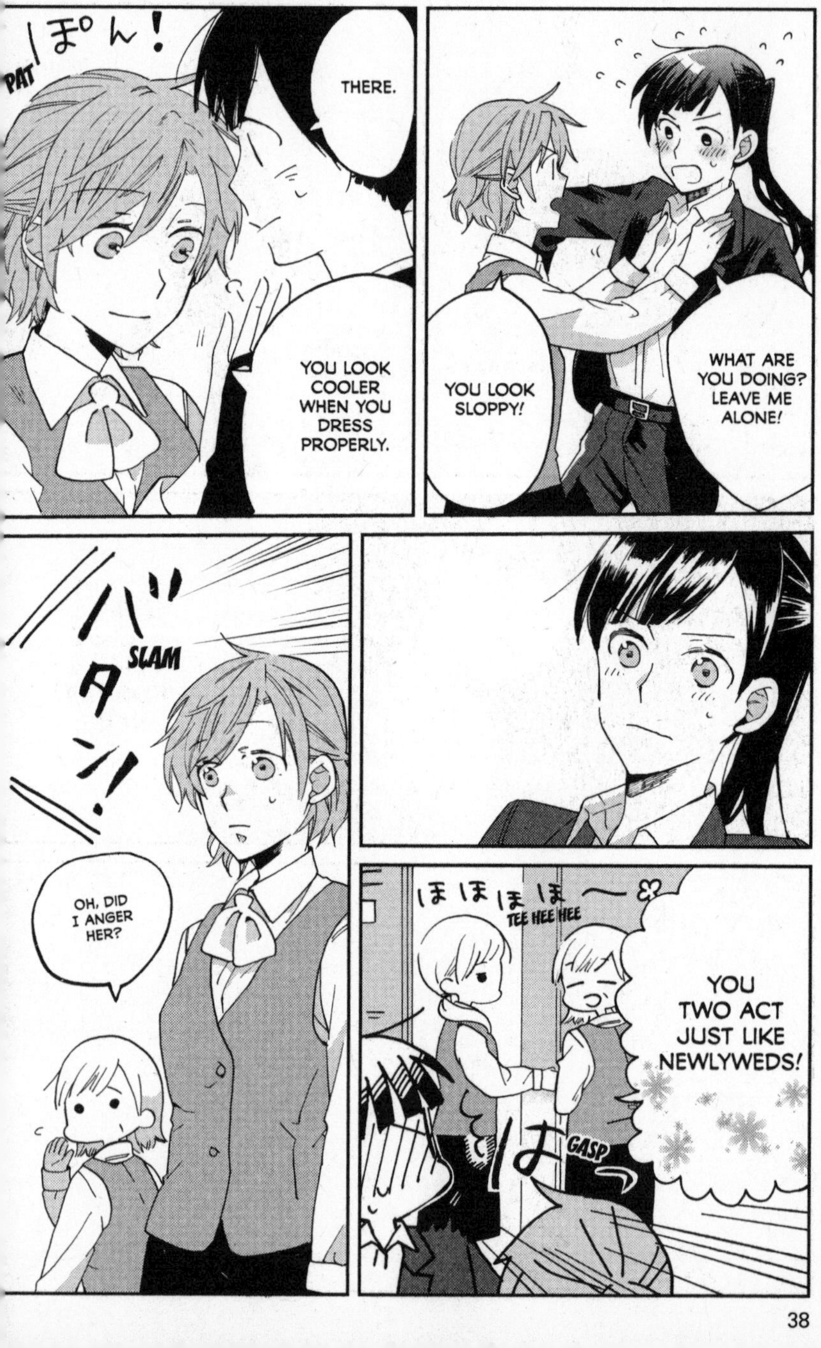
WHAT ARE YOU DOING? LEAVE ME ALONE!
YOU LOOK SLOPPY!
ぽん!
PAT
THERE.
YOU LOOK COOLER WHEN YOU DRESS PROPERLY.
ほほほほ〜
TEE HEE HEE
YOU TWO ACT JUST LIKE NEWLYWEDS!
は
GASP
バタン!
SLAM
OH, DID I ANGER HER?

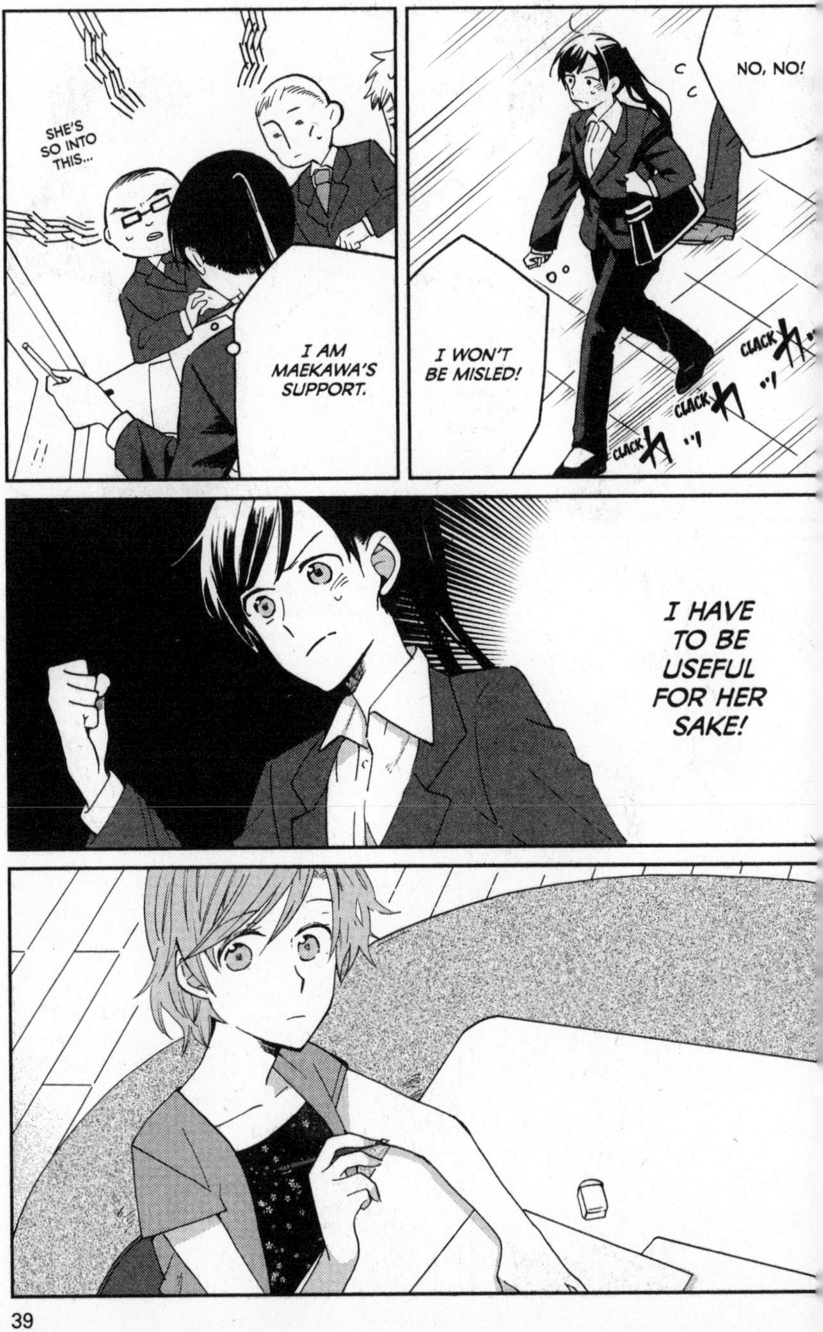
NO, NO!
I WON'T BE MISLED!
CLACK
CLACK
CLACK
I AM MAEKAWA'S SUPPORT.
SHE'S SO INTO THIS...
I HAVE TO BE USEFUL FOR HER SAKE!

FWOOSH
WHAT ARE YOU DOING?
I'M GOING TO COOK FOR YOU!
YOU SHOULDN'T TREAT FOOD THAT WAY.
SHIMIZU-SAN, YOU SEEM LIKE THE TYPE WHO TRIES TO BE CREATIVE AND RUINS THE FOOD.
DON'T WORRY, I WON'T BE ADVENTUROUS.
HUH?
WHAT AM I SUPPOSED TO DO WITH THIS?
CLANG
OUCH.
TA-DA!
ALL DONE!
IT'S SALTY.
I HATE SHIITAKE MUSH-ROOMS.
TOSS
HEY!

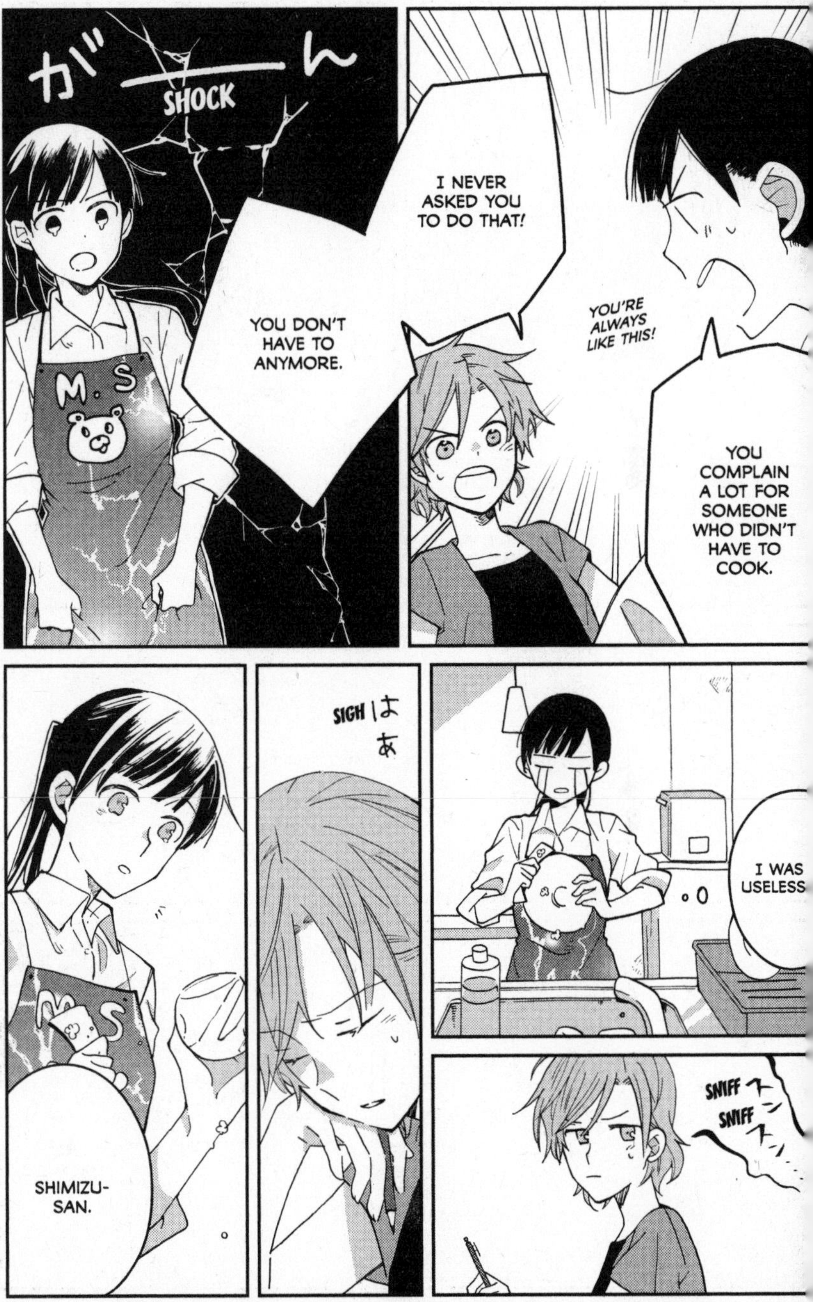
I NEVER ASKED YOU TO DO THAT!
YOU DON'T HAVE TO ANYMORE.
YOU'RE ALWAYS LIKE THIS!
YOU COMPLAIN A LOT FOR SOMEONE WHO DIDN'T HAVE TO COOK.
ガーん
SHOCK
I WAS USELESS
SNIFF スン
SNIFF スン
SIGH はあ
SHIMIZU-SAN.

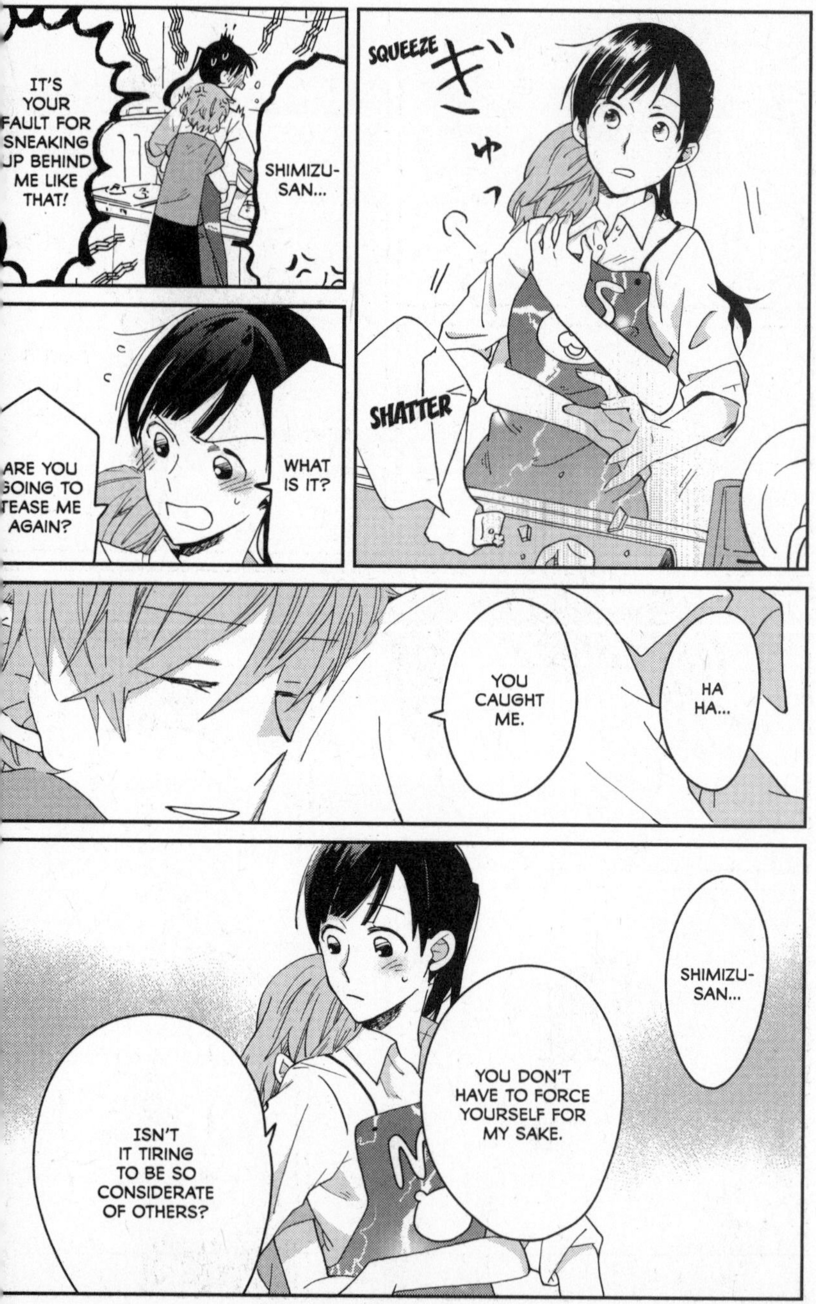
SQUEEZE
ぎゅっ
SHATTER
SHIMIZU-SAN...
IT'S YOUR FAULT FOR SNEAKING UP BEHIND ME LIKE THAT!
WHAT IS IT?
ARE YOU GOING TO TEASE ME AGAIN?
HA HA...
YOU CAUGHT ME.
SHIMIZU-SAN...
YOU DON'T HAVE TO FORCE YOURSELF FOR MY SAKE.
ISN'T IT TIRING TO BE SO CONSIDERATE OF OTHERS?

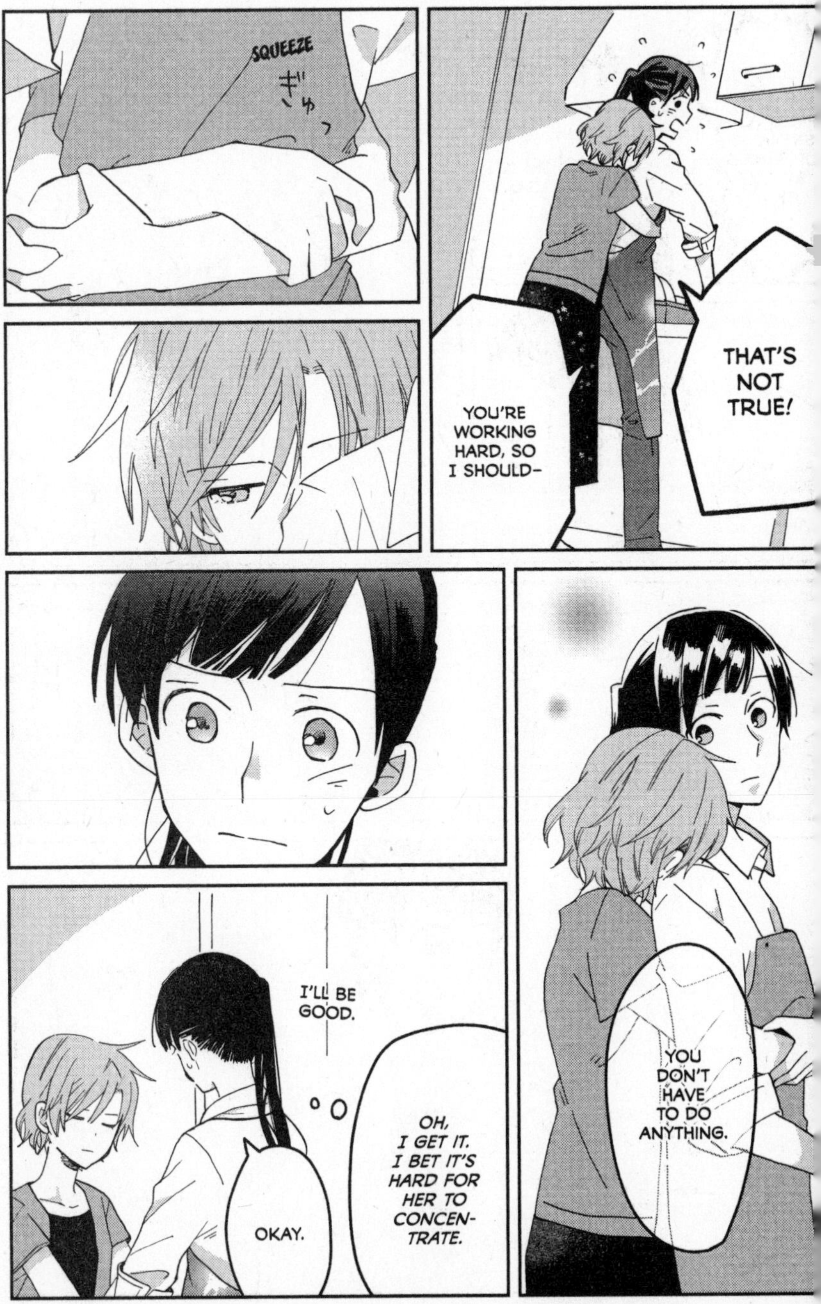
THAT'S NOT TRUE!
YOU'RE WORKING HARD, SO I SHOULD-
SQUEEZE
ぎゅっ
YOU DON'T HAVE TO DO ANYTHING.
OH, I GET IT. I BET IT'S HARD FOR HER TO CONCEN-TRATE.
I'LL BE GOOD.
OKAY.

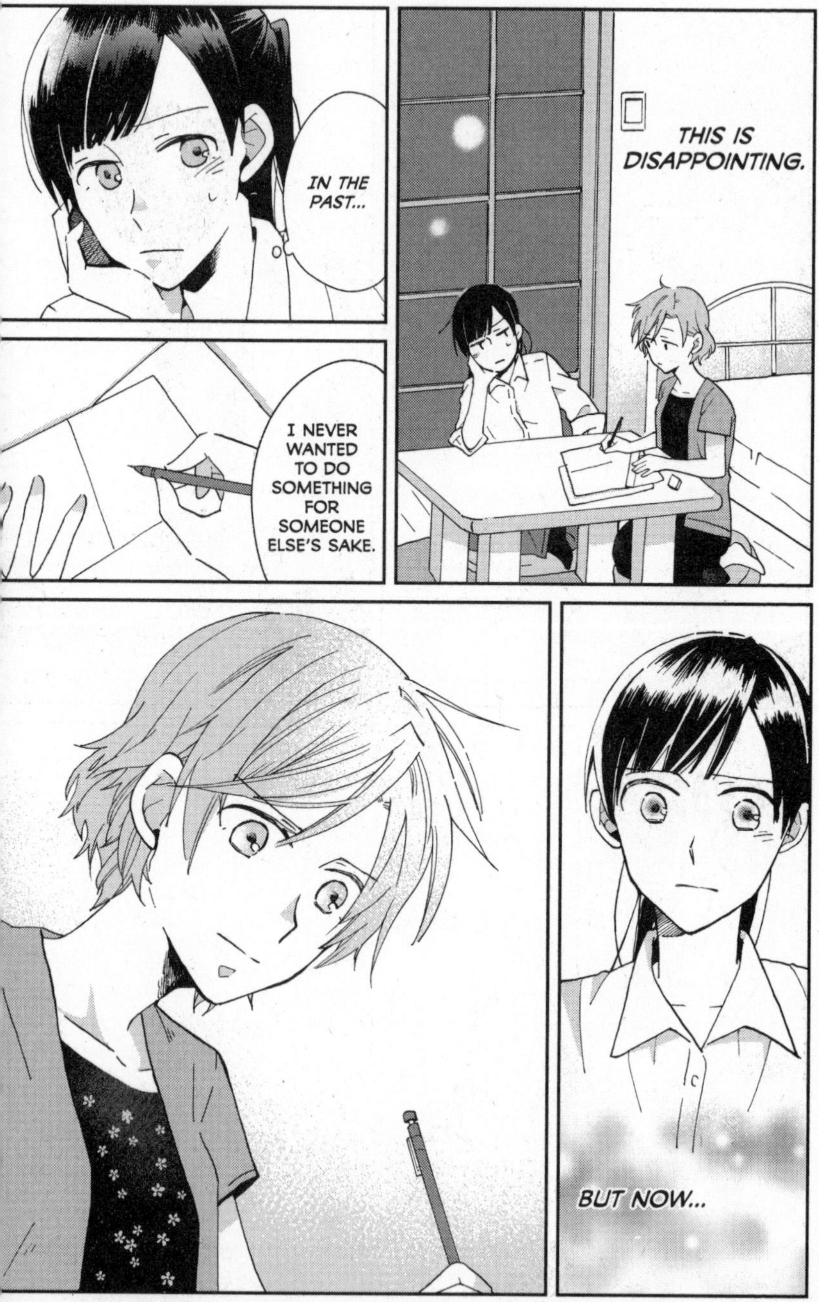
THIS IS DISAPPOINTING.
IN THE PAST...
I NEVER WANTED TO DO SOMETHING FOR SOMEONE ELSE'S SAKE.
BUT NOW...

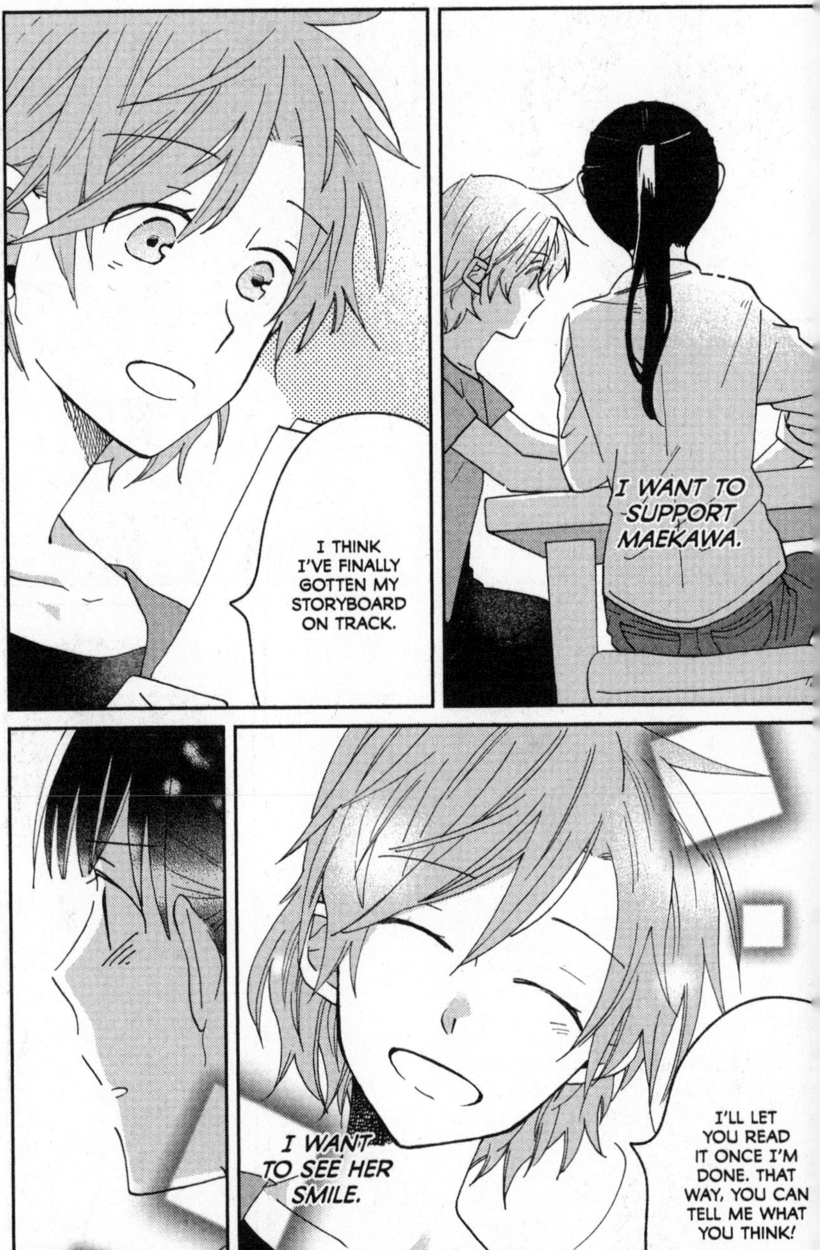
I WANT TO SUPPORT MAEKAWA.
I THINK I'VE FINALLY GOTTEN MY STORYBOARD ON TRACK.
I'LL LET YOU READ IT ONCE I'M DONE. THAT WAY, YOU CAN TELL ME WHAT YOU THINK!
I WANT TO SEE HER SMILE.

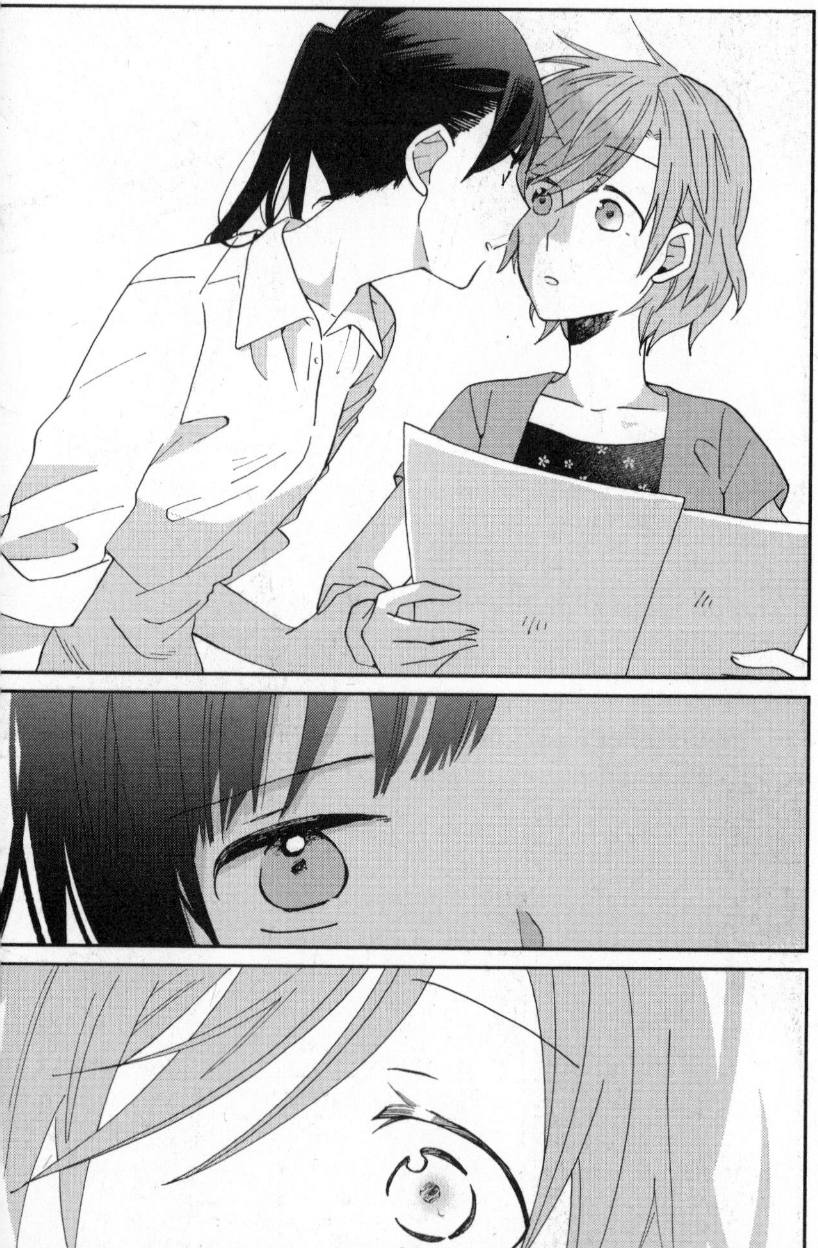

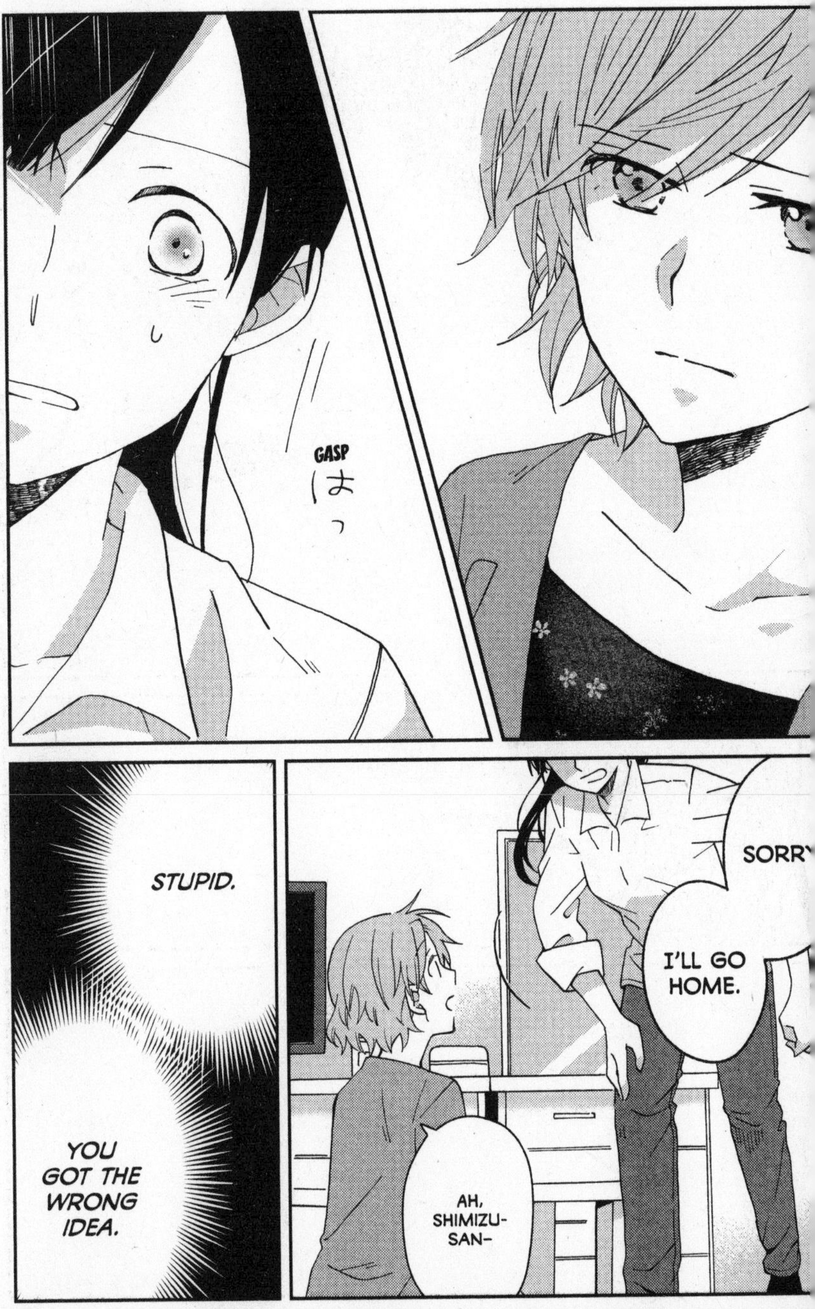
GASP
はっ
SORRY
I'LL GO HOME.
AH, SHIMIZU-SAN-
STUPID.
YOU GOT THE WRONG IDEA.

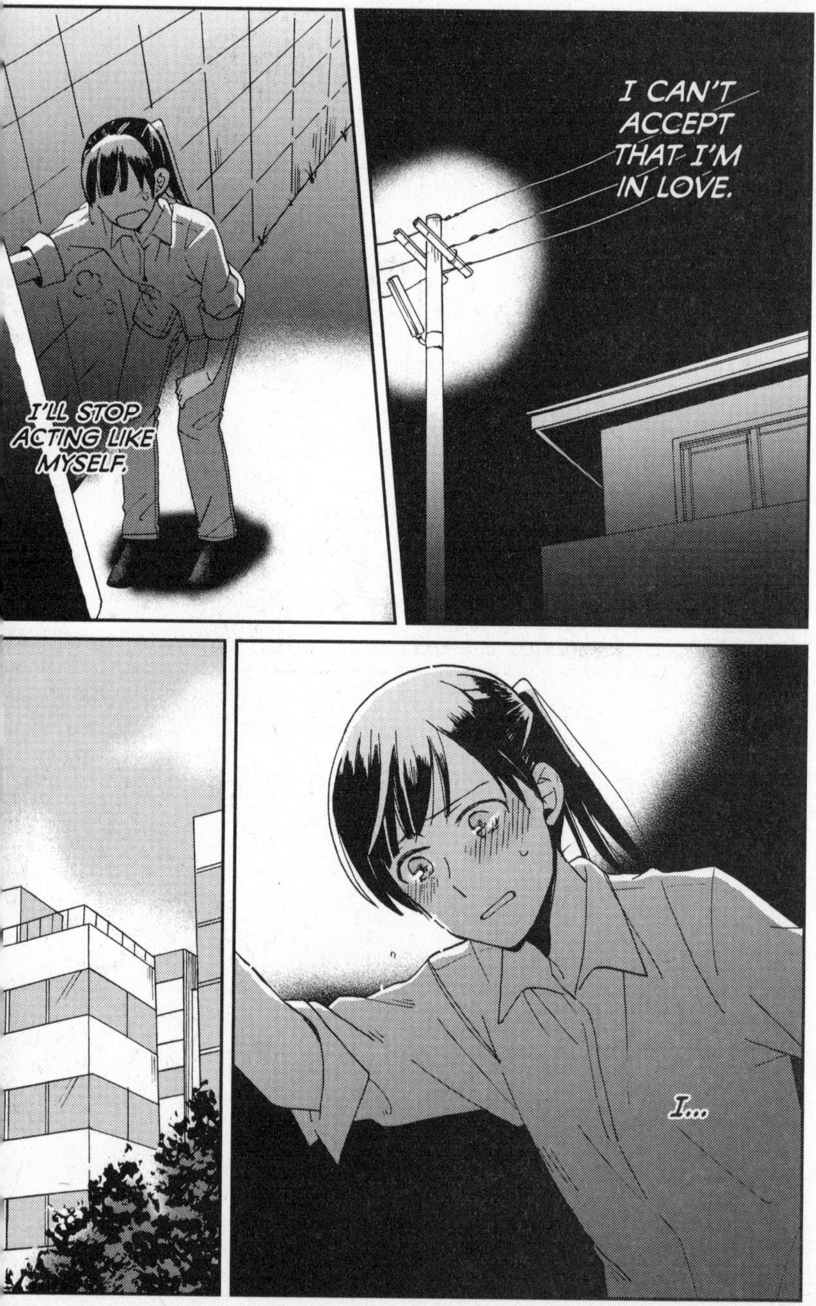
I CAN'T ACCEPT THAT I'M IN LOVE.
I'LL STOP ACTING LIKE MYSELF.
I...

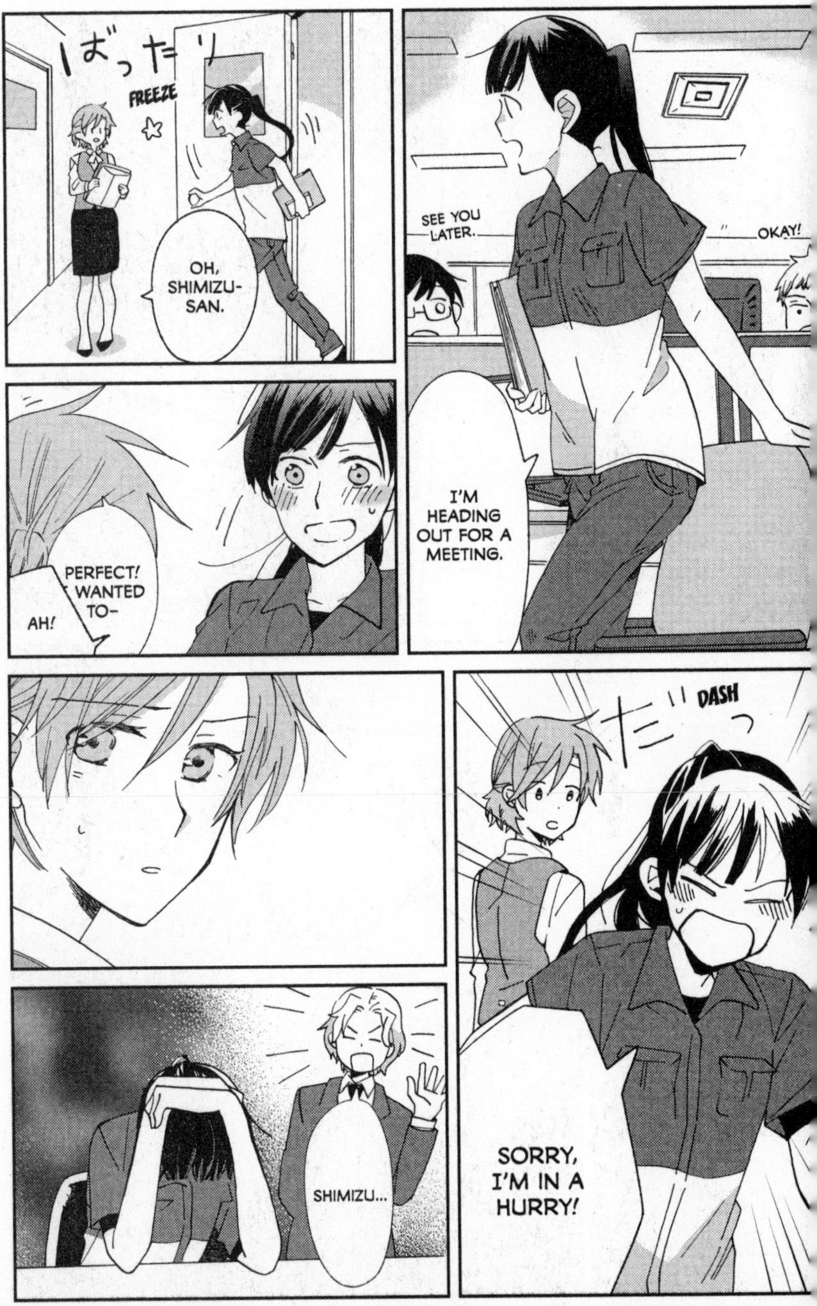
I'M HEADING OUT FOR A MEETING.
SEE YOU LATER.
OKAY!
ばったり
FREEZE
OH, SHIMIZU-SAN.
PERFECT! I WANTED TO-
AH!
だっ
DASH
SORRY, I'M IN A HURRY!
SHIMIZU...

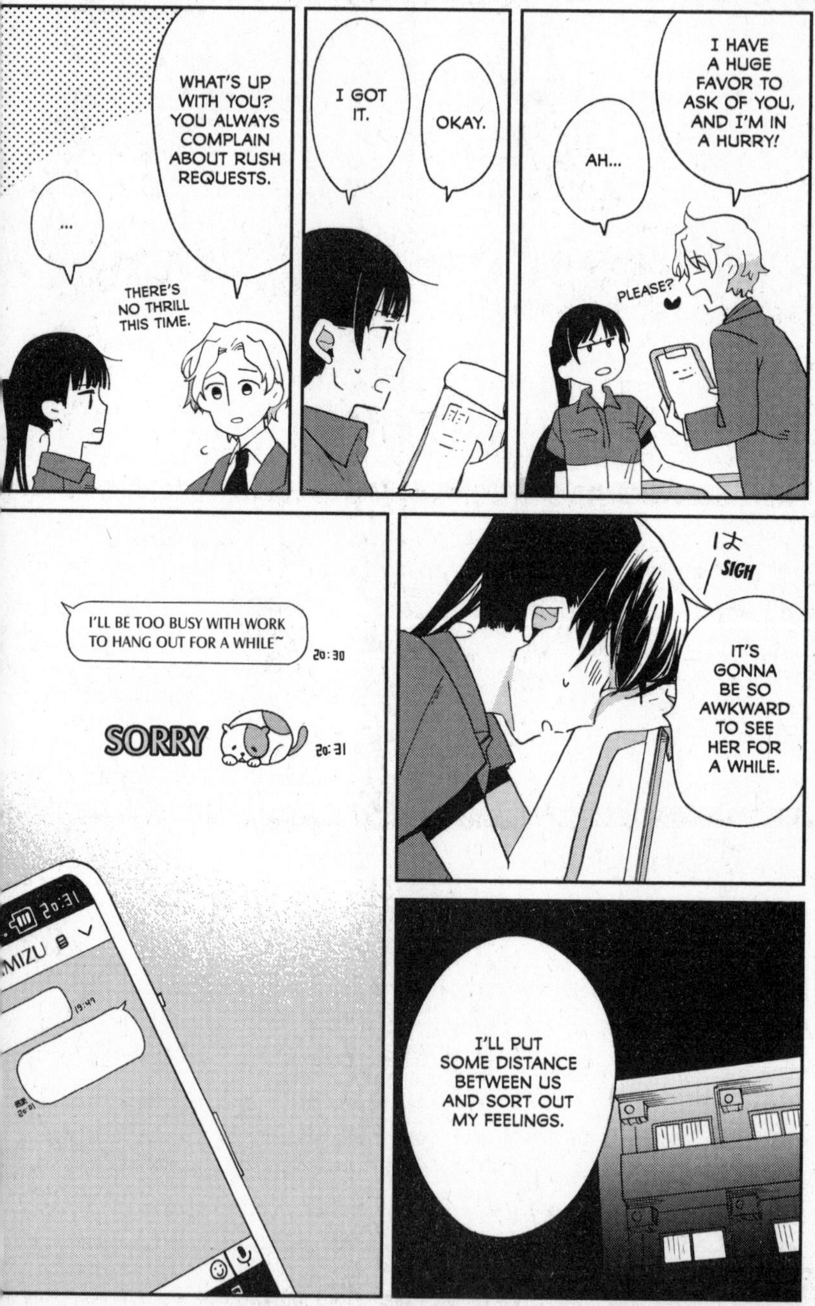
I HAVE A HUGE FAVOR TO ASK OF YOU, AND I'M IN A HURRY!
AH...
PLEASE?
OKAY.
I GOT IT.
WHAT'S UP WITH YOU? YOU ALWAYS COMPLAIN ABOUT RUSH REQUESTS.
...
THERE'S NO THRILL THIS TIME.
は
SIGH
IT'S GONNA BE SO AWKWARD TO SEE HER FOR A WHILE.
I'LL PUT SOME DISTANCE BETWEEN US AND SORT OUT MY FEELINGS.
I'LL BE TOO BUSY WITH WORK TO HANG OUT FOR A WHILE~
20:30
SORRY
20:31
20:31

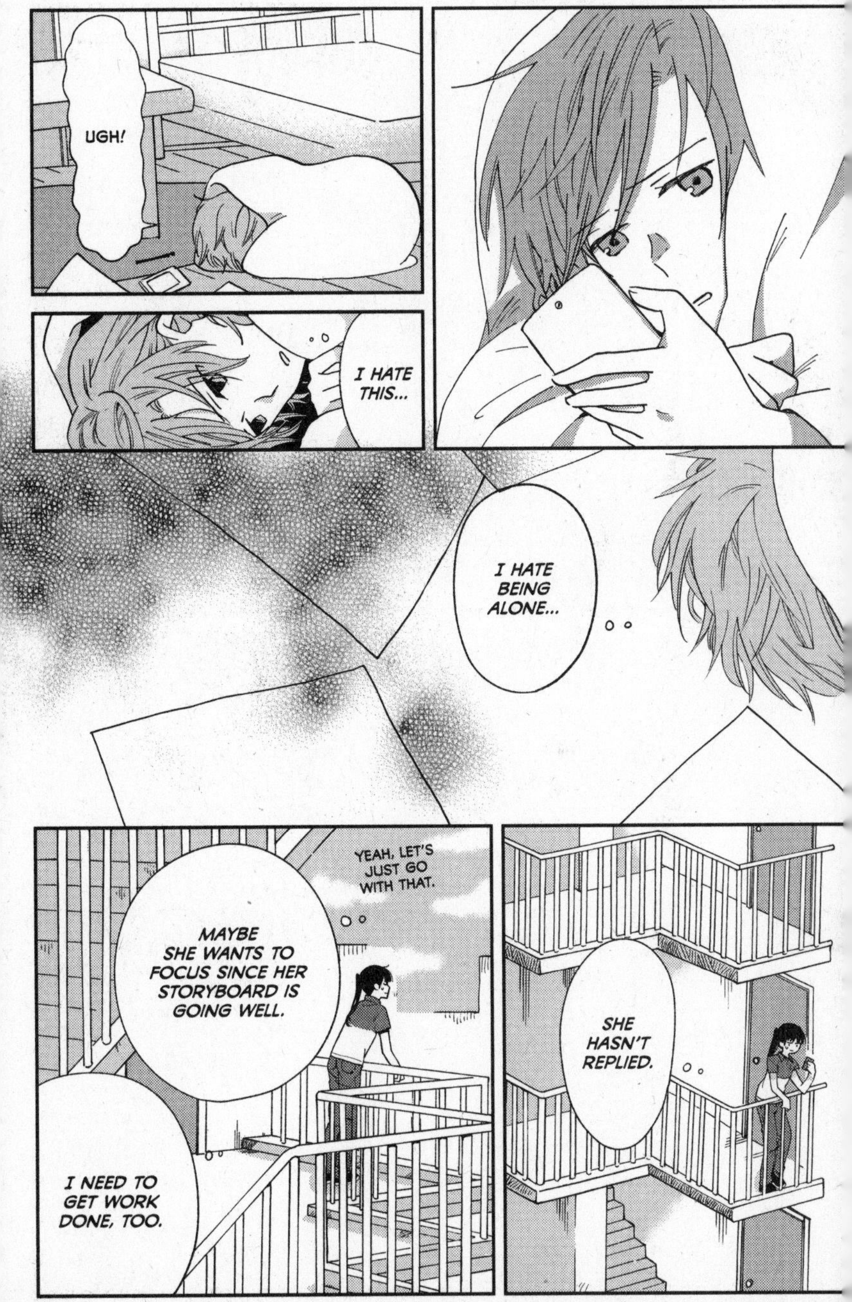
UGH!
I HATE THIS...
I HATE BEING ALONE...
SHE HASN'T REPLIED.
MAYBE SHE WANTS TO FOCUS SINCE HER STORYBOARD IS GOING WELL.
YEAH, LET'S JUST GO WITH THAT.
I NEED TO GET WORK DONE, TOO.

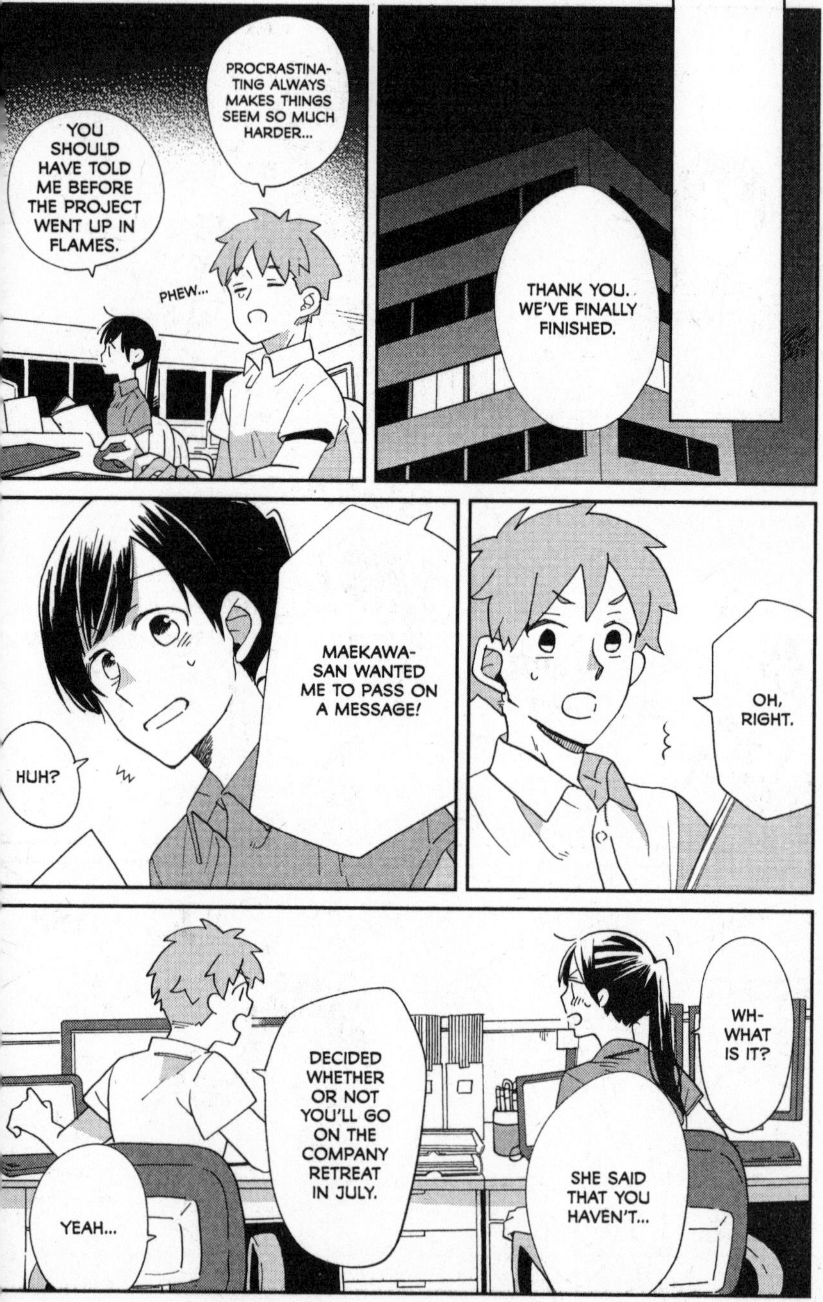
THANK YOU. WE'VE FINALLY FINISHED.
PROCRASTINA-TING ALWAYS MAKES THINGS SEEM SO MUCH HARDER...
YOU SHOULD HAVE TOLD ME BEFORE THE PROJECT WENT UP IN FLAMES.
PHEW...
OH, RIGHT.
MAEKAWA-SAN WANTED ME TO PASS ON A MESSAGE!
HUH?
WH-WHAT IS IT?
SHE SAID THAT YOU HAVEN'T...
DECIDED WHETHER OR NOT YOU'LL GO ON THE COMPANY RETREAT IN JULY.
YEAH...

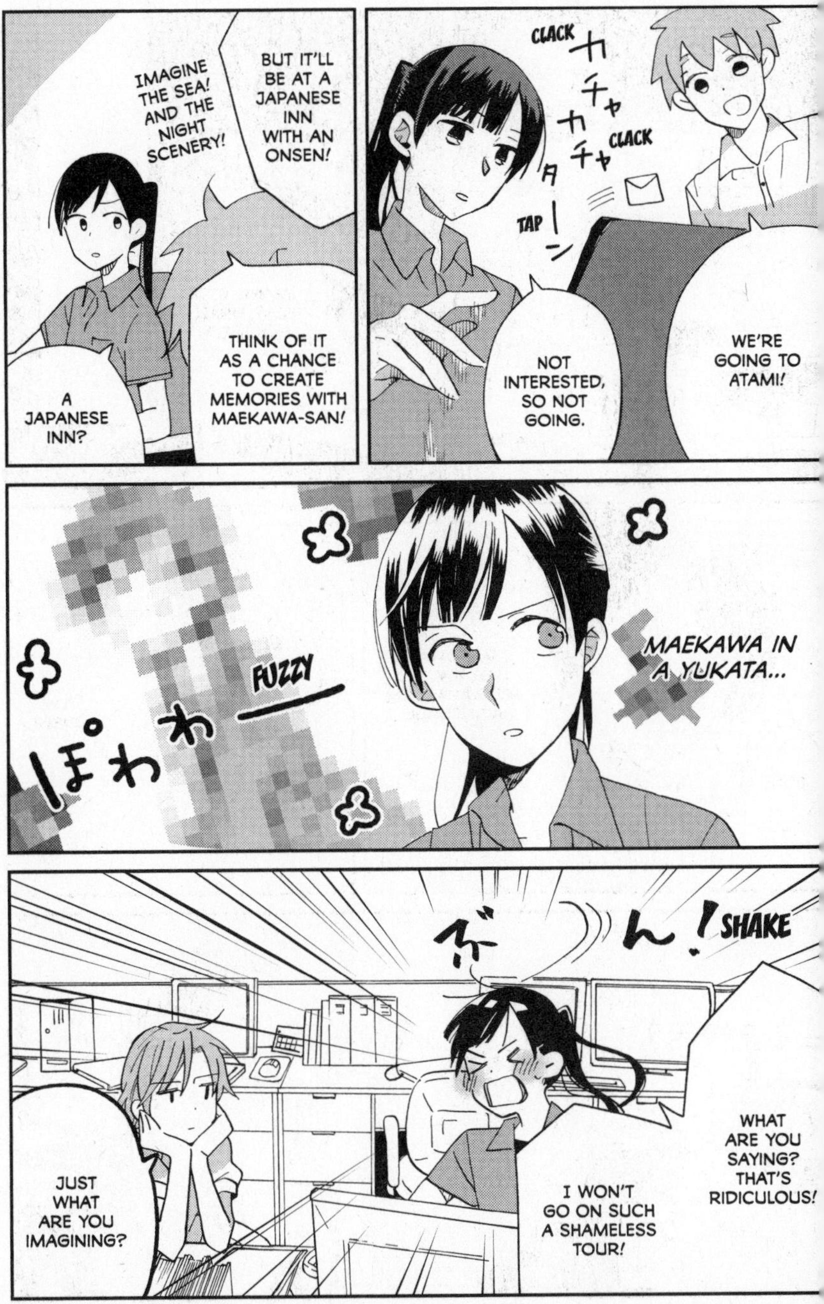
CLACK
カチャカチャ
CLACK
TAP
ターン
WE'RE GOING TO ATAMI!
NOT INTERESTED, SO NOT GOING.
BUT IT'LL BE AT A JAPANESE INN WITH AN ONSEN!
IMAGINE THE SEA! AND THE NIGHT SCENERY!
THINK OF IT AS A CHANCE TO CREATE MEMORIES WITH MAEKAWA-SAN!
A JAPANESE INN?
MAEKAWA IN A YUKATA...
FUZZY
ぽわわー
ぶん!
SHAKE
WHAT ARE YOU SAYING? THAT'S RIDICULOUS!
I WON'T GO ON SUCH A SHAMELESS TOUR!
JUST WHAT ARE YOU IMAGINING?

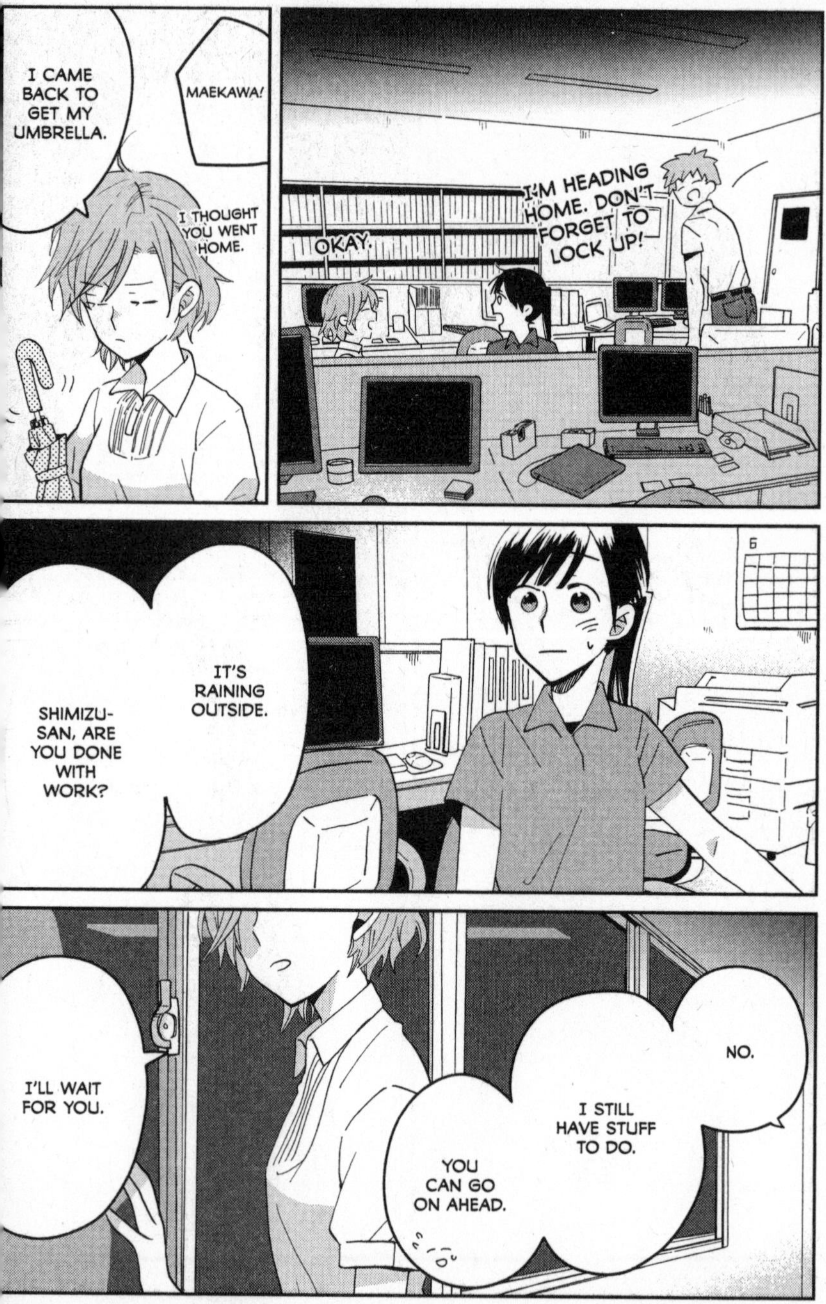

I'M HEADING HOME. DON'T FORGET TO LOCK UP!
OKAY.
MAEKAWA!
I THOUGHT YOU WENT HOME.
I CAME BACK TO GET MY UMBRELLA.
IT'S RAINING OUTSIDE.
SHIMIZU-SAN, ARE YOU DONE WITH WORK?
NO.
I STILL HAVE STUFF TO DO.
YOU CAN GO ON AHEAD.
I'LL WAIT FOR YOU.

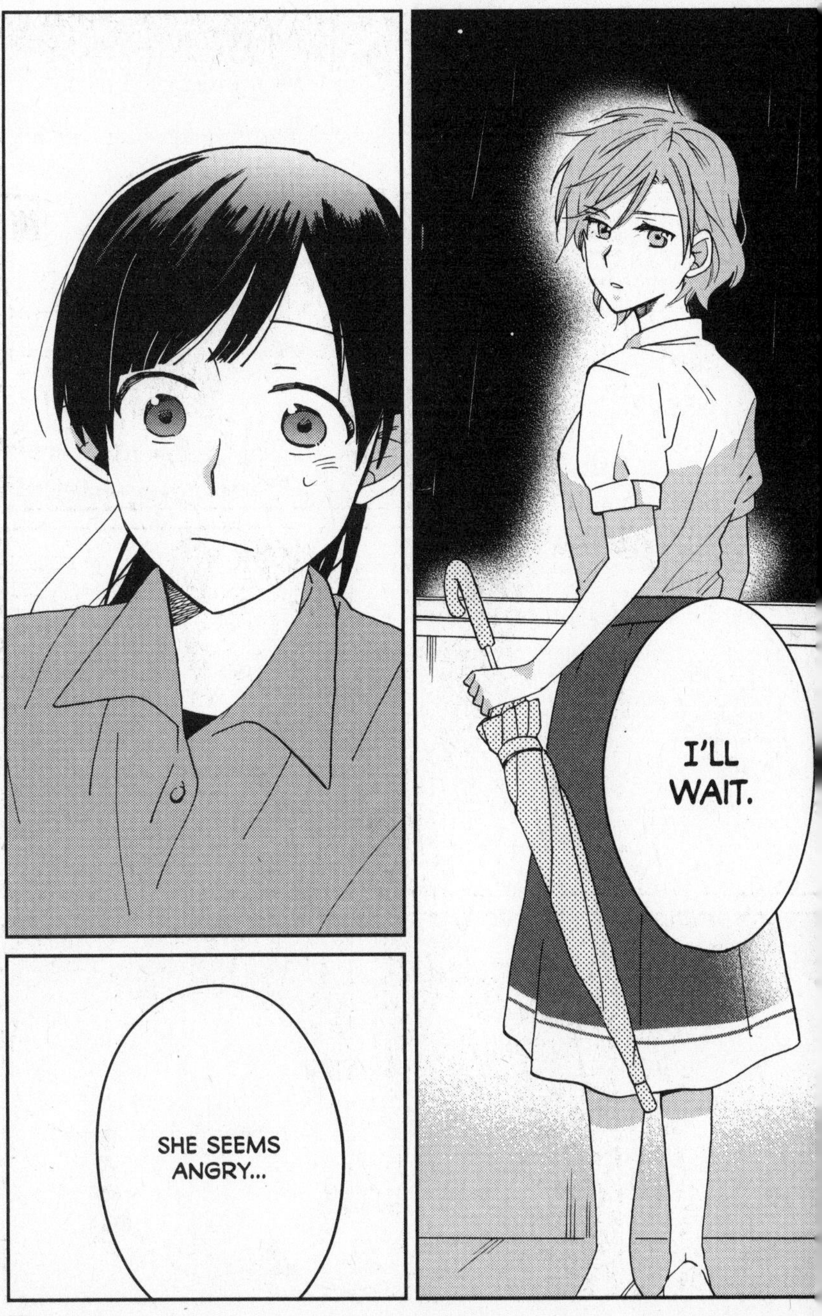
I'LL WAIT.
SHE SEEMS ANGRY...

CONTINUED ON PAGE 78 (AFTER CHAPTER 11)...

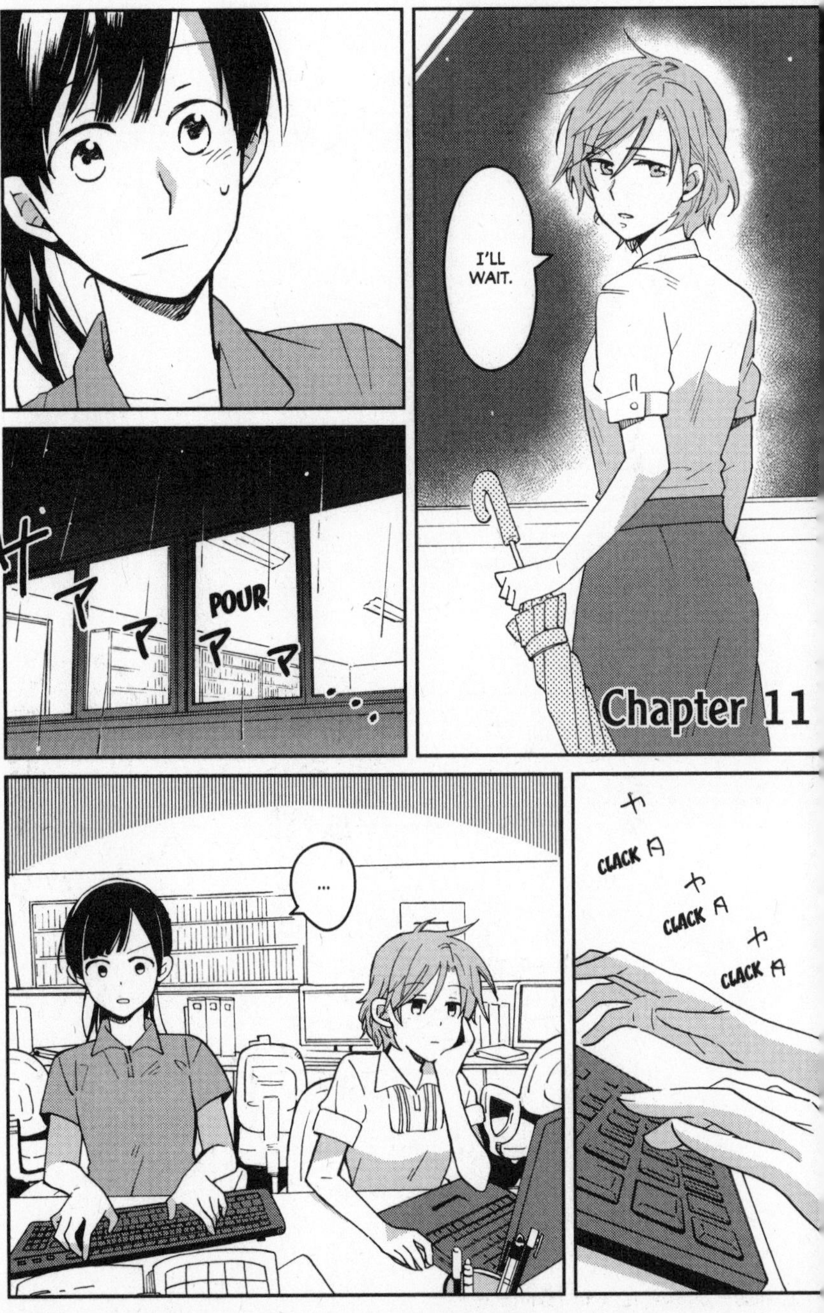

I'LL WAIT.
Chapter 11
ザアアアア
POUR
カ CLACK タ
カ CLACK タ
カ CLACK タ
...

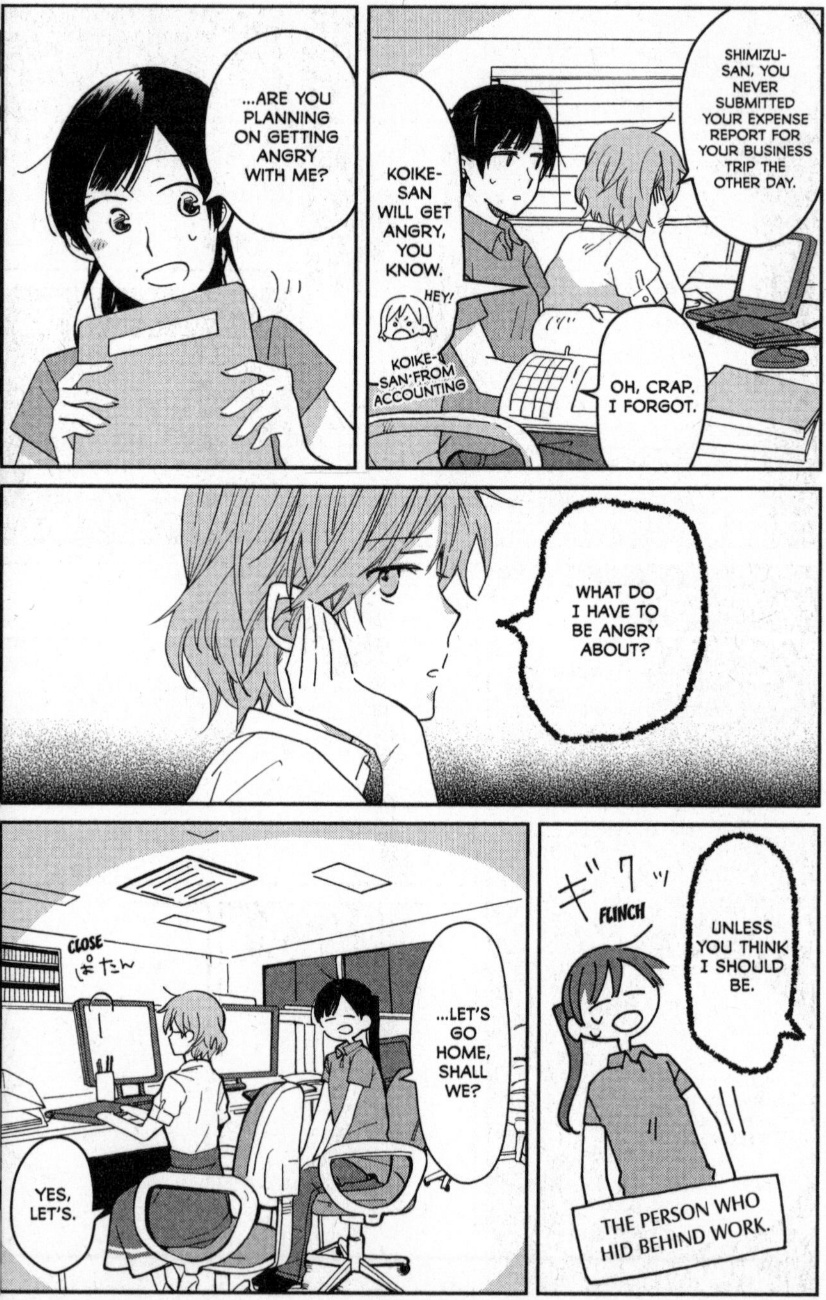
SHIMIZU-SAN, YOU NEVER SUBMITTED YOUR EXPENSE REPORT FOR YOUR BUSINESS TRIP THE OTHER DAY.
OH, CRAP. I FORGOT.
KOIKE-SAN WILL GET ANGRY, YOU KNOW.
HEY!
KOIKE-SAN·FROM ACCOUNTING
...ARE YOU PLANNING ON GETTING ANGRY WITH ME?
WHAT DO I HAVE TO BE ANGRY ABOUT?
UNLESS YOU THINK I SHOULD BE.
ギクッ
FLINCH
THE PERSON WHO HID BEHIND WORK.
...LET'S GO HOME, SHALL WE?
CLOSE
ぱたん
YES, LET'S.

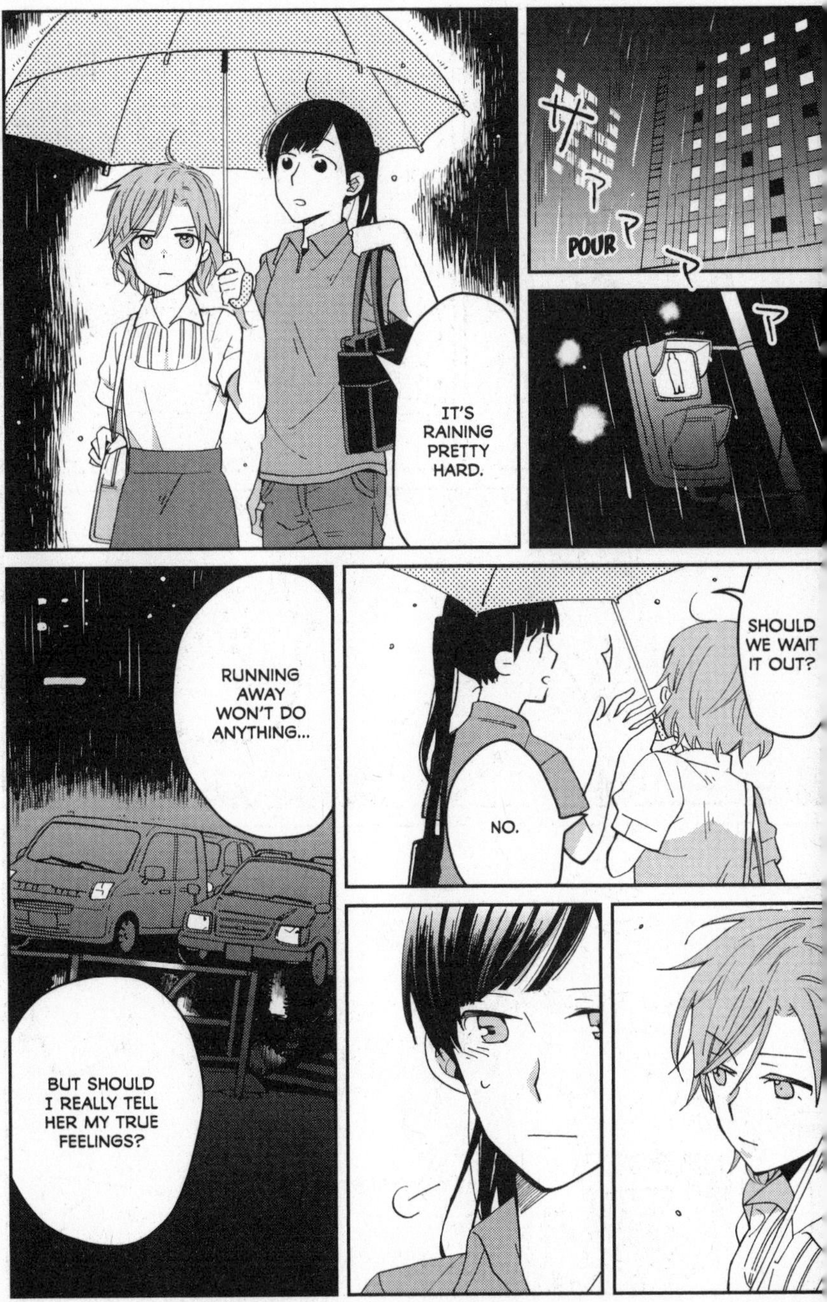
POUR
IT'S RAINING PRETTY HARD.
SHOULD WE WAIT IT OUT?
NO.
RUNNING AWAY WON'T DO ANYTHING...
BUT SHOULD I REALLY TELL HER MY TRUE FEELINGS?

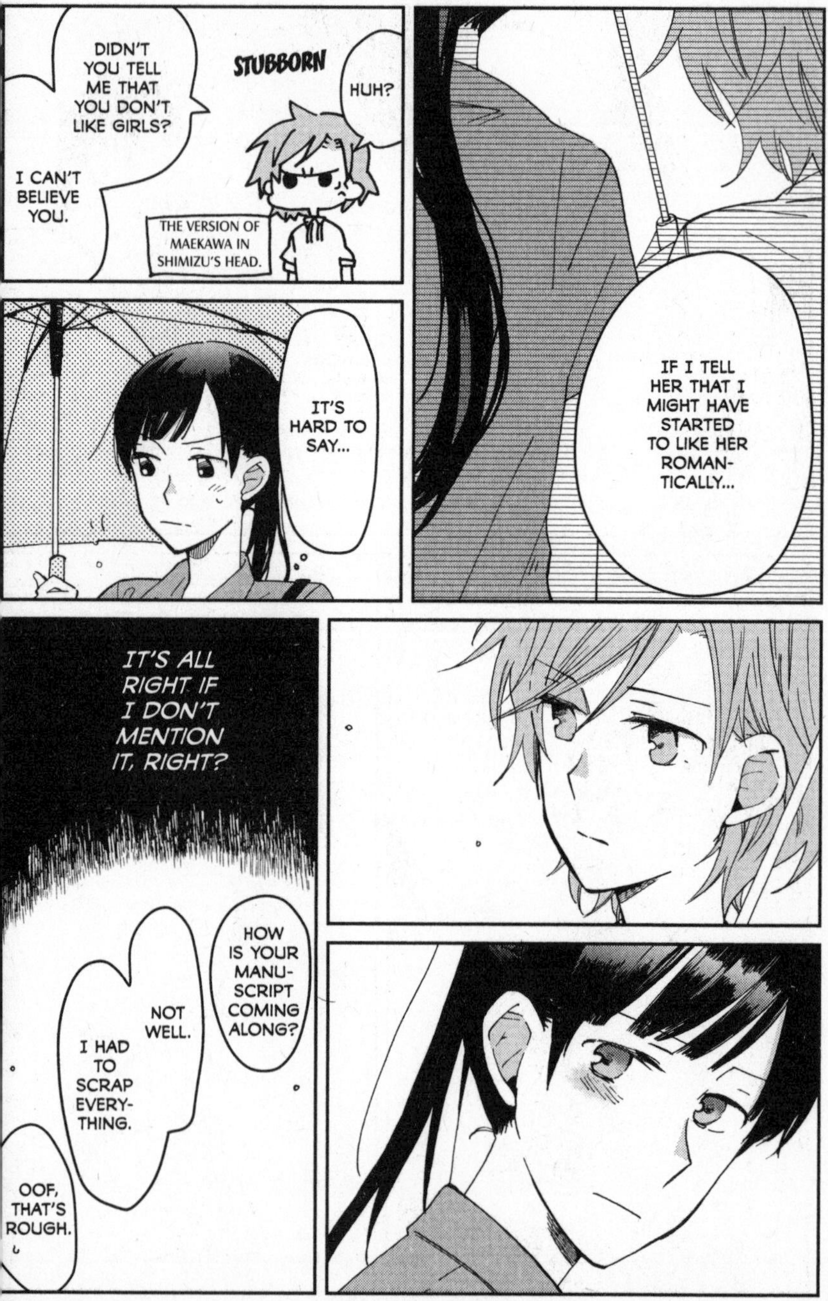
IF I TELL HER THAT I MIGHT HAVE STARTED TO LIKE HER ROMANTICALLY...
HUH?
STUBBORN
DIDN'T YOU TELL ME THAT YOU DON'T LIKE GIRLS?
I CAN'T BELIEVE YOU.
THE VERSION OF MAEKAWA IN SHIMIZU'S HEAD.
IT'S HARD TO SAY...
IT'S ALL RIGHT IF I DON'T MENTION IT, RIGHT?
HOW IS YOUR MANUSCRIPT COMING ALONG?
NOT WELL.
I HAD TO SCRAP EVERYTHING.
OOF, THAT'S ROUGH.

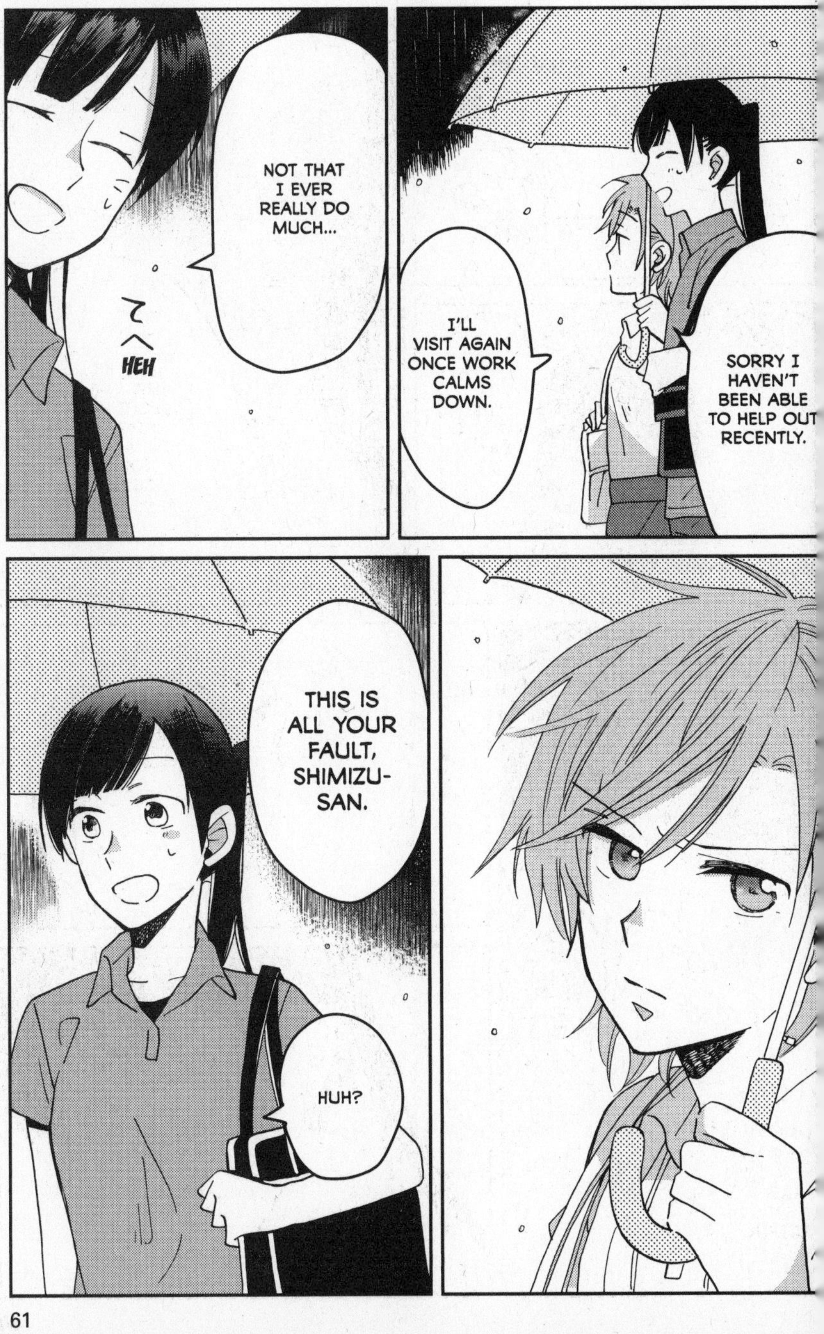
SORRY I HAVEN'T BEEN ABLE TO HELP OUT RECENTLY.
I'LL VISIT AGAIN ONCE WORK CALMS DOWN.
NOT THAT I EVER REALLY DO MUCH...
てへ
HEH
THIS IS ALL YOUR FAULT, SHIMIZU-SAN.
HUH?

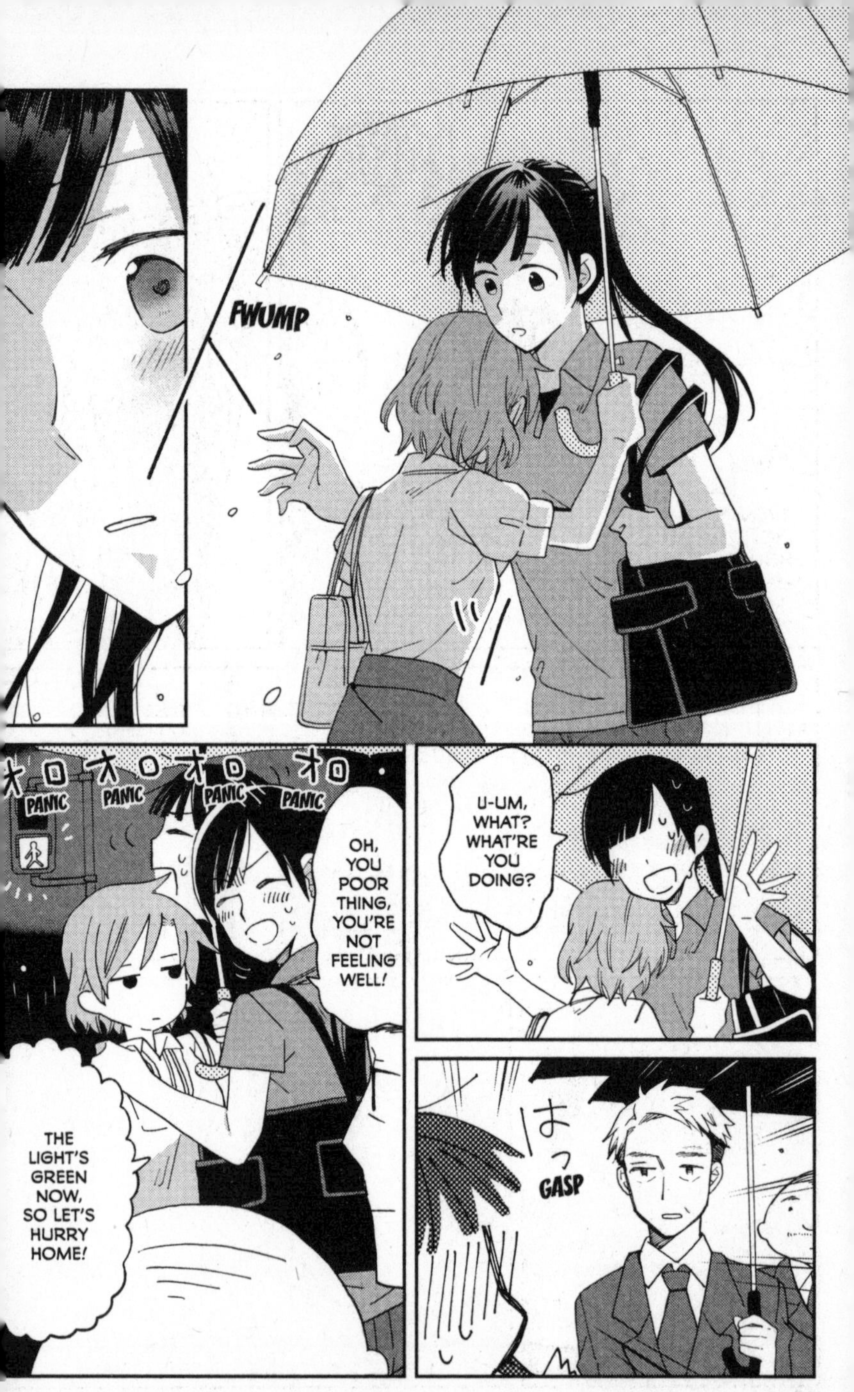
FWUMP
U-UM, WHAT? WHAT'RE YOU DOING?
GASP
PANIC PANIC PANIC PANIC
OH, YOU POOR THING, YOU'RE NOT FEELING WELL!
THE LIGHT'S GREEN NOW, SO LET'S HURRY HOME!

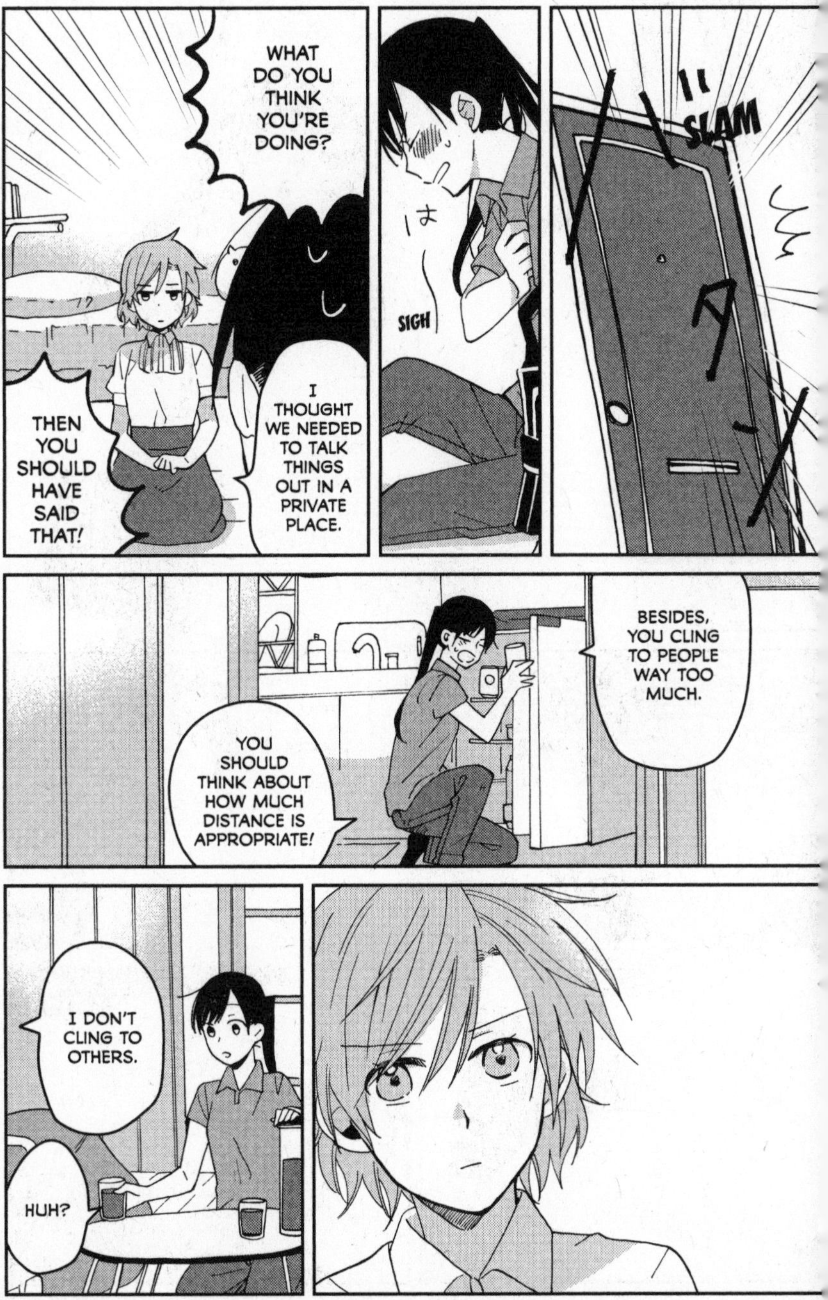
SLAM
SIGH
は
WHAT DO YOU THINK YOU'RE DOING?
I THOUGHT WE NEEDED TO TALK THINGS OUT IN A PRIVATE PLACE.
THEN YOU SHOULD HAVE SAID THAT!
BESIDES, YOU CLING TO PEOPLE WAY TOO MUCH.
YOU SHOULD THINK ABOUT HOW MUCH DISTANCE IS APPROPRIATE!
I DON'T CLING TO OTHERS.
HUH?

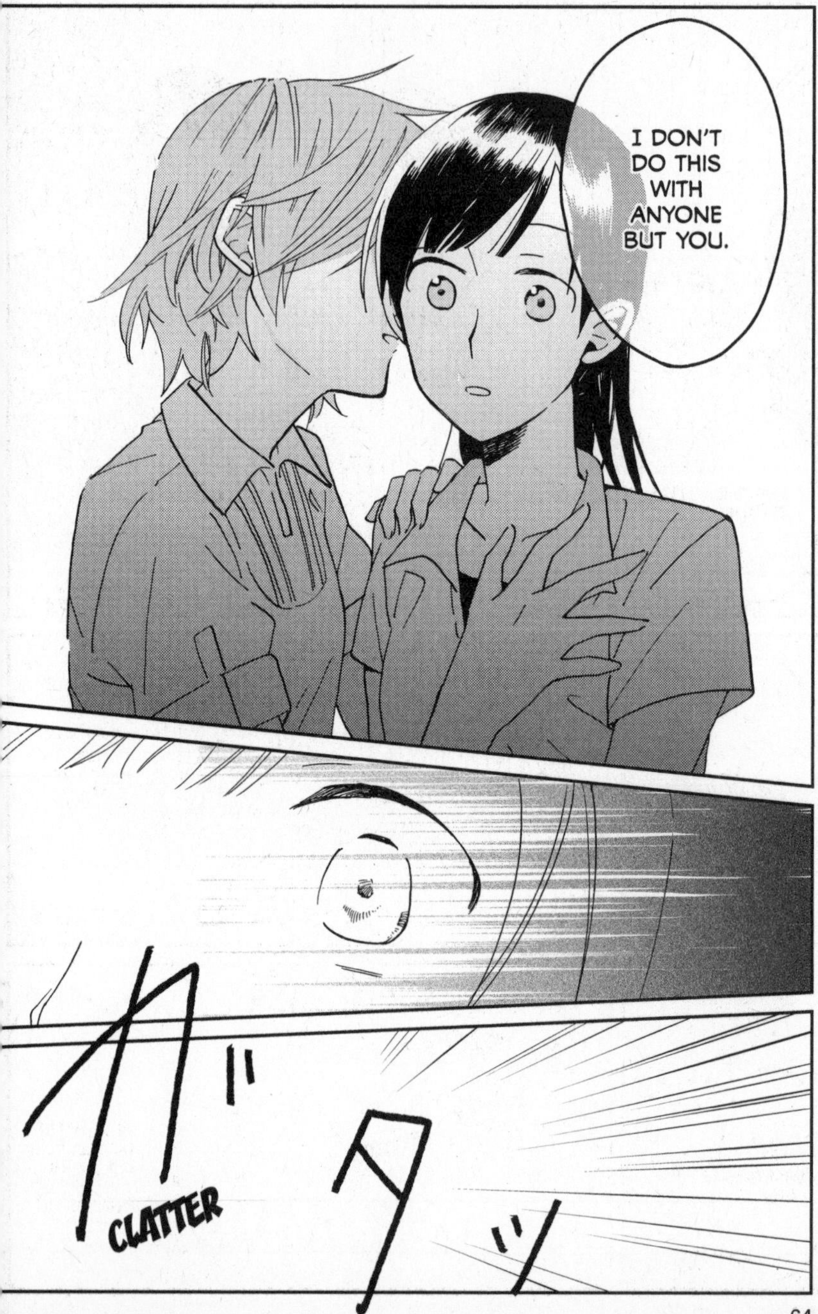
I DON'T DO THIS WITH ANYONE BUT YOU.
ガタッ
CLATTER

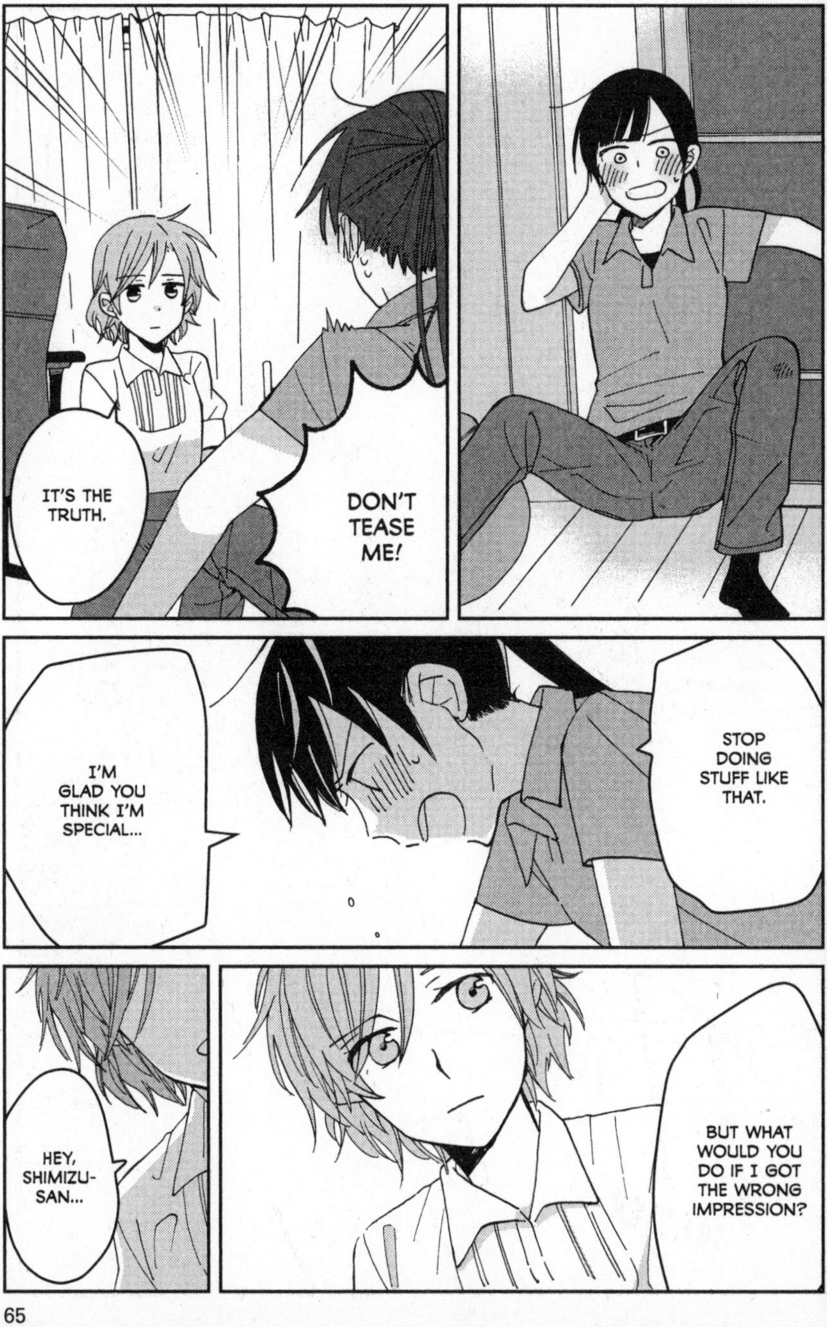
DON'T TEASE ME!
IT'S THE TRUTH.
STOP DOING STUFF LIKE THAT.
I'M GLAD YOU THINK I'M SPECIAL...
BUT WHAT WOULD YOU DO IF I GOT THE WRONG IMPRESSION?
HEY, SHIMIZU-SAN...

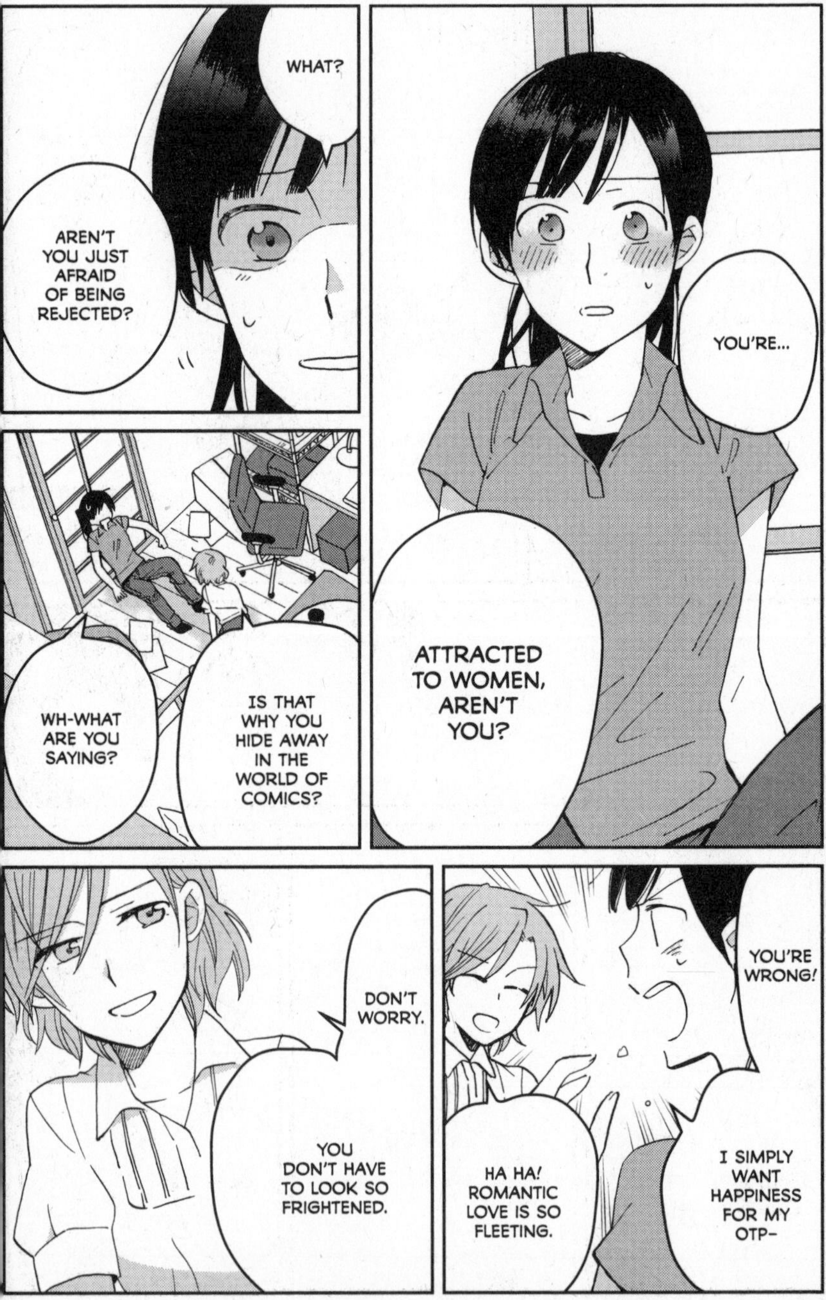
YOU'RE...
ATTRACTED TO WOMEN, AREN'T YOU?
WHAT?
AREN'T YOU JUST AFRAID OF BEING REJECTED?
IS THAT WHY YOU HIDE AWAY IN THE WORLD OF COMICS?
WH-WHAT ARE YOU SAYING?
YOU'RE WRONG!
I SIMPLY WANT HAPPINESS FOR MY OTP–
HA HA! ROMANTIC LOVE IS SO FLEETING.
DON'T WORRY.
YOU DON'T HAVE TO LOOK SO FRIGHTENED.

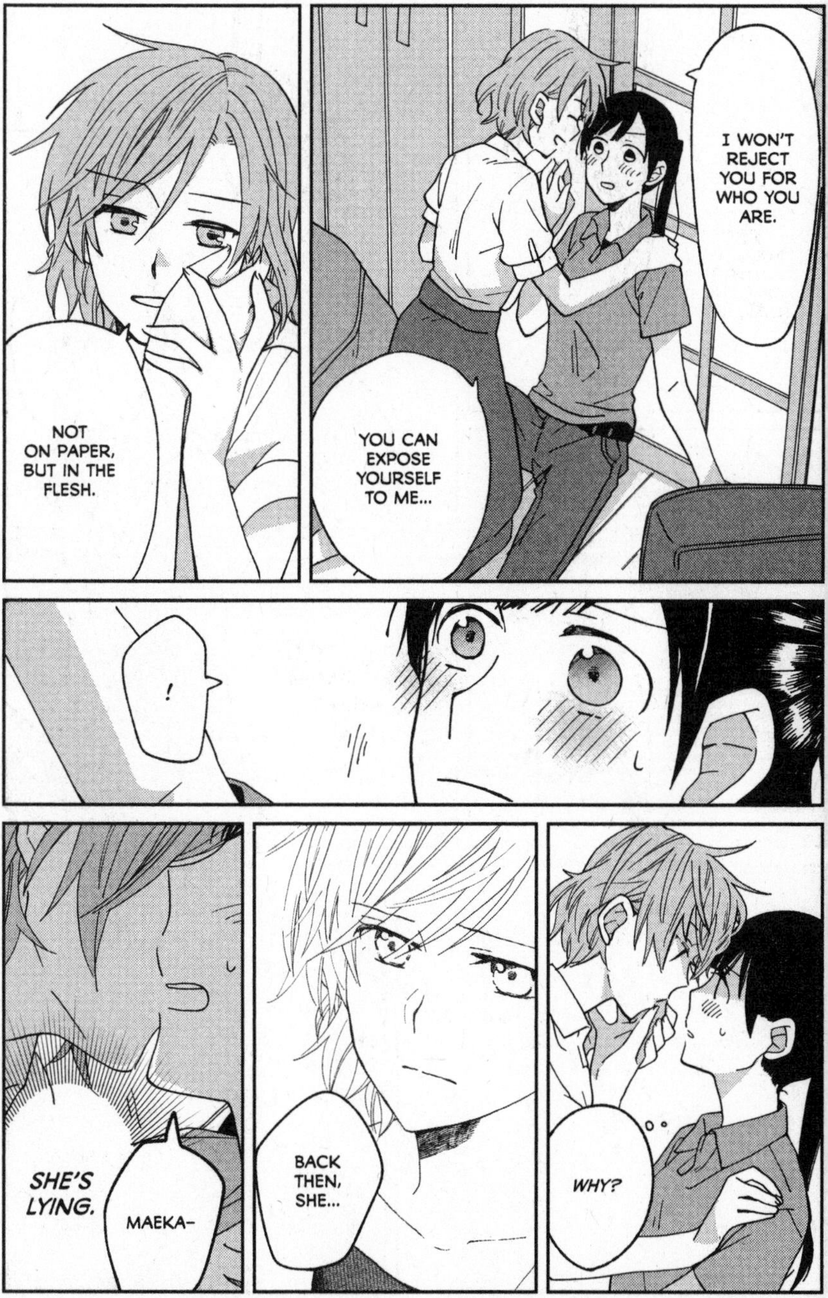
I WON'T REJECT YOU FOR WHO YOU ARE.
YOU CAN EXPOSE YOURSELF TO ME...
NOT ON PAPER, BUT IN THE FLESH.
!
WHY?
BACK THEN, SHE...
MAEKA-
SHE'S LYING.

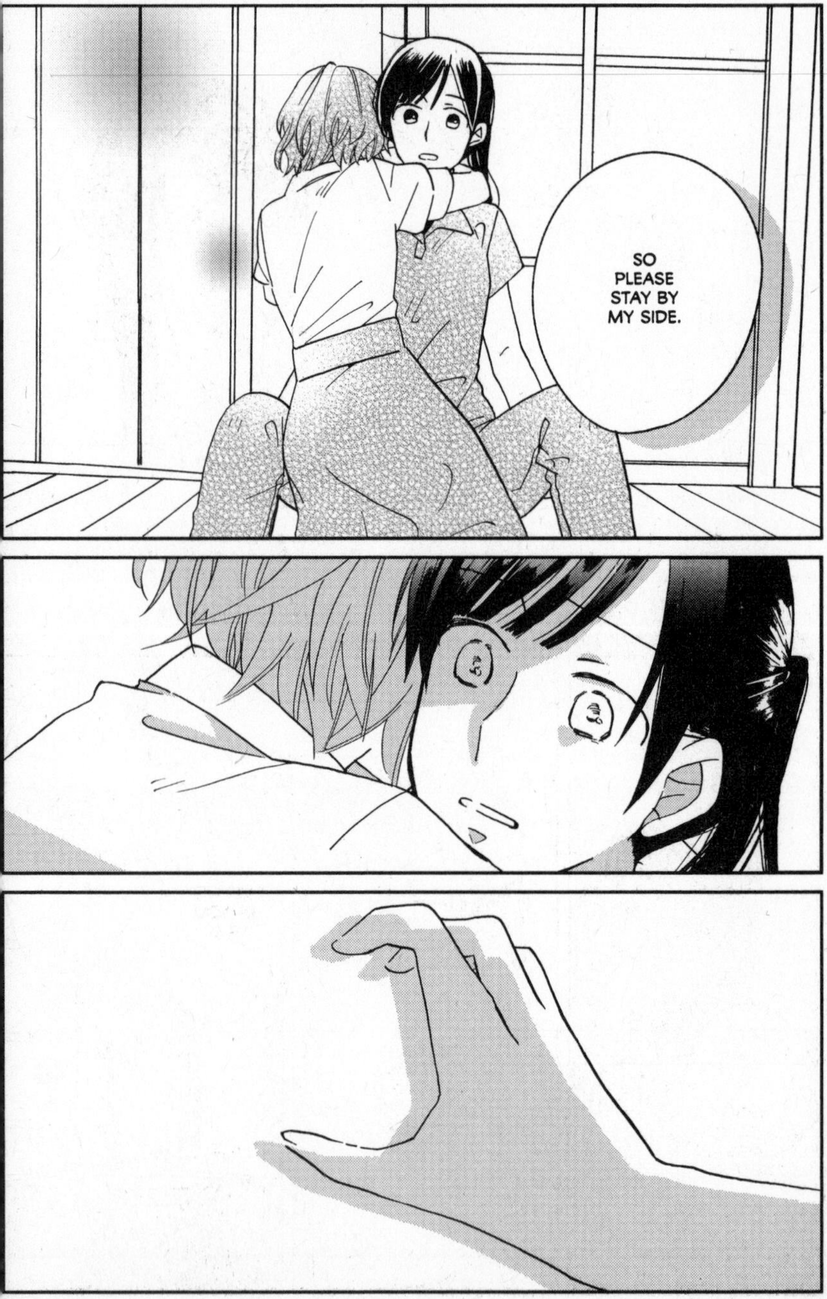
SO PLEASE STAY BY MY SIDE.

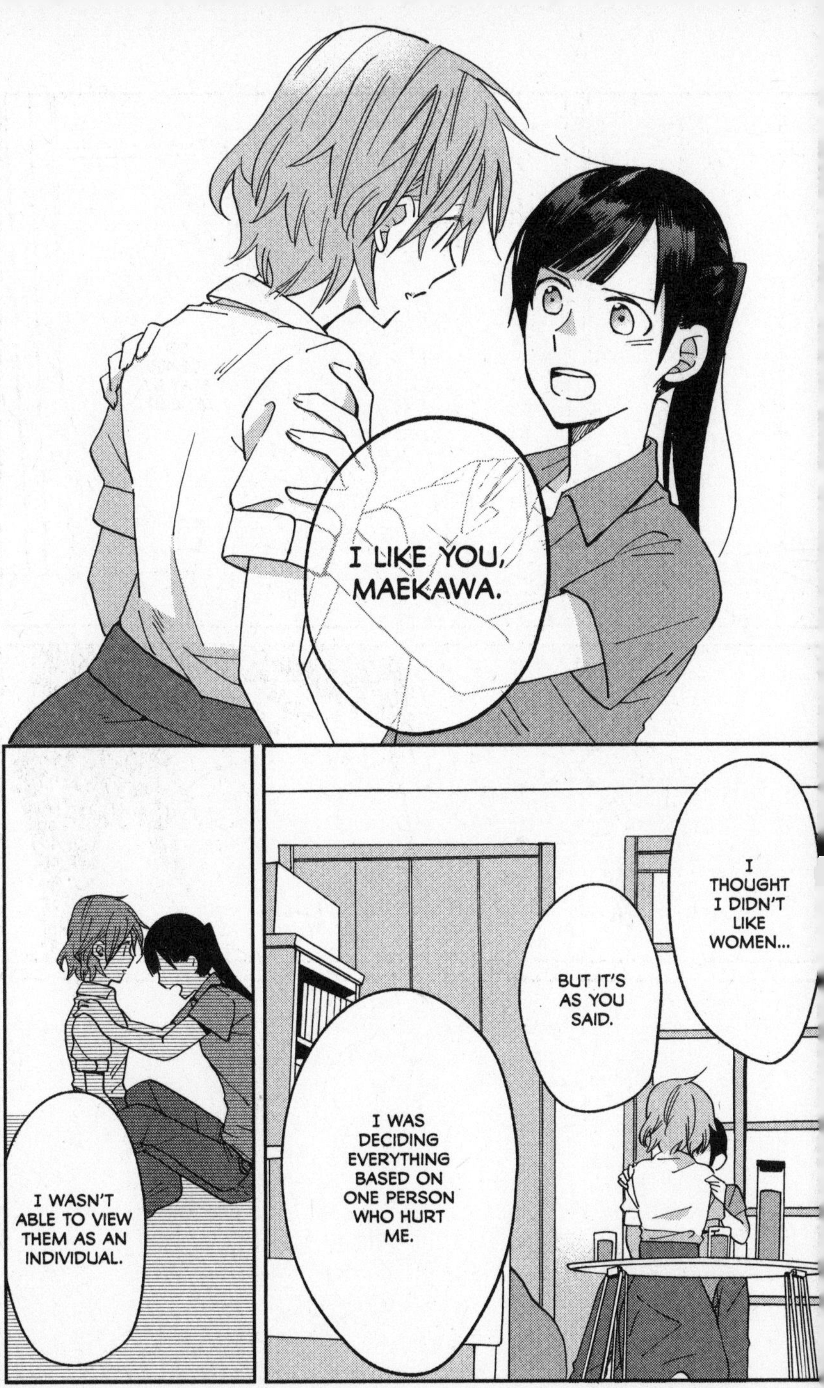
I LIKE YOU, MAEKAWA.
I THOUGHT I DIDN'T LIKE WOMEN...
BUT IT'S AS YOU SAID.
I WAS DECIDING EVERYTHING BASED ON ONE PERSON WHO HURT ME.
I WASN'T ABLE TO VIEW THEM AS AN INDIVIDUAL.

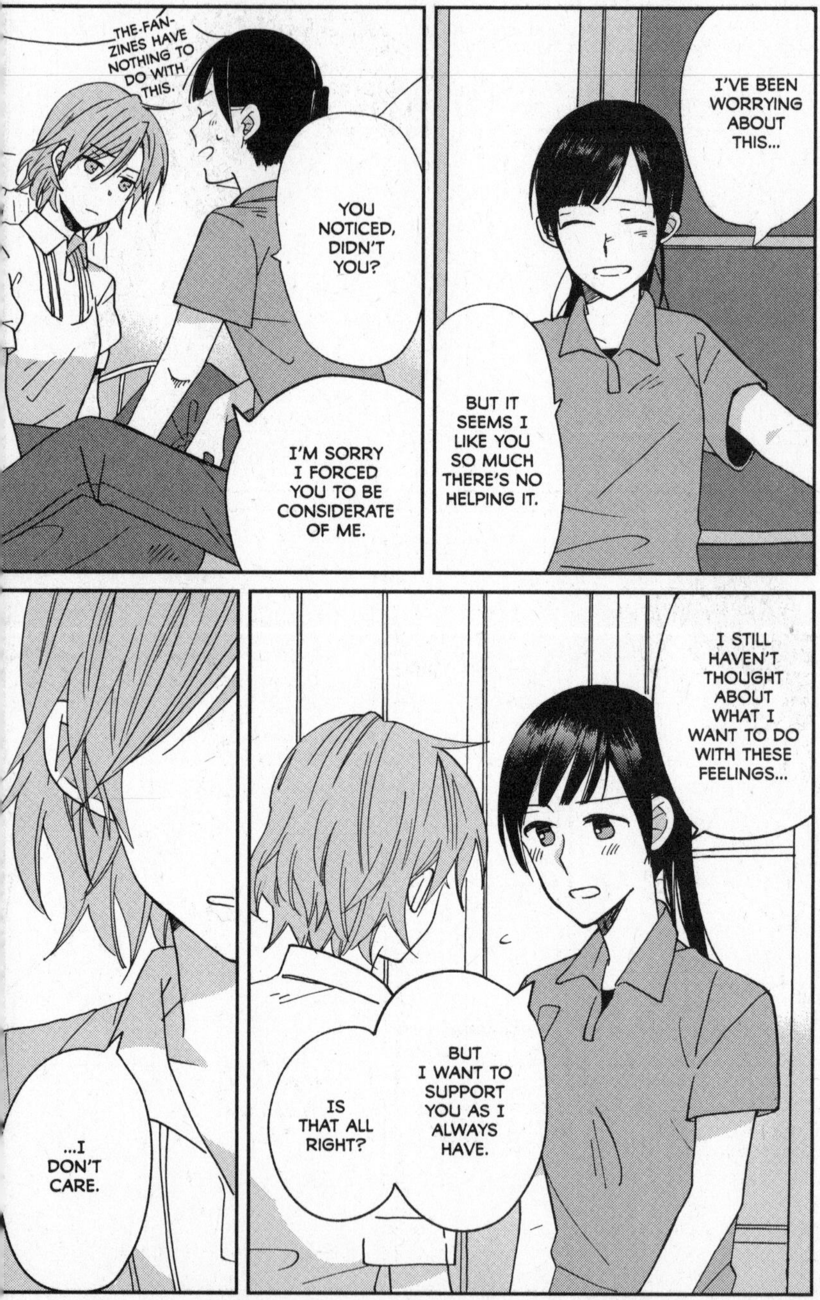
I'VE BEEN WORRYING ABOUT THIS...
BUT IT SEEMS I LIKE YOU SO MUCH THERE'S NO HELPING IT.
THE-FANZINES HAVE NOTHING TO DO WITH THIS.
YOU NOTICED, DIDN'T YOU?
I'M SORRY I FORCED YOU TO BE CONSIDERATE OF ME.
I STILL HAVEN'T THOUGHT ABOUT WHAT I WANT TO DO WITH THESE FEELINGS...
BUT I WANT TO SUPPORT YOU AS I ALWAYS HAVE.
IS THAT ALL RIGHT?
...I DON'T CARE.

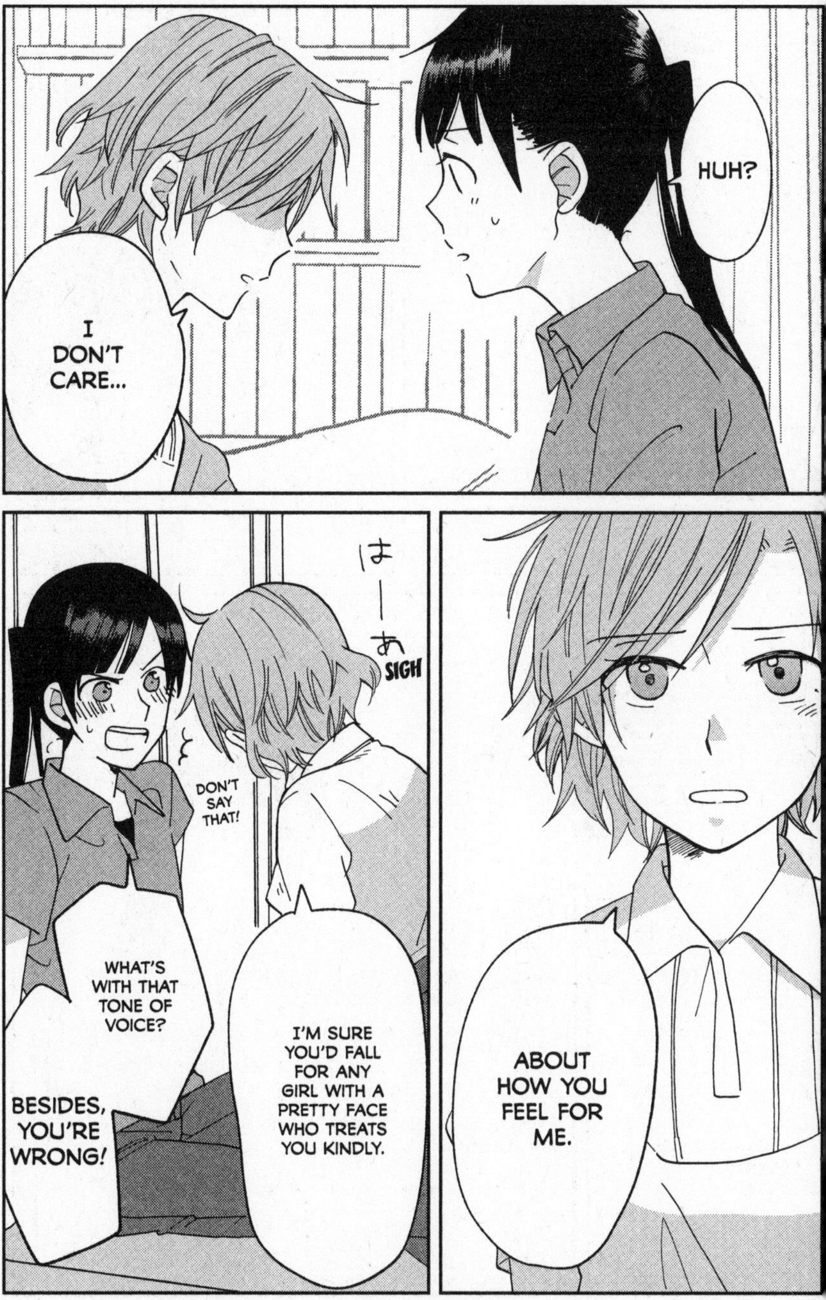
HUH?
I DON'T CARE...
ABOUT HOW YOU FEEL FOR ME.
はーあ
SIGH
DON'T SAY THAT!
I'M SURE YOU'D FALL FOR ANY GIRL WITH A PRETTY FACE WHO TREATS YOU KINDLY.
WHAT'S WITH THAT TONE OF VOICE?
BESIDES, YOU'RE WRONG!

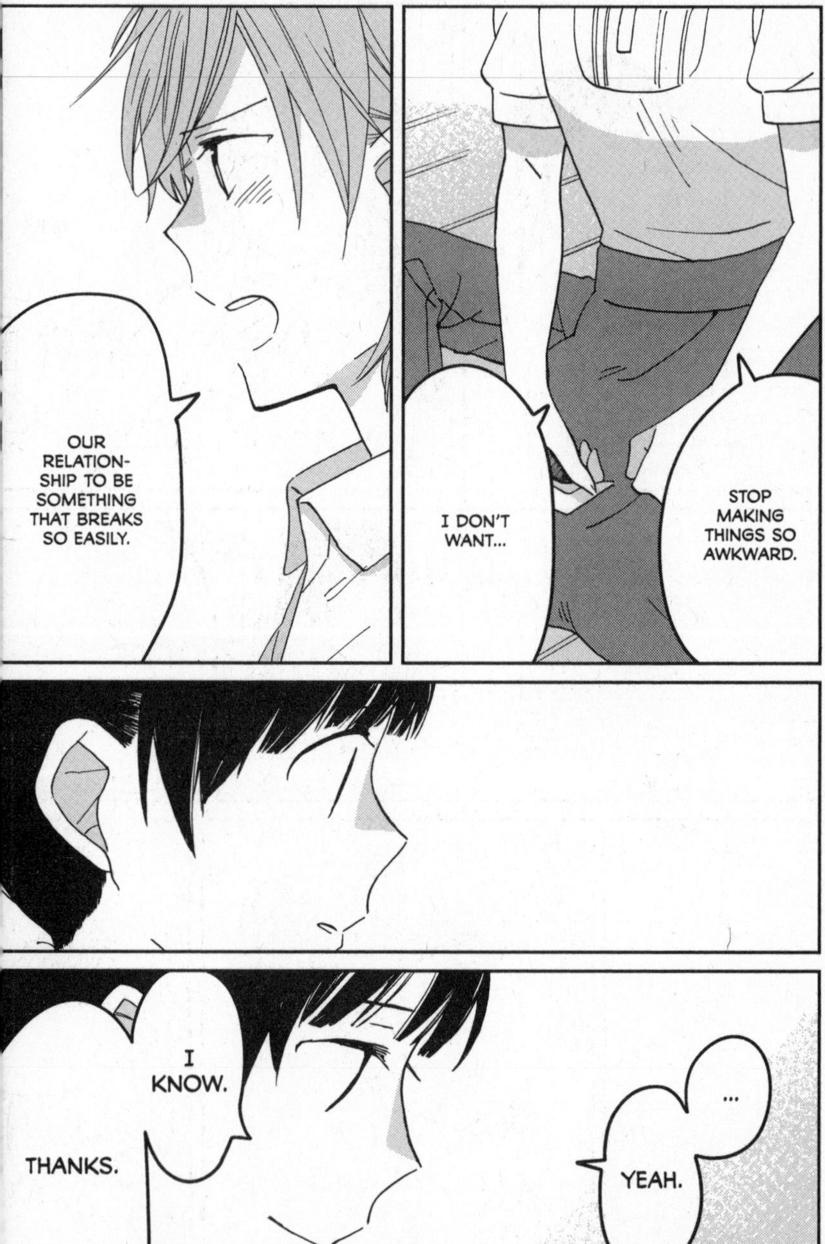
STOP MAKING THINGS SO AWKWARD.
I DON'T WANT...
OUR RELATION-SHIP TO BE SOMETHING THAT BREAKS SO EASILY.
...
YEAH.
I KNOW.
THANKS.

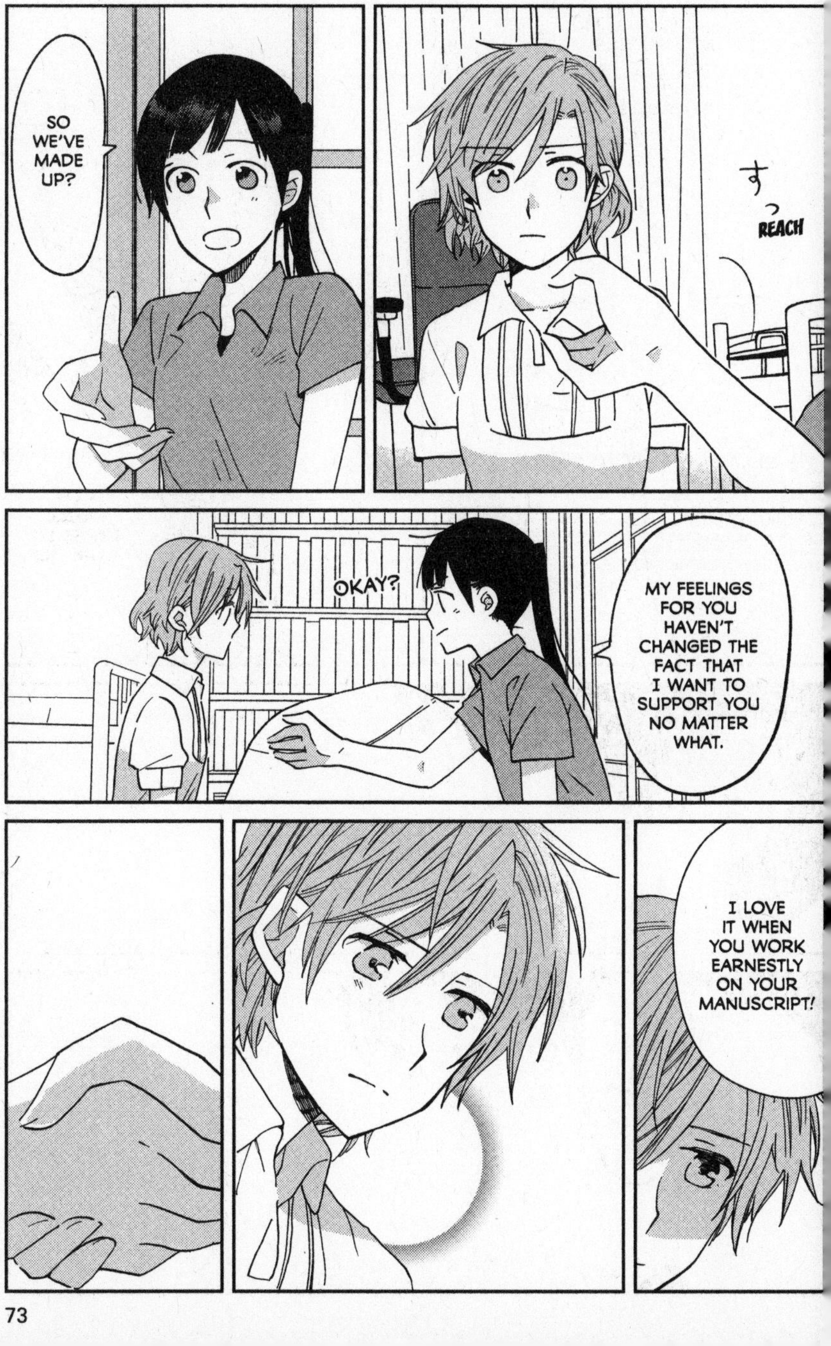
すっ
REACH
SO WE'VE MADE UP?
MY FEELINGS FOR YOU HAVEN'T CHANGED THE FACT THAT I WANT TO SUPPORT YOU NO MATTER WHAT.
OKAY?
I LOVE IT WHEN YOU WORK EARNESTLY ON YOUR MANUSCRIPT!

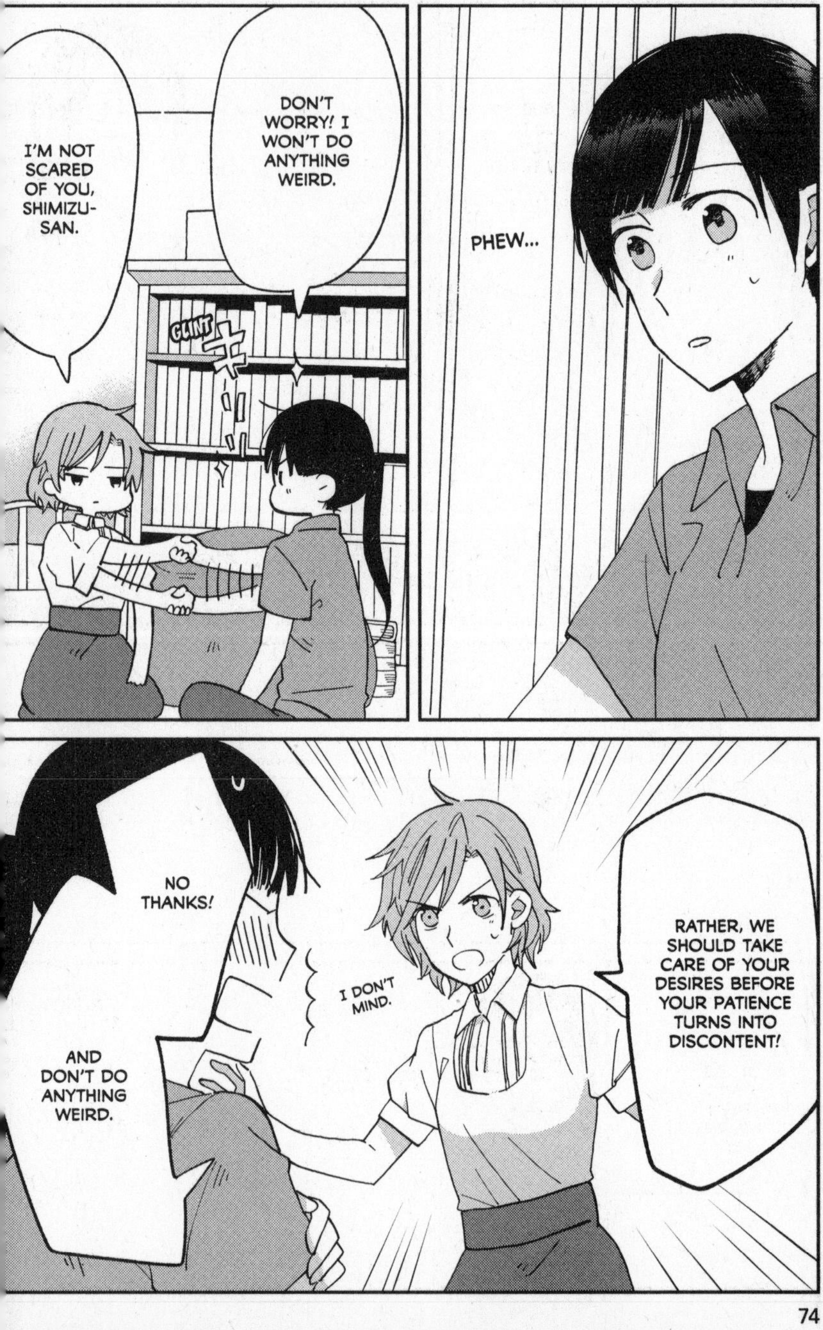
PHEW...
DON'T WORRY! I WON'T DO ANYTHING WEIRD.
I'M NOT SCARED OF YOU, SHIMIZU-SAN.
GLINT
RATHER, WE SHOULD TAKE CARE OF YOUR DESIRES BEFORE YOUR PATIENCE TURNS INTO DISCONTENT!
I DON'T MIND.
NO THANKS!
AND DON'T DO ANYTHING WEIRD.

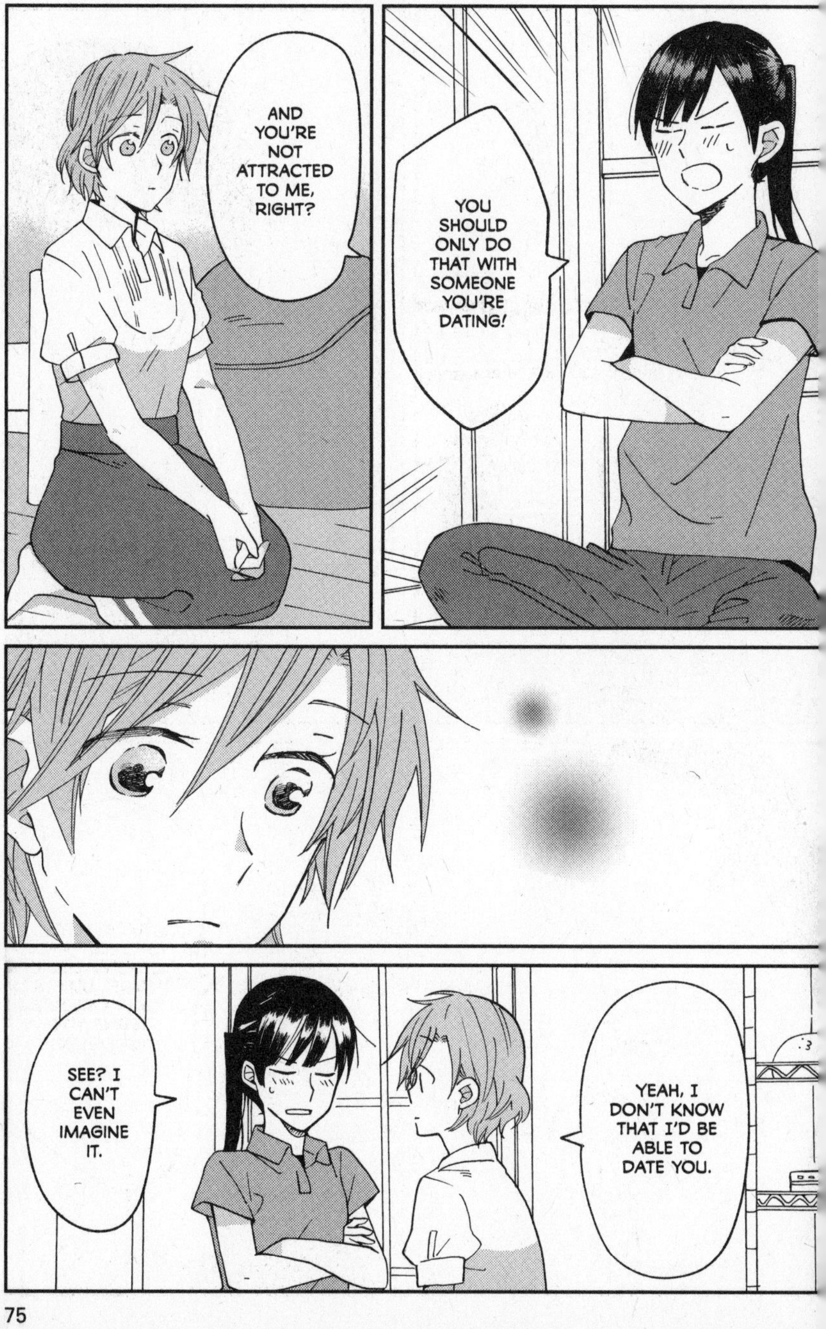
YOU SHOULD ONLY DO THAT WITH SOMEONE YOU'RE DATING!
AND YOU'RE NOT ATTRACTED TO ME, RIGHT?
YEAH, I DON'T KNOW THAT I'D BE ABLE TO DATE YOU.
SEE? I CAN'T EVEN IMAGINE IT.

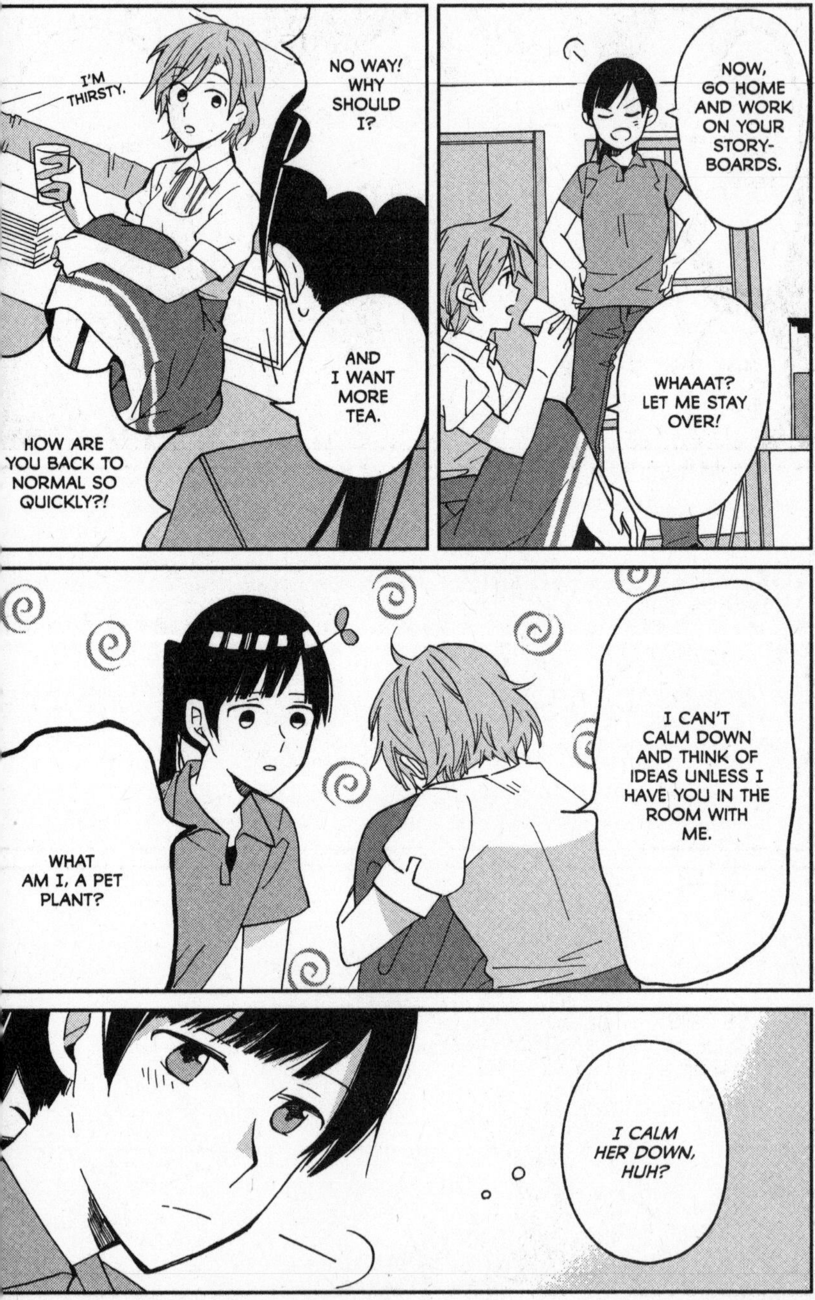

NOW, GO HOME AND WORK ON YOUR STORY-BOARDS.
WHAAAT? LET ME STAY OVER!
NO WAY! WHY SHOULD I?
I'M THIRSTY.
AND I WANT MORE TEA.
HOW ARE YOU BACK TO NORMAL SO QUICKLY?!
I CAN'T CALM DOWN AND THINK OF IDEAS UNLESS I HAVE YOU IN THE ROOM WITH ME.
WHAT AM I, A PET PLANT?
I CALM HER DOWN, HUH?

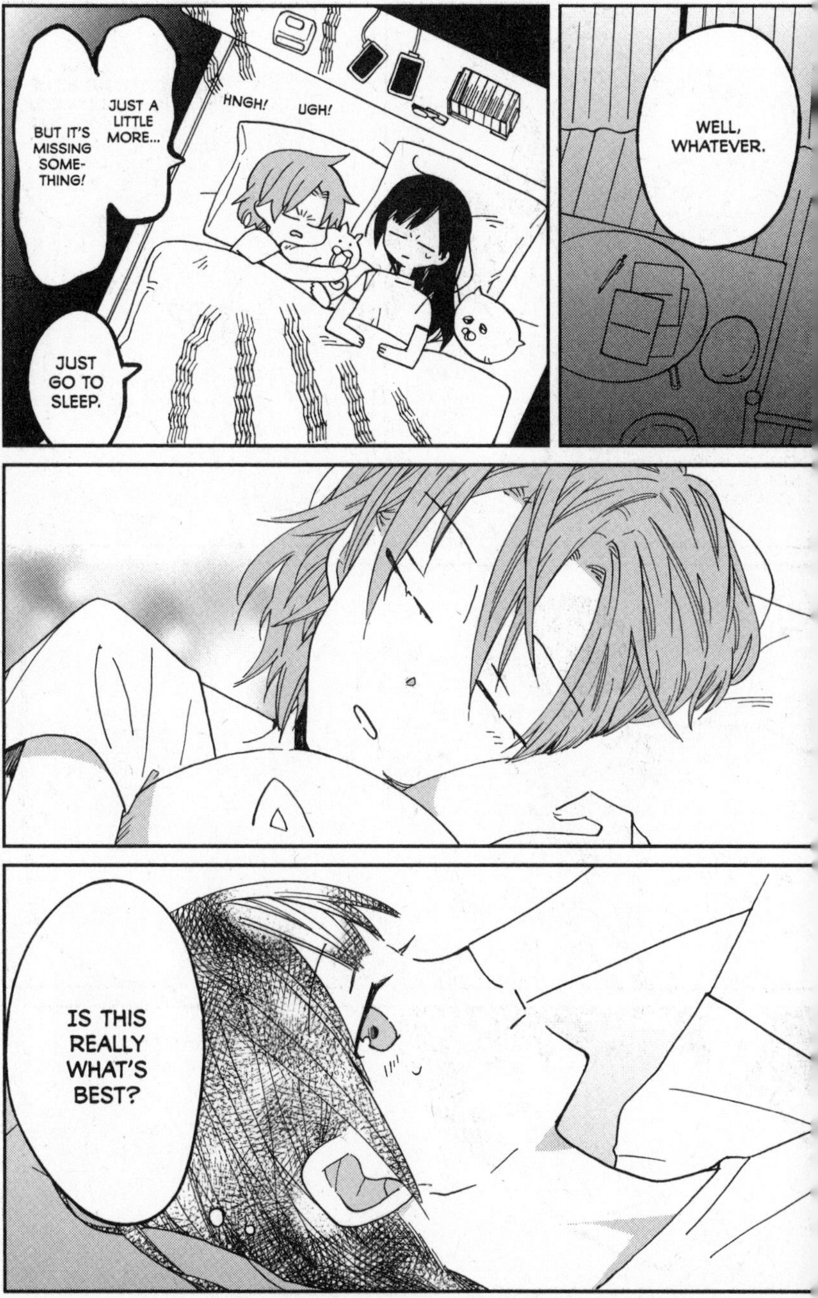
WELL, WHATEVER.
UGH!
HNGH!
JUST A LITTLE MORE...
BUT IT'S MISSING SOME-THING!
JUST GO TO SLEEP.
IS THIS REALLY WHAT'S BEST?

"MA..."

CONTINUED ON PAGE 129 (AFTER CHAPTER 13).

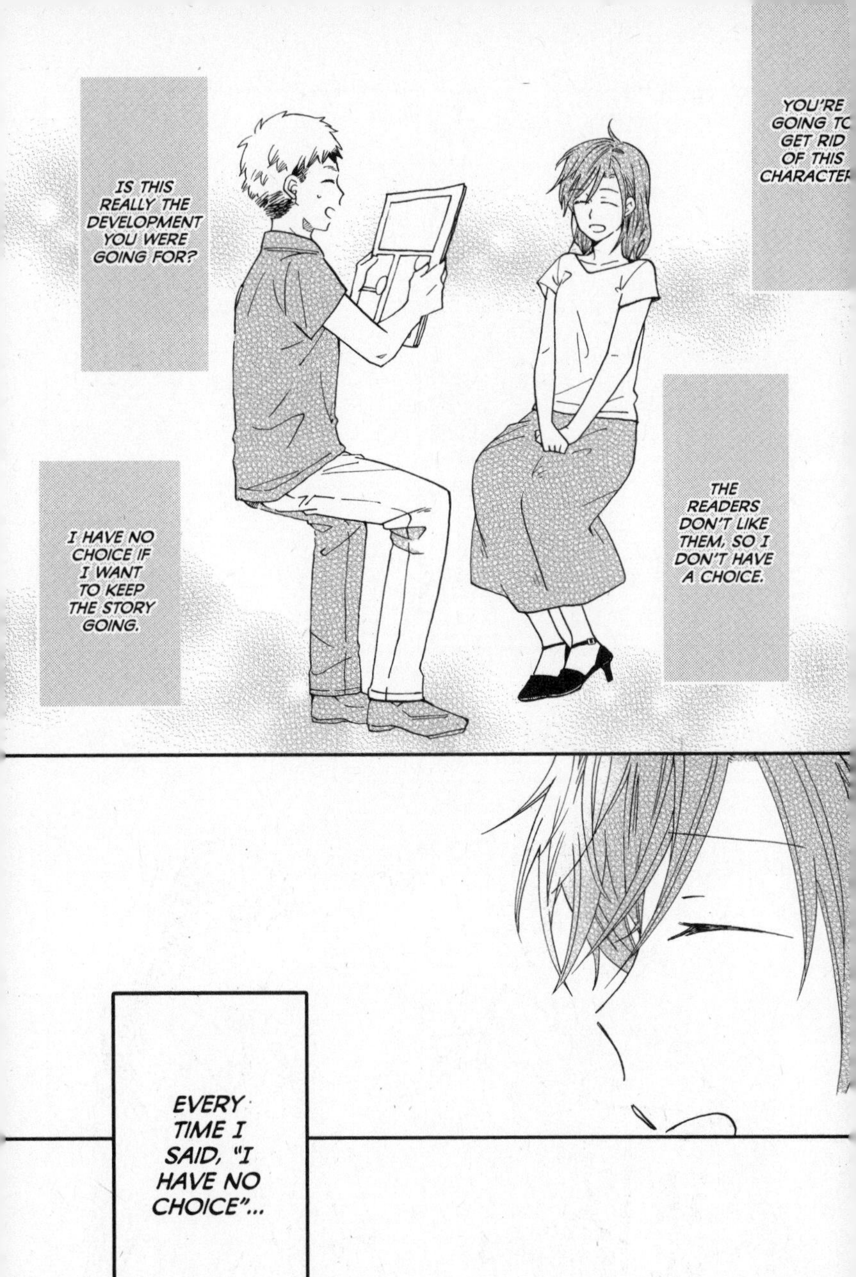
YOU'RE GOING TO GET RID OF THIS CHARACTER
IS THIS REALLY THE DEVELOPMENT YOU WERE GOING FOR?
THE READERS DON'T LIKE THEM, SO I DON'T HAVE A CHOICE.
I HAVE NO CHOICE IF I WANT TO KEEP THE STORY GOING.
EVERY TIME I SAID, "I HAVE NO CHOICE"...

Chapter 12

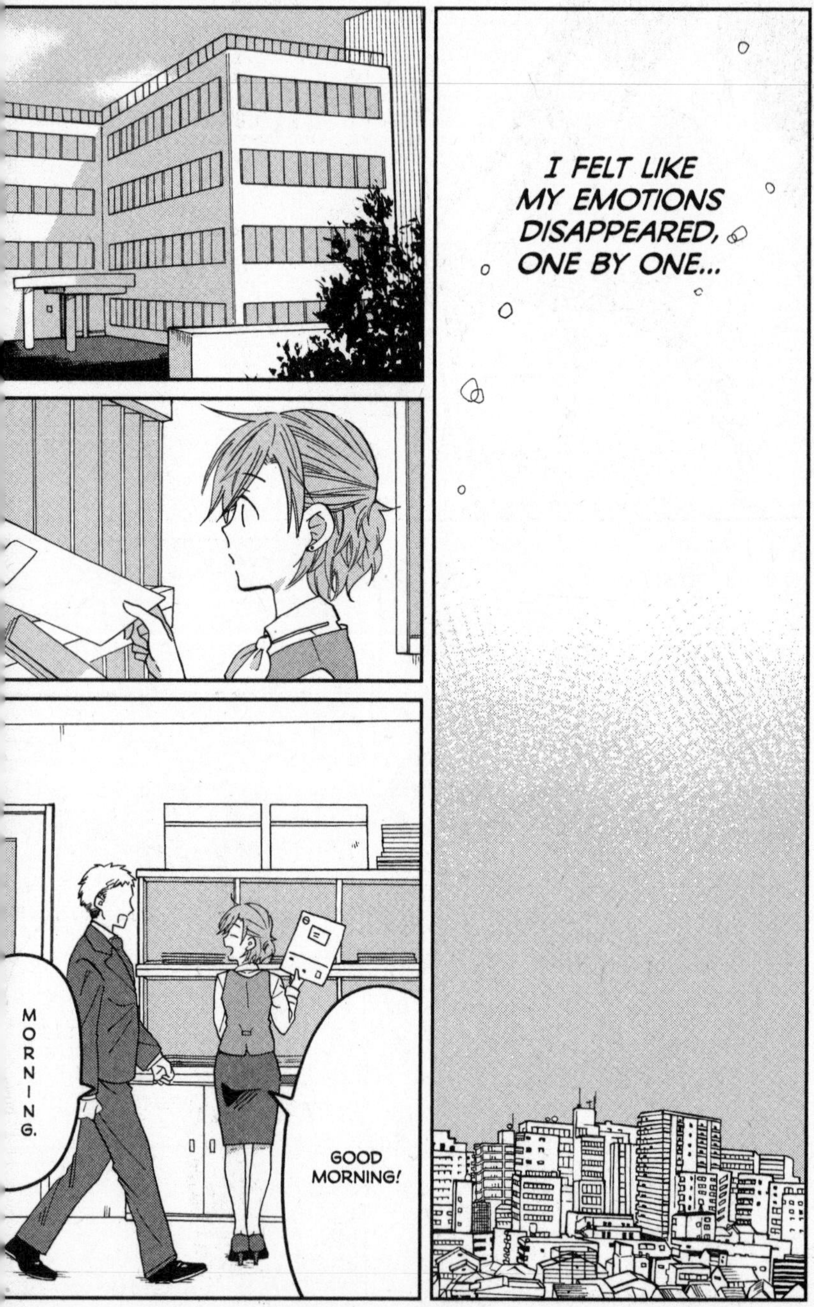
I FELT LIKE MY EMOTIONS DISAPPEARED, ONE BY ONE...
GOOD MORNING!
MORNING.

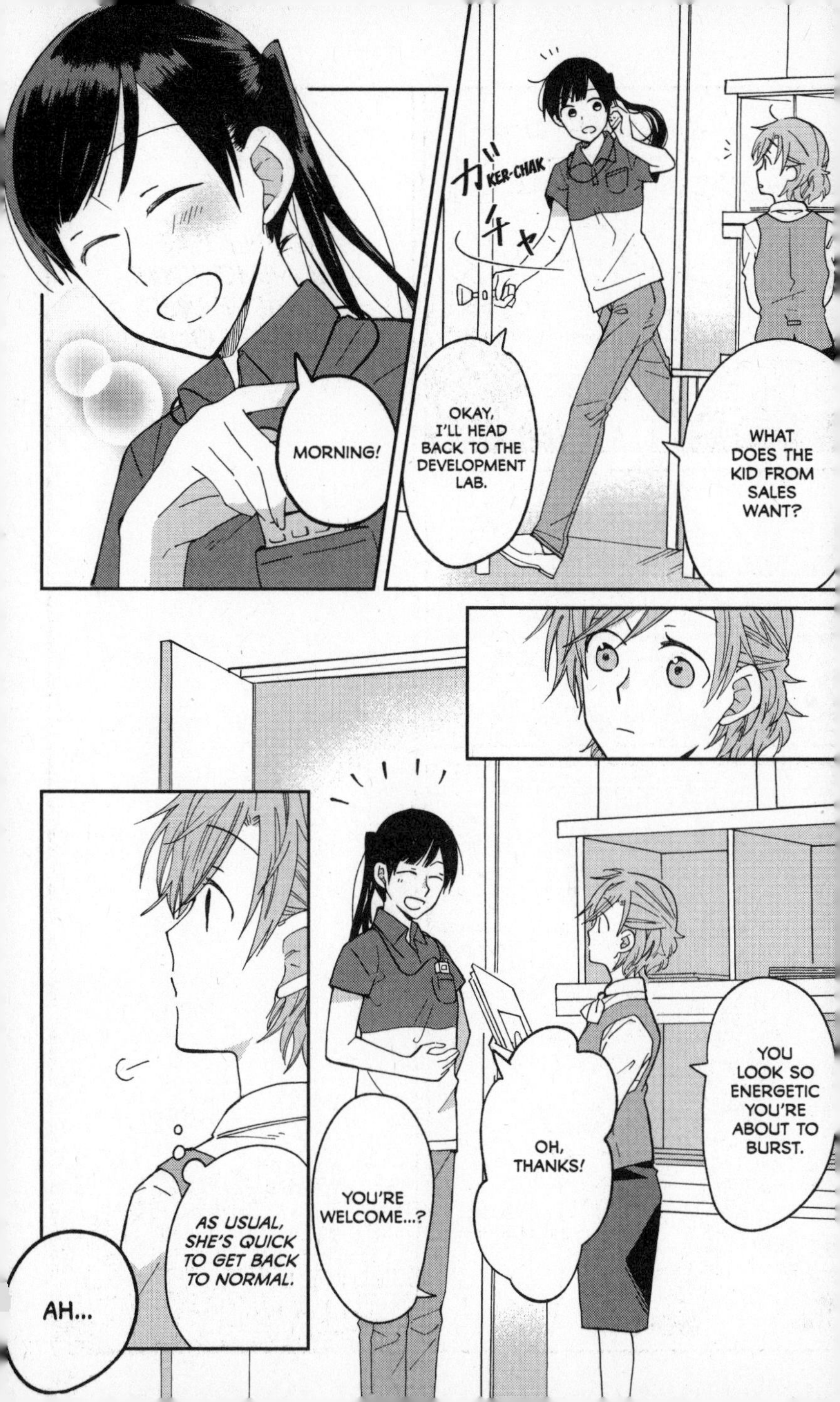

ガチャ KER-CHAK
WHAT DOES THE KID FROM SALES WANT?
OKAY, I'LL HEAD BACK TO THE DEVELOPMENT LAB.
MORNING!
YOU LOOK SO ENERGETIC YOU'RE ABOUT TO BURST.
OH, THANKS!
YOU'RE WELCOME...?
AS USUAL, SHE'S QUICK TO GET BACK TO NORMAL.
AH...

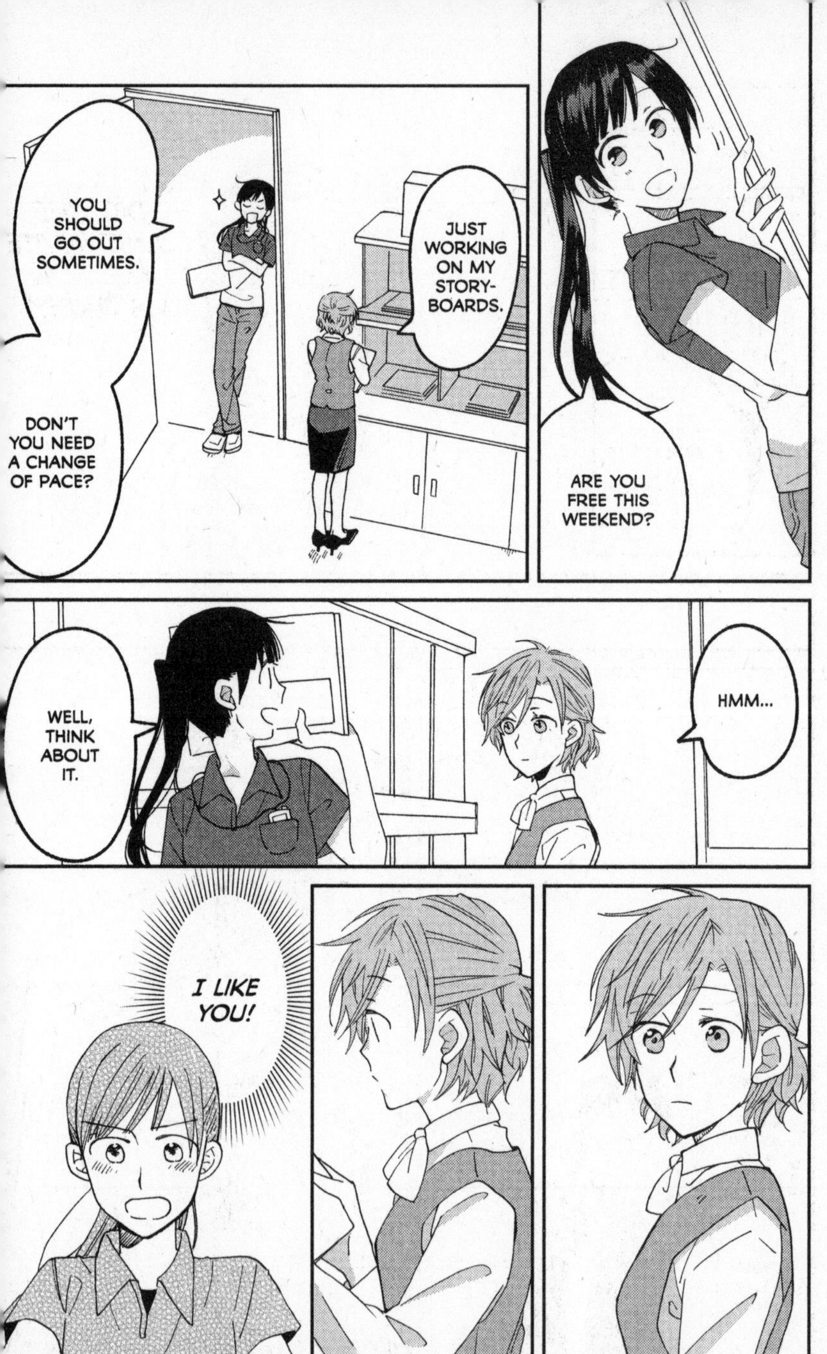
ARE YOU FREE THIS WEEKEND?
JUST WORKING ON MY STORY-BOARDS.
YOU SHOULD GO OUT SOMETIMES.
DON'T YOU NEED A CHANGE OF PACE?
HMM...
WELL, THINK ABOUT IT.
I LIKE YOU!

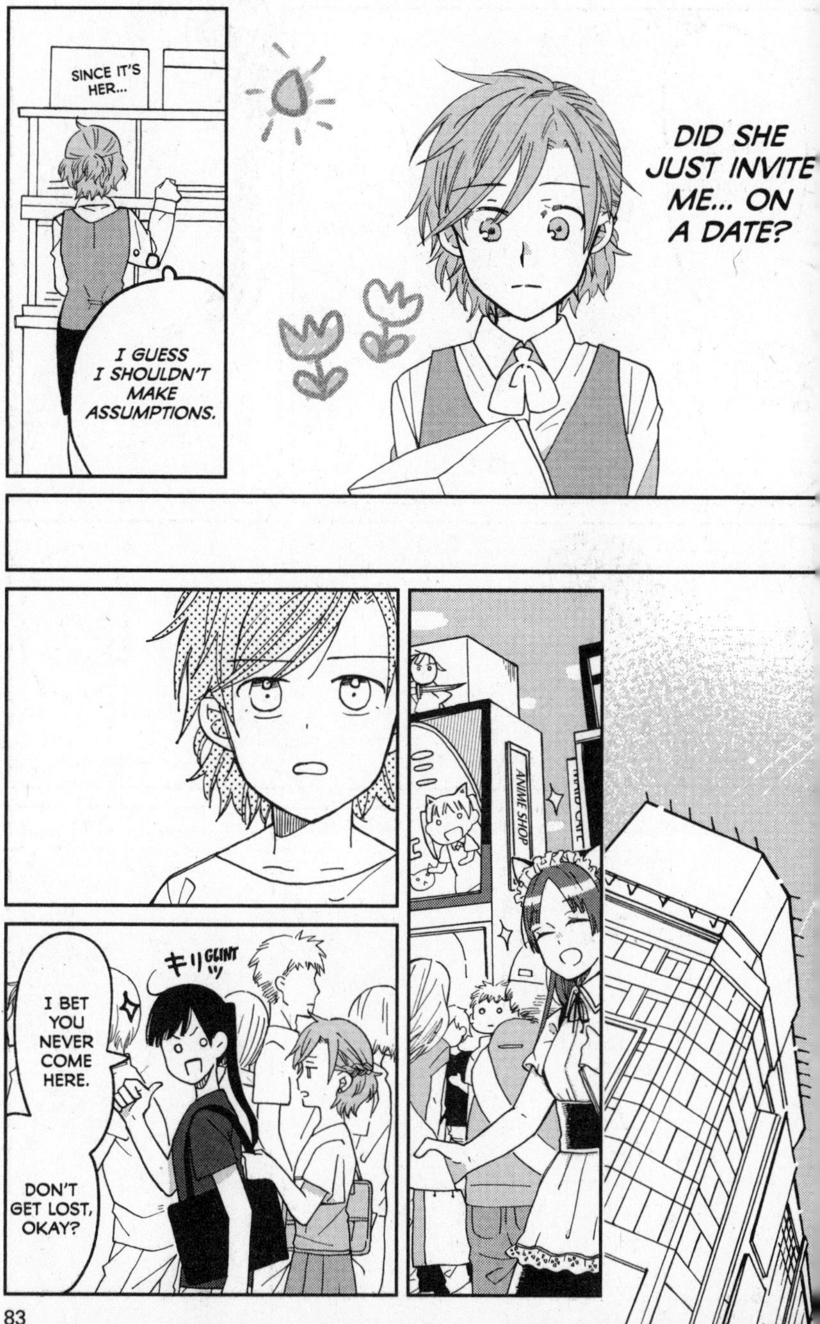
DID SHE JUST INVITE ME... ON A DATE?
SINCE IT'S HER...
I GUESS I SHOULDN'T MAKE ASSUMPTIONS.
ANIME SHOP
キリッ GLINT
I BET YOU NEVER COME HERE.
DON'T GET LOST, OKAY?

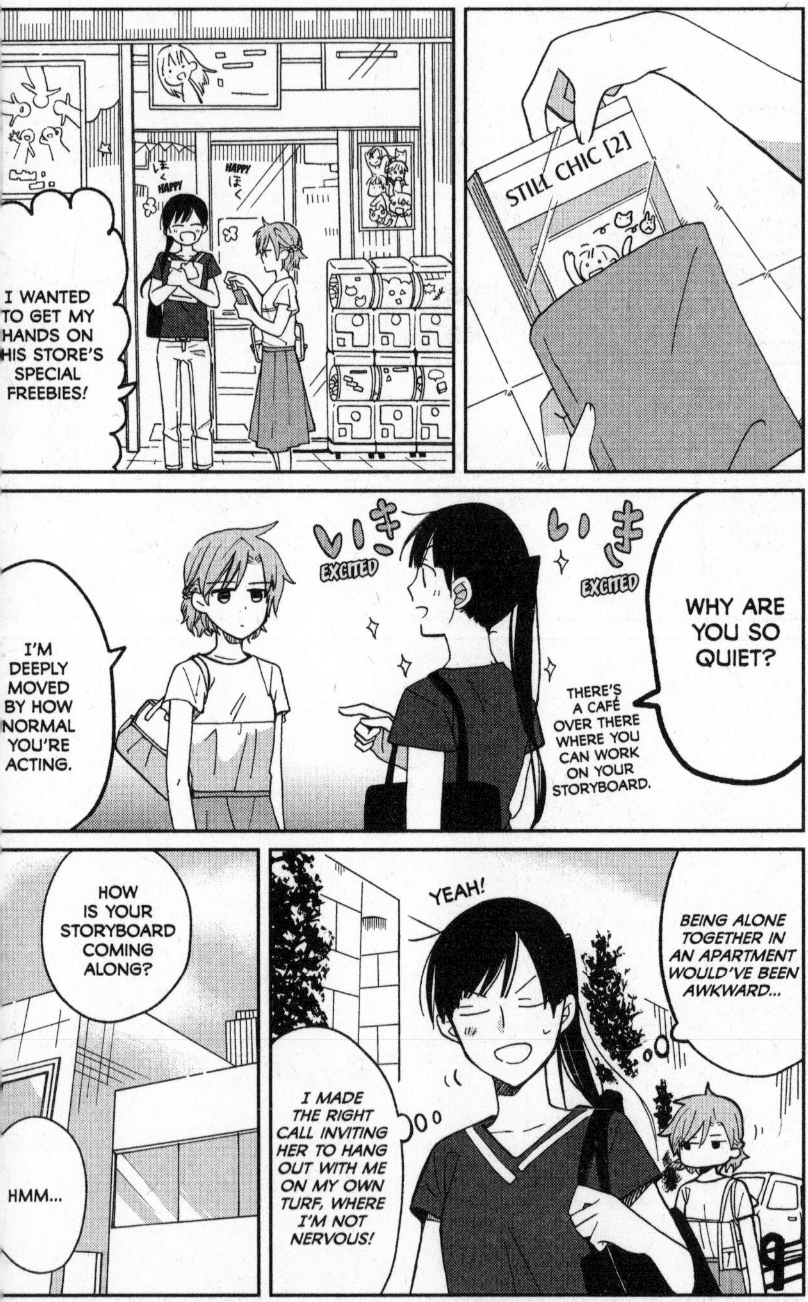
STILL CHIC [2]
I WANTED TO GET MY HANDS ON HIS STORE'S SPECIAL FREEBIES!
HAPPY ほく
ほく HAPPY
WHY ARE YOU SO QUIET?
いき EXCITED
いき EXCITED
THERE'S A CAFÉ OVER THERE WHERE YOU CAN WORK ON YOUR STORYBOARD.
I'M DEEPLY MOVED BY HOW NORMAL YOU'RE ACTING.
BEING ALONE TOGETHER IN AN APARTMENT WOULD'VE BEEN AWKWARD...
YEAH!
I MADE THE RIGHT CALL INVITING HER TO HANG OUT WITH ME ON MY OWN TURF, WHERE I'M NOT NERVOUS!
HOW IS YOUR STORYBOARD COMING ALONG?
HMM...

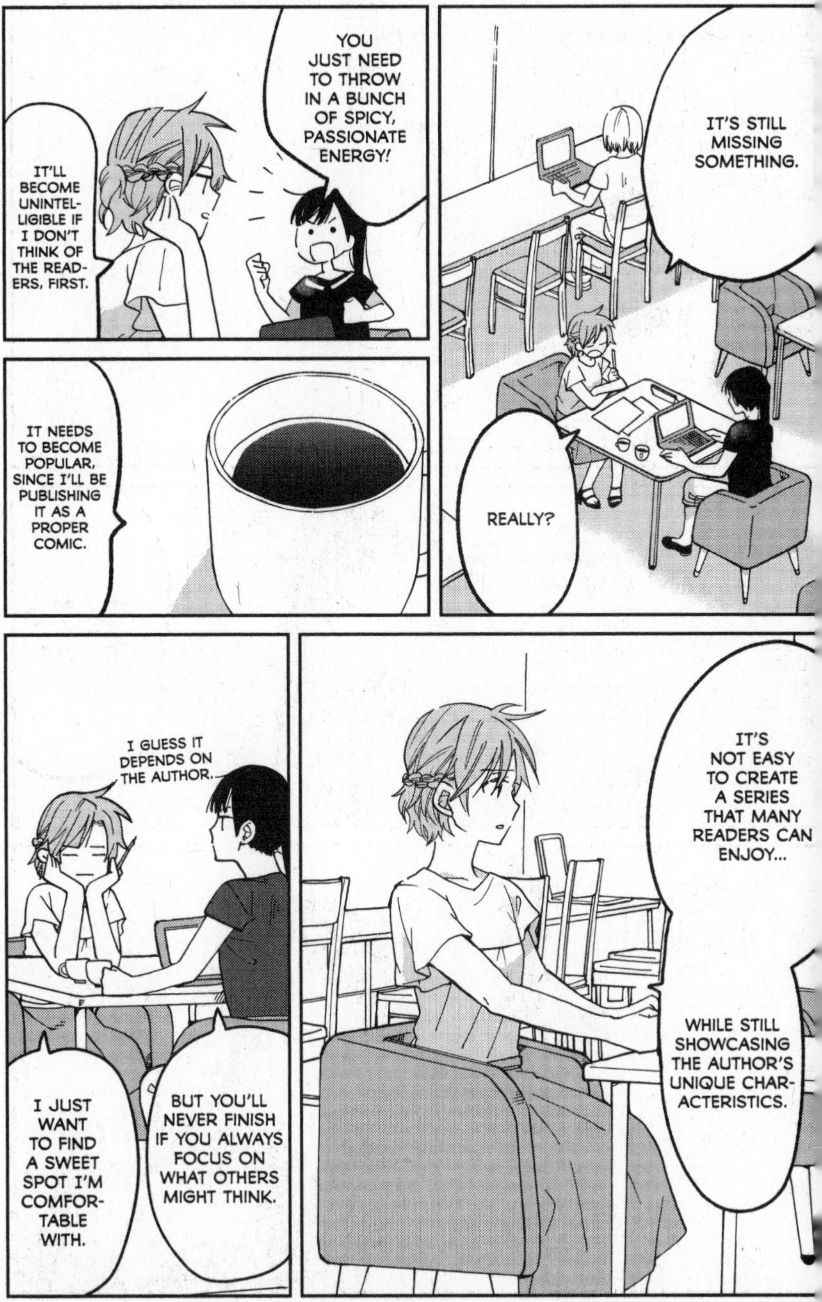
IT'S STILL MISSING SOMETHING.
REALLY?
YOU JUST NEED TO THROW IN A BUNCH OF SPICY, PASSIONATE ENERGY!
IT'LL BECOME UNINTEL-LIGIBLE IF I DON'T THINK OF THE READ-ERS, FIRST.
IT NEEDS TO BECOME POPULAR, SINCE I'LL BE PUBLISHING IT AS A PROPER COMIC.
IT'S NOT EASY TO CREATE A SERIES THAT MANY READERS CAN ENJOY...
WHILE STILL SHOWCASING THE AUTHOR'S UNIQUE CHAR-ACTERISTICS.
I GUESS IT DEPENDS ON THE AUTHOR.
BUT YOU'LL NEVER FINISH IF YOU ALWAYS FOCUS ON WHAT OTHERS MIGHT THINK.
I JUST WANT TO FIND A SWEET SPOT I'M COMFOR-TABLE WITH.

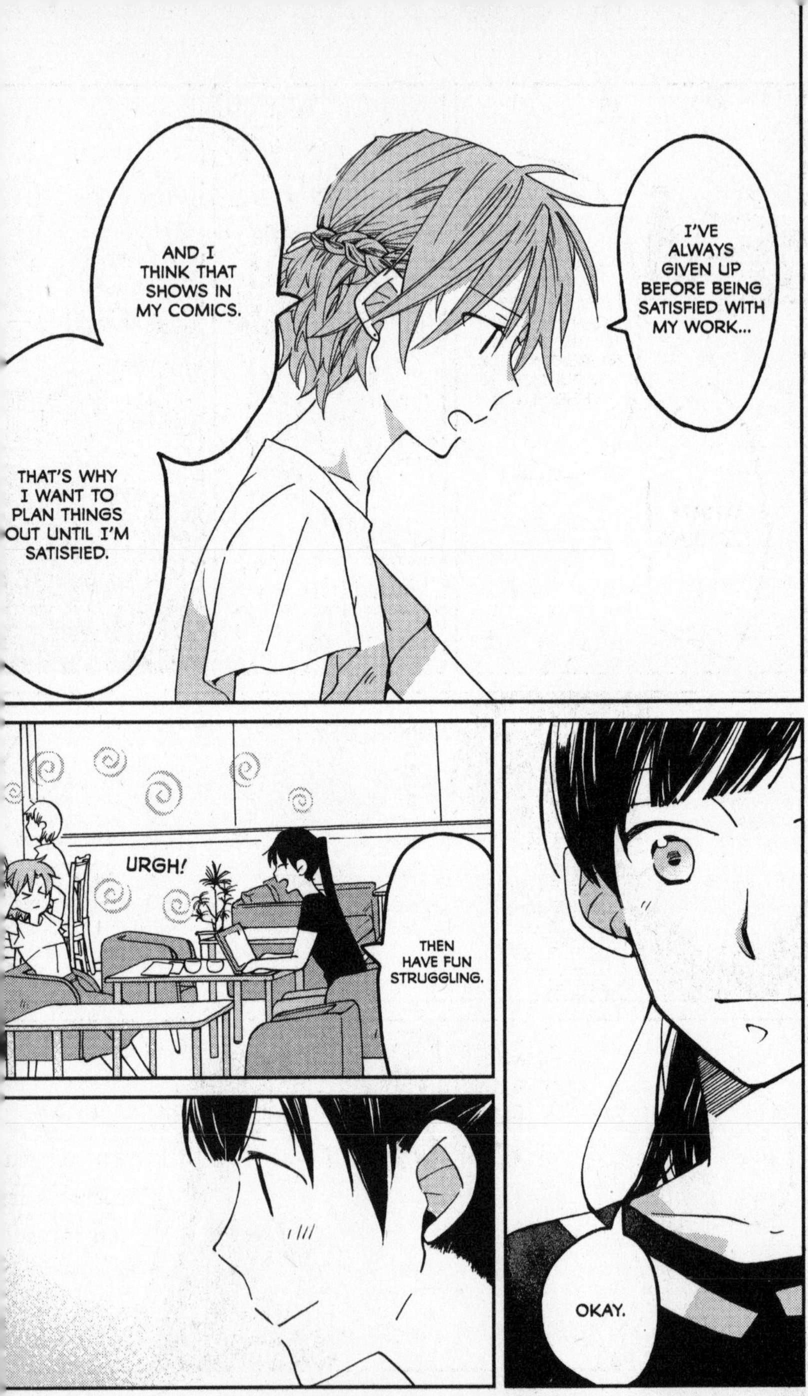
I'VE ALWAYS GIVEN UP BEFORE BEING SATISFIED WITH MY WORK...
AND I THINK THAT SHOWS IN MY COMICS.
THAT'S WHY I WANT TO PLAN THINGS OUT UNTIL I'M SATISFIED.
OKAY.
THEN HAVE FUN STRUGGLING.
URGH!

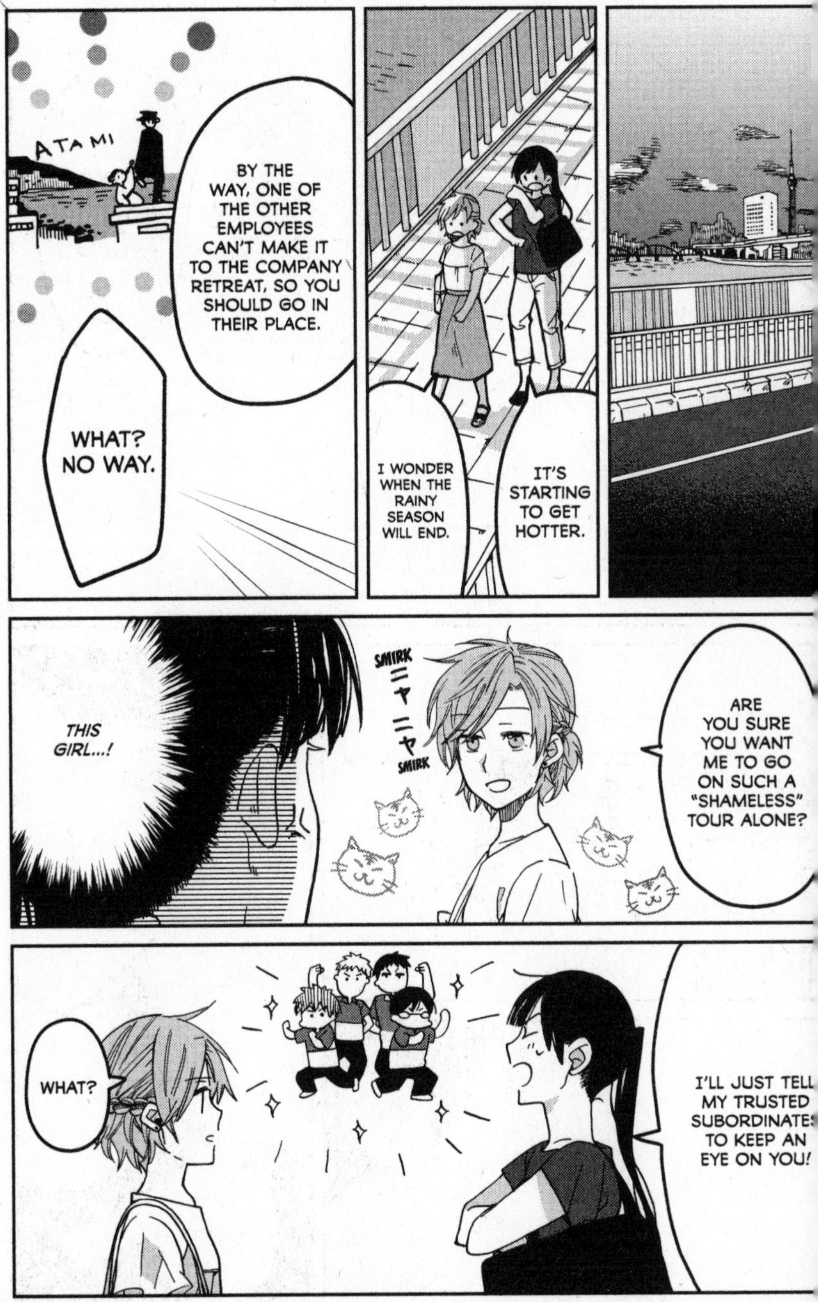
IT'S STARTING TO GET HOTTER.
I WONDER WHEN THE RAINY SEASON WILL END.
BY THE WAY, ONE OF THE OTHER EMPLOYEES CAN'T MAKE IT TO THE COMPANY RETREAT, SO YOU SHOULD GO IN THEIR PLACE.
ATAMI
WHAT? NO WAY.
ARE YOU SURE YOU WANT ME TO GO ON SUCH A "SHAMELESS" TOUR ALONE?
SMIRK ニヤ
ニヤ SMIRK
THIS GIRL...!
I'LL JUST TELL MY TRUSTED SUBORDINATES TO KEEP AN EYE ON YOU!
WHAT?

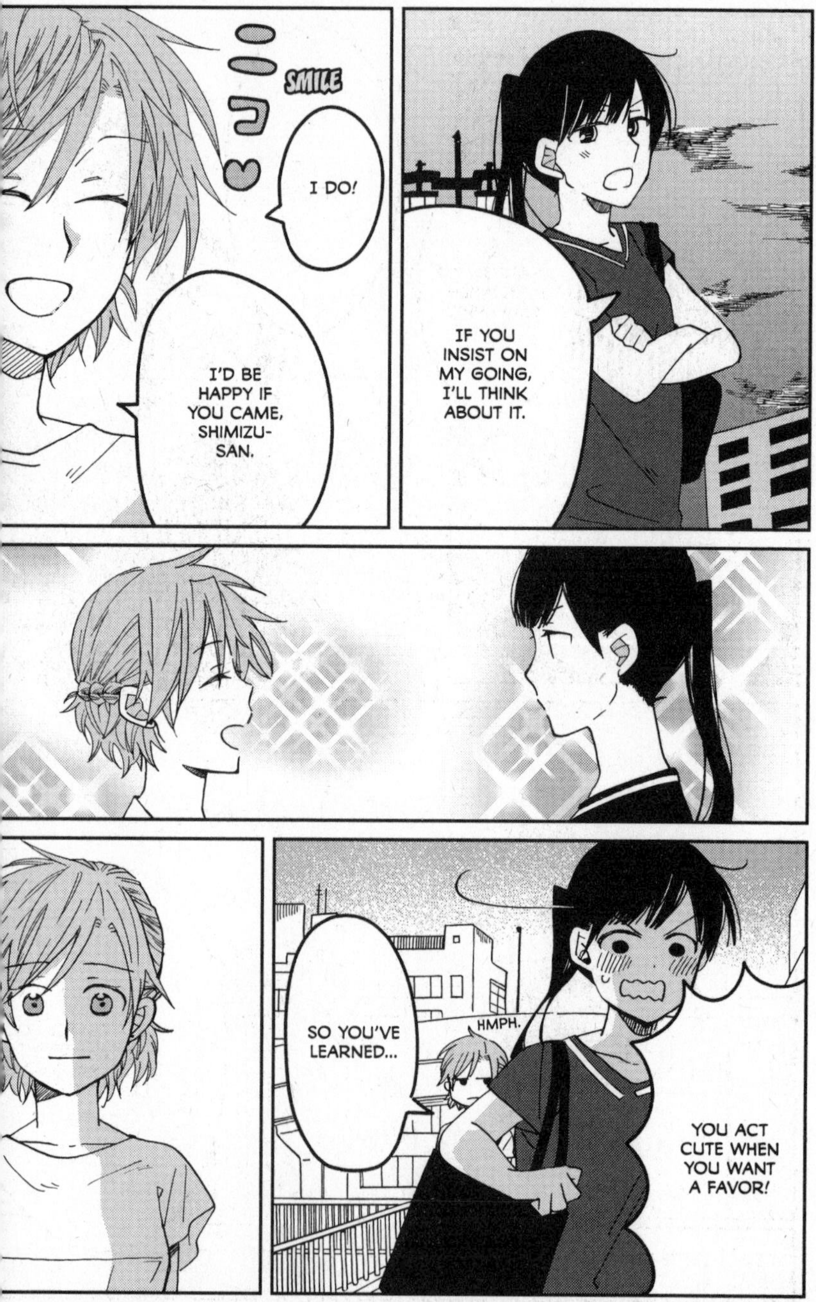
IF YOU INSIST ON MY GOING, I'LL THINK ABOUT IT.
SMILE
I DO!
I'D BE HAPPY IF YOU CAME, SHIMIZU-SAN.
YOU ACT CUTE WHEN YOU WANT A FAVOR!
SO YOU'VE LEARNED...
HMPH.

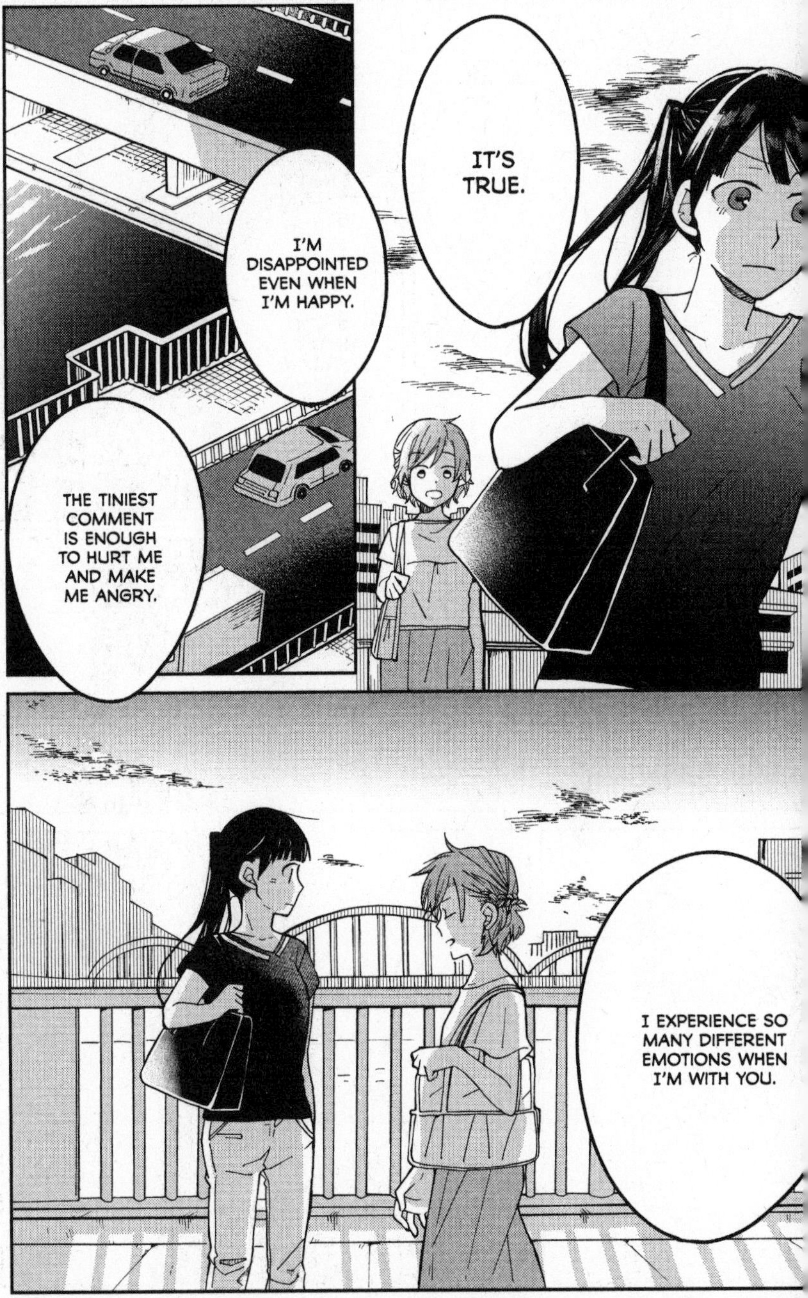
IT'S TRUE.
I'M DISAPPOINTED EVEN WHEN I'M HAPPY.
THE TINIEST COMMENT IS ENOUGH TO HURT ME AND MAKE ME ANGRY.
I EXPERIENCE SO MANY DIFFERENT EMOTIONS WHEN I'M WITH YOU.

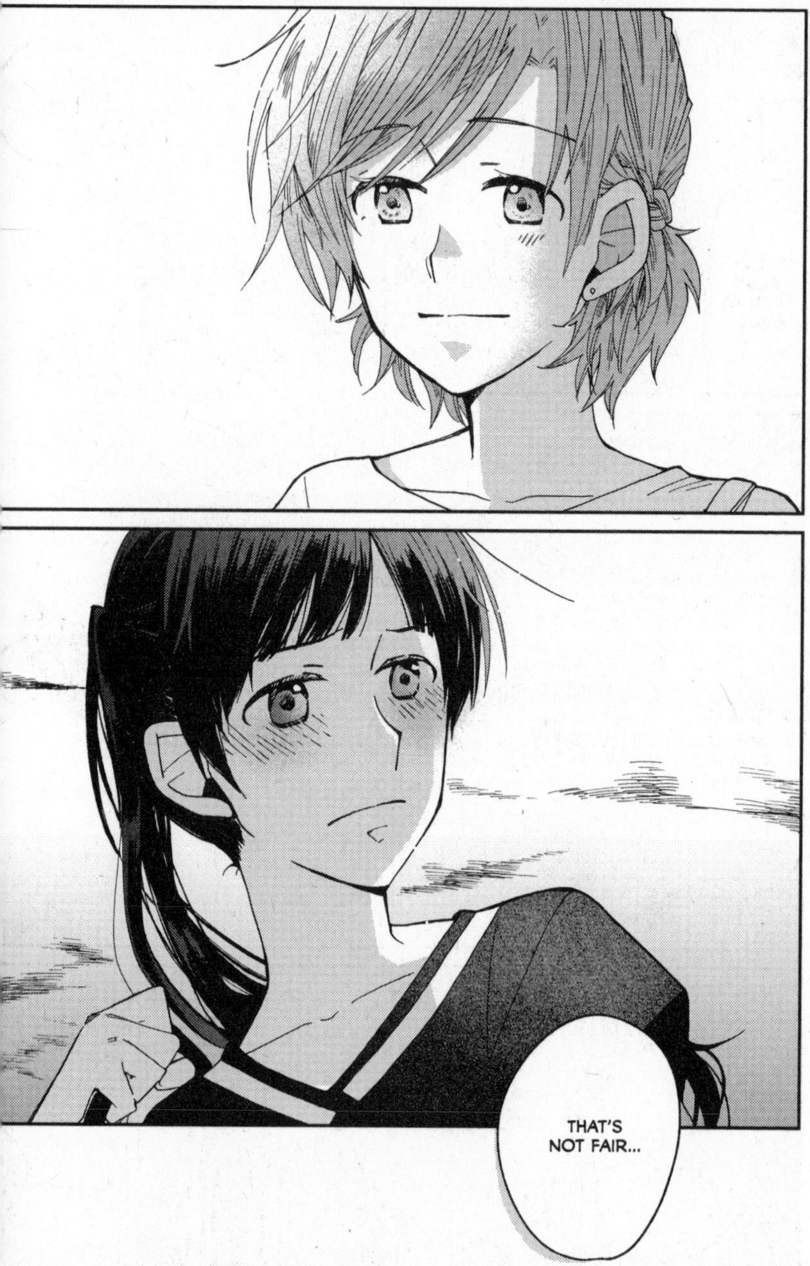
THAT'S NOT FAIR...

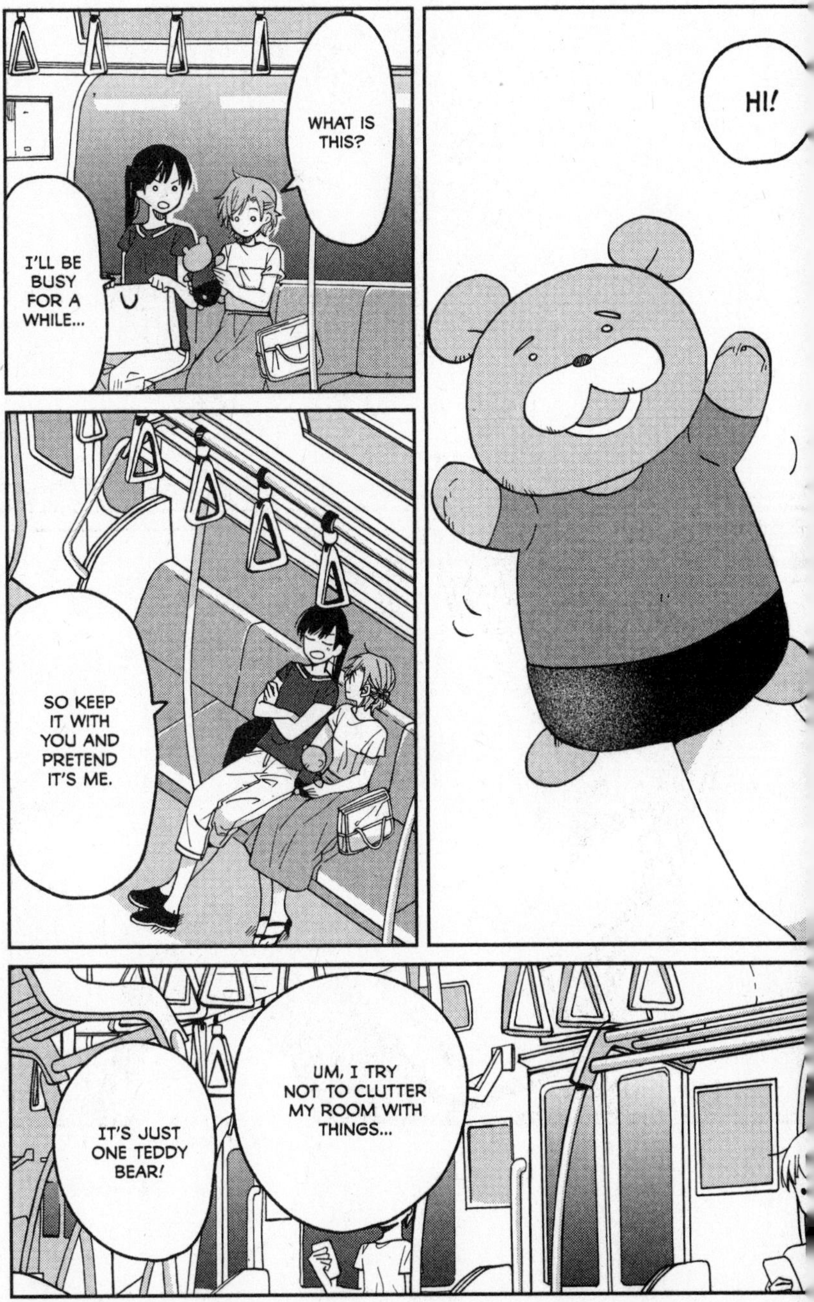
HI!
WHAT IS THIS?
I'LL BE BUSY FOR A WHILE...
SO KEEP IT WITH YOU AND PRETEND IT'S ME.
UM, I TRY NOT TO CLUTTER MY ROOM WITH THINGS...
IT'S JUST ONE TEDDY BEAR!

TA-DA!

LOOK, I BOUGHT A MATCHING ONE FOR MYSELF!

EW...

OKAY, I'LL IMAGINE IT'S YOU WHILE USING IT TO RELIEVE STRESS.

DON'T TORMENT THE FAKE ME!

SMACK

WORK HARD ON YOUR MANUSCRIPT, OKAY?

CROSS-COUNTER PUNCH!

OKAY.

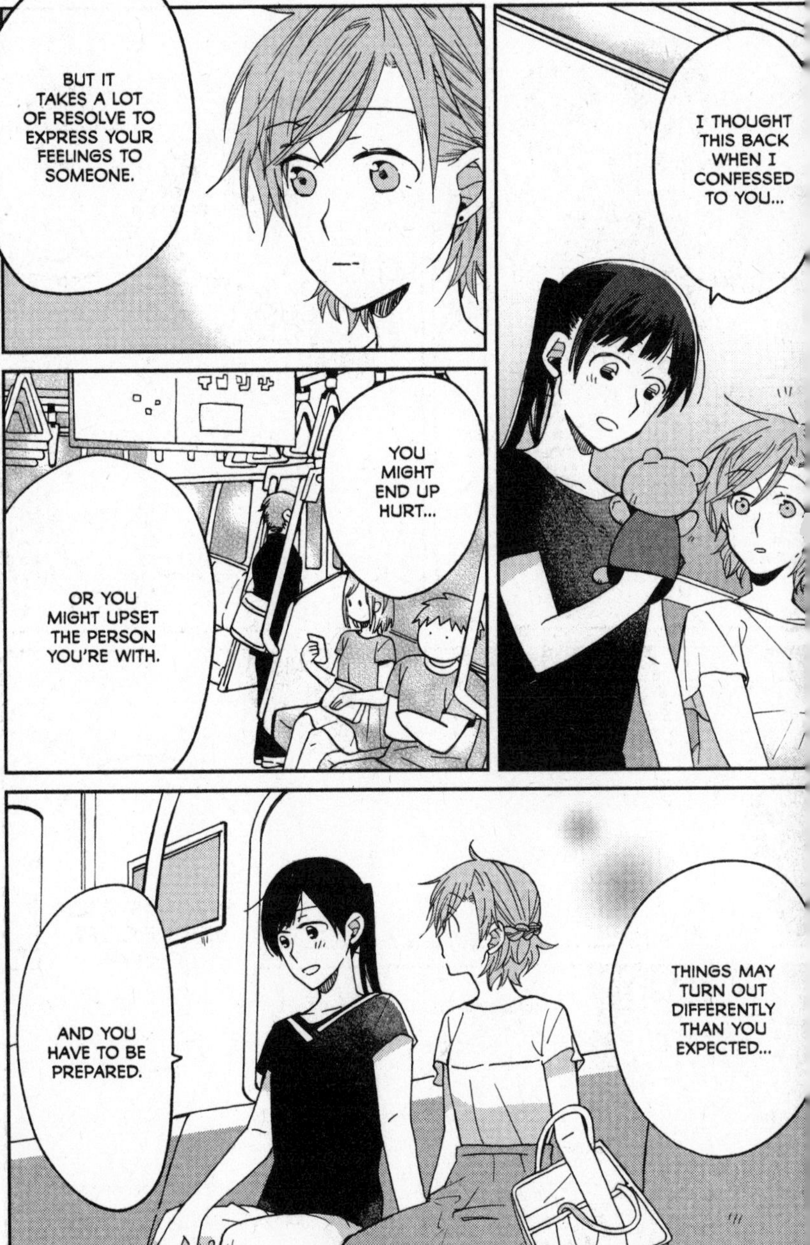
I THOUGHT THIS BACK WHEN I CONFESSED TO YOU...
BUT IT TAKES A LOT OF RESOLVE TO EXPRESS YOUR FEELINGS TO SOMEONE.
YOU MIGHT END UP HURT...
OR YOU MIGHT UPSET THE PERSON YOU'RE WITH.
THINGS MAY TURN OUT DIFFERENTLY THAN YOU EXPECTED...
AND YOU HAVE TO BE PREPARED.

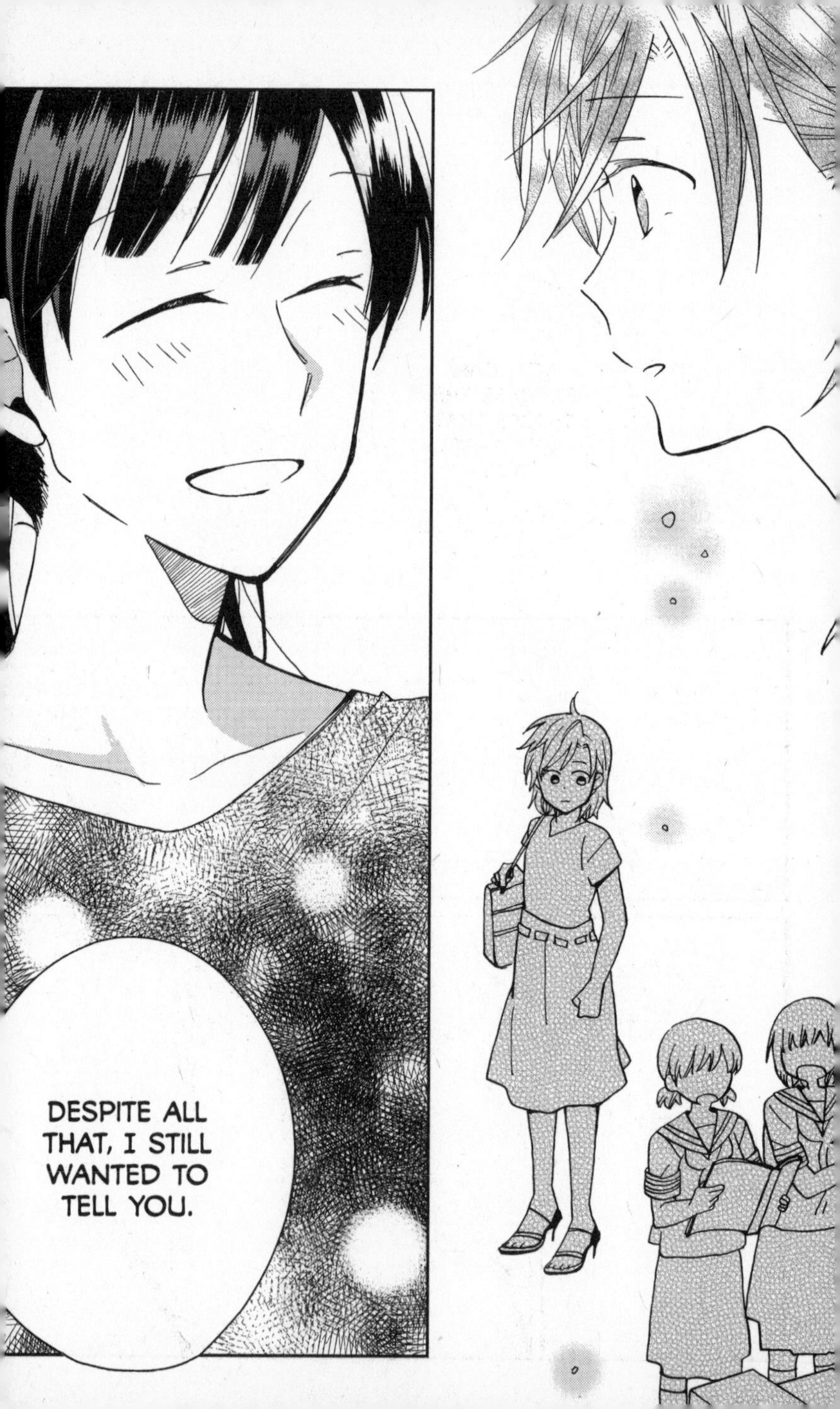
DESPITE ALL THAT, I STILL WANTED TO TELL YOU.

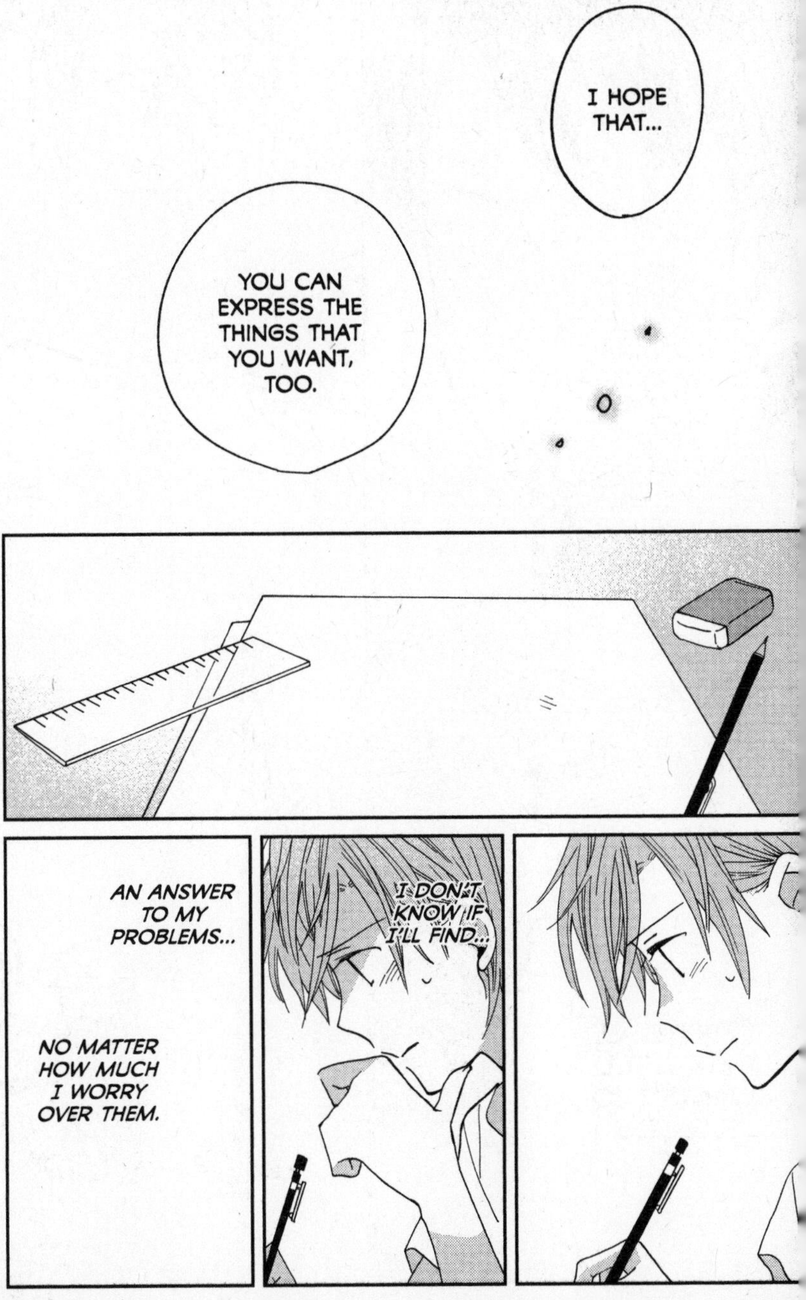
I HOPE THAT...
YOU CAN EXPRESS THE THINGS THAT YOU WANT, TOO.
I DON'T KNOW IF I'LL FIND...
AN ANSWER TO MY PROBLEMS...
NO MATTER HOW MUCH I WORRY OVER THEM.

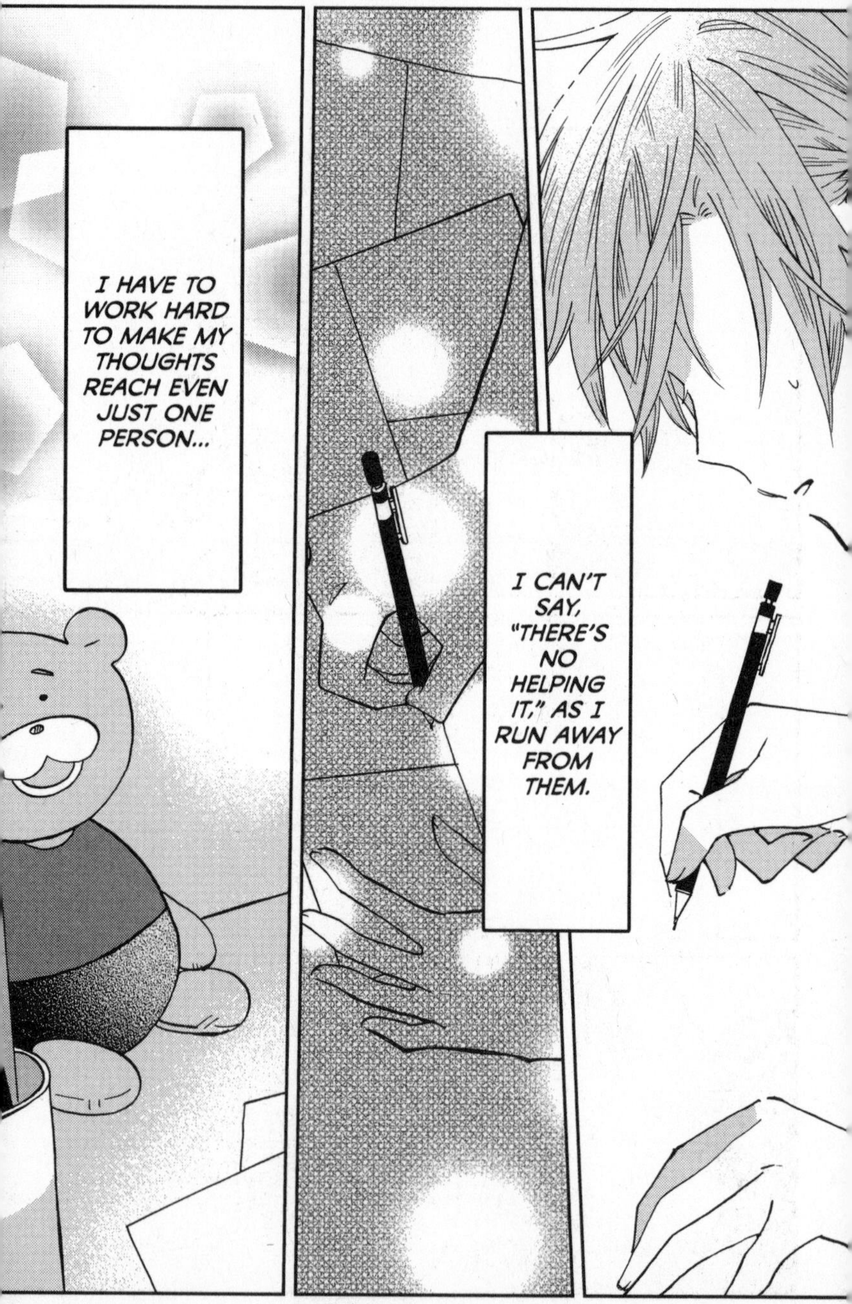
I CAN'T SAY, "THERE'S NO HELPING IT," AS I RUN AWAY FROM THEM.
I HAVE TO WORK HARD TO MAKE MY THOUGHTS REACH EVEN JUST ONE PERSON...

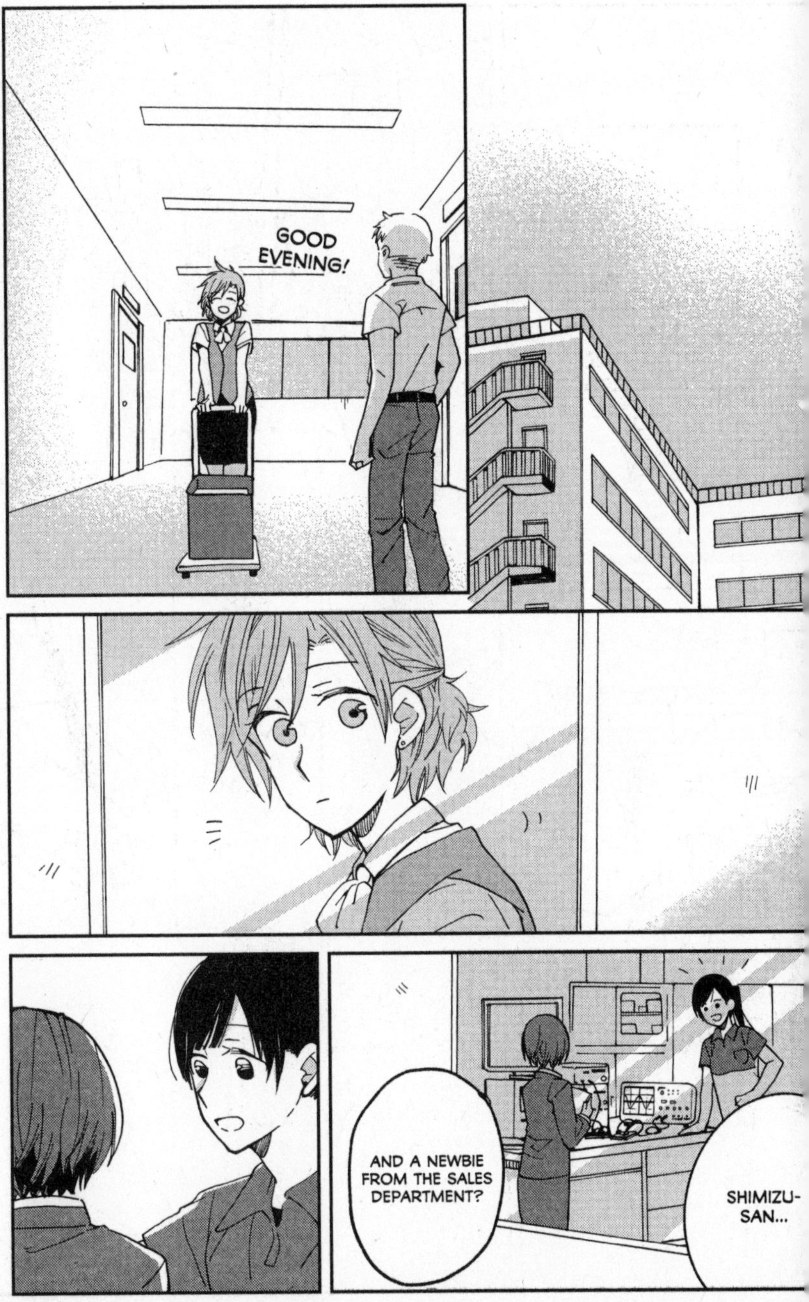
GOOD EVENING!
SHIMIZU-SAN...
AND A NEWBIE FROM THE SALES DEPARTMENT?

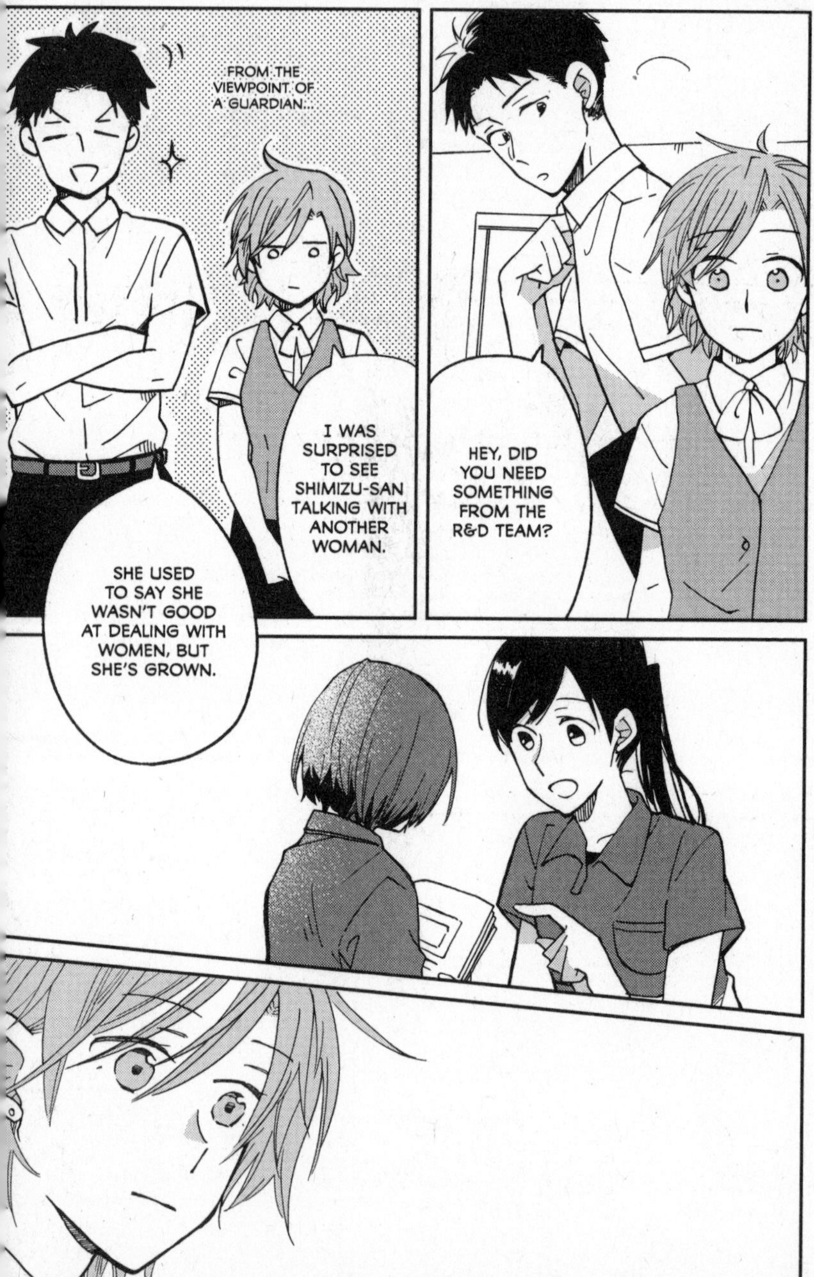
HEY, DID YOU NEED SOMETHING FROM THE R&D TEAM?
FROM THE VIEWPOINT OF A GUARDIAN...
I WAS SURPRISED TO SEE SHIMIZU-SAN TALKING WITH ANOTHER WOMAN.
SHE USED TO SAY SHE WASN'T GOOD AT DEALING WITH WOMEN, BUT SHE'S GROWN.

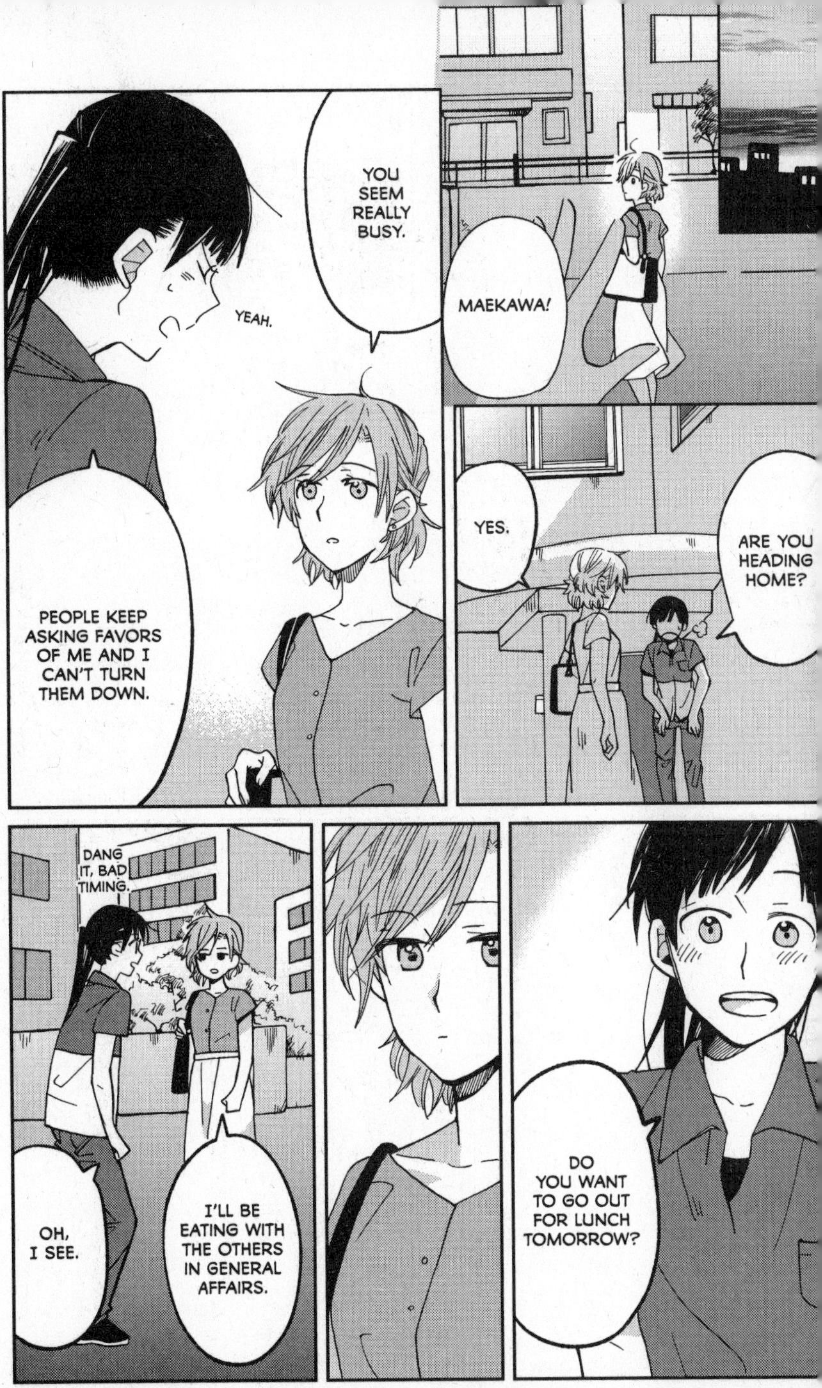
MAEKAWA!
ARE YOU HEADING HOME?
YES.
YOU SEEM REALLY BUSY.
YEAH.
PEOPLE KEEP ASKING FAVORS OF ME AND I CAN'T TURN THEM DOWN.
DO YOU WANT TO GO OUT FOR LUNCH TOMORROW?
I'LL BE EATING WITH THE OTHERS IN GENERAL AFFAIRS.
OH, I SEE.
DANG IT, BAD TIMING.

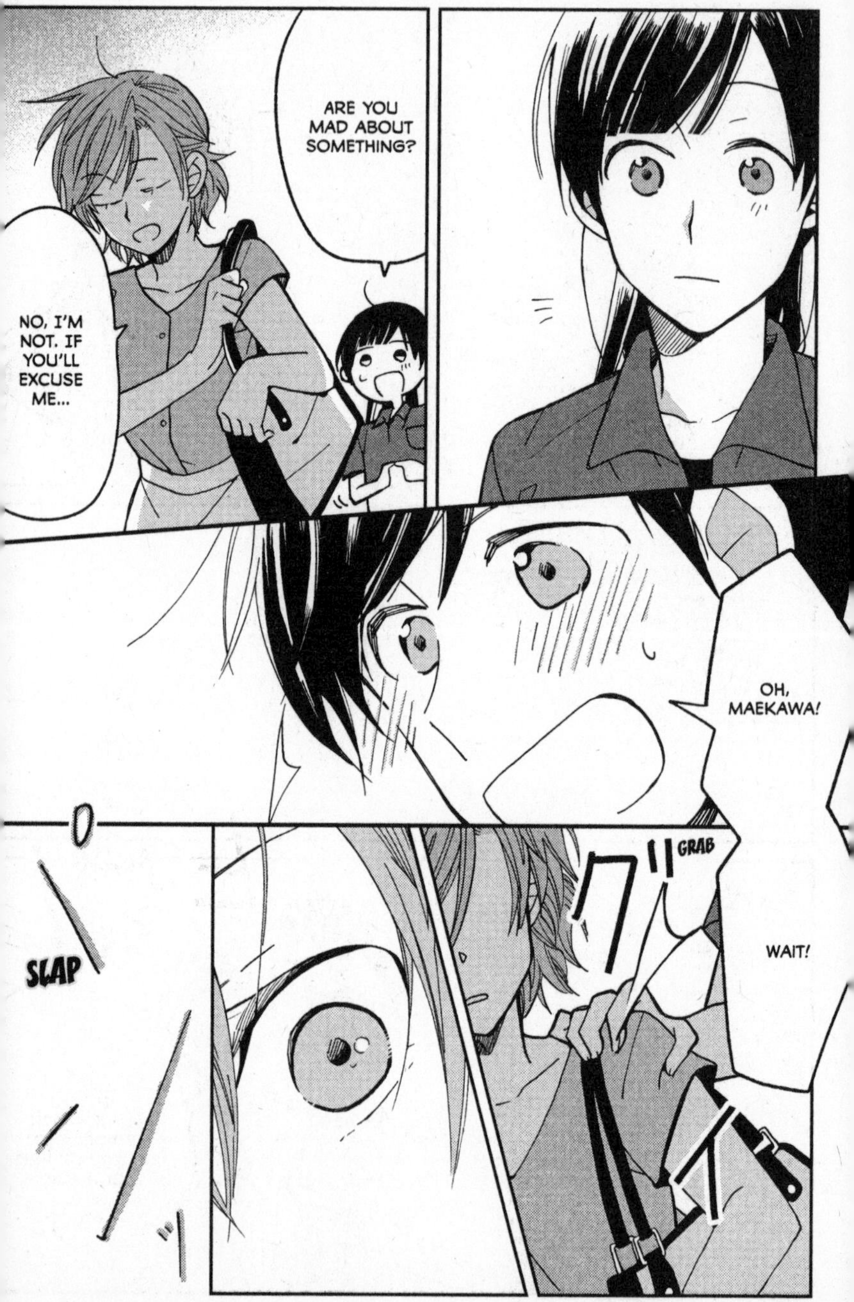
ARE YOU MAD ABOUT SOMETHING?
NO, I'M NOT. IF YOU'LL EXCUSE ME...
OH, MAEKAWA!
GRAB
WAIT!
SLAP

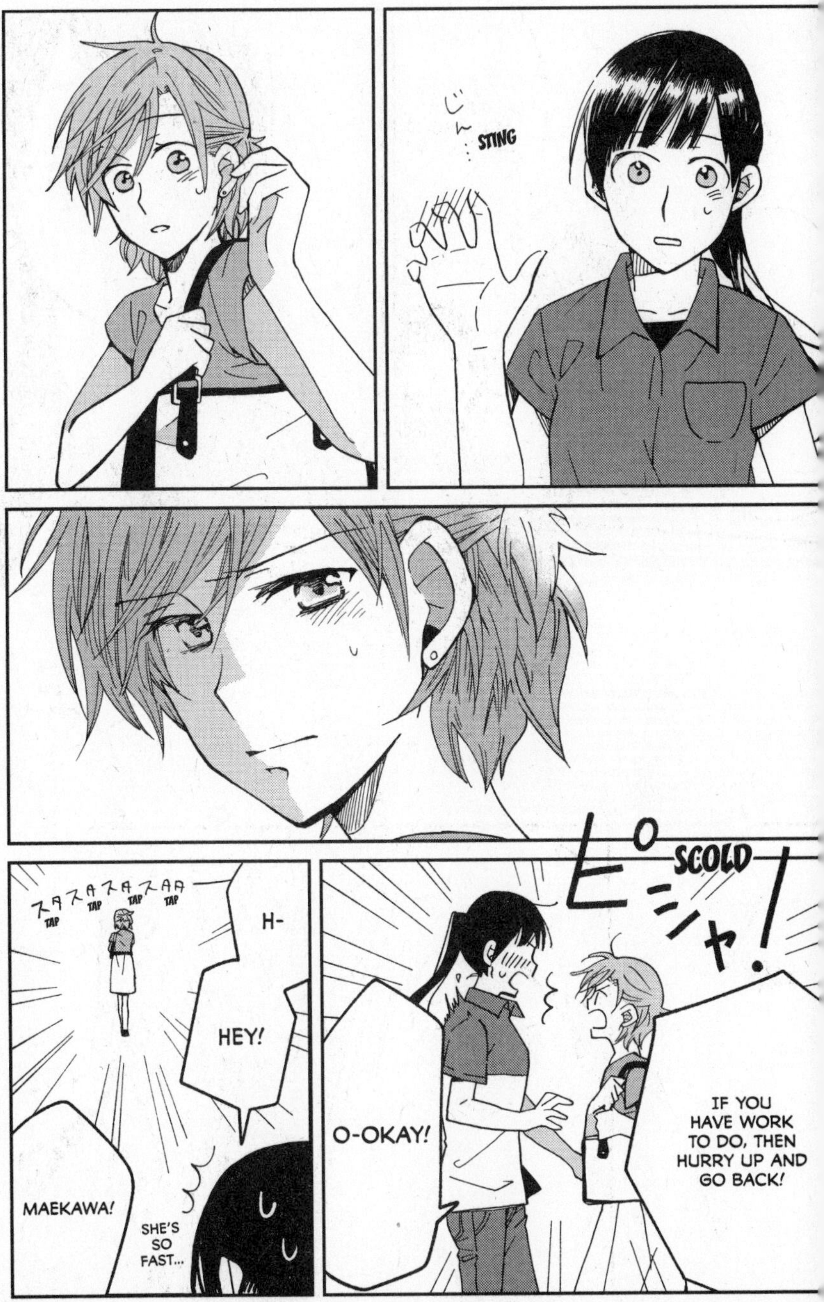
じん…
STING
ピシャ!
SCOLD
IF YOU HAVE WORK TO DO, THEN HURRY UP AND GO BACK!
O-OKAY!
スタスタスタスタ
TAP TAP TAP TAP
H-
HEY!
MAEKAWA!
SHE'S SO FAST...

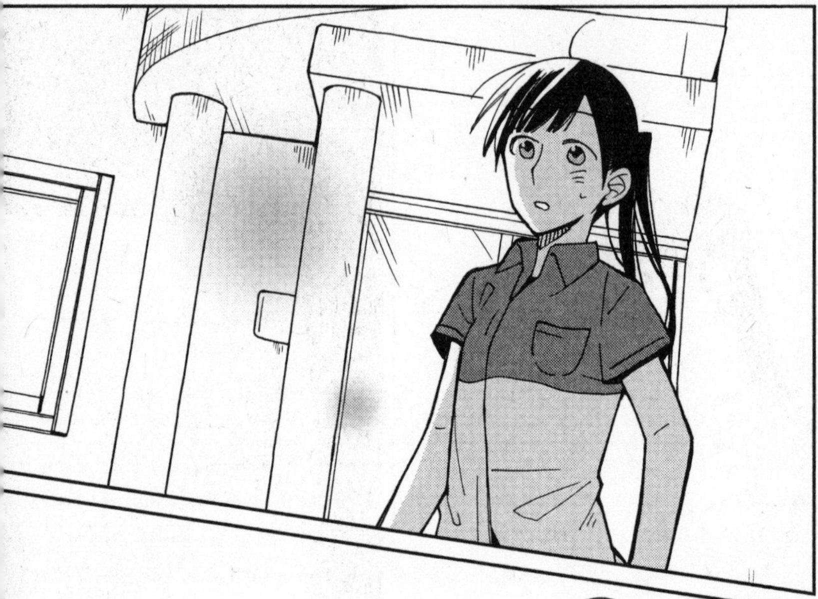
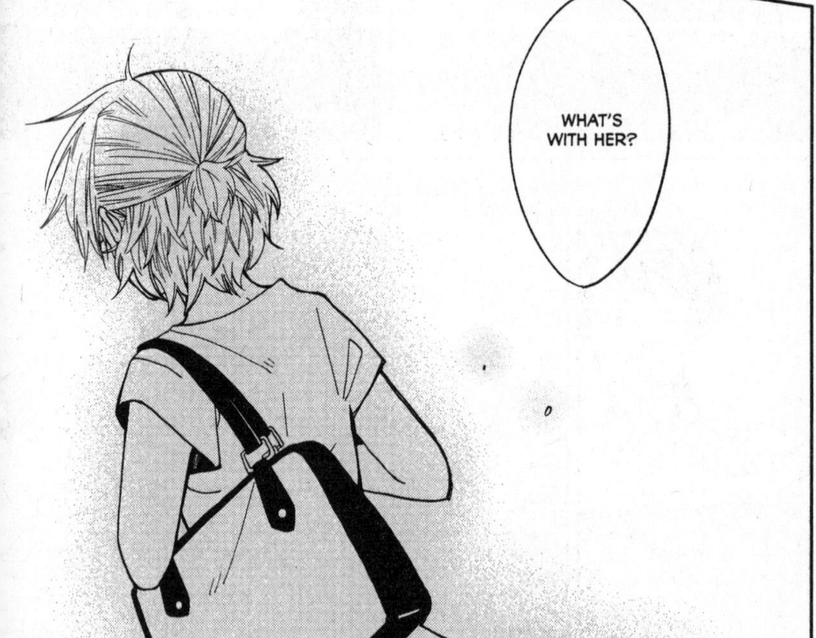
WHAT'S WITH HER?

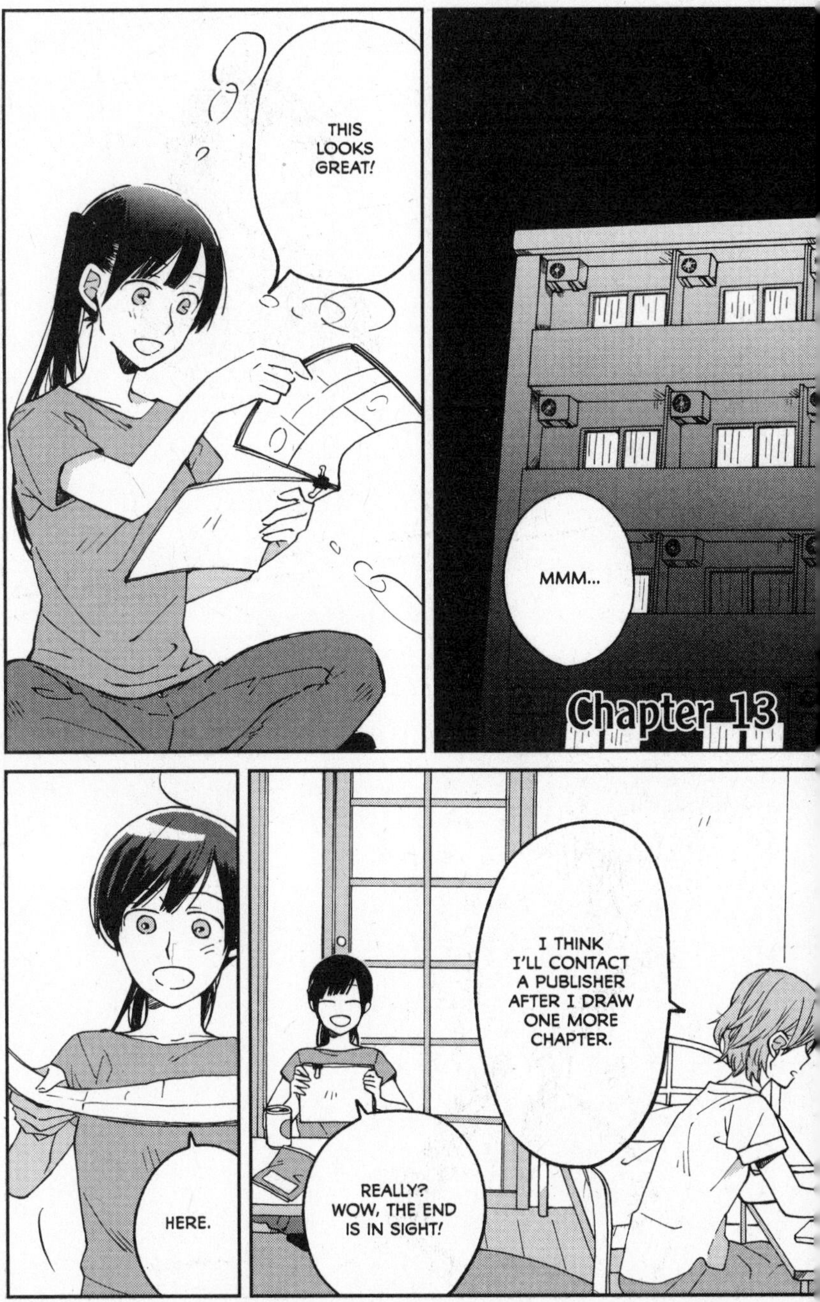
MMM...
Chapter 13
THIS LOOKS GREAT!
I THINK I'LL CONTACT A PUBLISHER AFTER I DRAW ONE MORE CHAPTER.
REALLY? WOW, THE END IS IN SIGHT!
HERE.

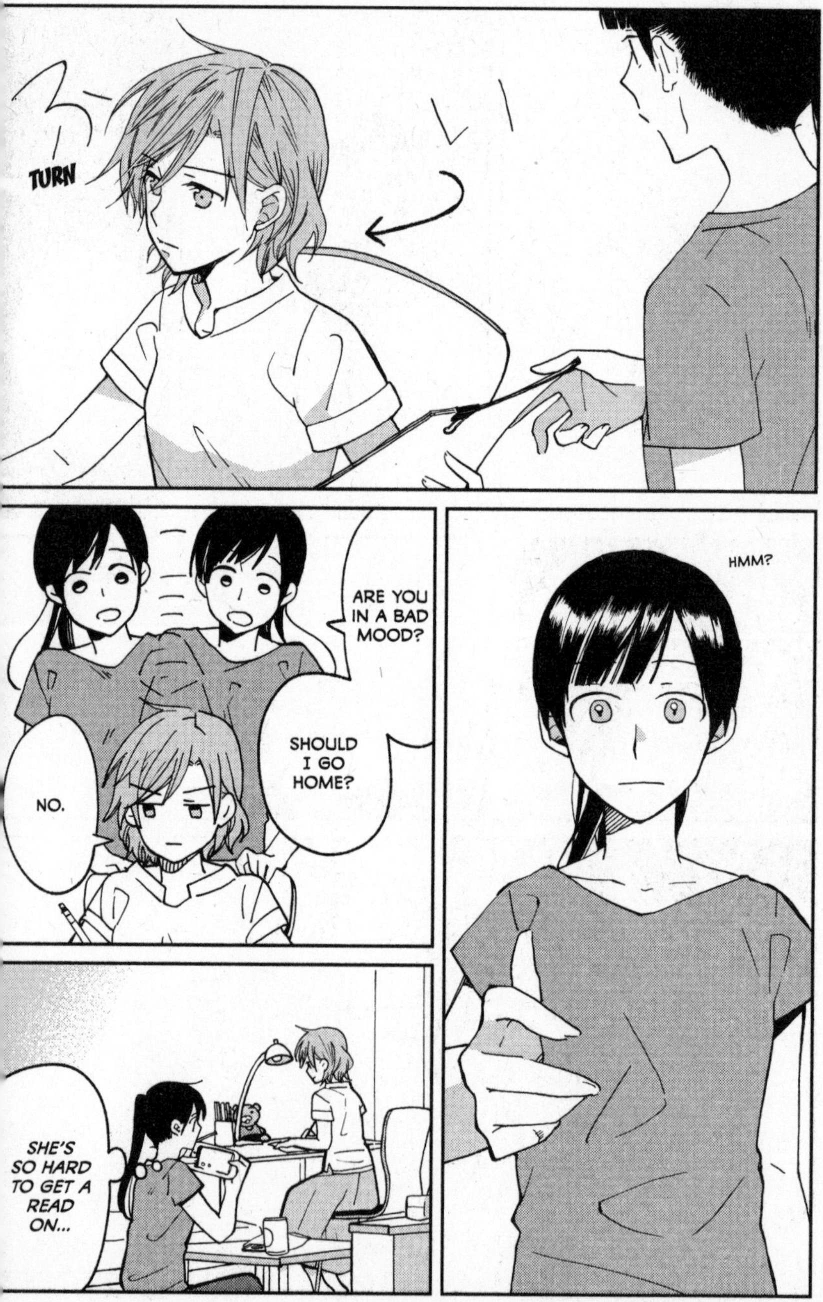
TURN
HMM?
ARE YOU IN A BAD MOOD?
SHOULD I GO HOME?
NO.
SHE'S SO HARD TO GET A READ ON...

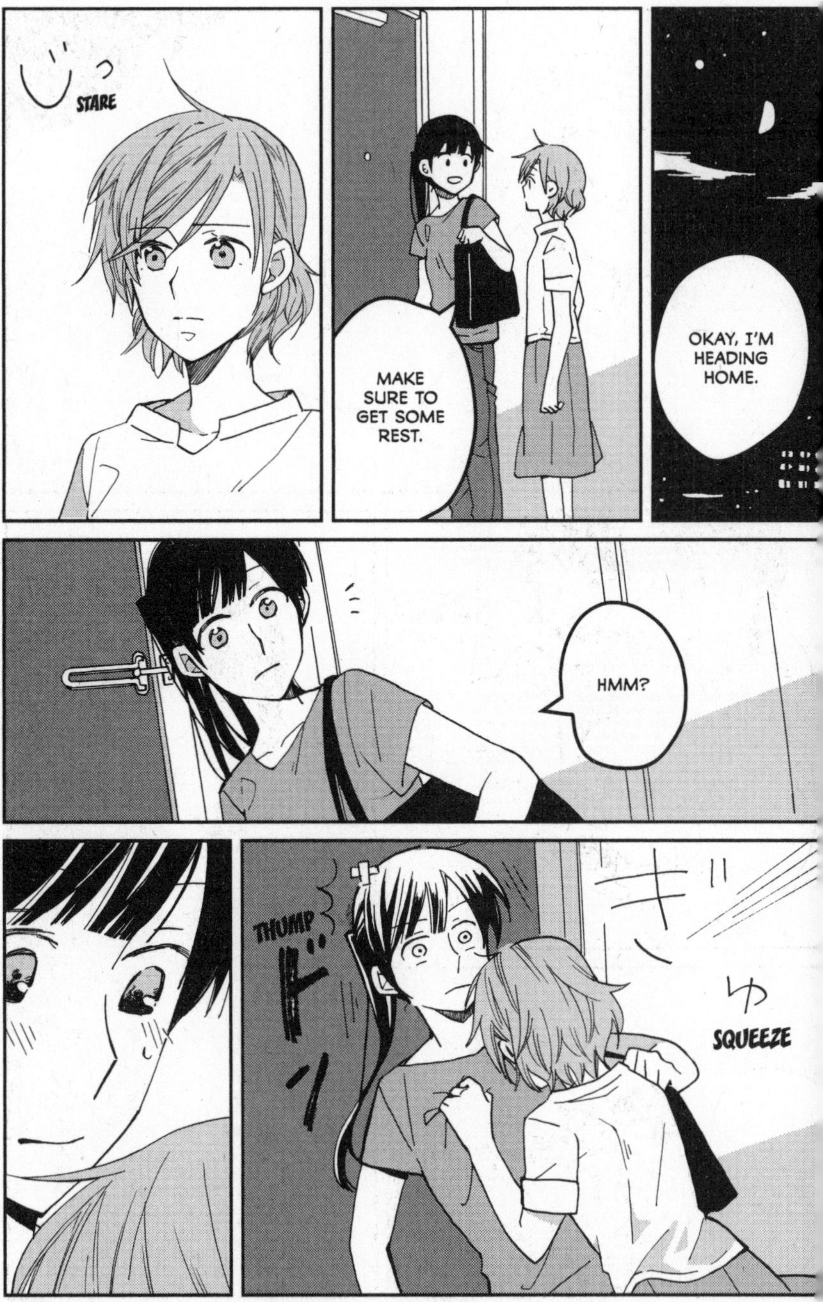
OKAY, I'M HEADING HOME.
MAKE SURE TO GET SOME REST.
じっ
STARE
HMM?
ぎゅ
SQUEEZE
THUMP
ド

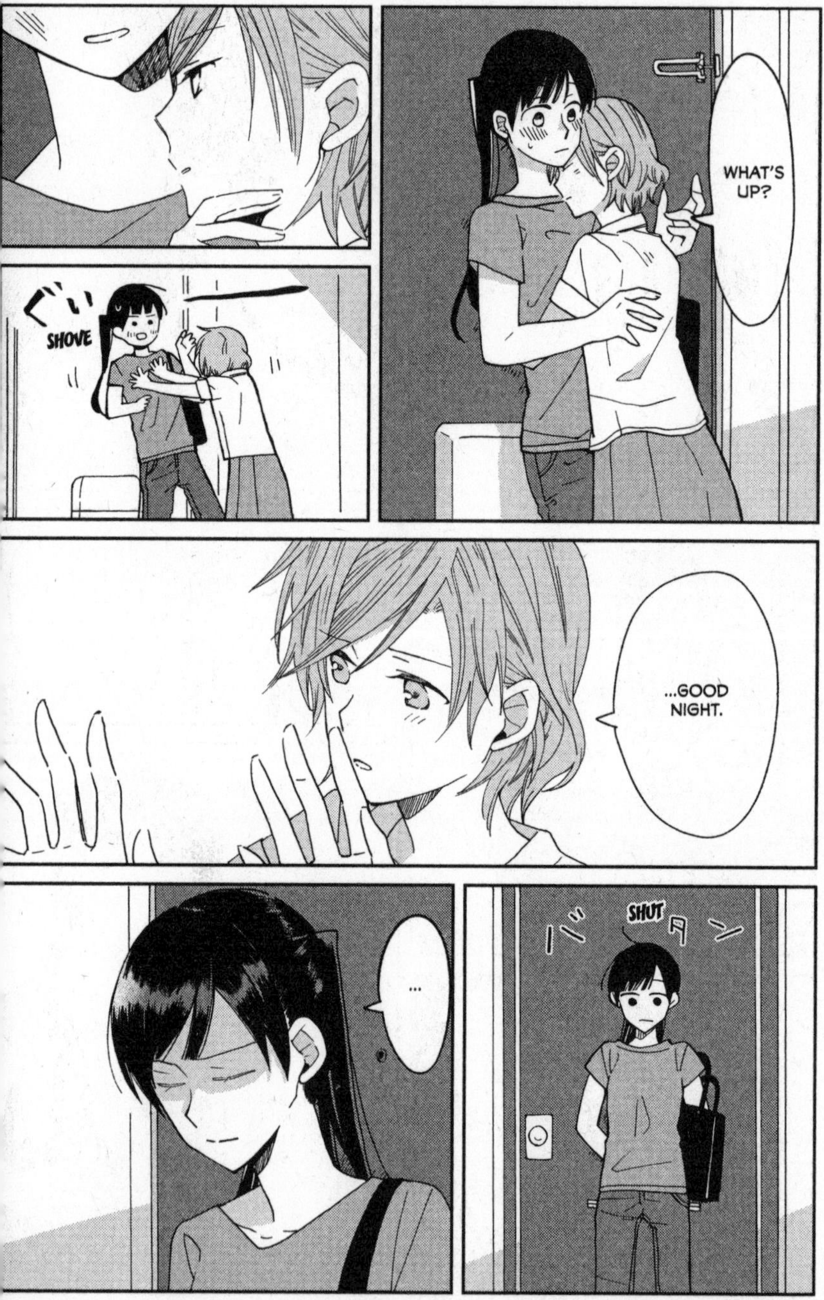
WHAT'S UP?
ぐい
SHOVE
...GOOD NIGHT.
バタン
SHUT
...

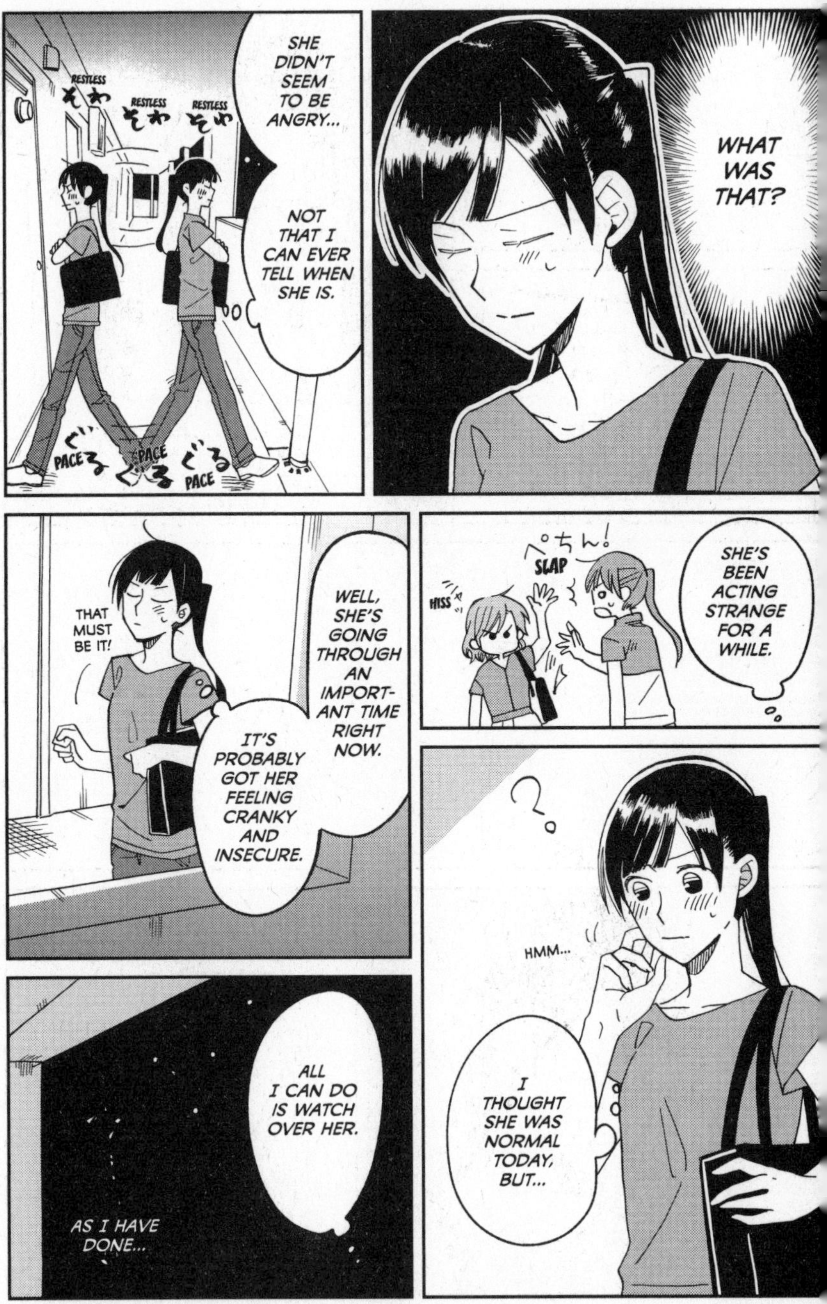
WHAT WAS THAT?
SHE DIDN'T SEEM TO BE ANGRY...
NOT THAT I CAN EVER TELL WHEN SHE IS.
RESTLESS そわ
RESTLESS そわ
RESTLESS そわ
PACE ぐる
PACE ぐる
PACE ぐる
SHE'S BEEN ACTING STRANGE FOR A WHILE.
ぺちん!
SLAP
HISS
WELL, SHE'S GOING THROUGH AN IMPORTANT TIME RIGHT NOW.
IT'S PROBABLY GOT HER FEELING CRANKY AND INSECURE.
THAT MUST BE IT!
HMM...
I THOUGHT SHE WAS NORMAL TODAY, BUT...
ALL I CAN DO IS WATCH OVER HER.
AS I HAVE DONE...

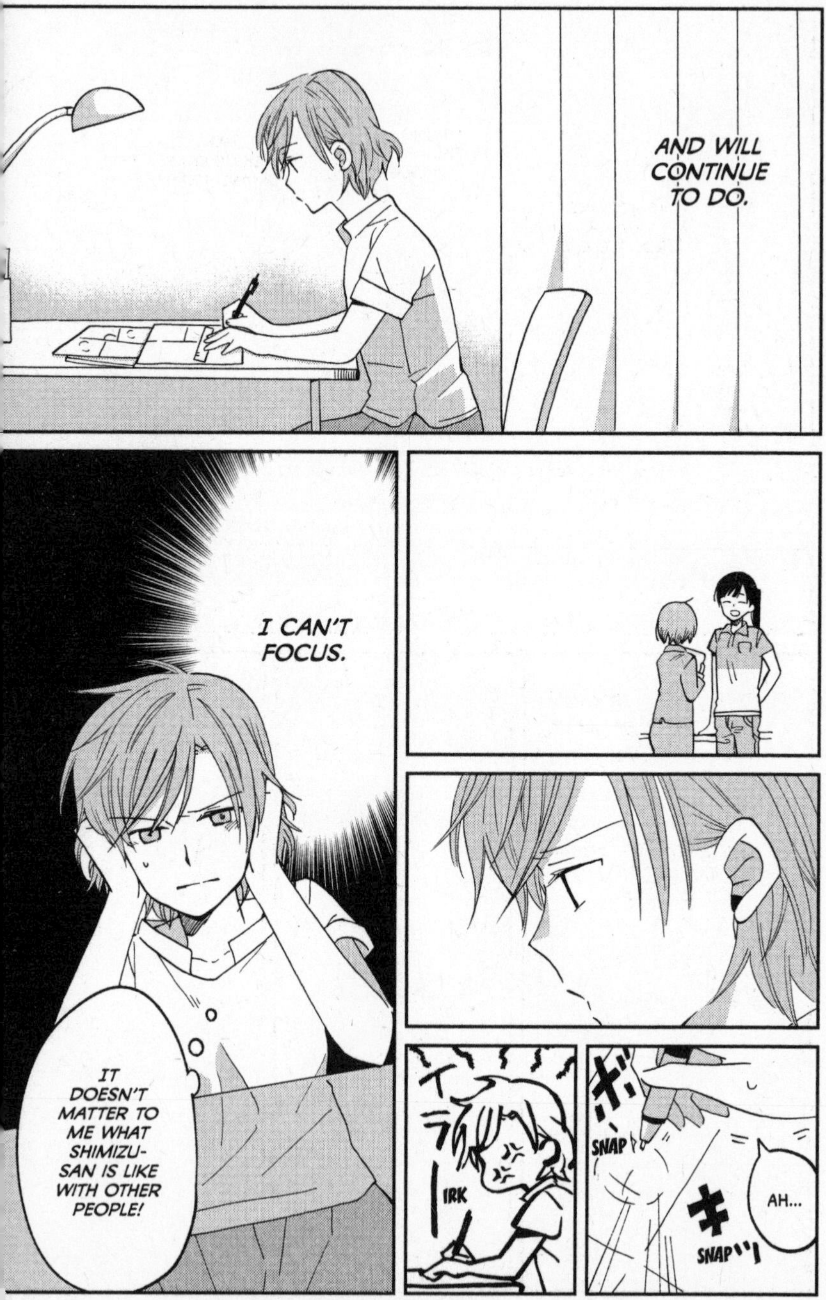
AND WILL CONTINUE TO DO.
ボ
SNAP
キ
SNAP
AH...
イラー
IRK
I CAN'T FOCUS.
IT DOESN'T MATTER TO ME WHAT SHIMIZU-SAN IS LIKE WITH OTHER PEOPLE!

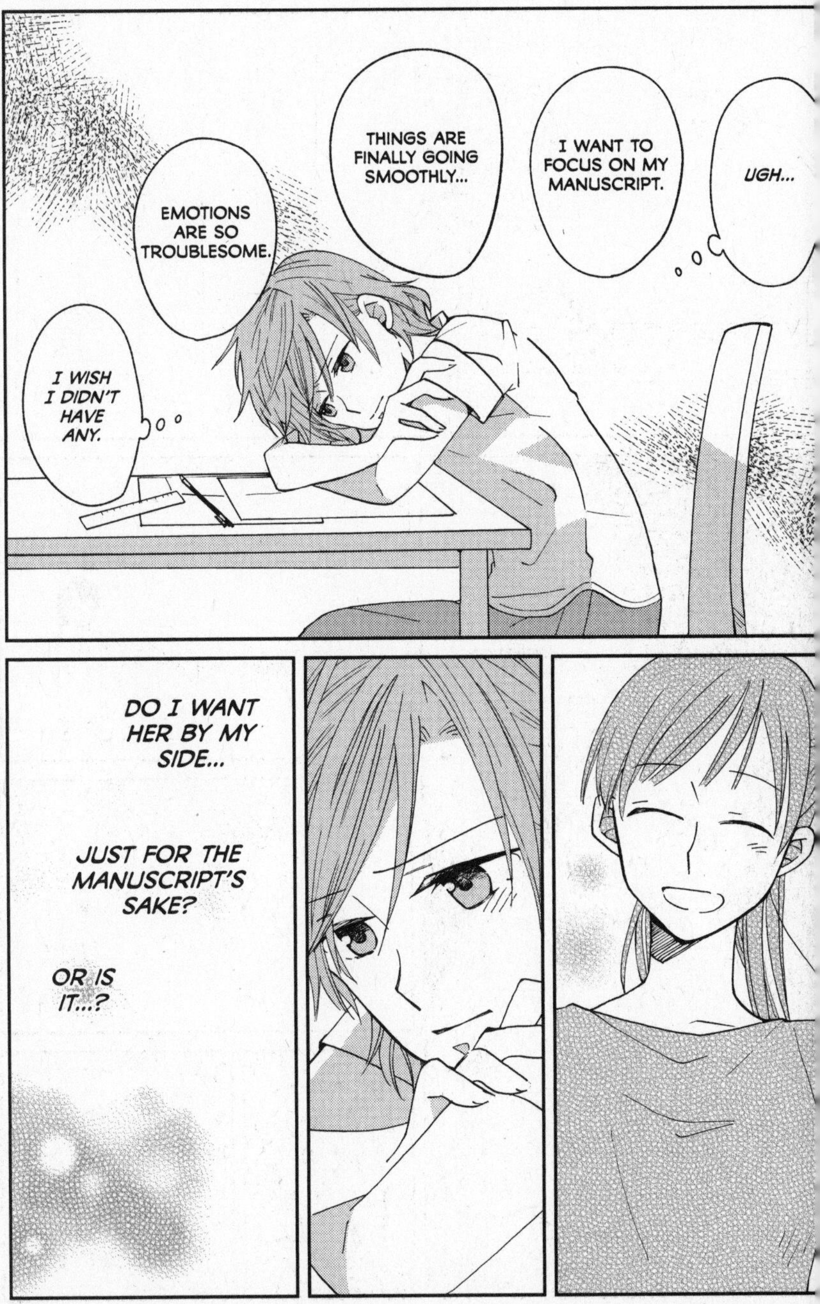
UGH...
I WANT TO FOCUS ON MY MANUSCRIPT.
THINGS ARE FINALLY GOING SMOOTHLY...
EMOTIONS ARE SO TROUBLESOME.
I WISH I DIDN'T HAVE ANY.
DO I WANT HER BY MY SIDE...
JUST FOR THE MANUSCRIPT'S SAKE?
OR IS IT...?

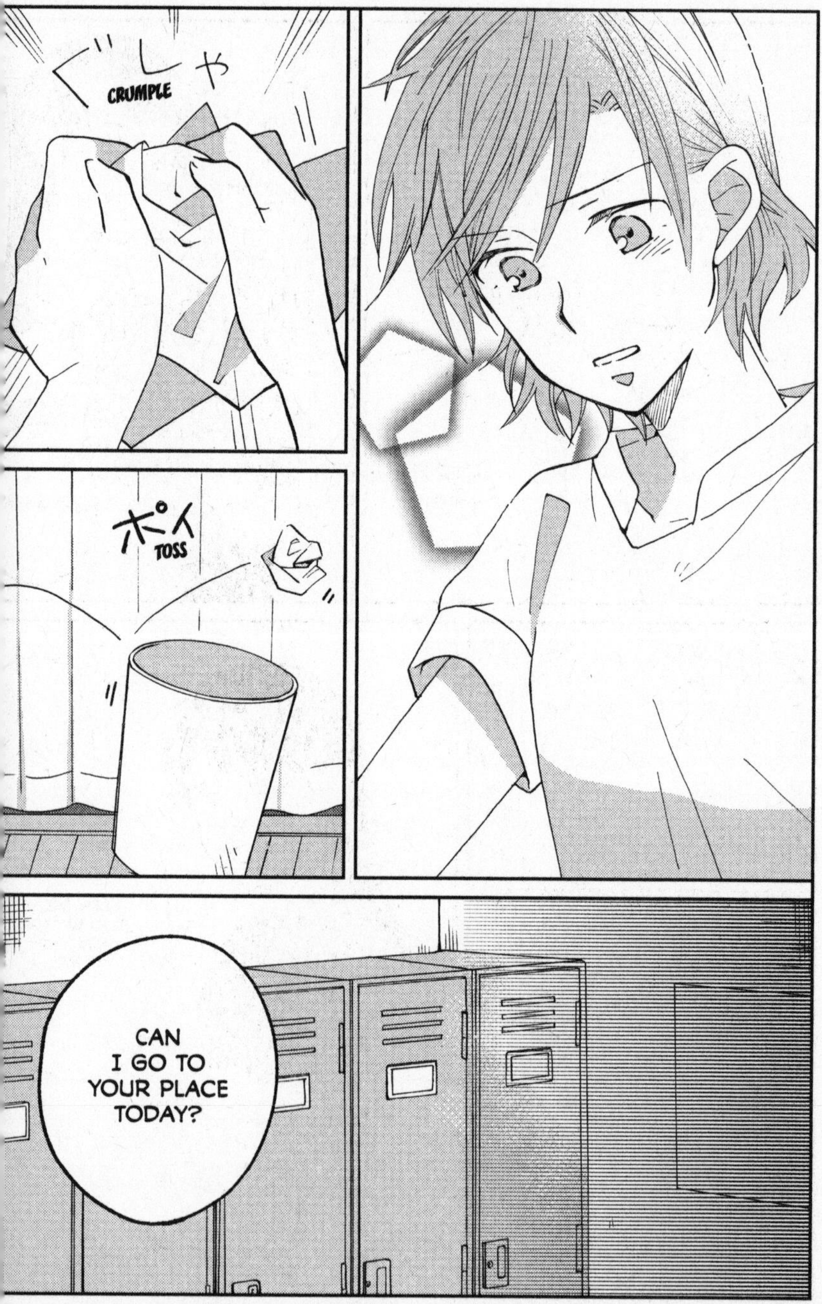
ぐしゃ
CRUMPLE
ポイ
TOSS
CAN I GO TO YOUR PLACE TODAY?

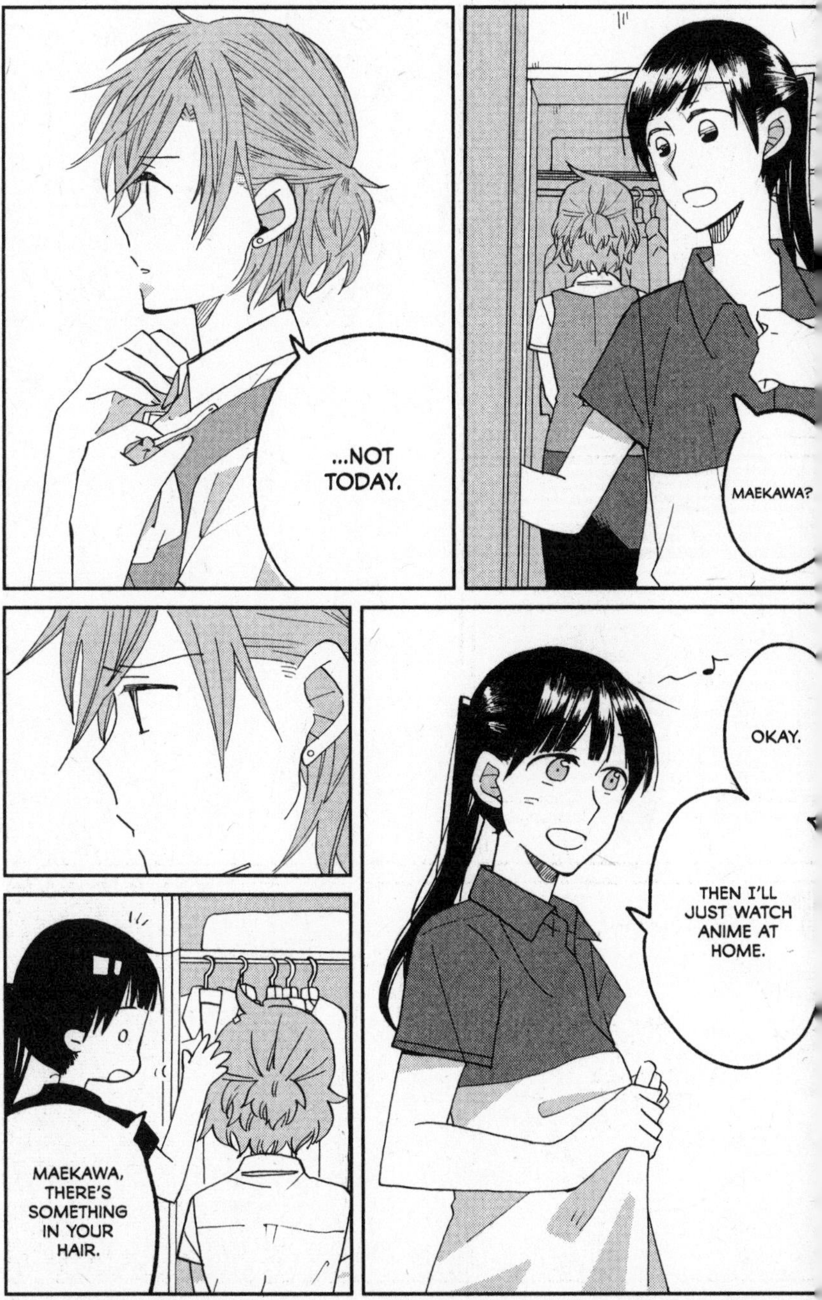
MAEKAWA?
...NOT TODAY.
OKAY.
THEN I'LL JUST WATCH ANIME AT HOME.
MAEKAWA, THERE'S SOMETHING IN YOUR HAIR.

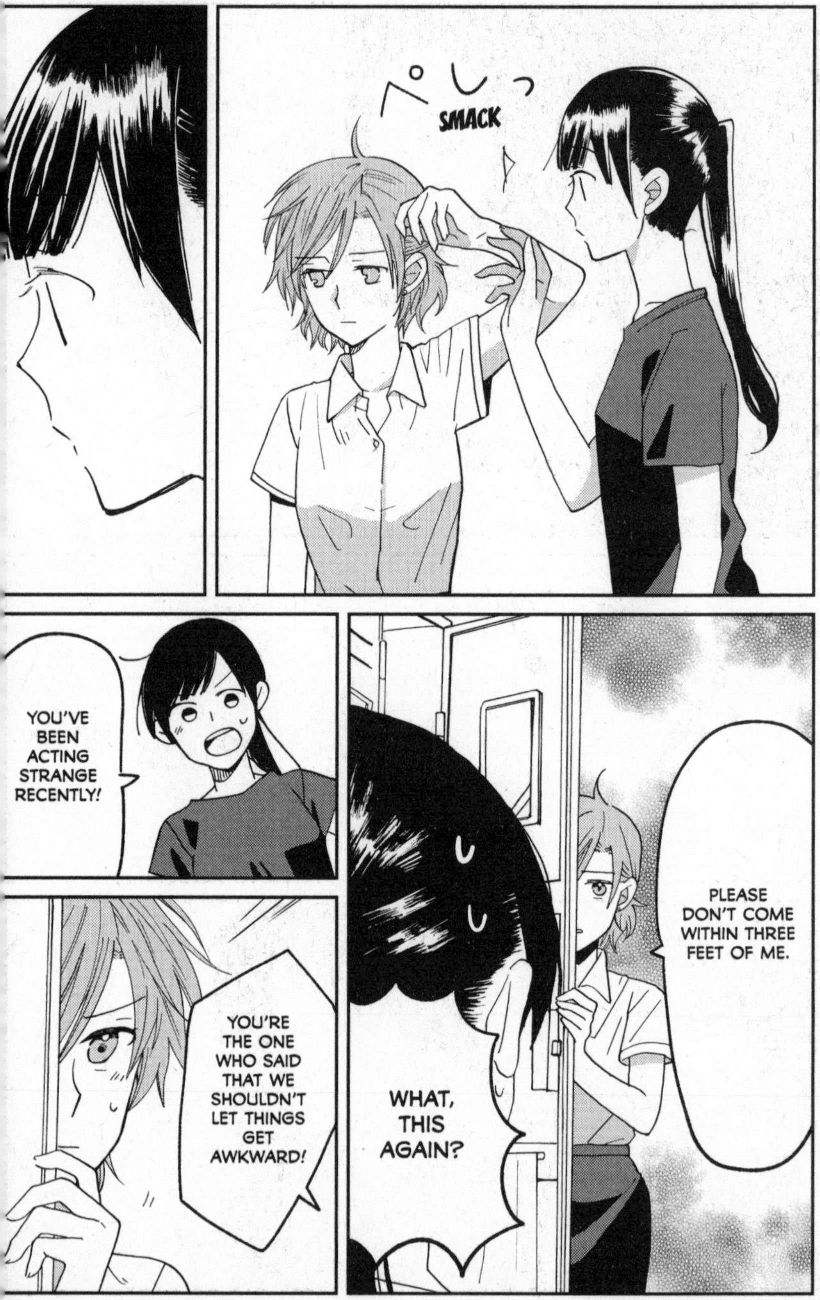
ぺしっ
SMACK
PLEASE DON'T COME WITHIN THREE FEET OF ME.
WHAT, THIS AGAIN?
YOU'VE BEEN ACTING STRANGE RECENTLY!
YOU'RE THE ONE WHO SAID THAT WE SHOULDN'T LET THINGS GET AWKWARD!

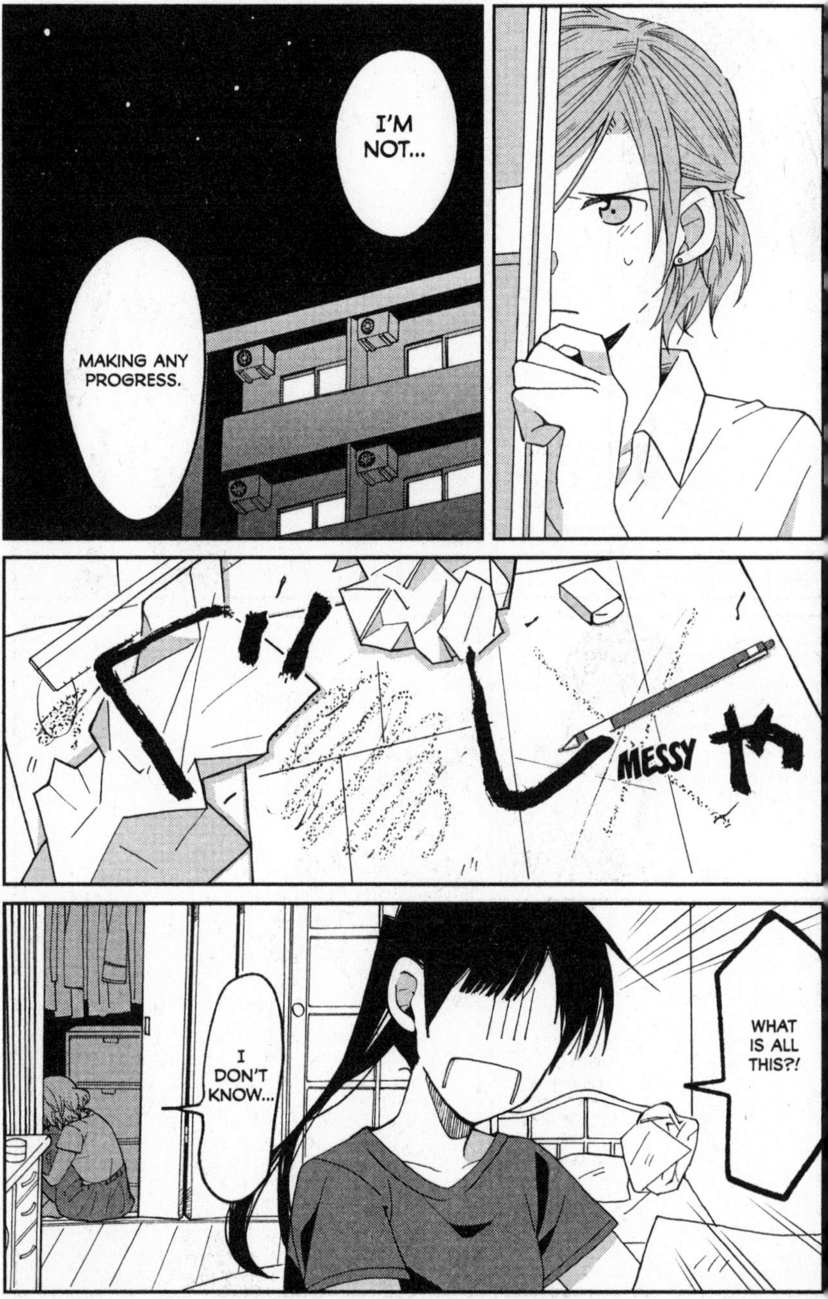
I'M NOT...
MAKING ANY PROGRESS.
ぐしゃ
MESSY
WHAT IS ALL THIS?!
I DON'T KNOW...

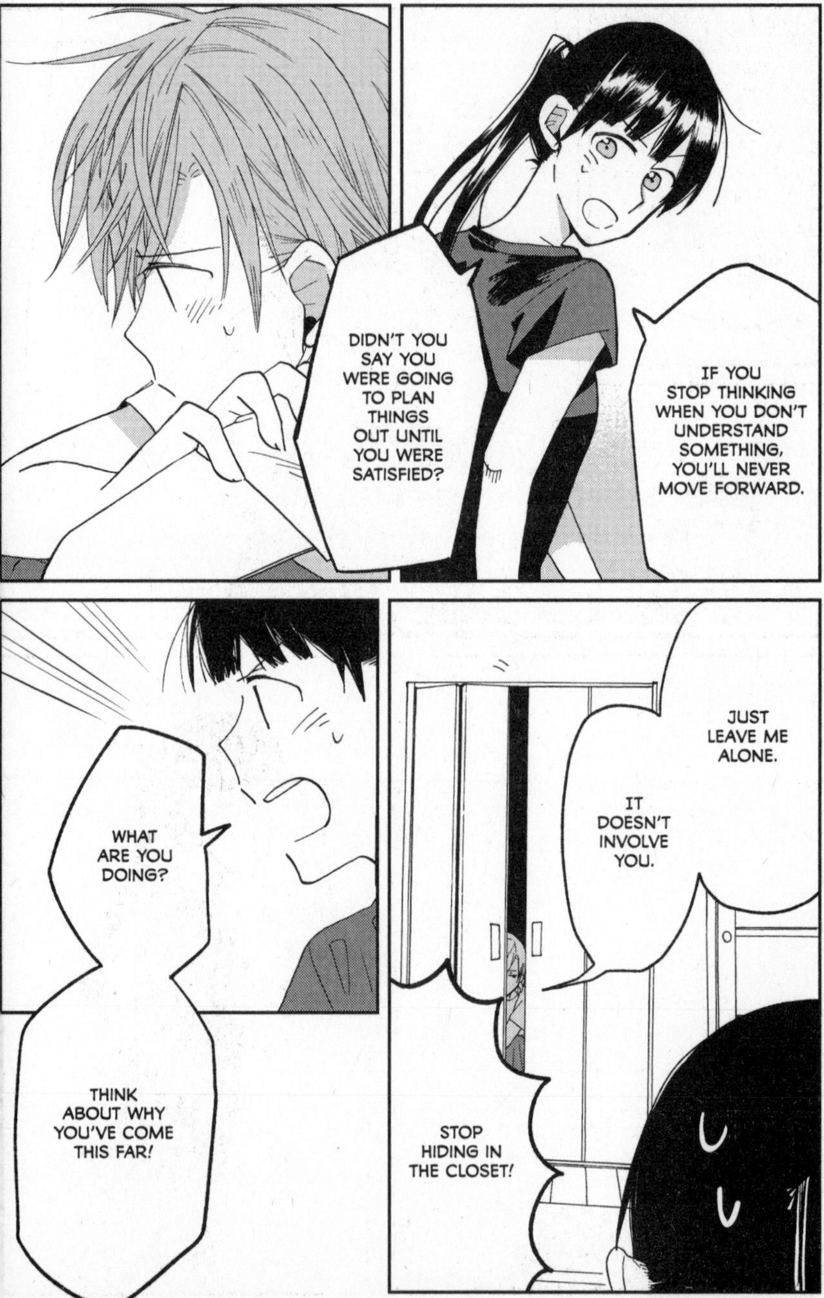
IF YOU STOP THINKING WHEN YOU DON'T UNDERSTAND SOMETHING, YOU'LL NEVER MOVE FORWARD.
DIDN'T YOU SAY YOU WERE GOING TO PLAN THINGS OUT UNTIL YOU WERE SATISFIED?
JUST LEAVE ME ALONE.
IT DOESN'T INVOLVE YOU.
STOP HIDING IN THE CLOSET!
WHAT ARE YOU DOING?
THINK ABOUT WHY YOU'VE COME THIS FAR!

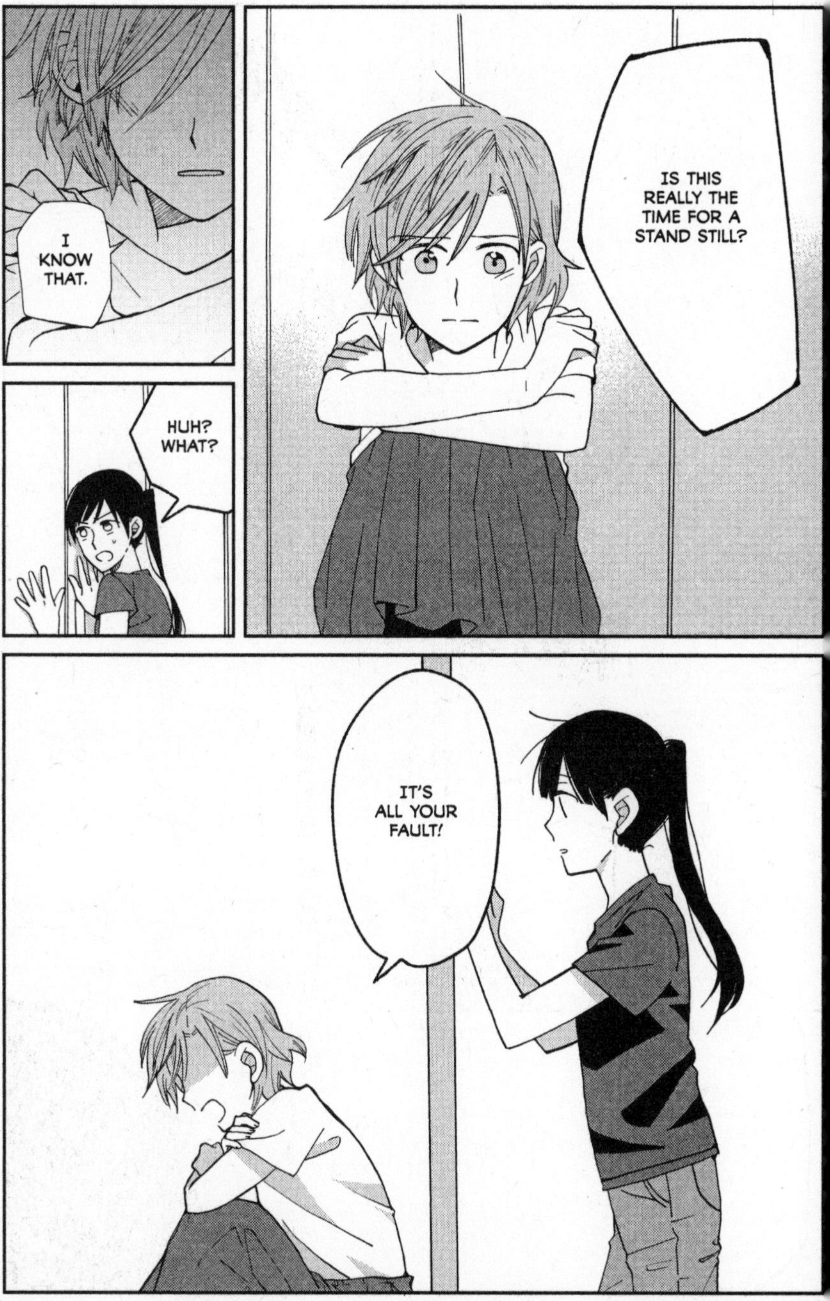
IS THIS REALLY THE TIME FOR A STAND STILL?
I KNOW THAT.
HUH? WHAT?
IT'S ALL YOUR FAULT!

MY FAULT?
DID I DO SOMETHING WRONG?
NO.
THAT'S NOT IT.
SHE'LL THINK I'M ANGRY AT HER AGAIN.
IT HURTS ME TO BE WITH YOU, SHIMIZU-SAN...
WHY?
DON'T ASK ME THAT.

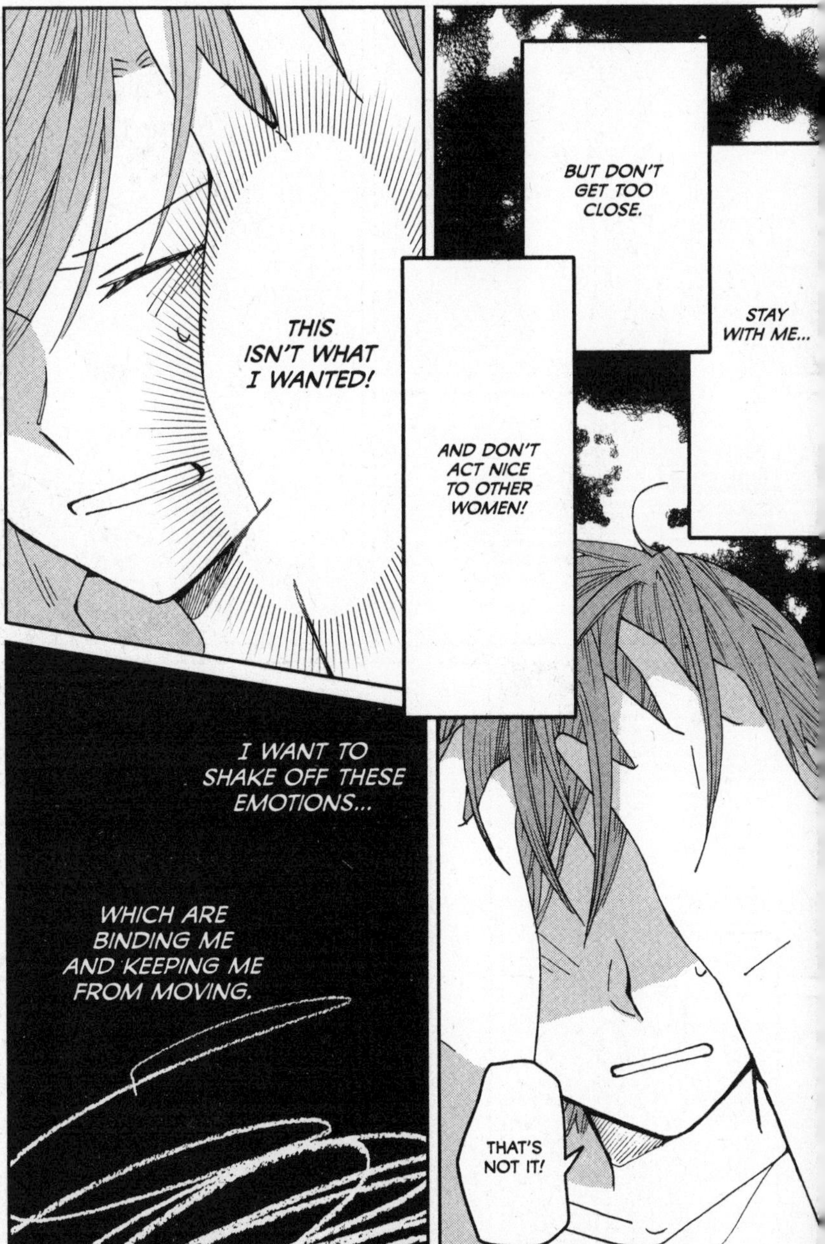
STAY WITH ME...
BUT DON'T GET TOO CLOSE.
AND DON'T ACT NICE TO OTHER WOMEN!
THAT'S NOT IT!
THIS ISN'T WHAT I WANTED!
I WANT TO SHAKE OFF THESE EMOTIONS...
WHICH ARE BINDING ME AND KEEPING ME FROM MOVING.

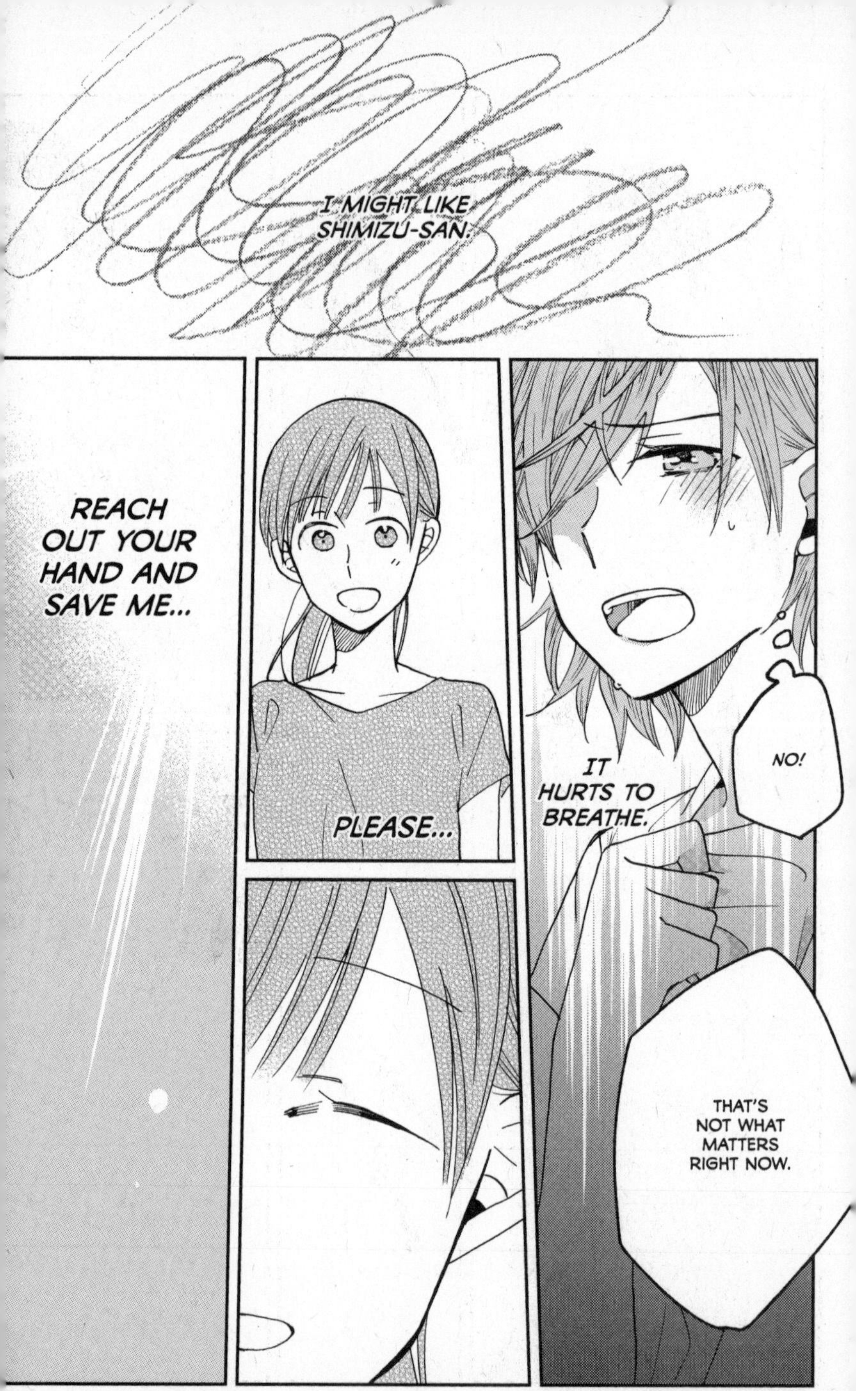
I MIGHT LIKE SHIMIZU-SAN.
NO!
IT HURTS TO BREATHE.
THAT'S NOT WHAT MATTERS RIGHT NOW.
PLEASE...
REACH OUT YOUR HAND AND SAVE ME...

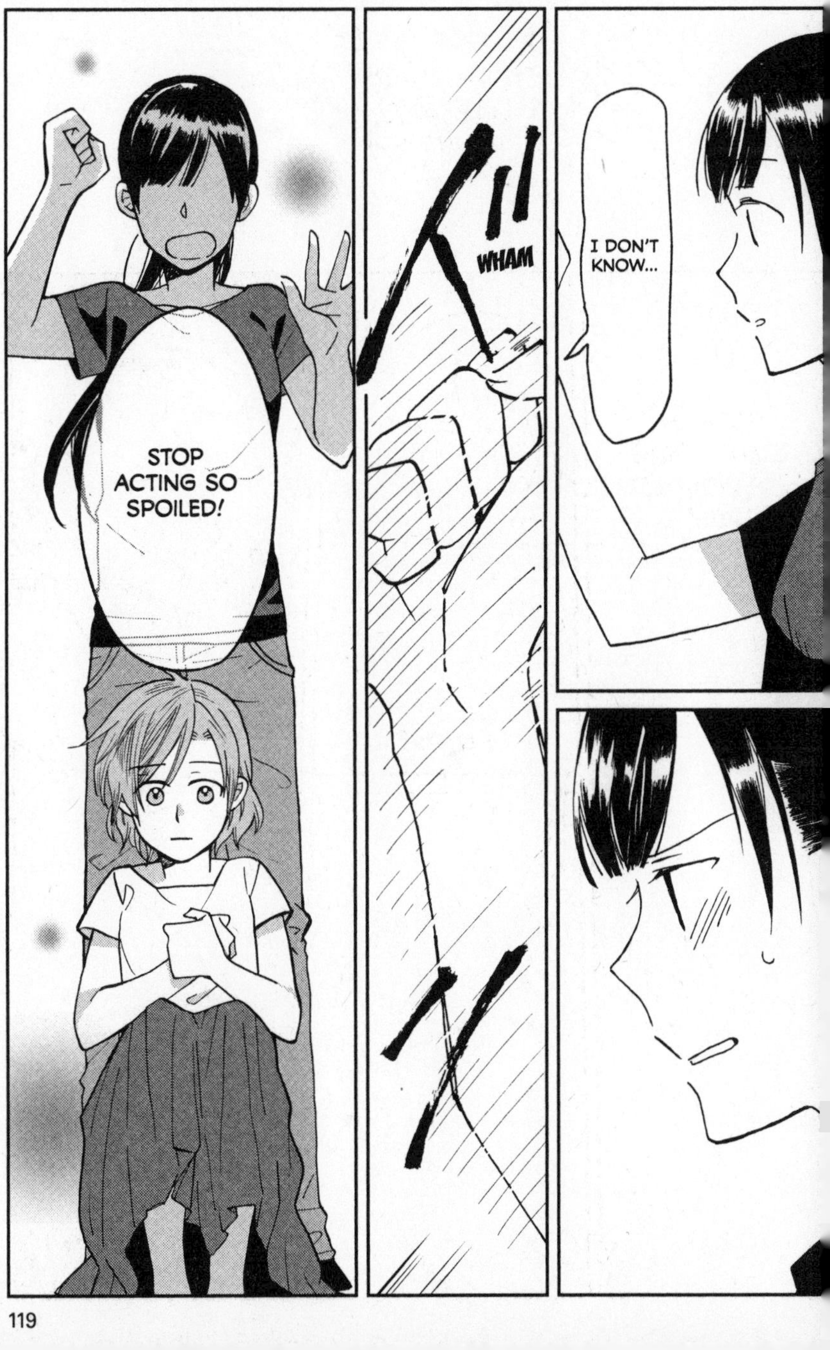
I DON'T KNOW...
WHAM
STOP ACTING SO SPOILED!

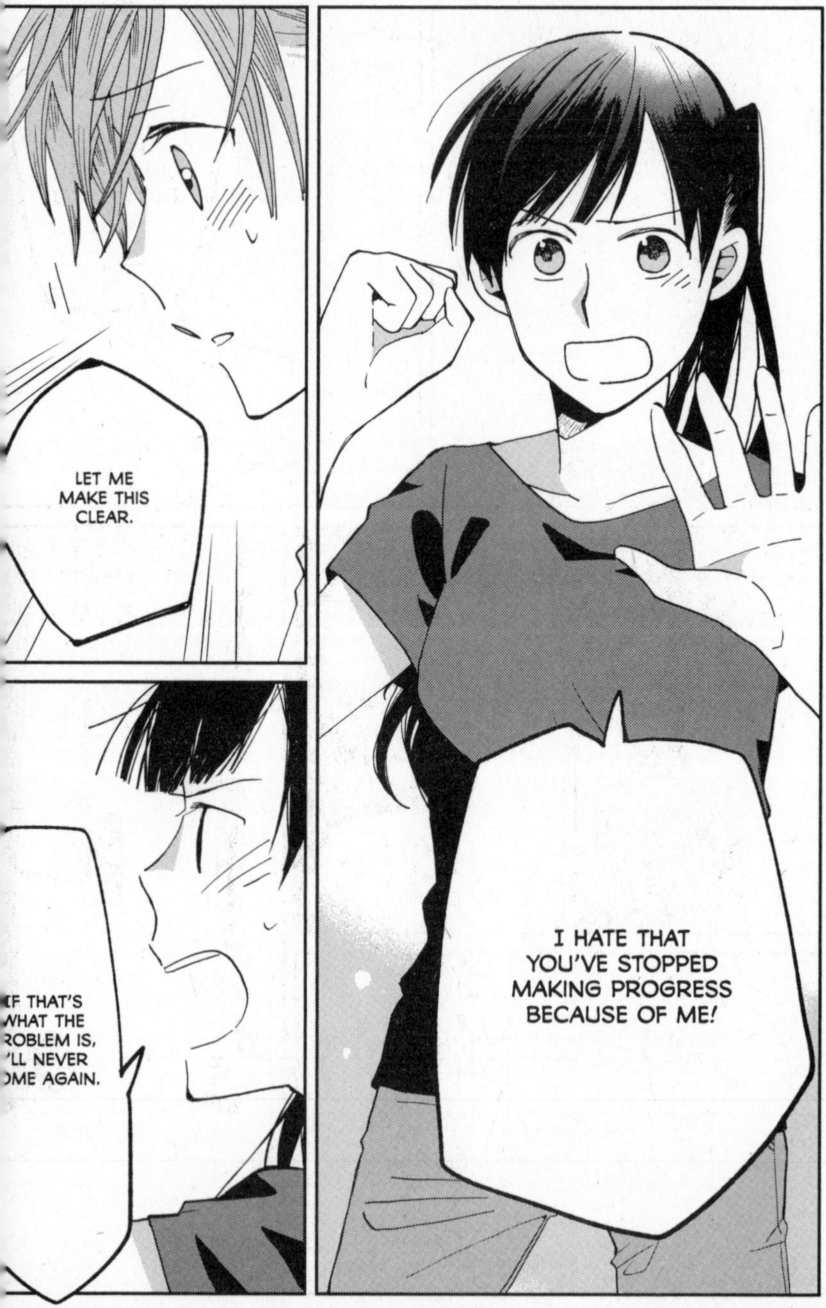
I HATE THAT YOU'VE STOPPED MAKING PROGRESS BECAUSE OF ME!
LET ME MAKE THIS CLEAR.
F THAT'S VHAT THE ROBLEM IS, 'LL NEVER OME AGAIN.

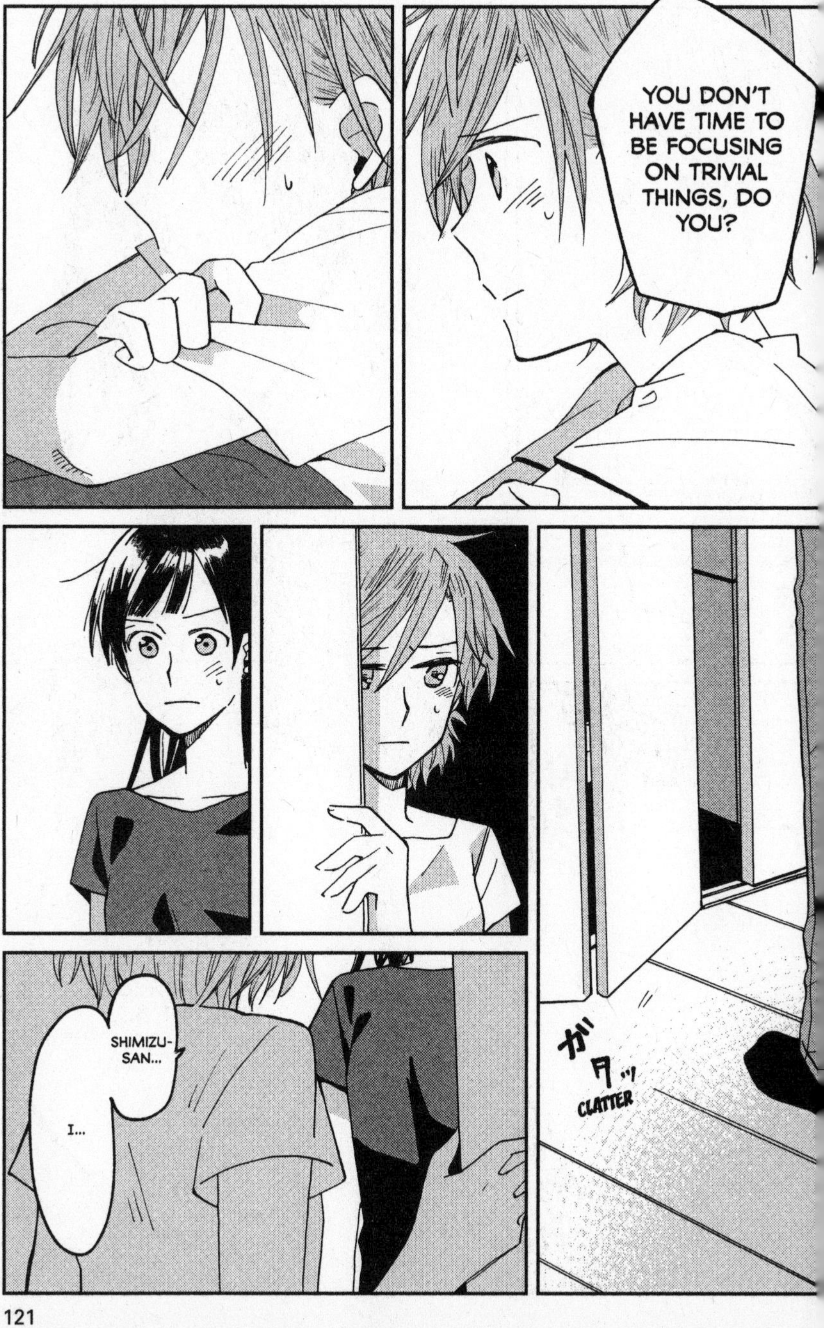
YOU DON'T HAVE TIME TO BE FOCUSING ON TRIVIAL THINGS, DO YOU?
ガタッ
CLATTER
SHIMIZU-SAN...
I...

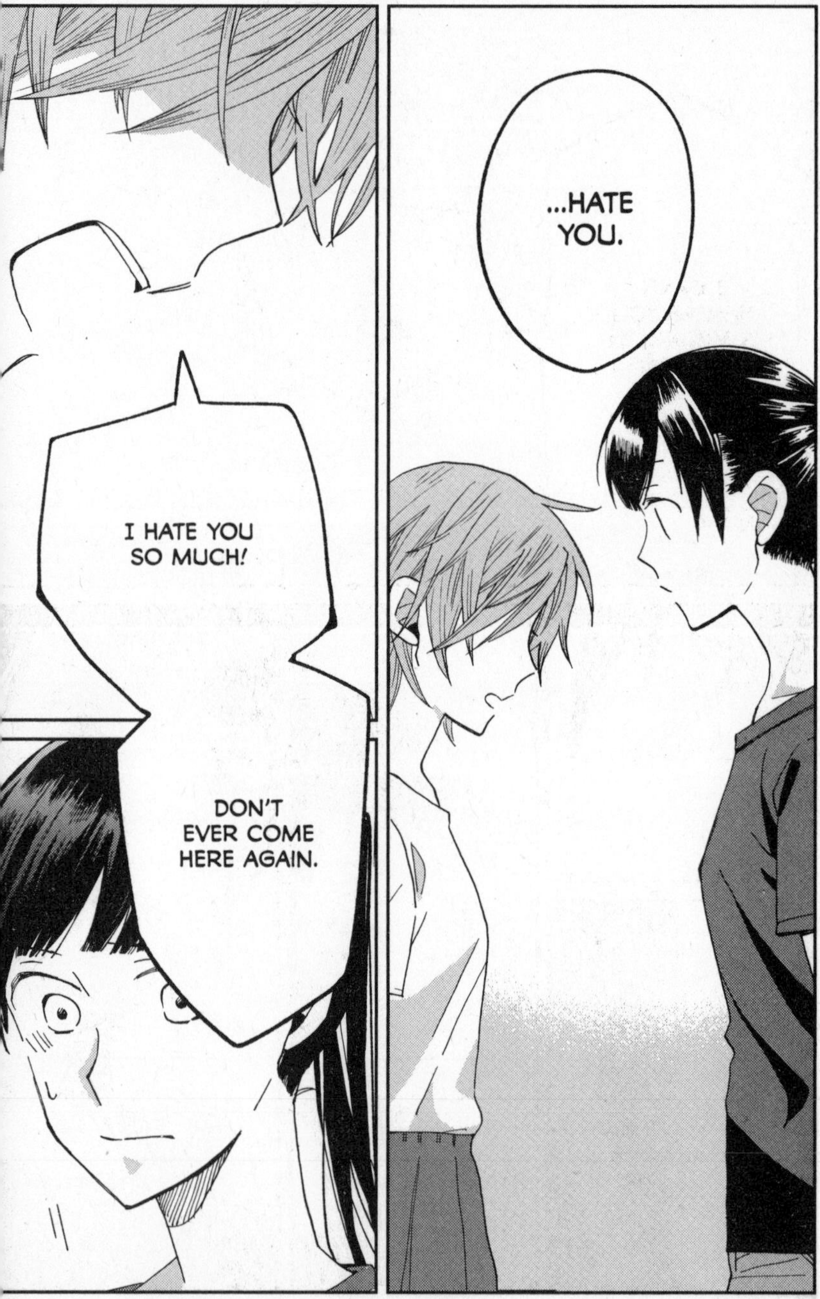
...HATE YOU.
I HATE YOU SO MUCH!
DON'T EVER COME HERE AGAIN.

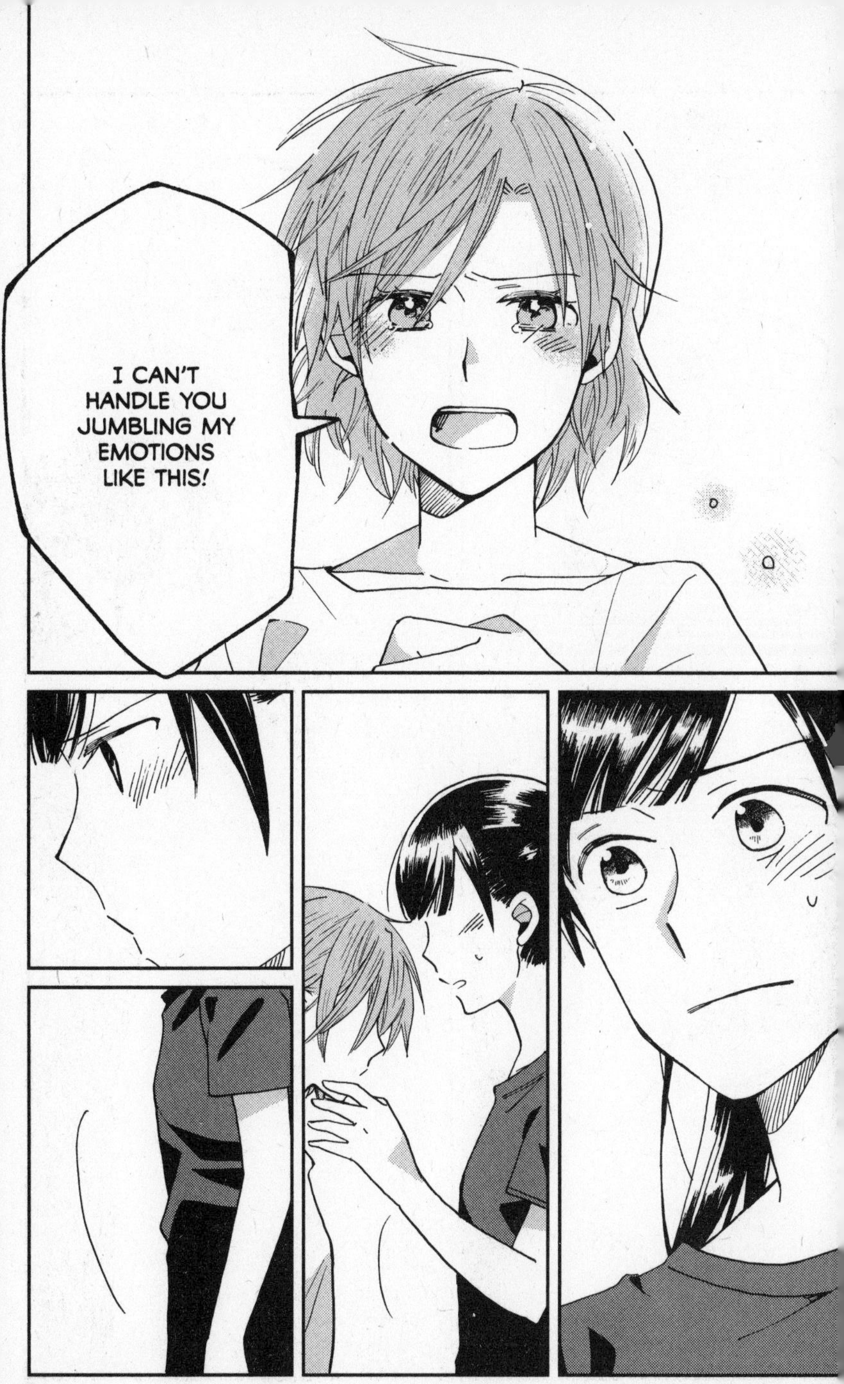
I CAN'T HANDLE YOU JUMBLING MY EMOTIONS LIKE THIS!

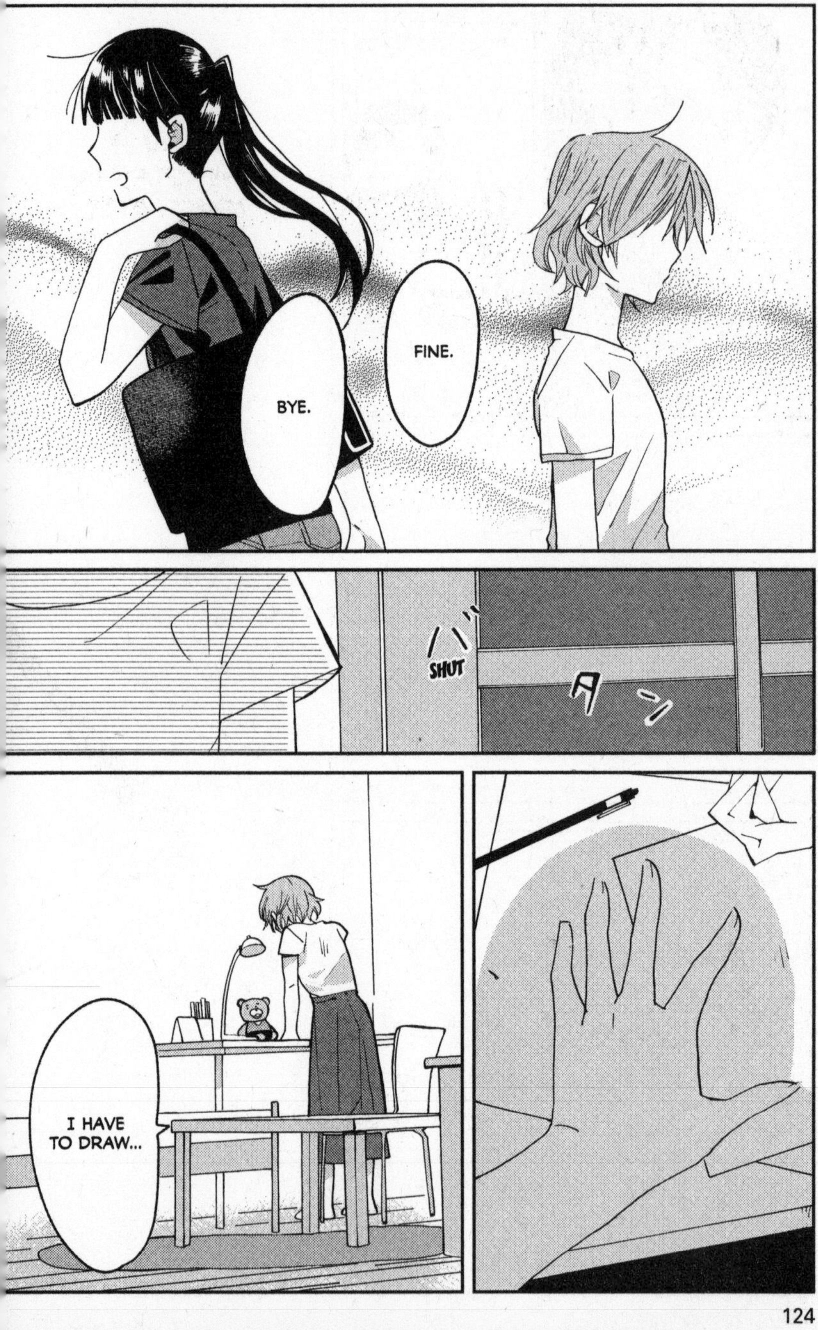
FINE.
BYE.
バ
SHUT
タン
I HAVE TO DRAW...

...MORN-
ING.

EVEN IF
SHIMIZU-SAN
ISN'T HERE.

GOOD
MORNING.

I HAVE
TO DRAW...

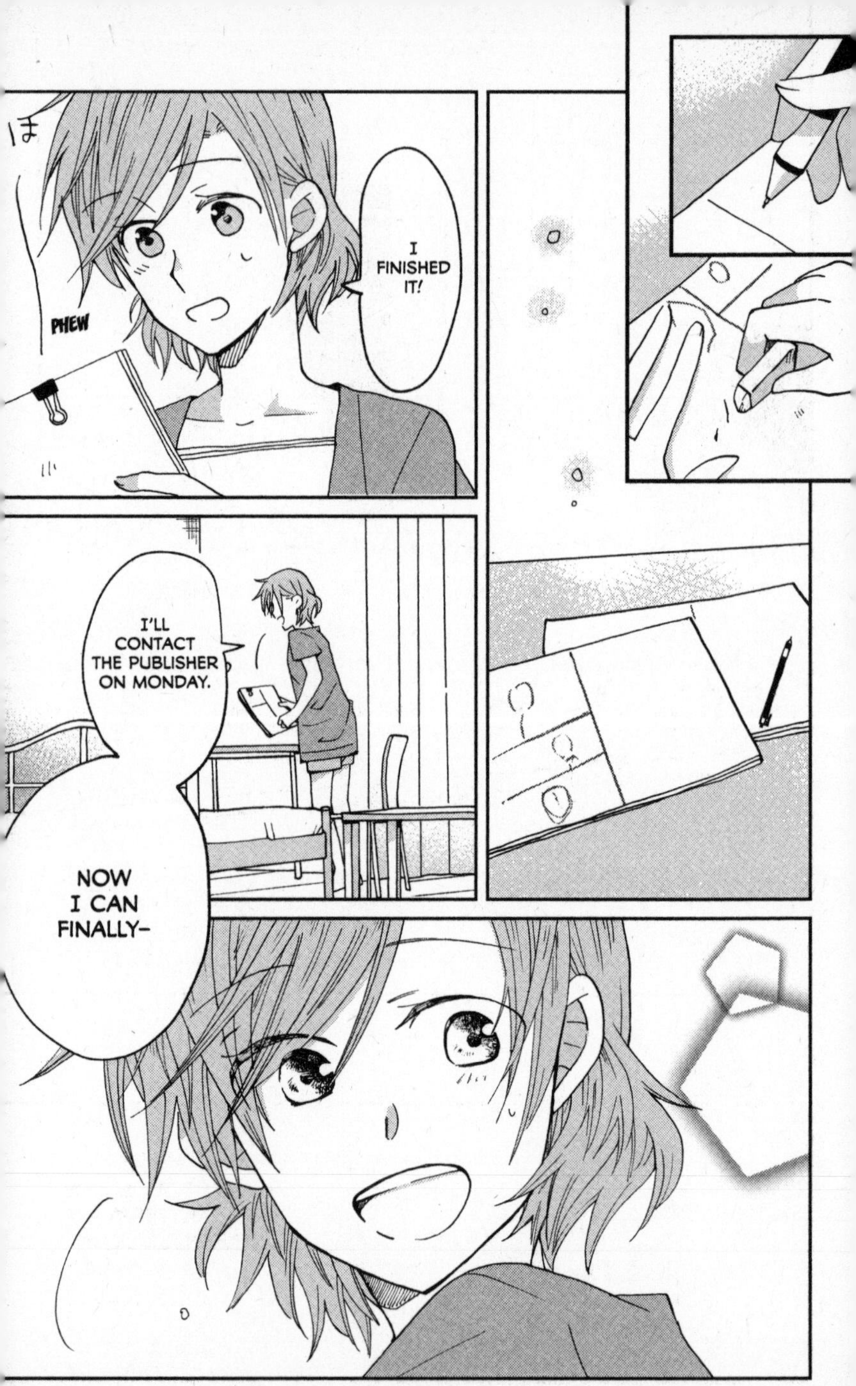
は
PHEW
I FINISHED IT!
I'LL CONTACT THE PUBLISHER ON MONDAY.
NOW I CAN FINALLY-

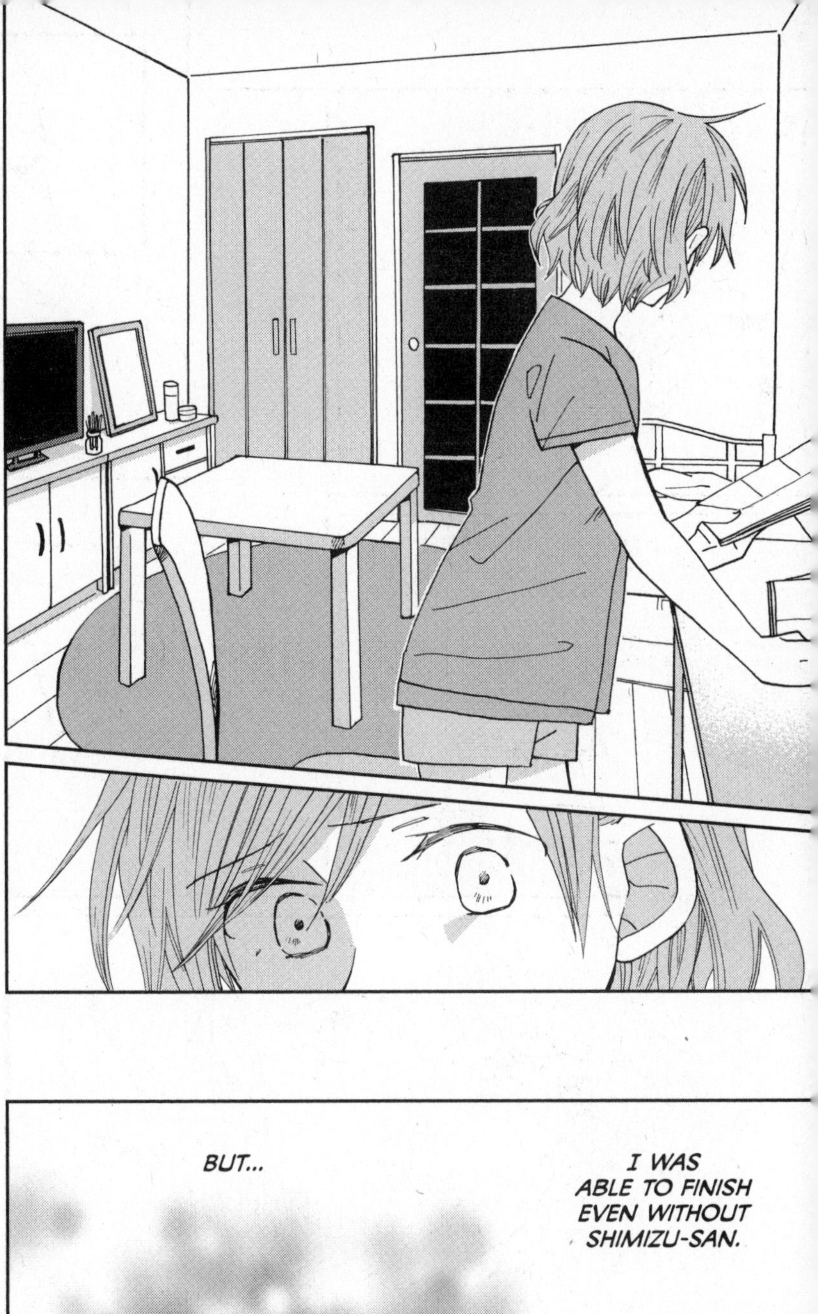
I WAS ABLE TO FINISH EVEN WITHOUT SHIMIZU-SAN.
BUT...

I WANTED HER TO BE HERE WHEN MY DREAM CAME TRUE...
THE COMPANY RETREAT IS THIS WEEKEND.
OH, I FORGOT.
SHIMIZU-SAN.

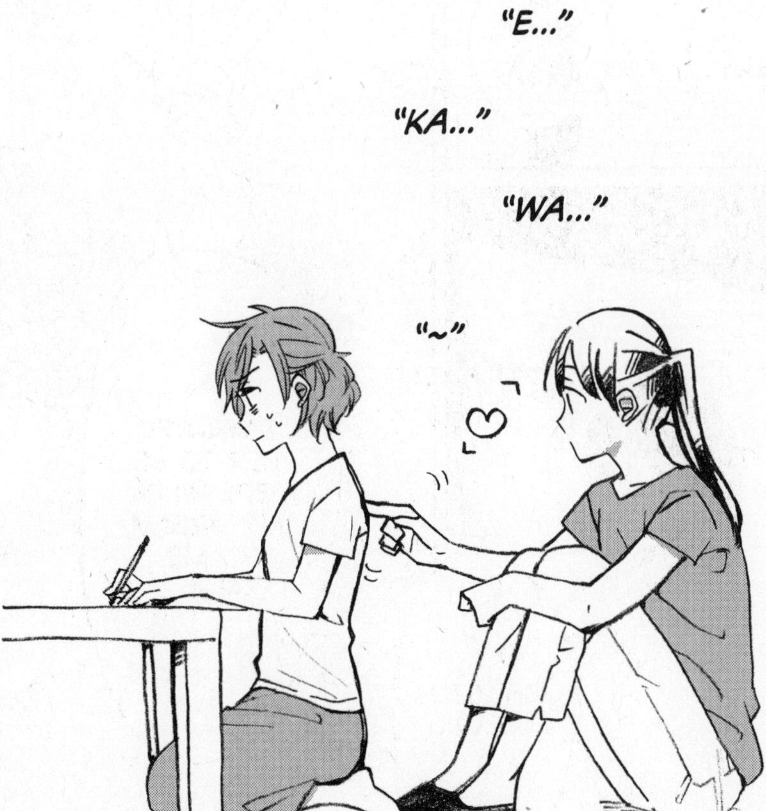

CONTINUED ON THE NEXT PAGE...

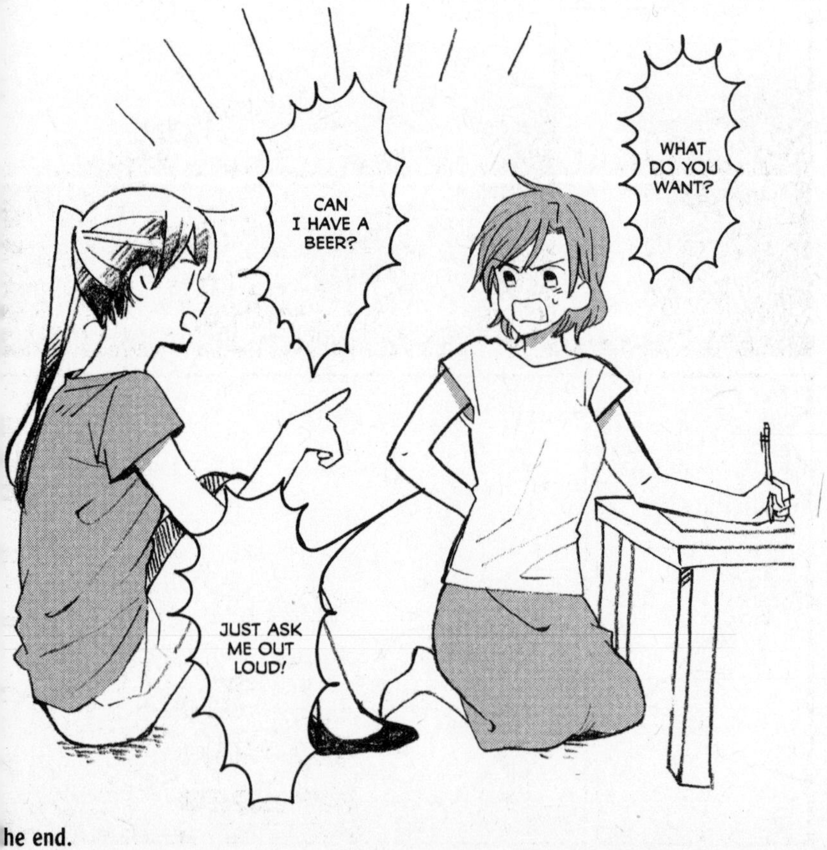
WHAT DO YOU WANT?
CAN I HAVE A BEER?
JUST ASK ME OUT LOUD!

he end.

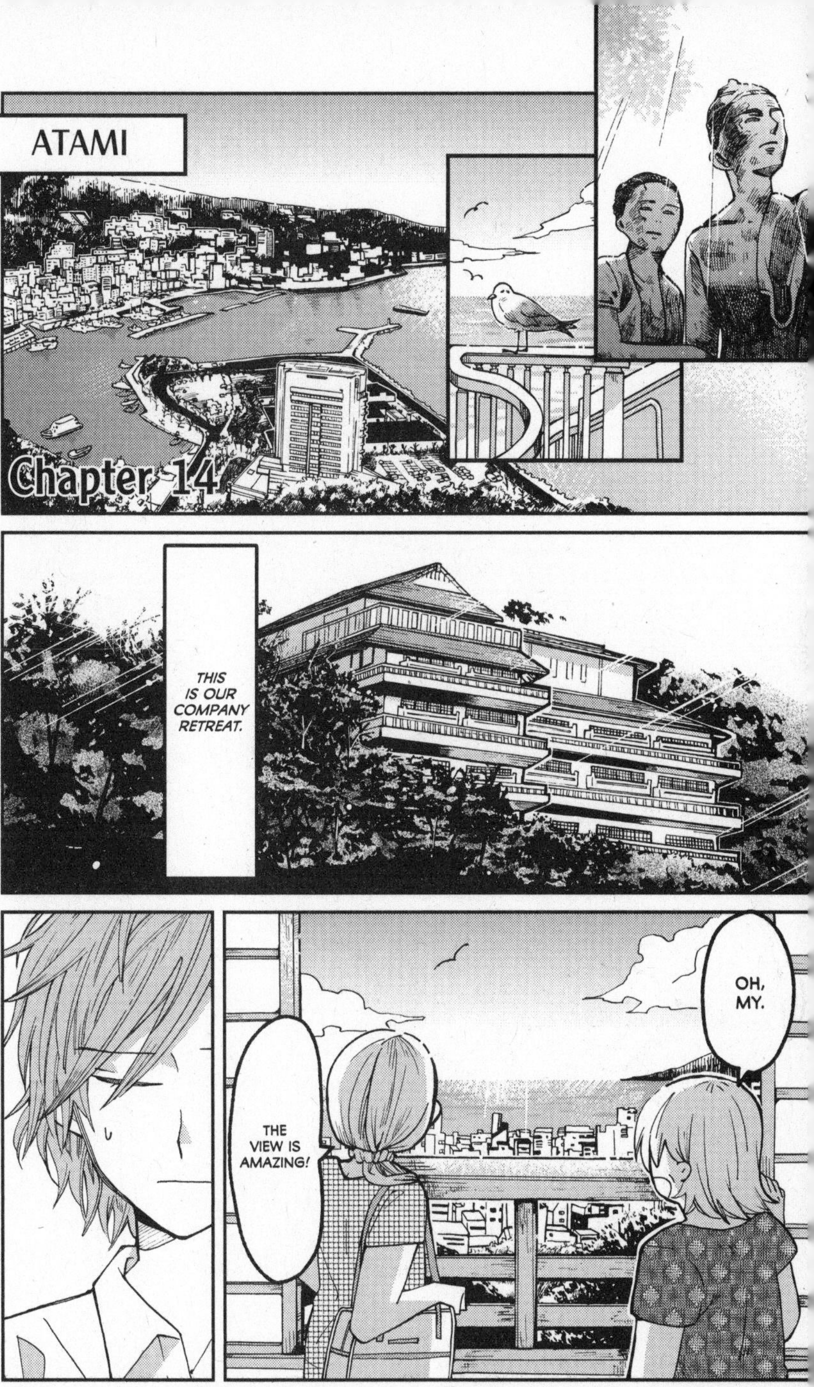
ATAMI
Chapter 14
THIS IS OUR COMPANY RETREAT.
OH, MY.
THE VIEW IS AMAZING!

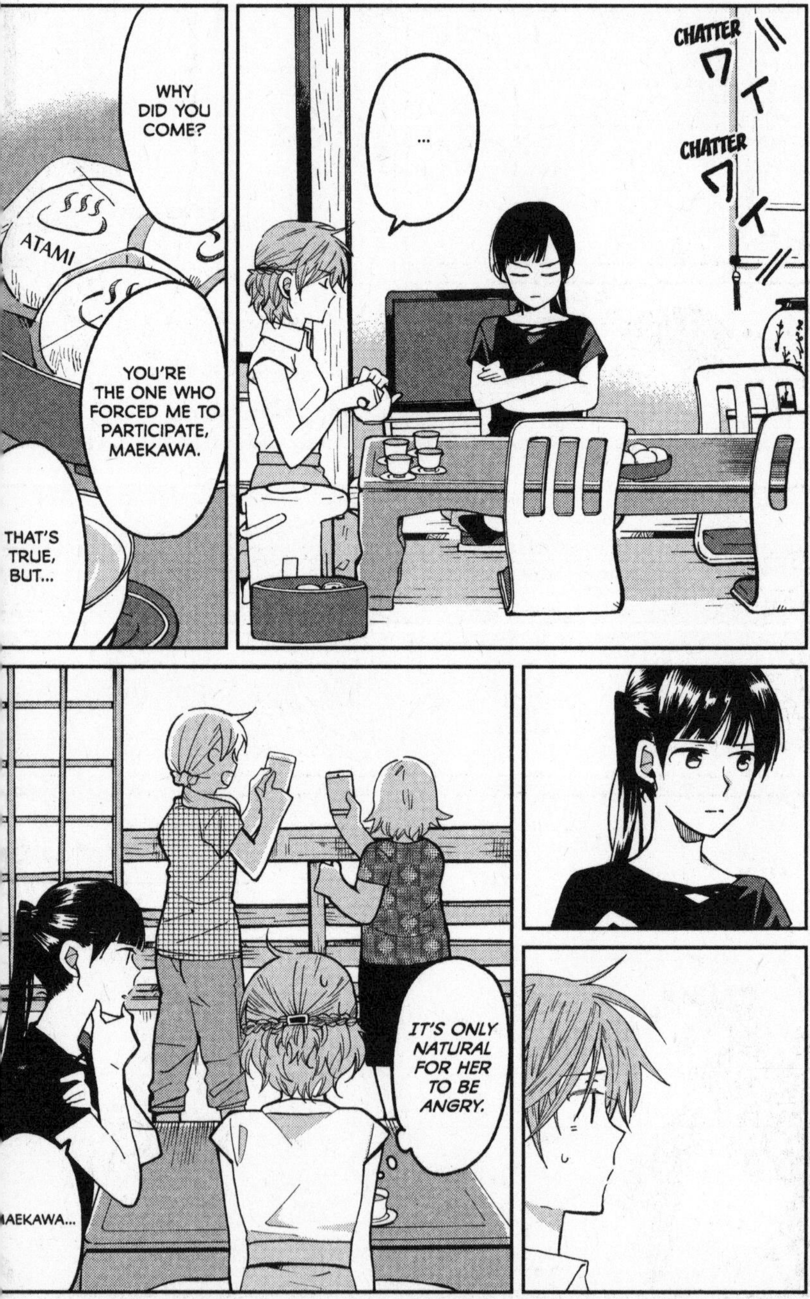

CHATTER
ワイ
CHATTER
ワイ
...
ATAMI
WHY DID YOU COME?
YOU'RE THE ONE WHO FORCED ME TO PARTICIPATE, MAEKAWA.
THAT'S TRUE, BUT...
IT'S ONLY NATURAL FOR HER TO BE ANGRY.
AEKAWA...

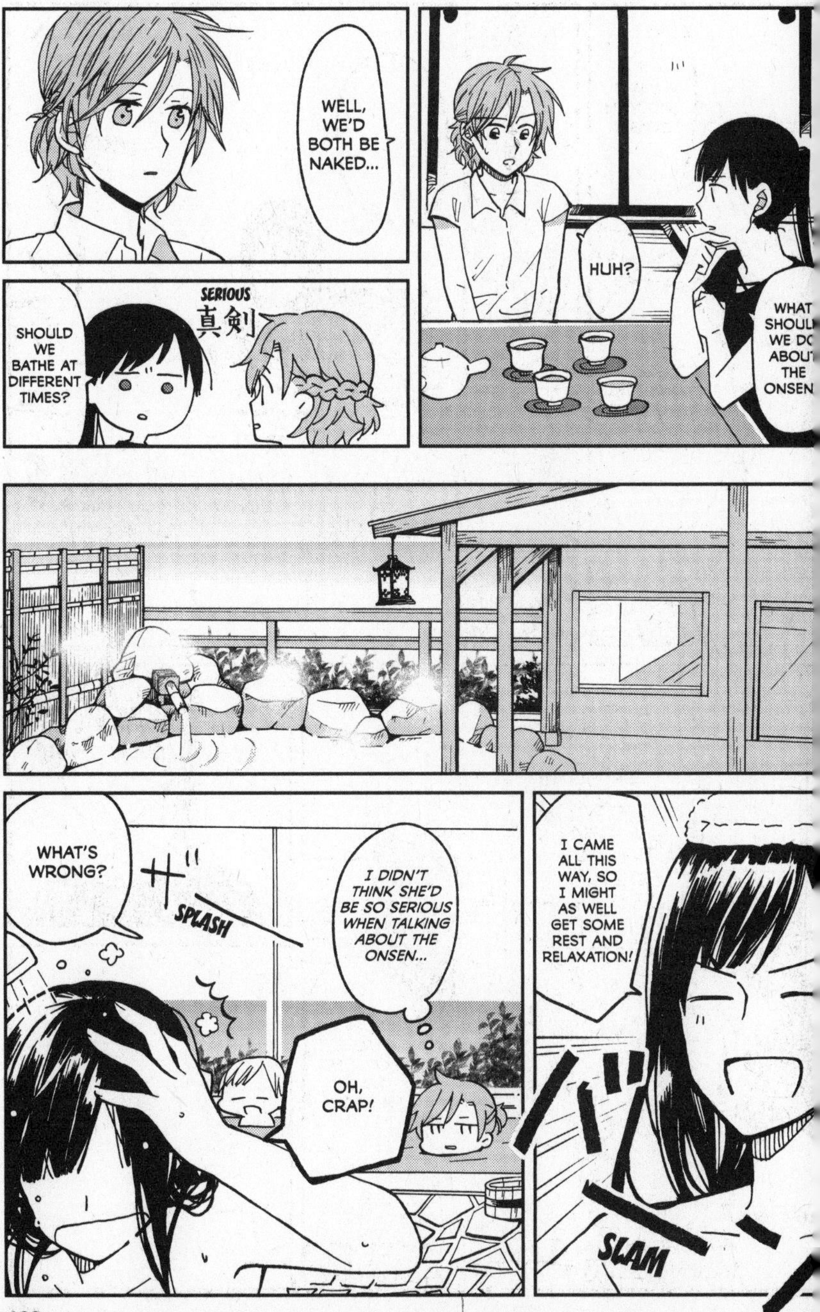
WHAT SHOUL WE DO ABOUT THE ONSEN
HUH?
WELL, WE'D BOTH BE NAKED...
SERIOUS 真剣
SHOULD WE BATHE AT DIFFERENT TIMES?
I CAME ALL THIS WAY, SO I MIGHT AS WELL GET SOME REST AND RELAXATION!
SLAM
I DIDN'T THINK SHE'D BE SO SERIOUS WHEN TALKING ABOUT THE ONSEN...
WHAT'S WRONG?
SPLASH
OH, CRAP!

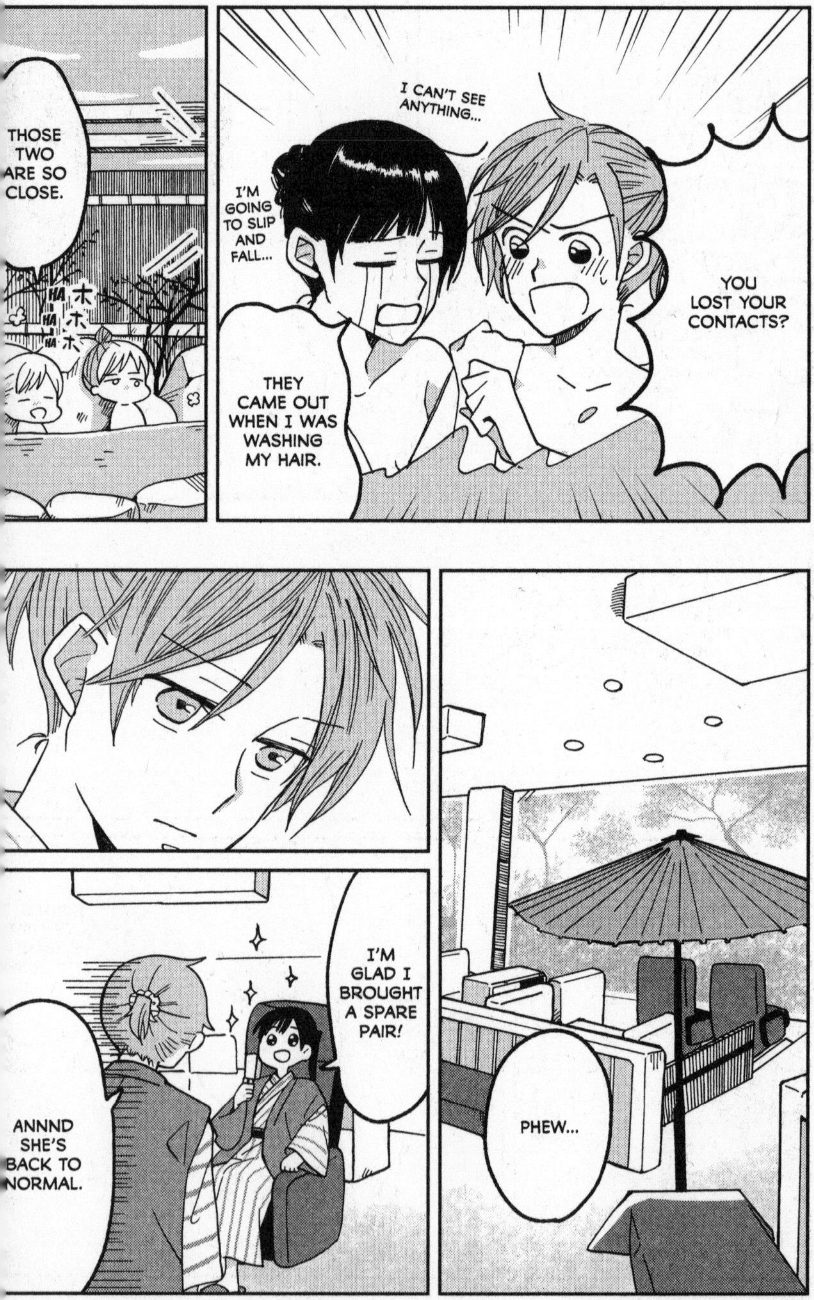
YOU LOST YOUR CONTACTS?
I CAN'T SEE ANYTHING...
I'M GOING TO SLIP AND FALL...
THEY CAME OUT WHEN I WAS WASHING MY HAIR.
THOSE TWO ARE SO CLOSE.
HA HA HA HA
ホホホ
PHEW...
I'M GLAD I BROUGHT A SPARE PAIR!
ANNND SHE'S BACK TO NORMAL.

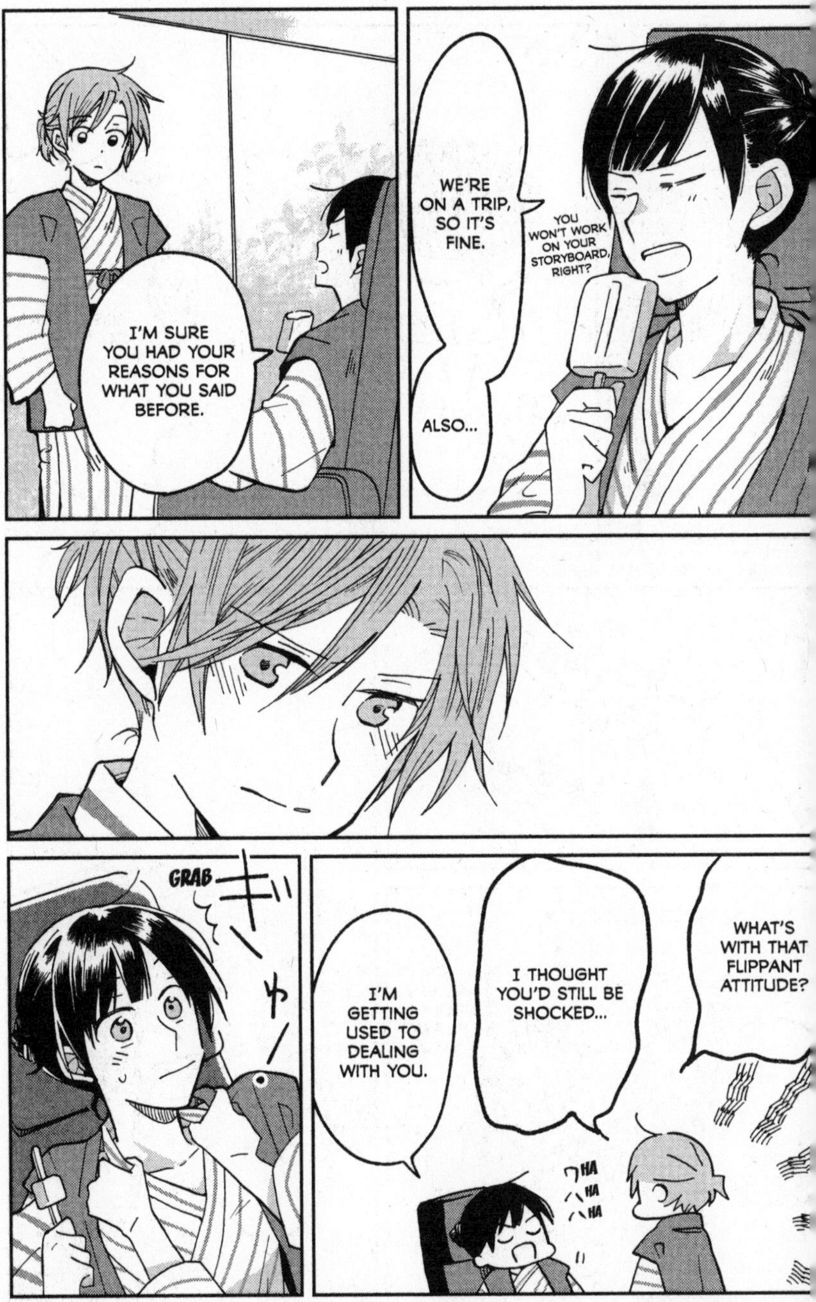

YOU WON'T WORK ON YOUR STORYBOARD, RIGHT?
WE'RE ON A TRIP, SO IT'S FINE.
ALSO...
I'M SURE YOU HAD YOUR REASONS FOR WHAT YOU SAID BEFORE.
WHAT'S WITH THAT FLIPPANT ATTITUDE?
I THOUGHT YOU'D STILL BE SHOCKED...
I'M GETTING USED TO DEALING WITH YOU.
HA HA HA
GRAB

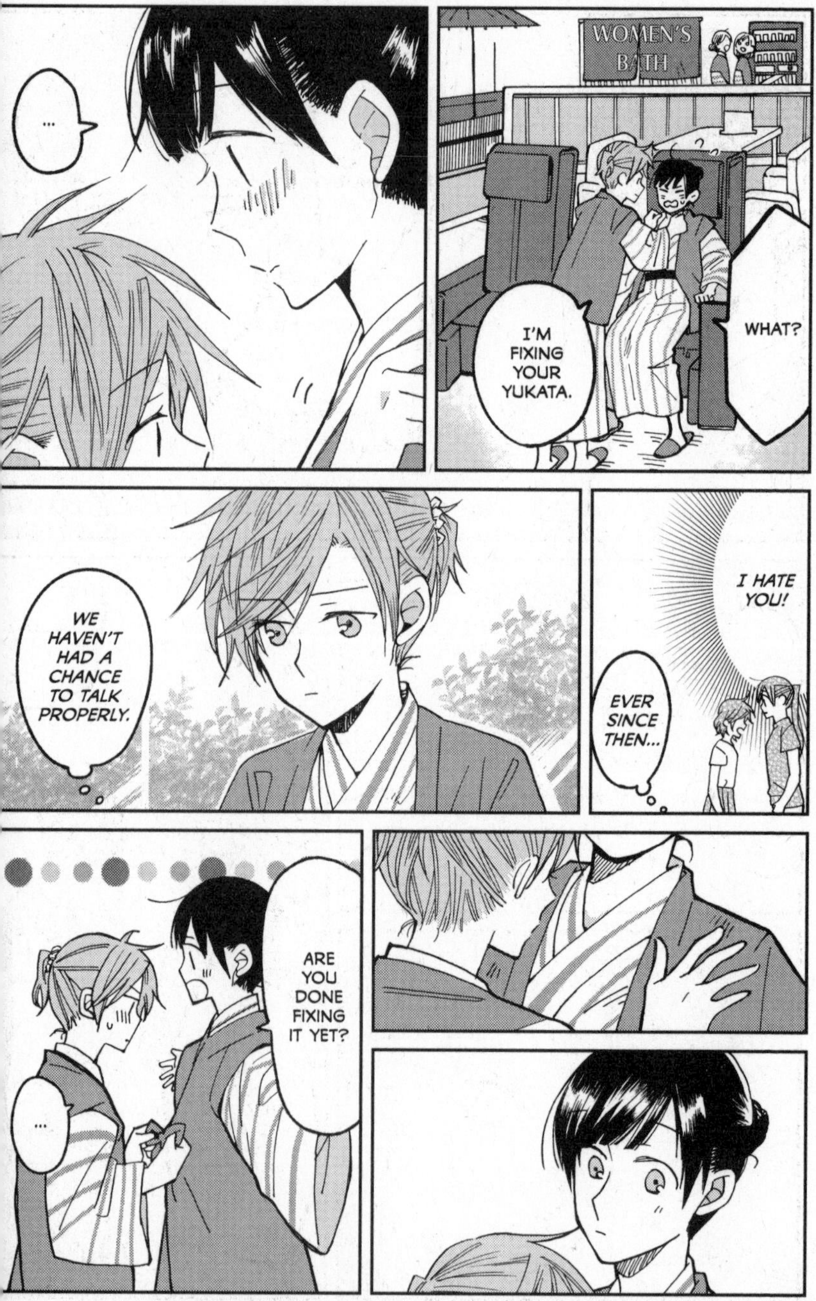
WOMEN'S BATH
WHAT?
I'M FIXING YOUR YUKATA.
...
I HATE YOU!
EVER SINCE THEN...
WE HAVEN'T HAD A CHANCE TO TALK PROPERLY.
ARE YOU DONE FIXING IT YET?
...

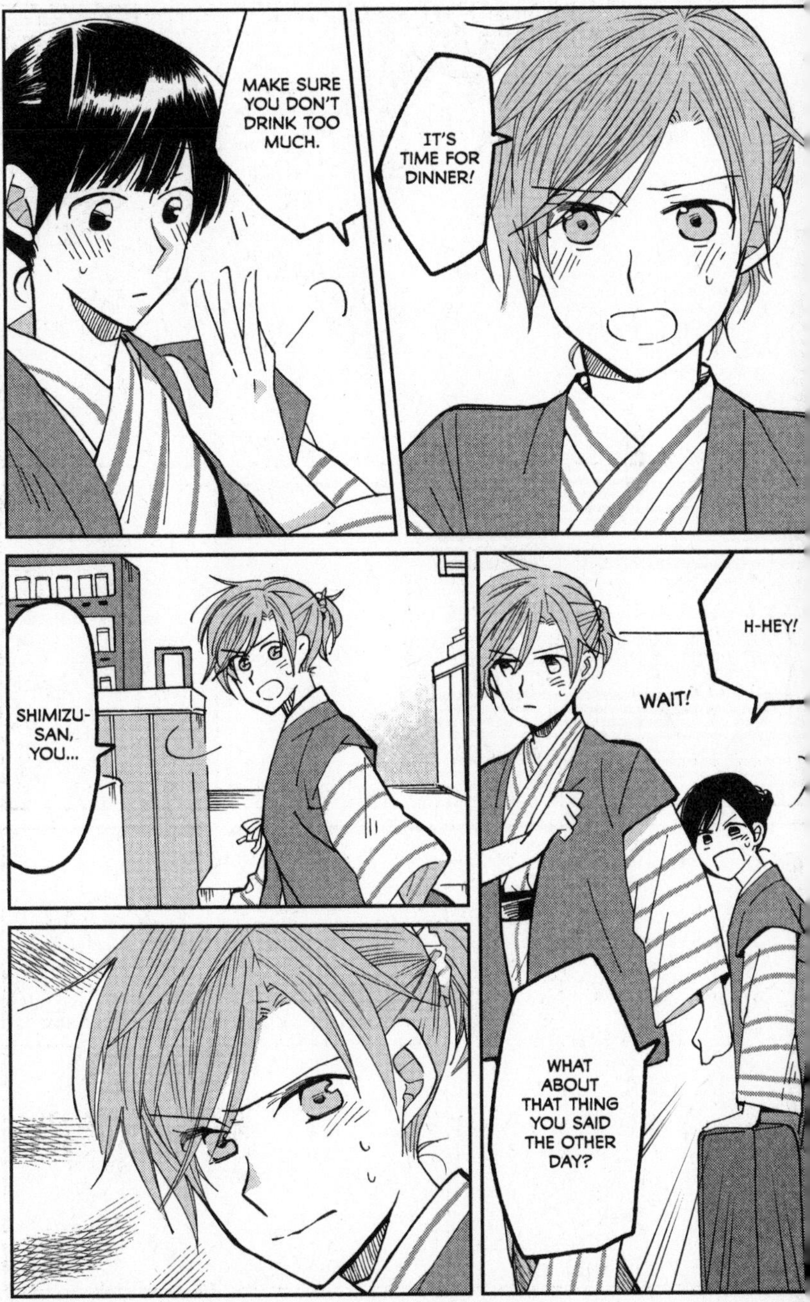
IT'S TIME FOR DINNER!
MAKE SURE YOU DON'T DRINK TOO MUCH.
H-HEY!
WAIT!
WHAT ABOUT THAT THING YOU SAID THE OTHER DAY?
SHIMIZU-SAN, YOU...

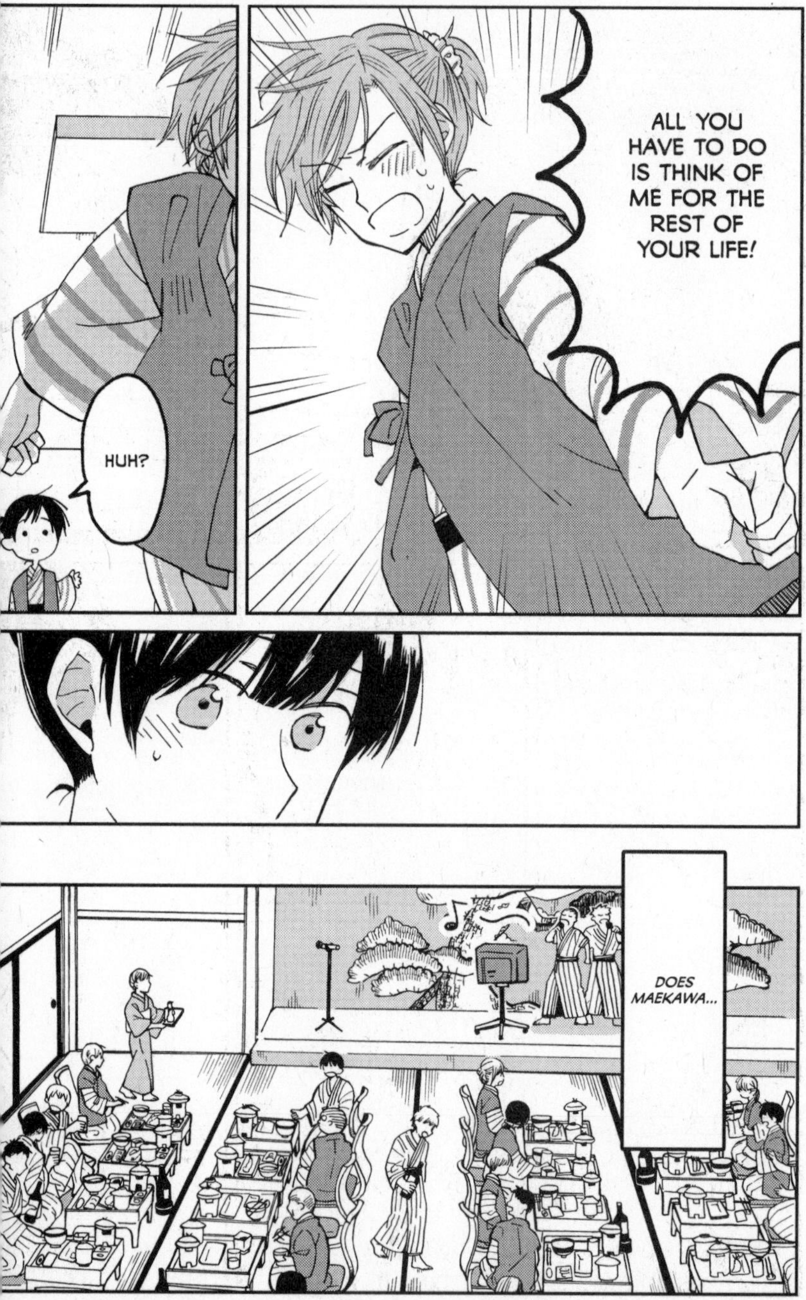
ALL YOU HAVE TO DO IS THINK OF ME FOR THE REST OF YOUR LIFE!
HUH?
DOES MAEKAWA...

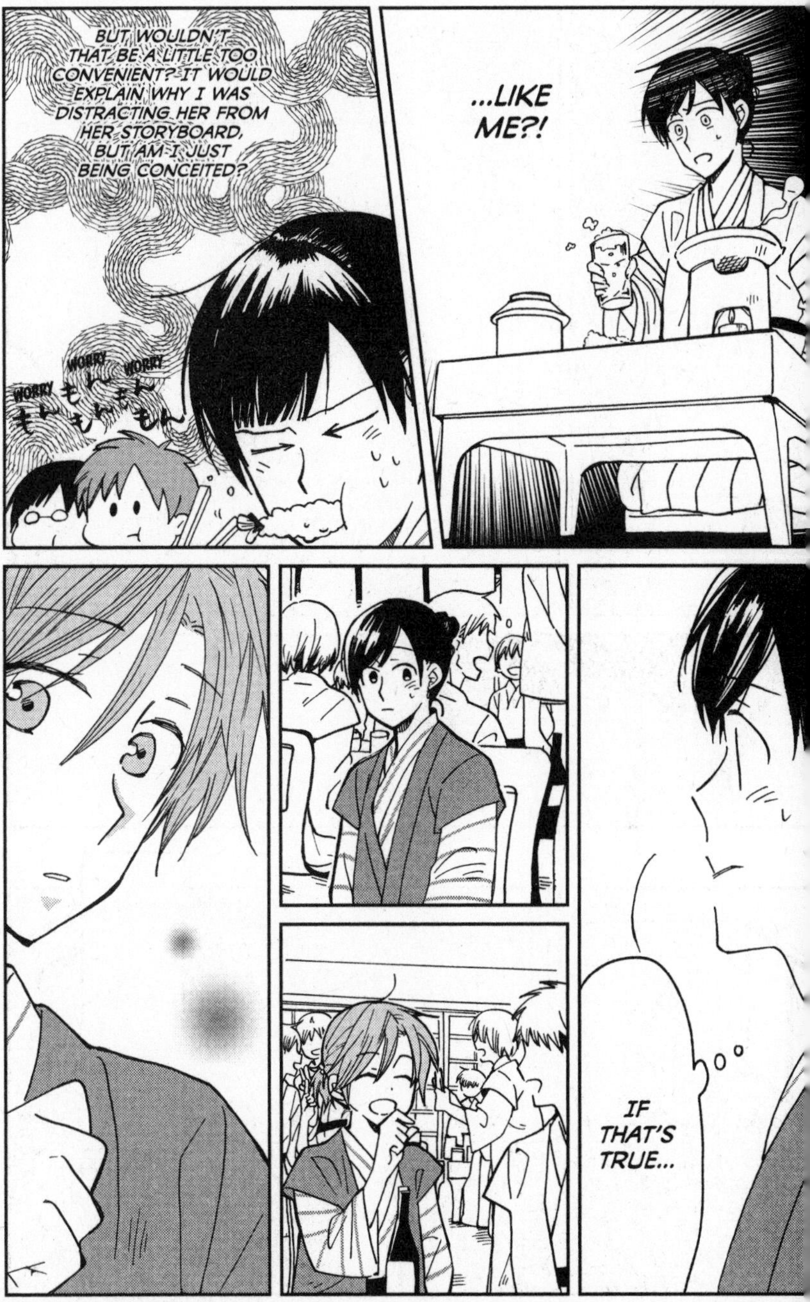
...LIKE ME?!
BUT WOULDN'T THAT BE A LITTLE TOO CONVENIENT? IT WOULD EXPLAIN WHY I WAS DISTRACTING HER FROM HER STORYBOARD, BUT AM I JUST BEING CONCEITED?
WORRY WORRY WORRY
もん もん もん もん もん
IF THAT'S TRUE...

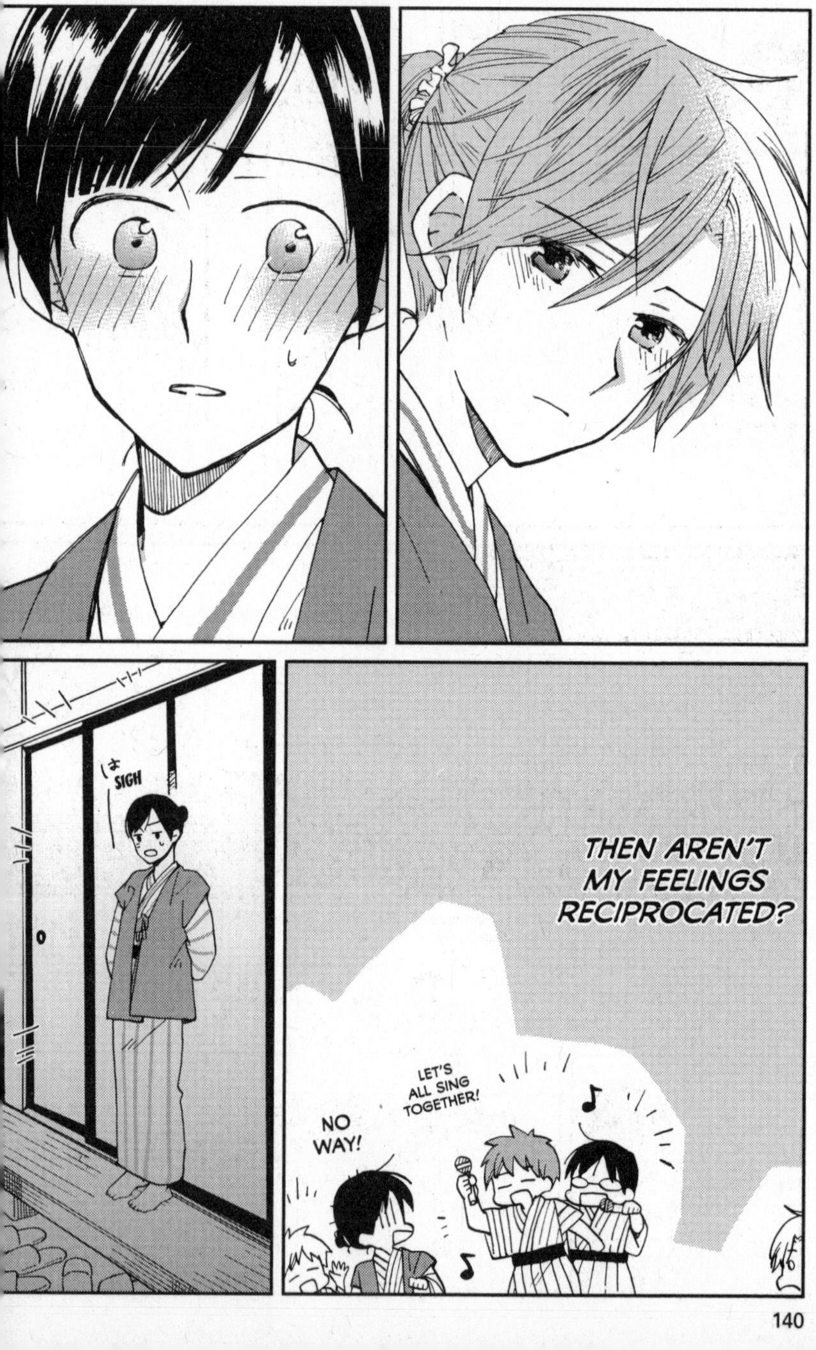
THEN AREN'T MY FEELINGS RECIPROCATED?
LET'S ALL SING TOGETHER!
NO WAY!
は SIGH

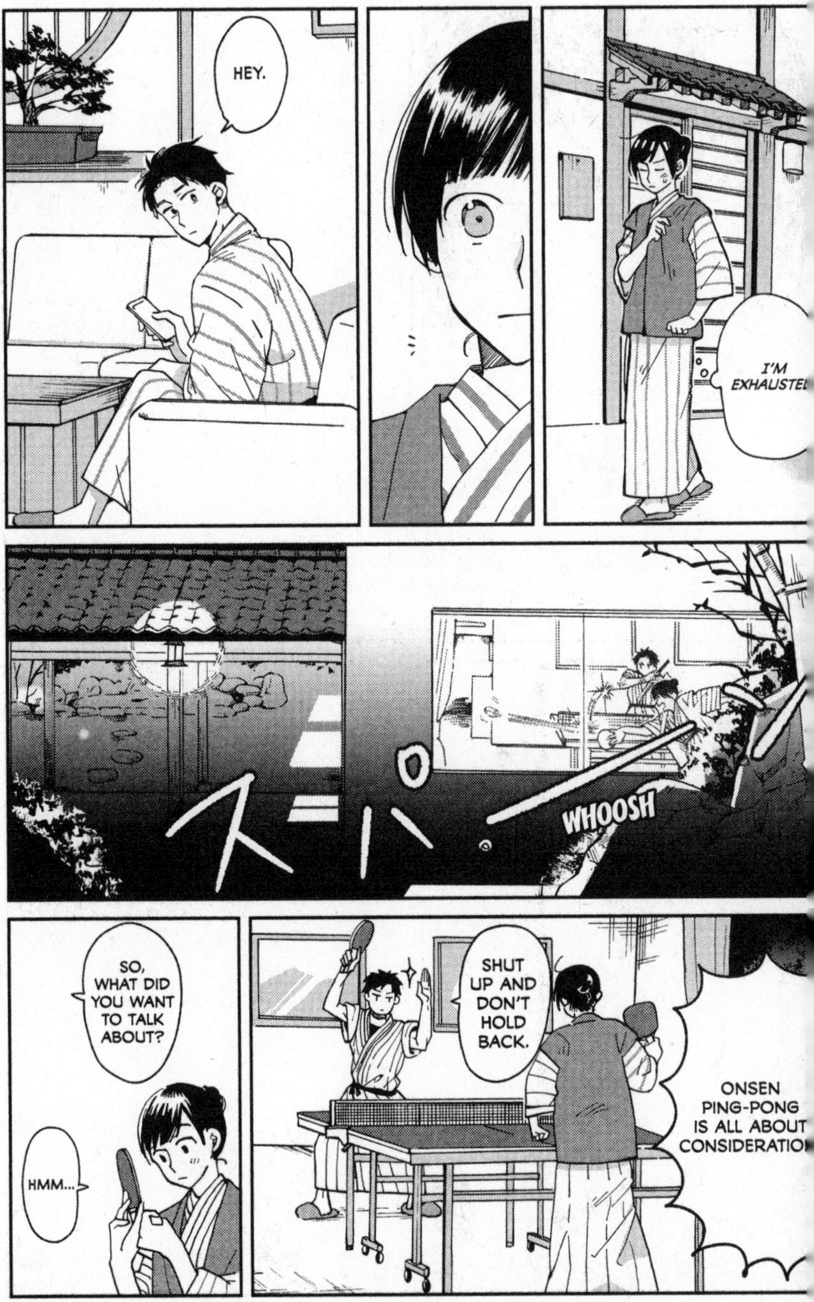
I'M EXHAUSTE
HEY.
WHOOSH
スパ
SHUT UP AND DON'T HOLD BACK.
ONSEN PING-PONG IS ALL ABOUT CONSIDERATIO
SO, WHAT DID YOU WANT TO TALK ABOUT?
HMM...

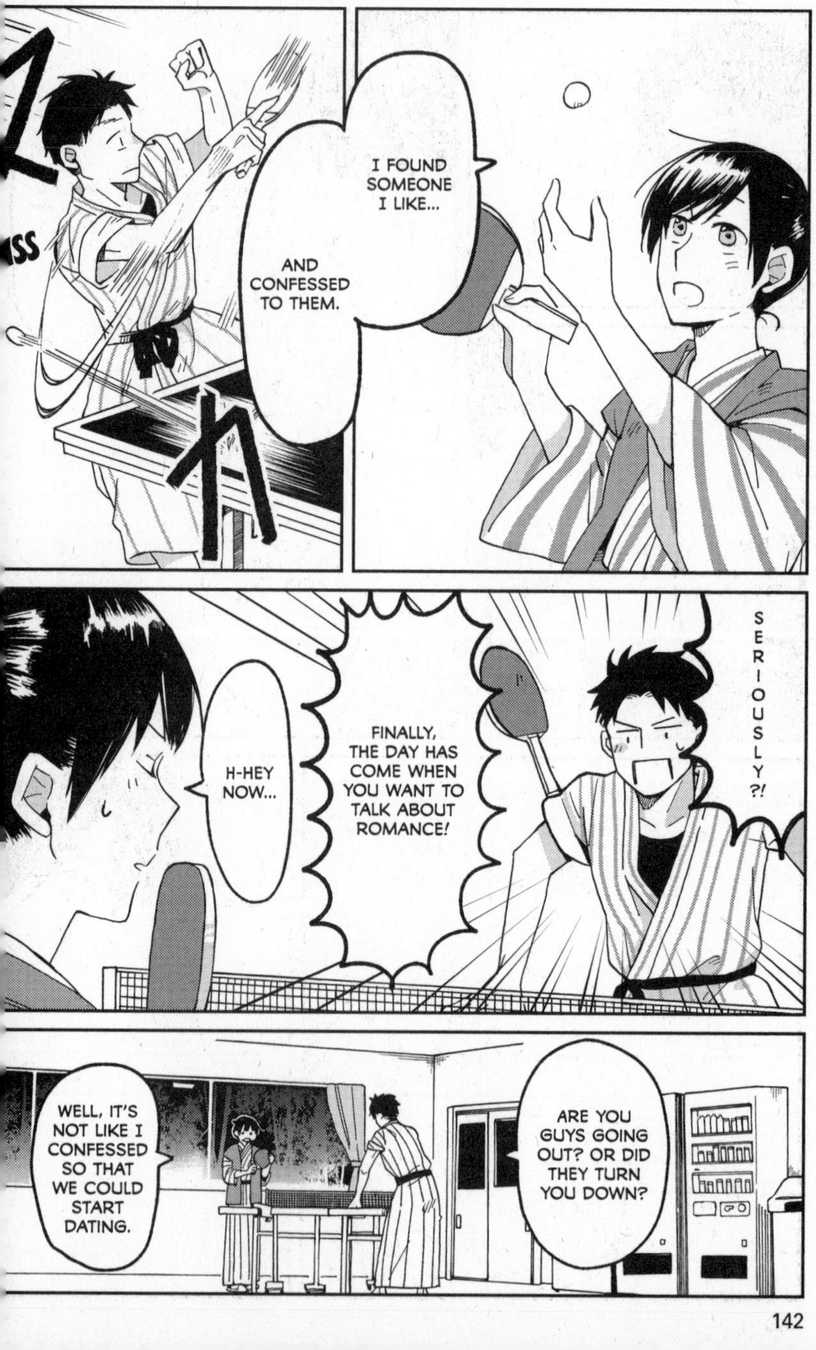
I FOUND SOMEONE I LIKE...
AND CONFESSED TO THEM.
SERIOUSLY?!
FINALLY, THE DAY HAS COME WHEN YOU WANT TO TALK ABOUT ROMANCE!
H-HEY NOW...
ARE YOU GUYS GOING OUT? OR DID THEY TURN YOU DOWN?
WELL, IT'S NOT LIKE I CONFESSED SO THAT WE COULD START DATING.

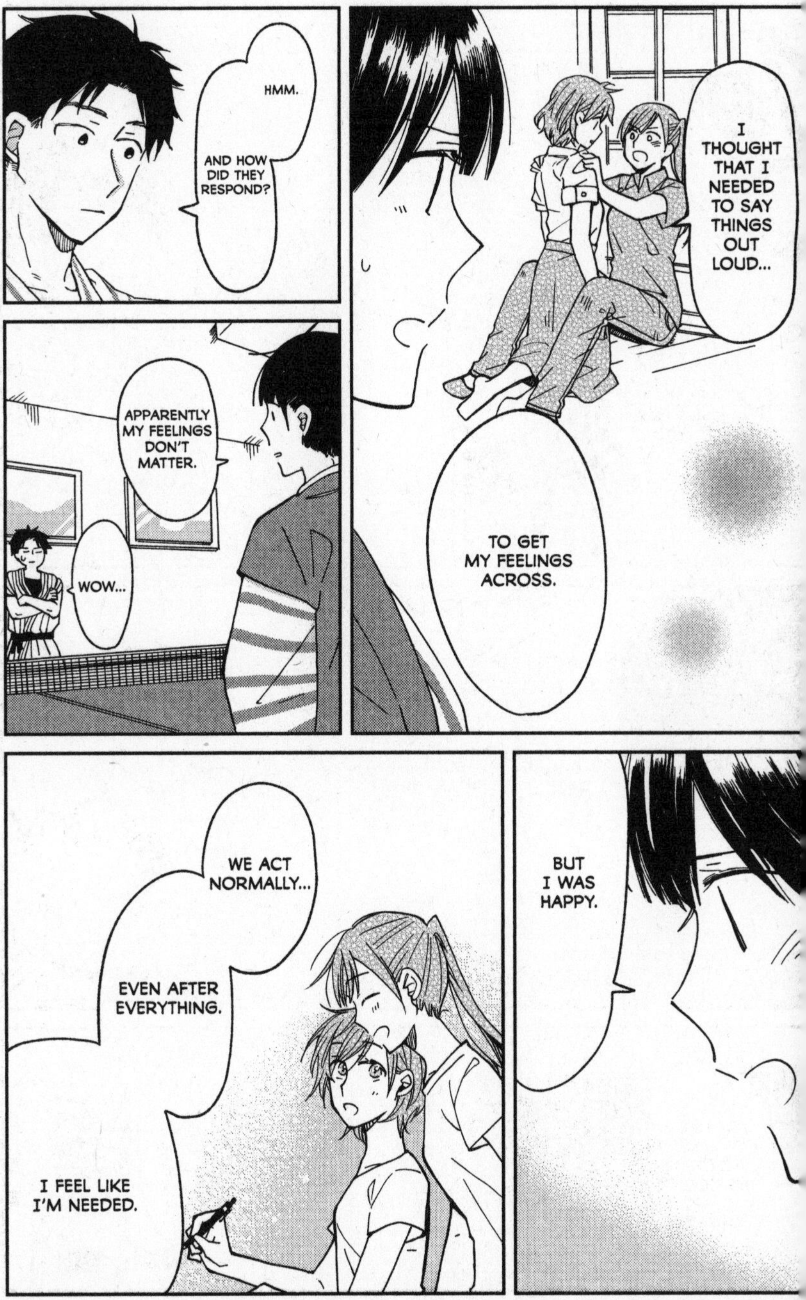
I THOUGHT THAT I NEEDED TO SAY THINGS OUT LOUD...
TO GET MY FEELINGS ACROSS.
HMM.
AND HOW DID THEY RESPOND?
APPARENTLY MY FEELINGS DON'T MATTER.
WOW...
BUT I WAS HAPPY.
WE ACT NORMALLY...
EVEN AFTER EVERYTHING.
I FEEL LIKE I'M NEEDED.

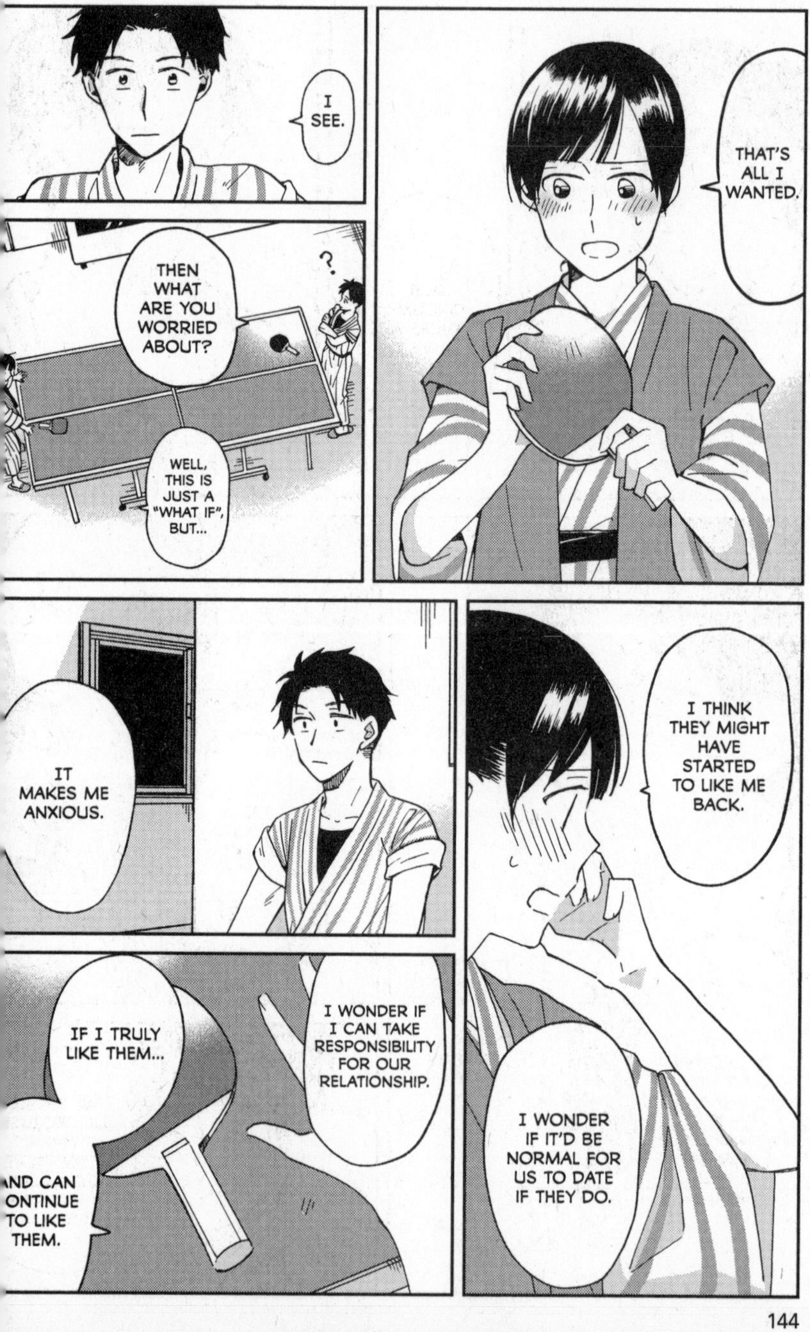
THAT'S ALL I WANTED.
I SEE.
THEN WHAT ARE YOU WORRIED ABOUT?
WELL, THIS IS JUST A "WHAT IF", BUT...
I THINK THEY MIGHT HAVE STARTED TO LIKE ME BACK.
I WONDER IF IT'D BE NORMAL FOR US TO DATE IF THEY DO.
IT MAKES ME ANXIOUS.
I WONDER IF I CAN TAKE RESPONSIBILITY FOR OUR RELATIONSHIP.
IF I TRULY LIKE THEM...
ND CAN ONTINUE TO LIKE THEM.

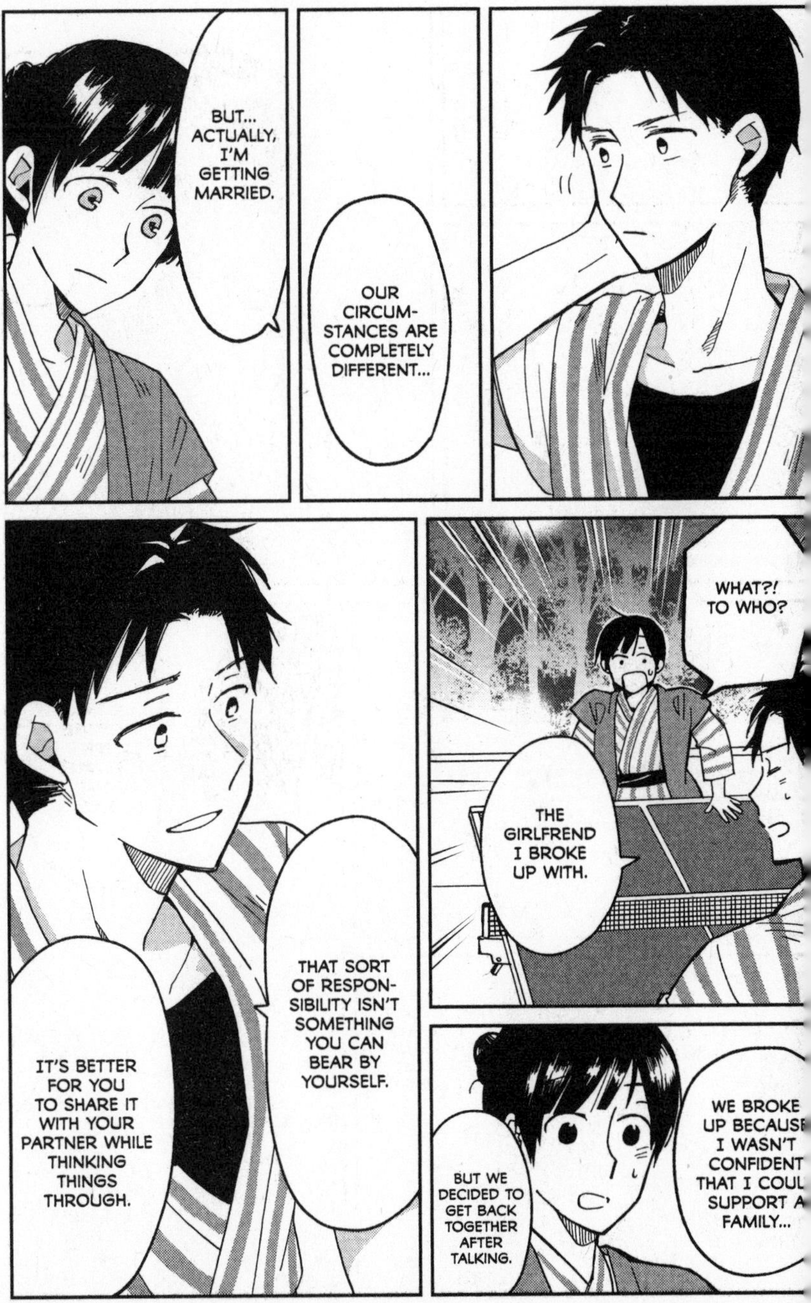
OUR CIRCUM-
STANCES ARE
COMPLETELY
DIFFERENT...
BUT...
ACTUALLY,
I'M
GETTING
MARRIED.
WHAT?!
TO WHO?
THE
GIRLFREND
I BROKE
UP WITH.
WE BROKE
UP BECAUS
I WASN'T
CONFIDENT
THAT I COUL
SUPPORT A
FAMILY...
BUT WE
DECIDED TO
GET BACK
TOGETHER
AFTER
TALKING.
THAT SORT
OF RESPON-
SIBILITY ISN'T
SOMETHING
YOU CAN
BEAR BY
YOURSELF.
IT'S BETTER
FOR YOU
TO SHARE IT
WITH YOUR
PARTNER WHILE
THINKING
THINGS
THROUGH.

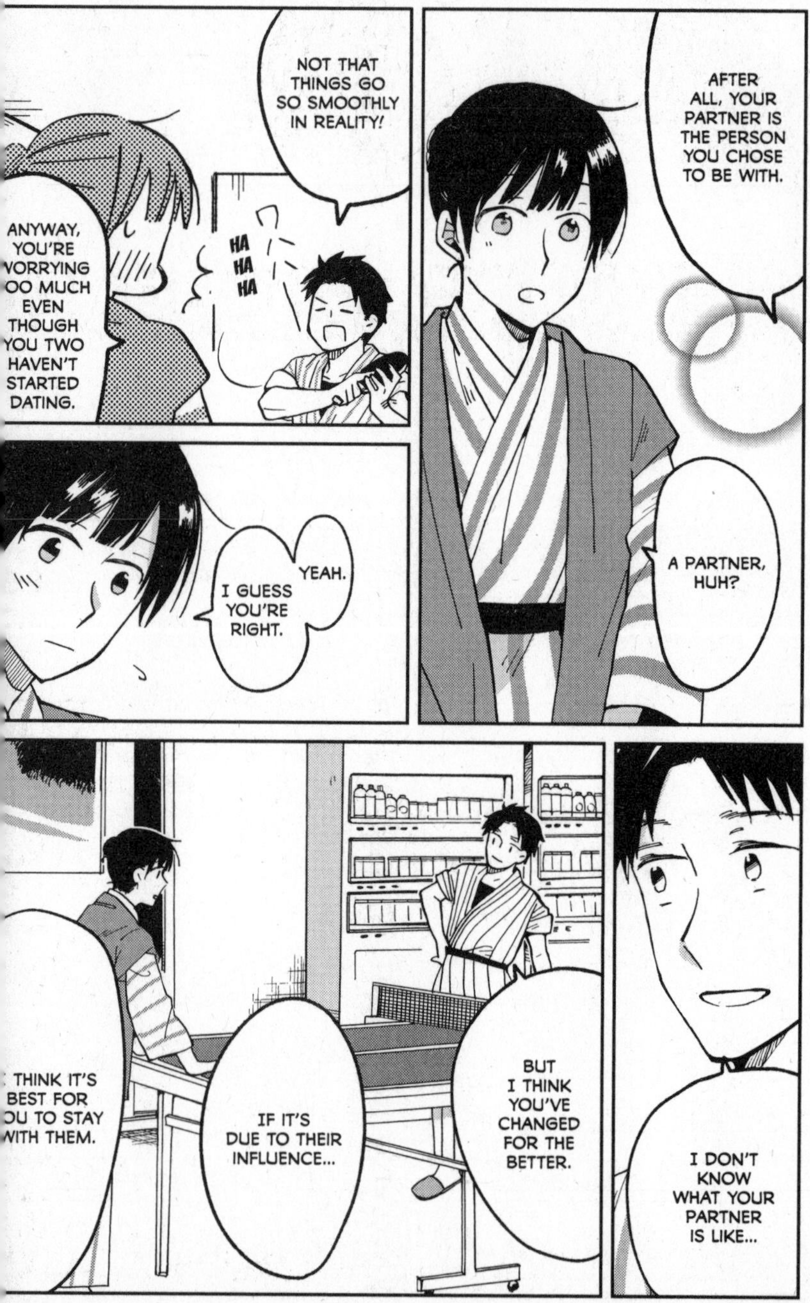

AFTER ALL, YOUR PARTNER IS THE PERSON YOU CHOSE TO BE WITH.
A PARTNER, HUH?
NOT THAT THINGS GO SO SMOOTHLY IN REALITY!
HA HA HA
ANYWAY, YOU'RE VORRYING OO MUCH EVEN THOUGH YOU TWO HAVEN'T STARTED DATING.
YEAH. I GUESS YOU'RE RIGHT.
I DON'T KNOW WHAT YOUR PARTNER IS LIKE...
BUT I THINK YOU'VE CHANGED FOR THE BETTER.
IF IT'S DUE TO THEIR INFLUENCE...
THINK IT'S BEST FOR OU TO STAY VITH THEM.

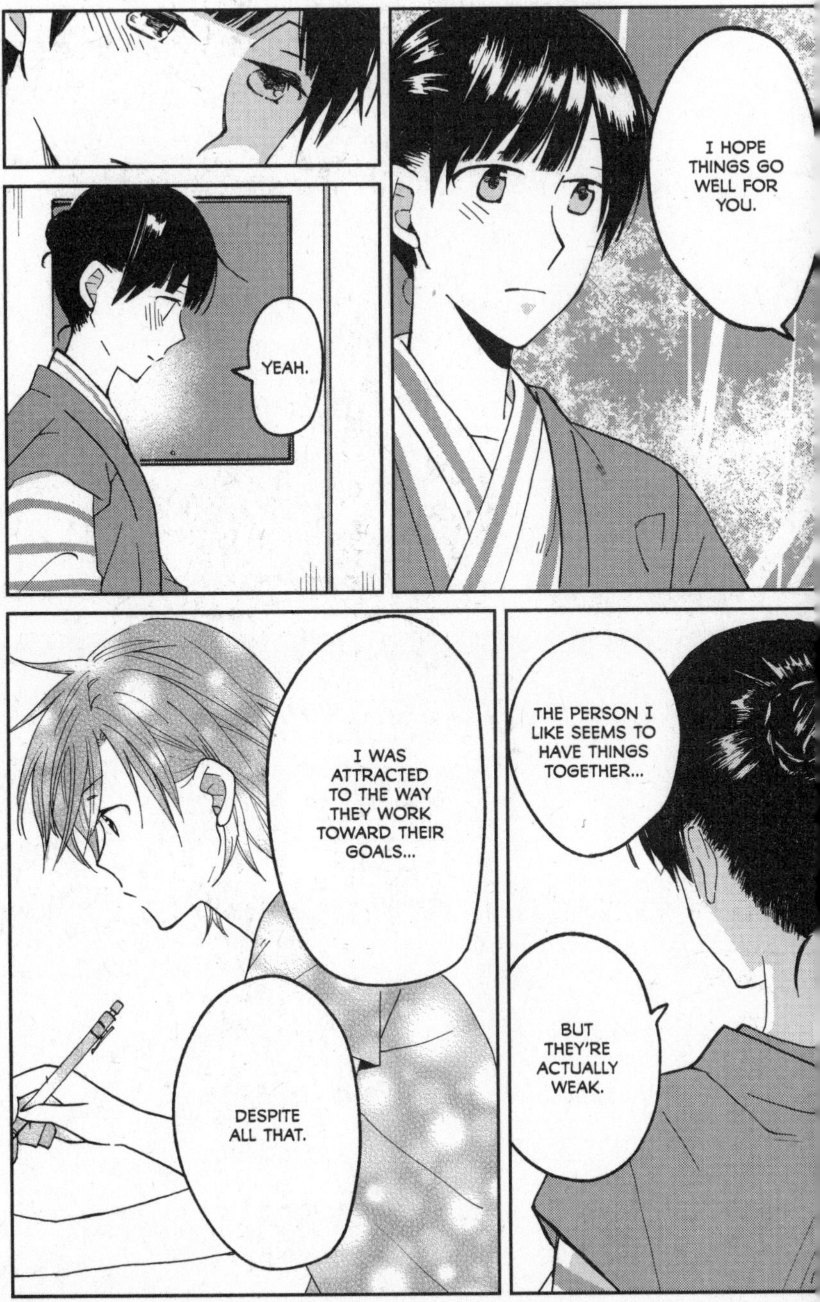
I HOPE THINGS GO WELL FOR YOU.
YEAH.
THE PERSON I LIKE SEEMS TO HAVE THINGS TOGETHER...
BUT THEY'RE ACTUALLY WEAK.
I WAS ATTRACTED TO THE WAY THEY WORK TOWARD THEIR GOALS...
DESPITE ALL THAT.

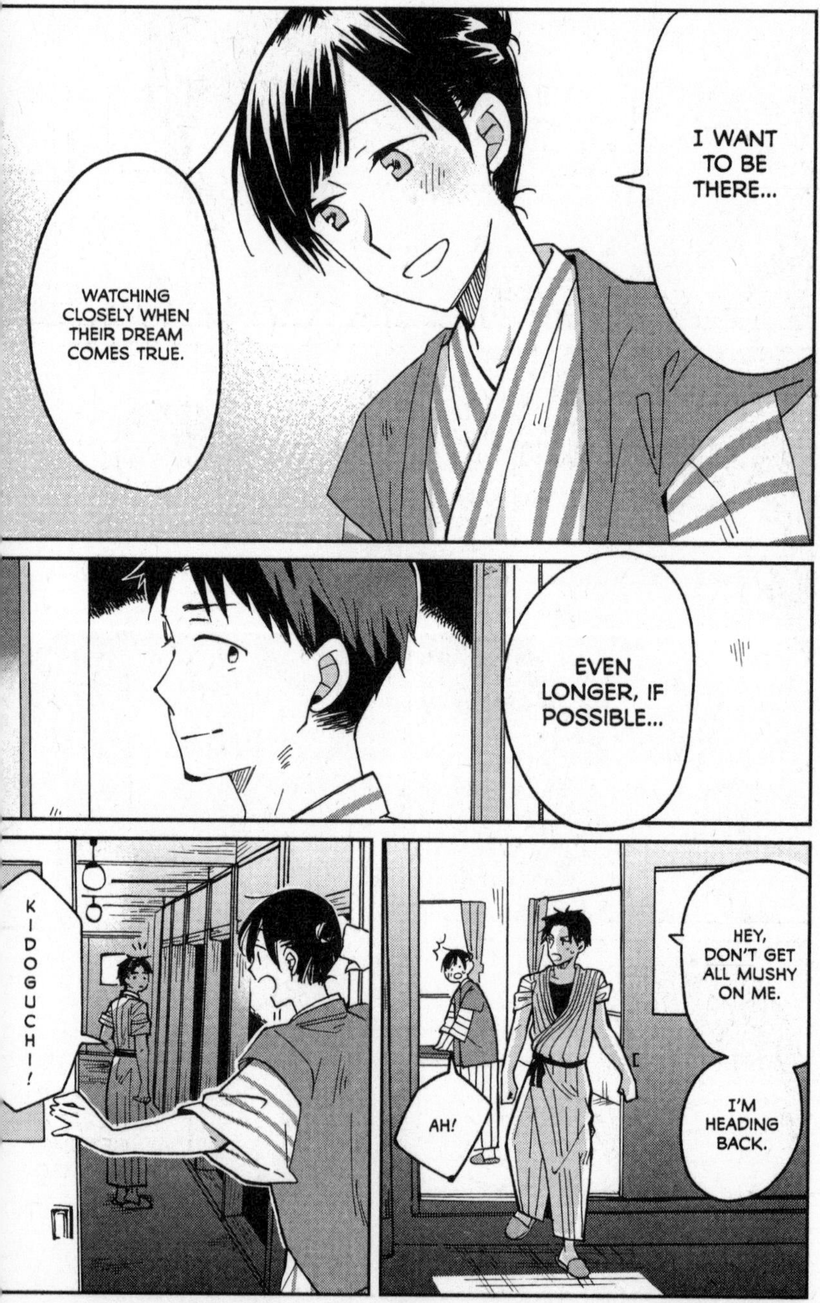
I WANT TO BE THERE...
WATCHING CLOSELY WHEN THEIR DREAM COMES TRUE.
EVEN LONGER, IF POSSIBLE...
HEY, DON'T GET ALL MUSHY ON ME.
I'M HEADING BACK.
AH!
KIDOGUCHI!

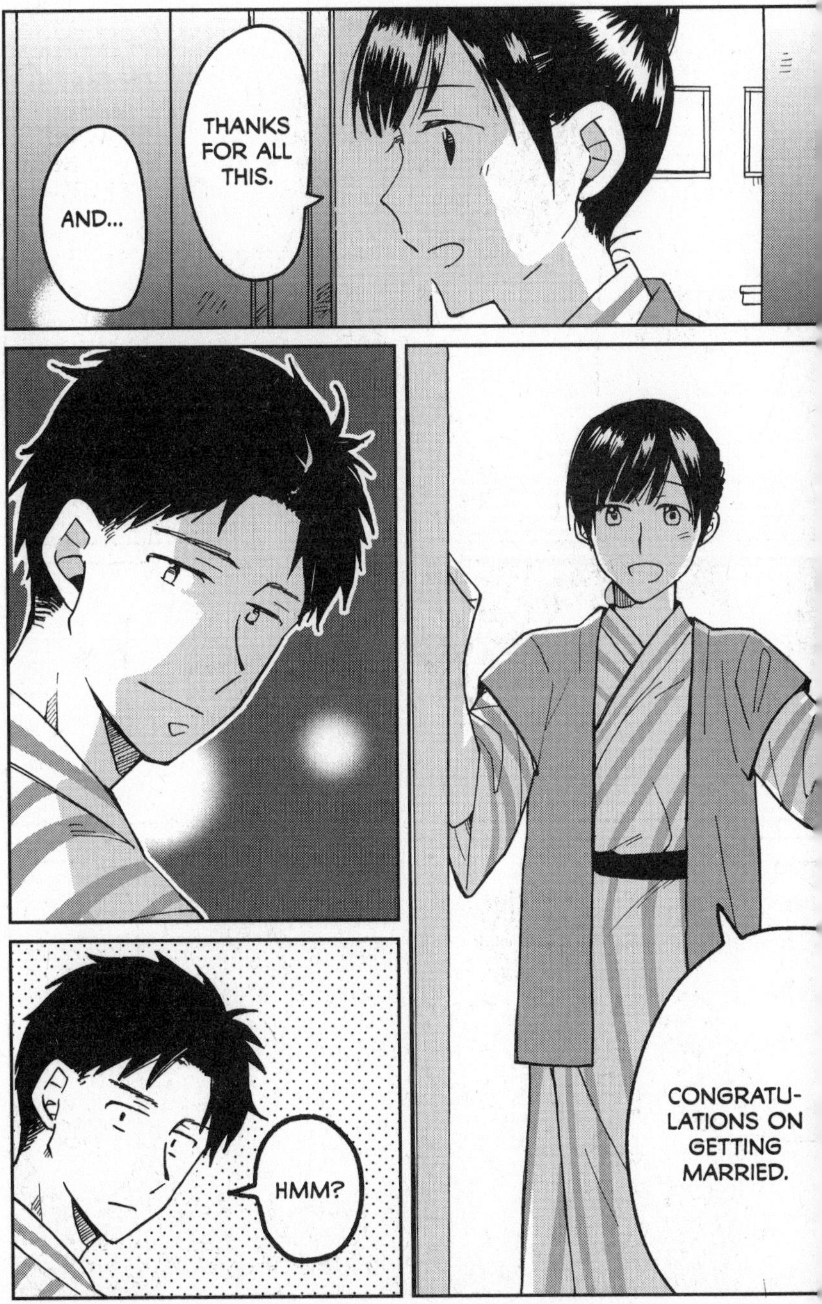
THANKS FOR ALL THIS.
AND...
CONGRATU-LATIONS ON GETTING MARRIED.
HMM?

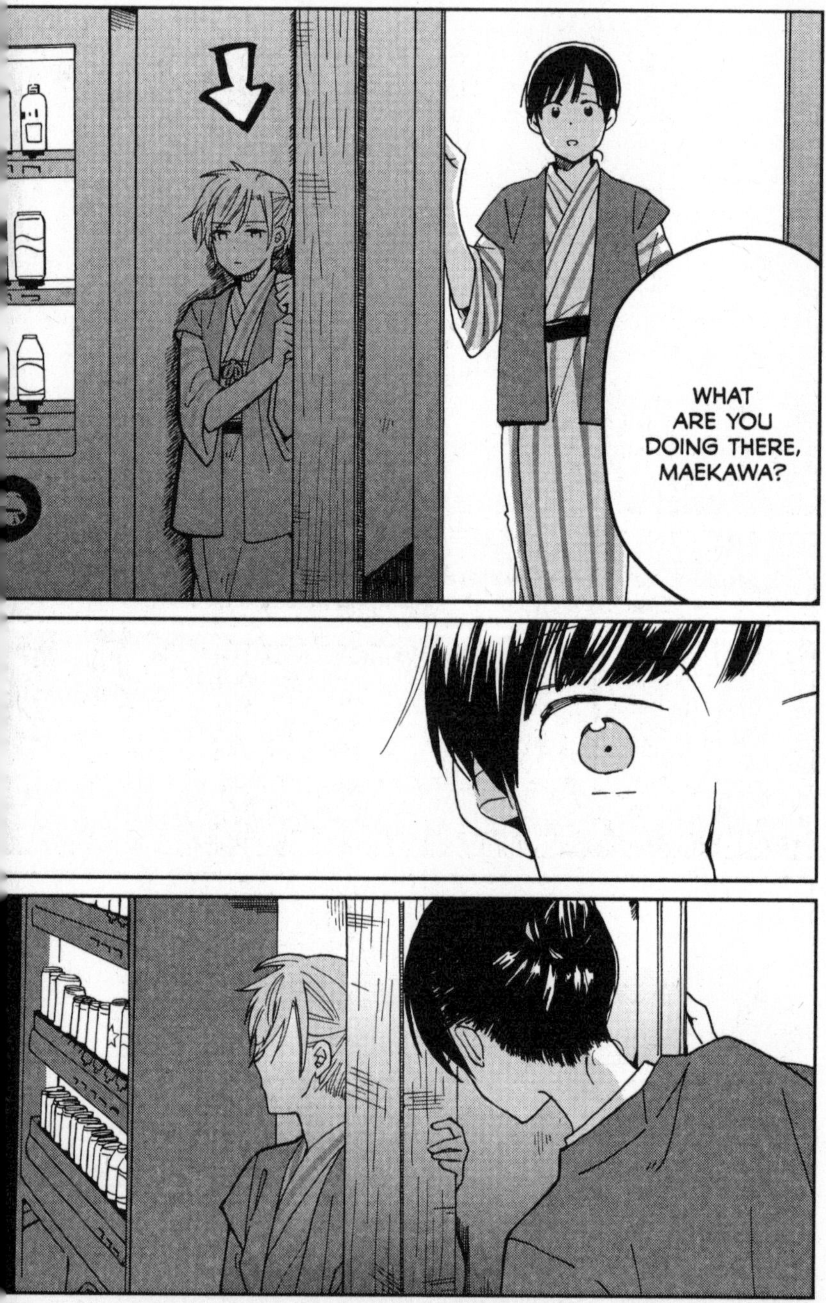
WHAT ARE YOU DOING THERE, MAEKAWA?

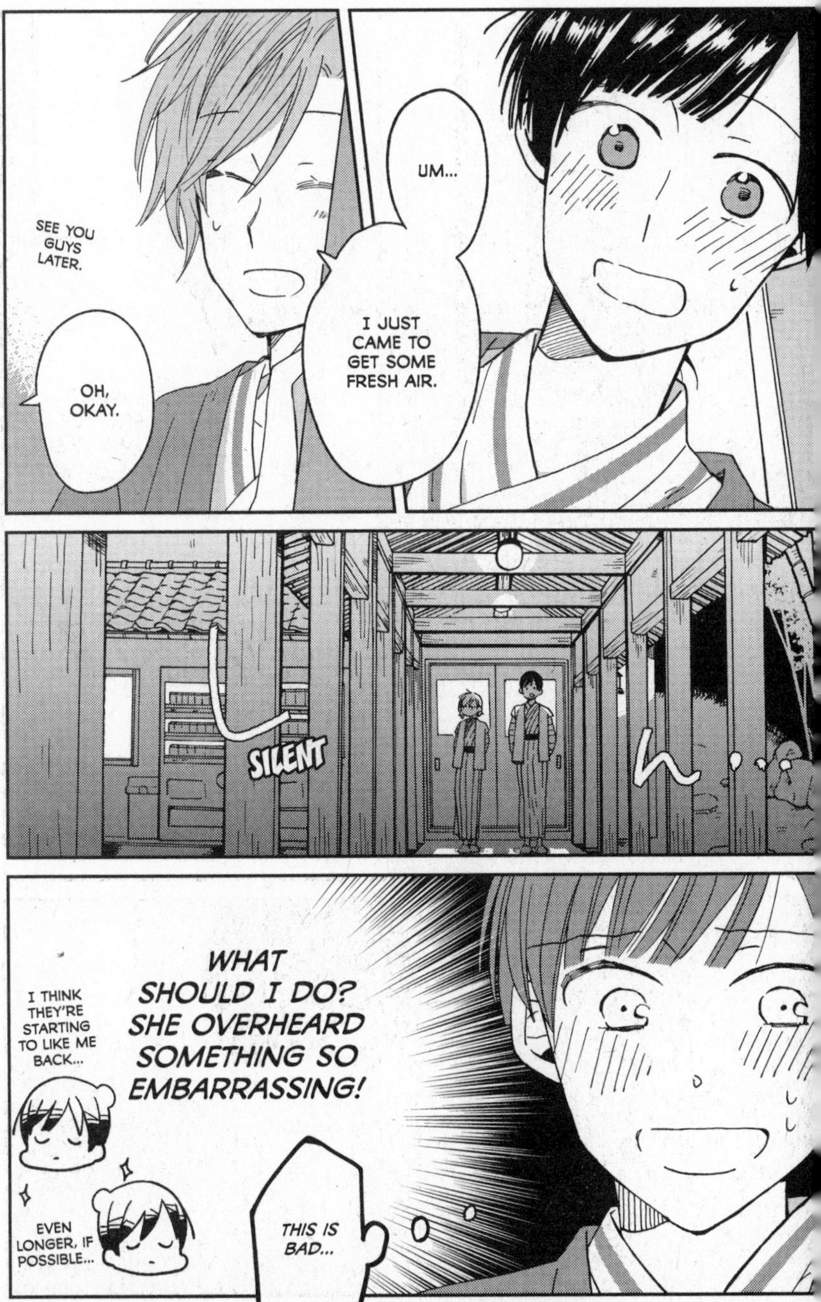
UM...
I JUST CAME TO GET SOME FRESH AIR.
SEE YOU GUYS LATER.
OH, OKAY.
SILENT
WHAT SHOULD I DO? SHE OVERHEARD SOMETHING SO EMBARRASSING!
THIS IS BAD...
I THINK THEY'RE STARTING TO LIKE ME BACK...
EVEN LONGER, IF POSSIBLE...

DID YOU HEAR US?
HOW GREAT FOR HIM, GETTING MARRIED.
HEY, UM, YOU KNOW LISTENING IN ON PEOPLE ISN'T NICE...
I DIDN'T KNOW YOU TALKED TO KIDOGUCHI-SAN ABOUT THAT SORT OF THING.
WELL, YEAH. HE'S THE EASIEST TO GET ADVICE FROM...
C-COME ON, LET'S GO BACK TO THE BANQUET HALL!

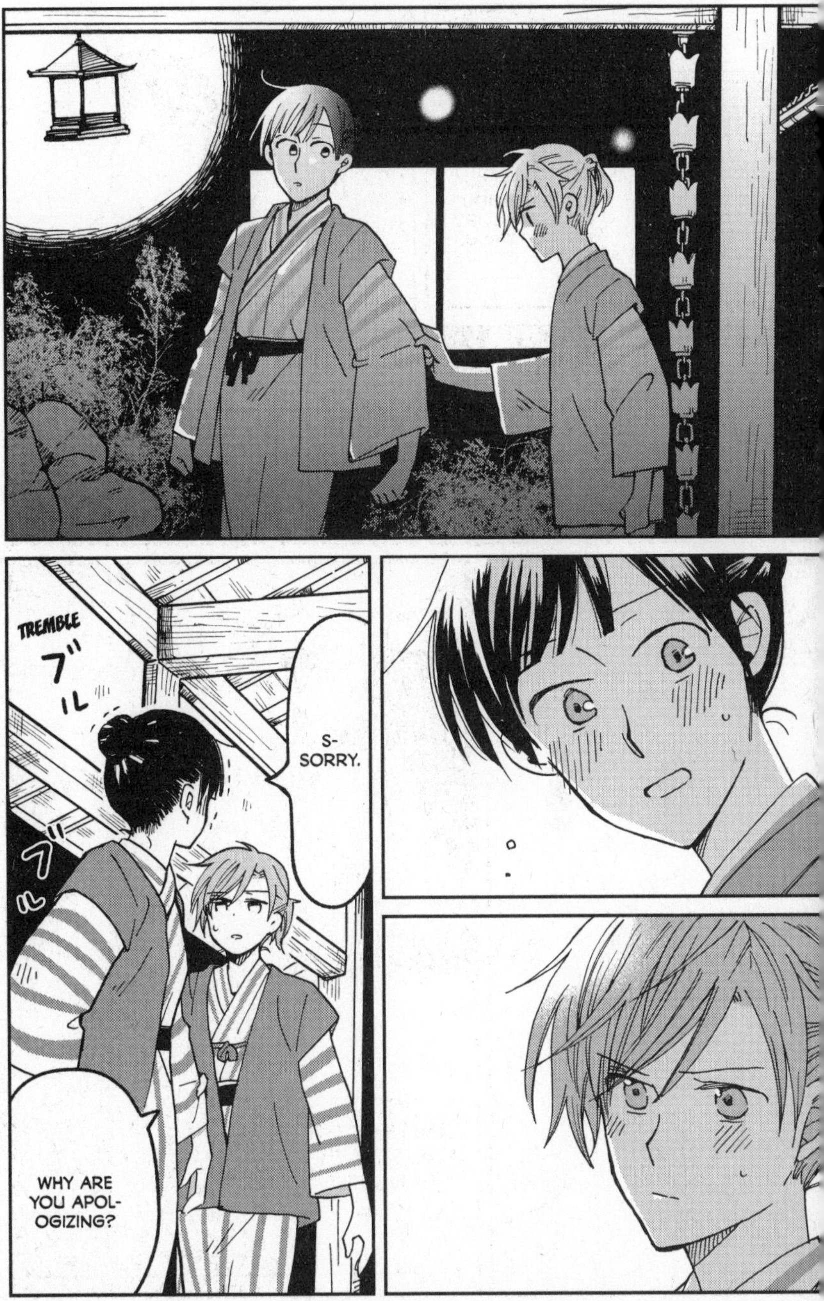
S-SORRY.
TREMBLE
ブル
ブル
WHY ARE YOU APOLOGIZING?

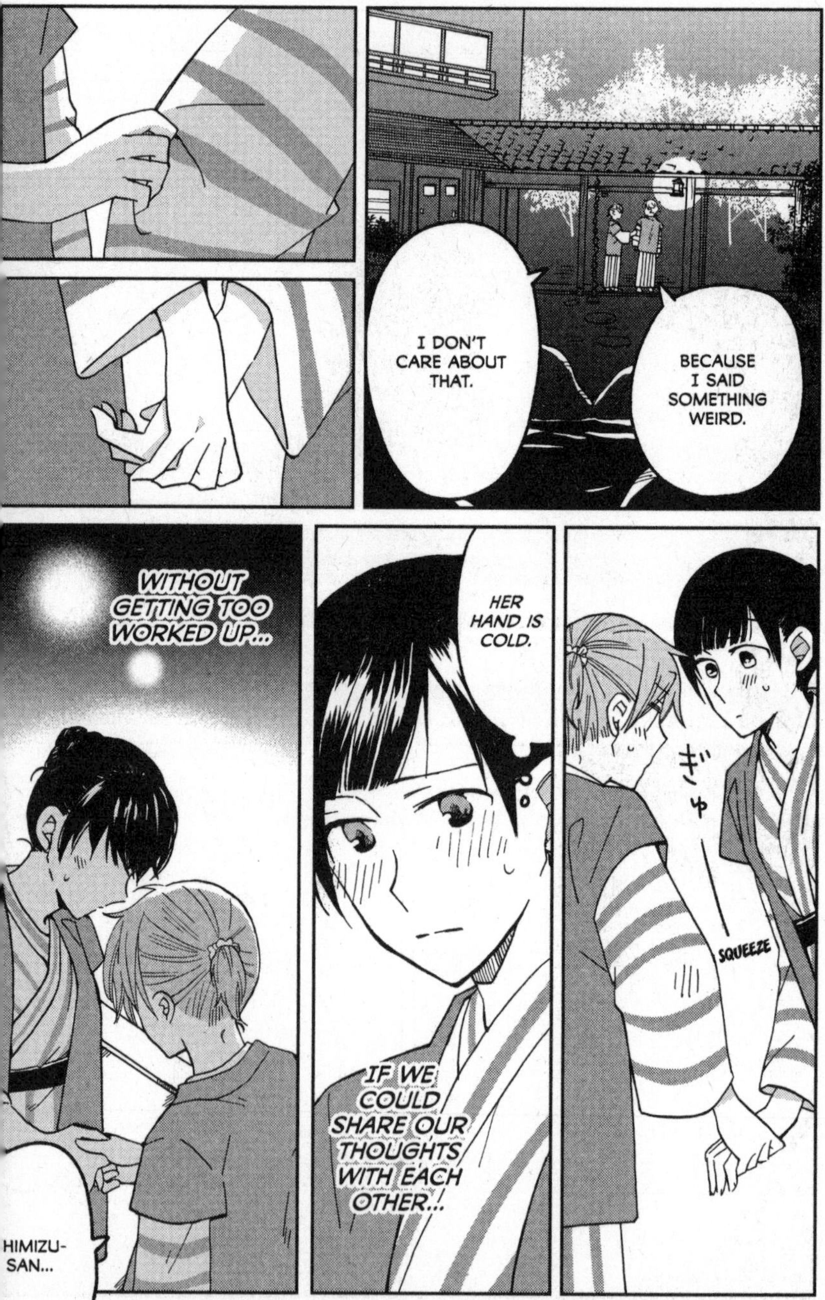
BECAUSE I SAID SOMETHING WEIRD.
I DON'T CARE ABOUT THAT.
ぎゅ
SQUEEZE
HER HAND IS COLD.
IF WE COULD SHARE OUR THOUGHTS WITH EACH OTHER...
WITHOUT GETTING TOO WORKED UP...
HIMIZU-SAN...

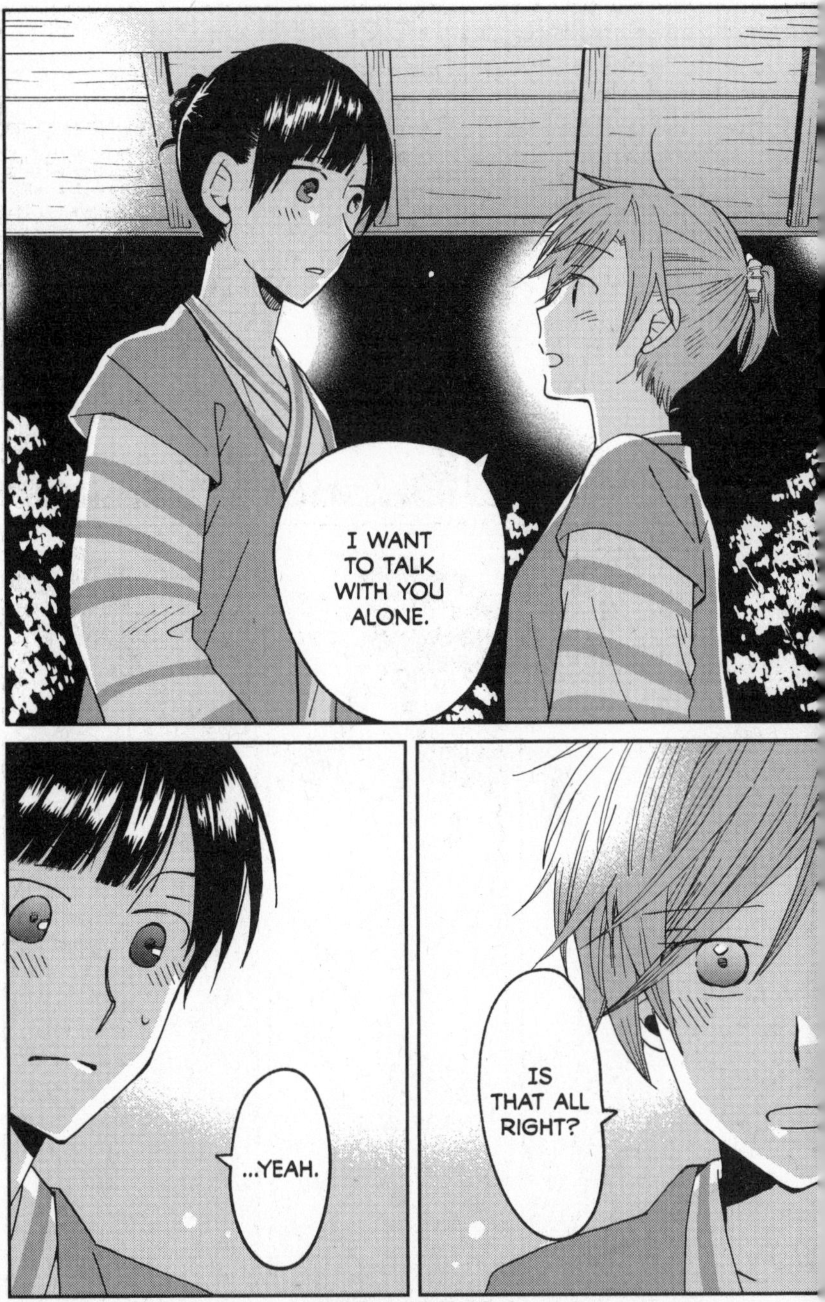
I WANT TO TALK WITH YOU ALONE.
IS THAT ALL RIGHT?
...YEAH.
Still Sick [2] The End

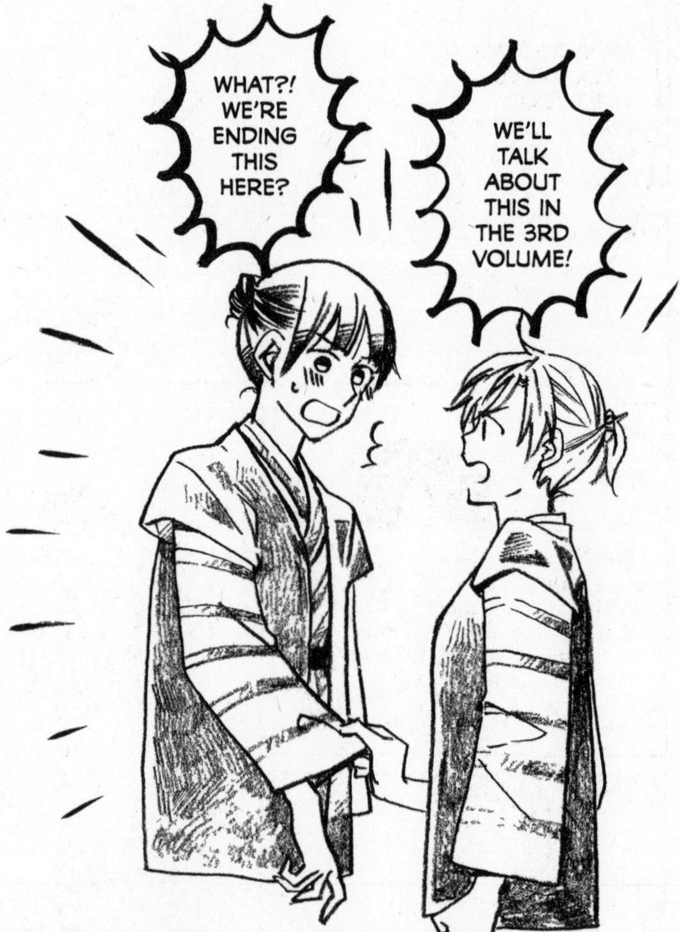
WE'LL TALK ABOUT THIS IN THE 3RD VOLUME!
WHAT?! WE'RE ENDING THIS HERE?

THE BONUS CHAPTER STARTS ON THE NEXT PAGE.
(IT TAKES PLACE A LITTLE AFTER CHAPTER 8.)

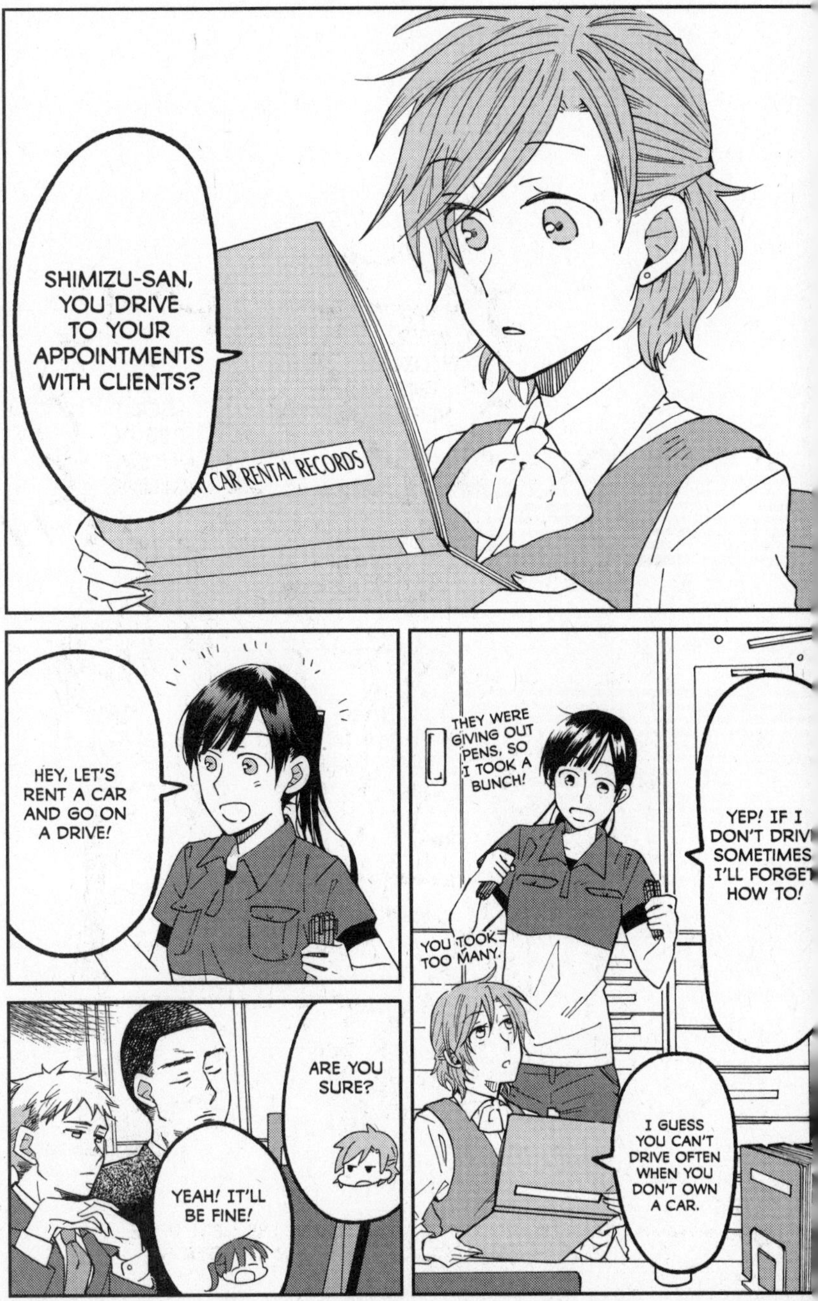

SHIMIZU-SAN, YOU DRIVE TO YOUR APPOINTMENTS WITH CLIENTS?
CAR RENTAL RECORDS
YEP! IF I DON'T DRIV SOMETIMES I'LL FORGET HOW TO!
THEY WERE GIVING OUT PENS, SO I TOOK A BUNCH!
YOU TOOK TOO MANY.
I GUESS YOU CAN'T DRIVE OFTEN WHEN YOU DON'T OWN A CAR.
HEY, LET'S RENT A CAR AND GO ON A DRIVE!
ARE YOU SURE?
YEAH! IT'LL BE FINE!

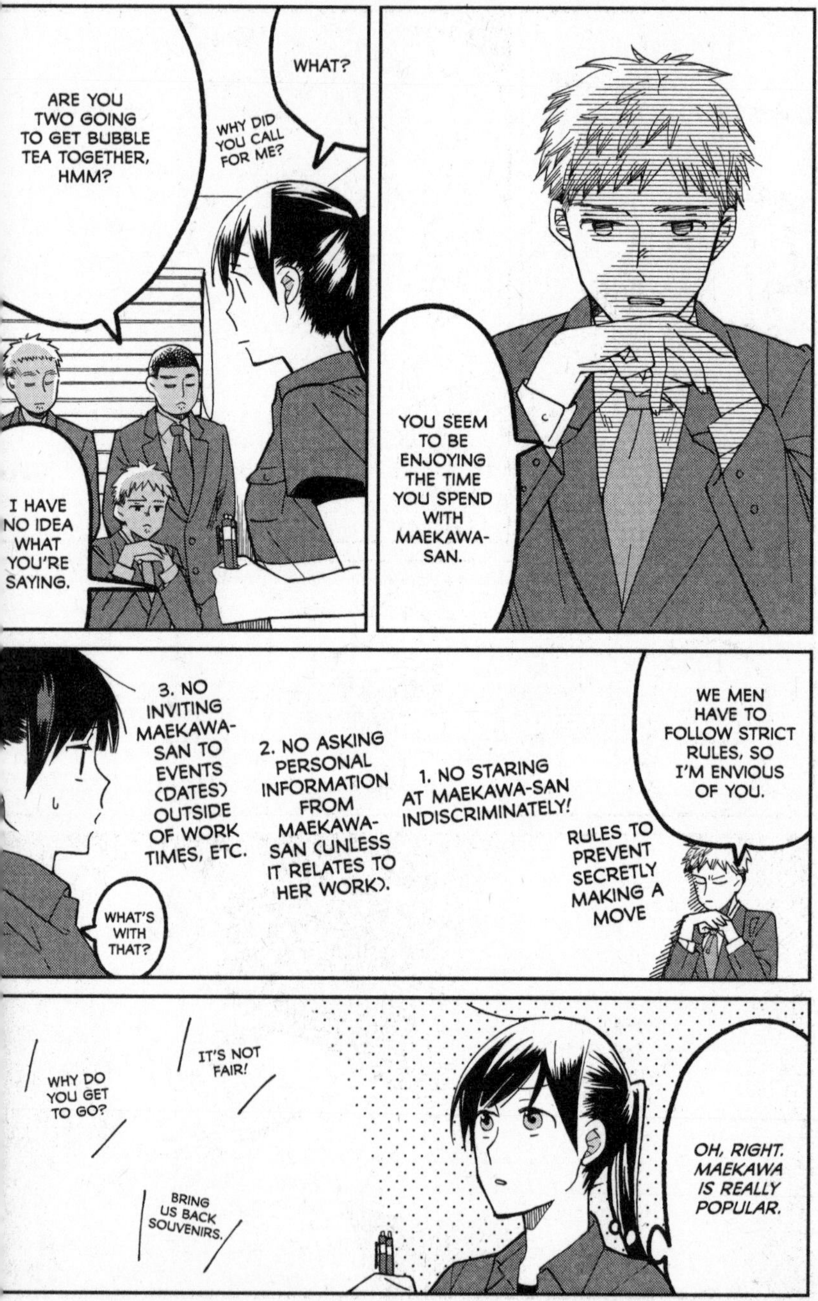
YOU SEEM TO BE ENJOYING THE TIME YOU SPEND WITH MAEKAWA-SAN.
WHAT?
WHY DID YOU CALL FOR ME?
ARE YOU TWO GOING TO GET BUBBLE TEA TOGETHER, HMM?
I HAVE NO IDEA WHAT YOU'RE SAYING.
WE MEN HAVE TO FOLLOW STRICT RULES, SO I'M ENVIOUS OF YOU.
RULES TO PREVENT SECRETLY MAKING A MOVE
1. NO STARING AT MAEKAWA-SAN INDISCRIMINATELY!
2. NO ASKING PERSONAL INFORMATION FROM MAEKAWA-SAN (UNLESS IT RELATES TO HER WORK).
3. NO INVITING MAEKAWA-SAN TO EVENTS (DATES) OUTSIDE OF WORK TIMES, ETC.
WHAT'S WITH THAT?
OH, RIGHT. MAEKAWA IS REALLY POPULAR.
IT'S NOT FAIR!
BRING US BACK SOUVENIRS.
WHY DO YOU GET TO GO?

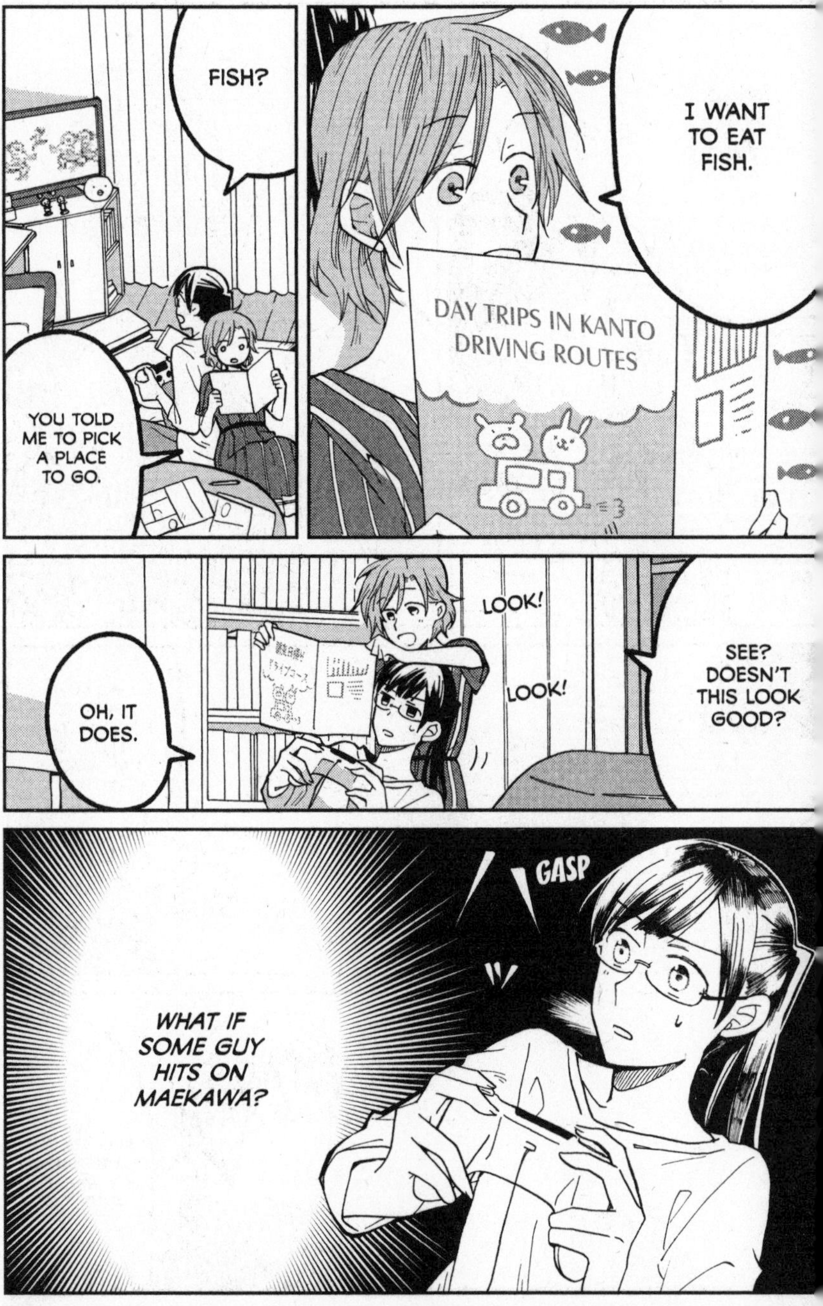
I WANT TO EAT FISH.
DAY TRIPS IN KANTO DRIVING ROUTES
FISH?
YOU TOLD ME TO PICK A PLACE TO GO.
SEE? DOESN'T THIS LOOK GOOD?
LOOK!
LOOK!
OH, IT DOES.
GASP
WHAT IF SOME GUY HITS ON MAEKAWA?

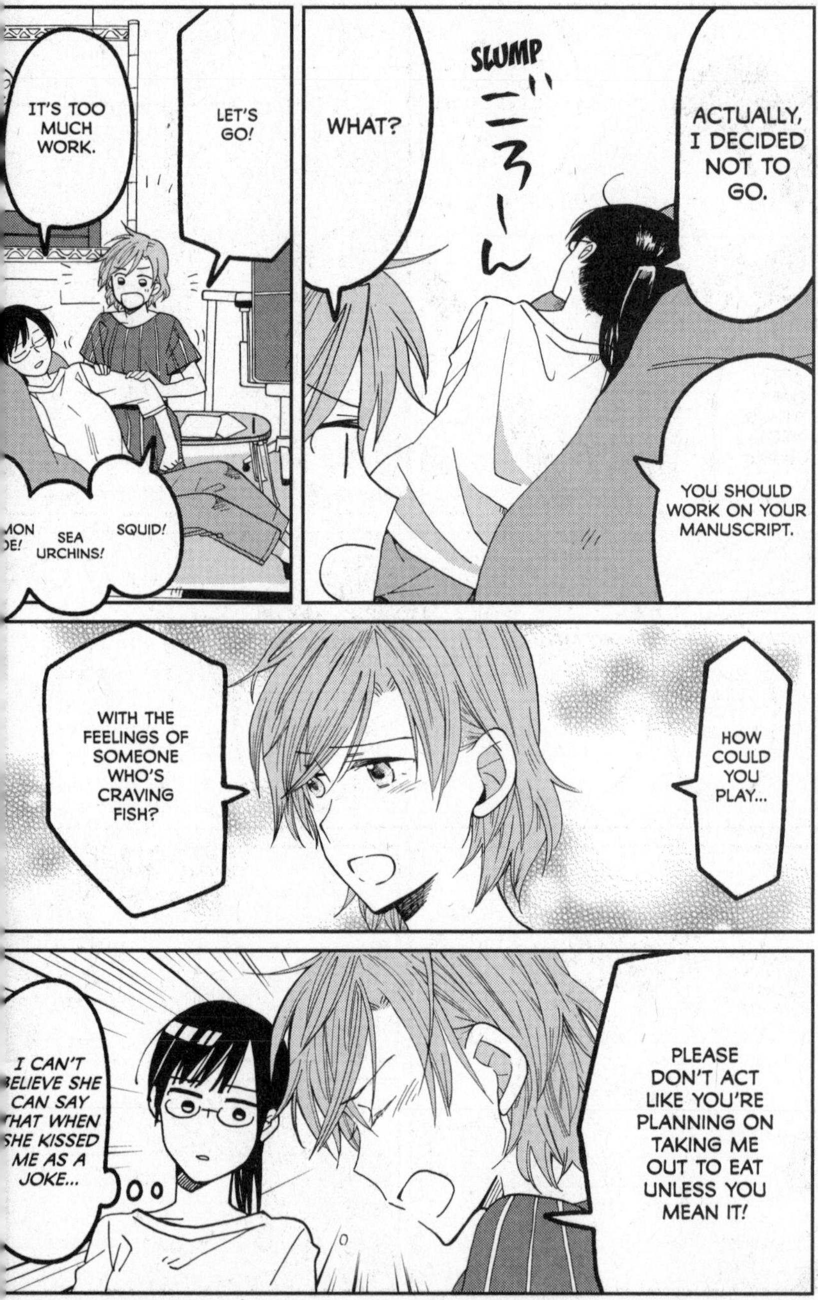

ACTUALLY, I DECIDED NOT TO GO.
YOU SHOULD WORK ON YOUR MANUSCRIPT.
SLUMP
WHAT?
LET'S GO!
IT'S TOO MUCH WORK.
SQUID!
SEA URCHINS!
HOW COULD YOU PLAY...
WITH THE FEELINGS OF SOMEONE WHO'S CRAVING FISH?
PLEASE DON'T ACT LIKE YOU'RE PLANNING ON TAKING ME OUT TO EAT UNLESS YOU MEAN IT!
I CAN'T ELIEVE SHE CAN SAY HAT WHEN HE KISSED ME AS A JOKE...

*PLEASE REFER TO CHAPTER 3.

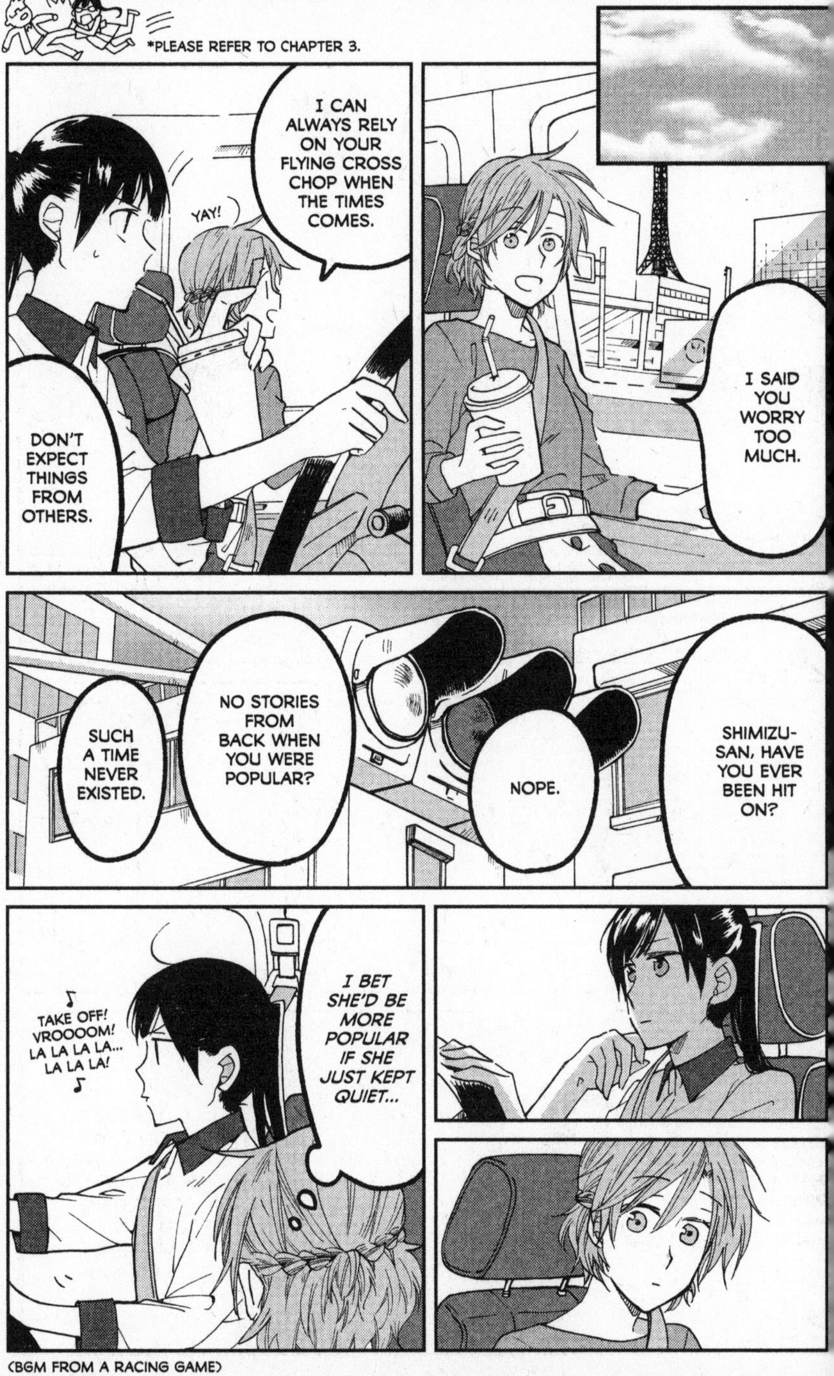
I SAID YOU WORRY TOO MUCH.
I CAN ALWAYS RELY ON YOUR FLYING CROSS CHOP WHEN THE TIMES COMES.
YAY!
DON'T EXPECT THINGS FROM OTHERS.
SHIMIZU-SAN, HAVE YOU EVER BEEN HIT ON?
NOPE.
NO STORIES FROM BACK WHEN YOU WERE POPULAR?
SUCH A TIME NEVER EXISTED.
I BET SHE'D BE MORE POPULAR IF SHE JUST KEPT QUIET...
TAKE OFF! VROOOOM! LA LA LA... LA LA LA!

(BGM FROM A RACING GAME)

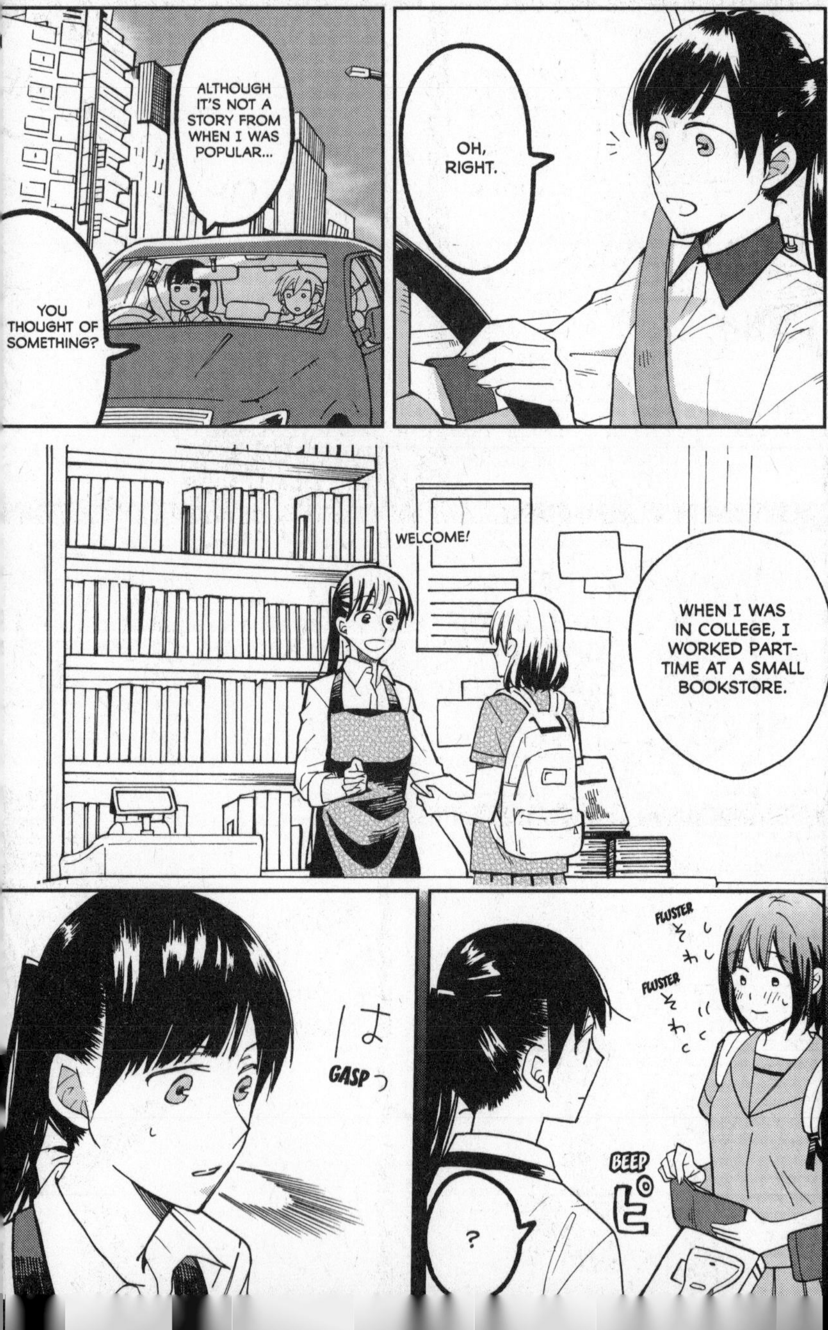
OH, RIGHT.
ALTHOUGH IT'S NOT A STORY FROM WHEN I WAS POPULAR...
YOU THOUGHT OF SOMETHING?
WHEN I WAS IN COLLEGE, I WORKED PART-TIME AT A SMALL BOOKSTORE.
WELCOME!
FLUSTER
そわ
FLUSTER
そわ
BEEP
ピ
?
はっ
GASP

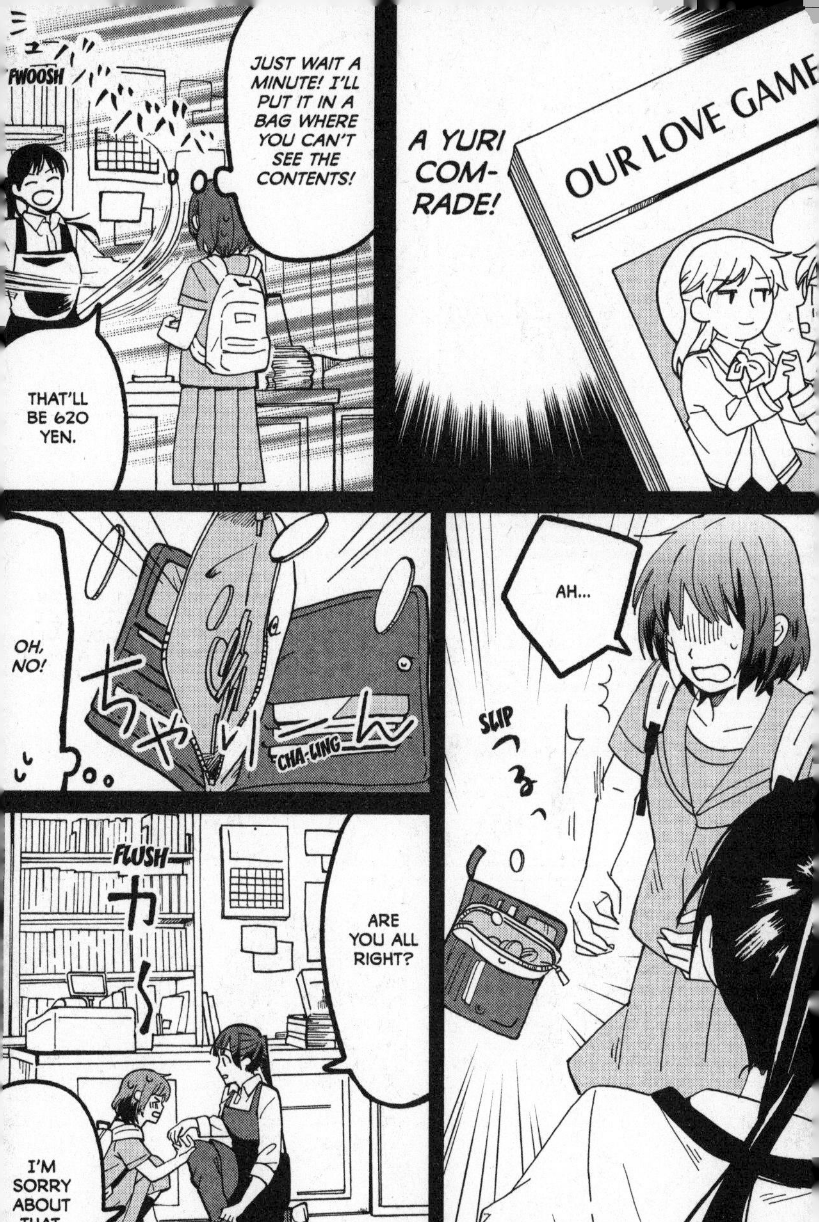
OUR LOVE GAME
A YURI COM-RADE!
JUST WAIT A MINUTE! I'LL PUT IT IN A BAG WHERE YOU CAN'T SEE THE CONTENTS!
FWOOSH
THAT'LL BE 620 YEN.
AH...
SLIP
OH, NO!
CHA-LING
FLUSH
ARE YOU ALL RIGHT?
I'M SORRY ABOUT THAT.

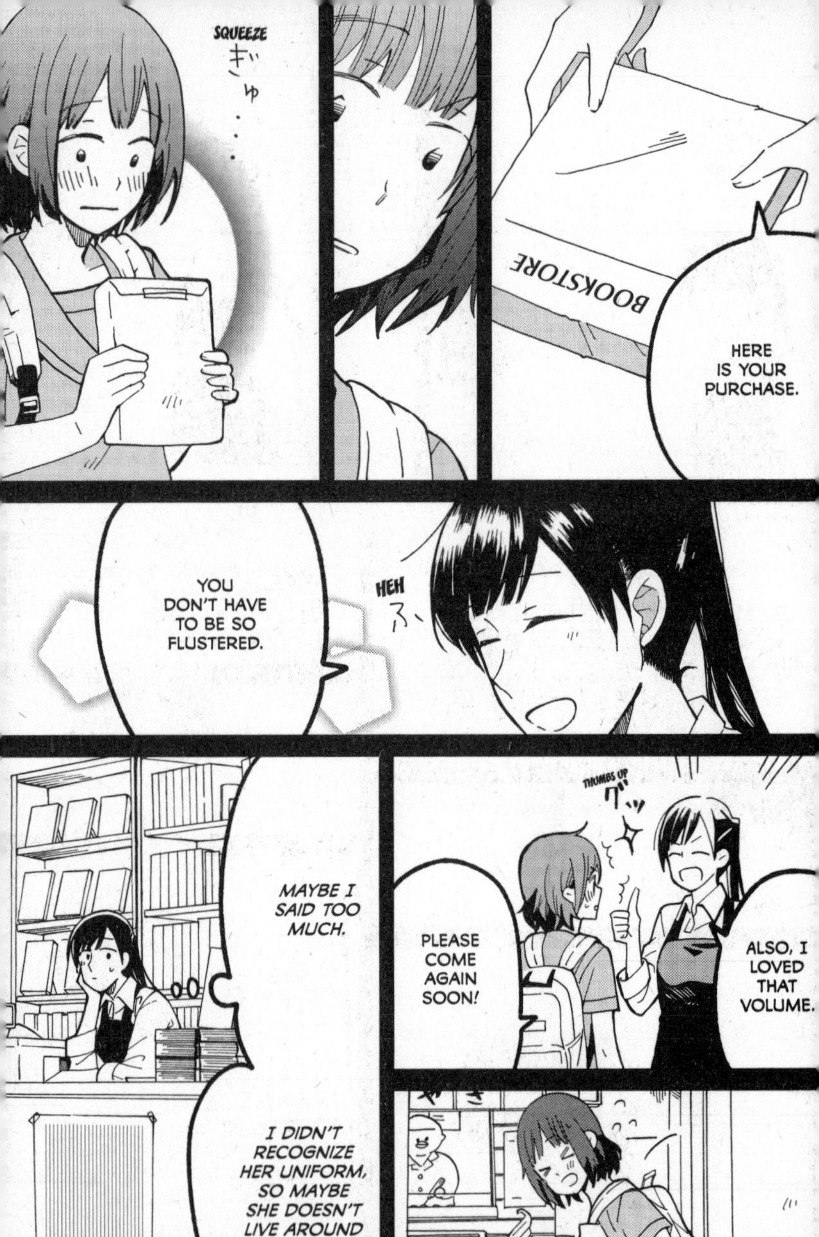
BOOKSTORE
HERE IS YOUR PURCHASE.
SQUEEZE
ぎゅ…
HEH
ふ
YOU DON'T HAVE TO BE SO FLUSTERED.
THUMBS UP
グッ
ALSO, I LOVED THAT VOLUME.
PLEASE COME AGAIN SOON!
MAYBE I SAID TOO MUCH.
I DIDN'T RECOGNIZE HER UNIFORM, SO MAYBE SHE DOESN'T LIVE AROUND HERE.

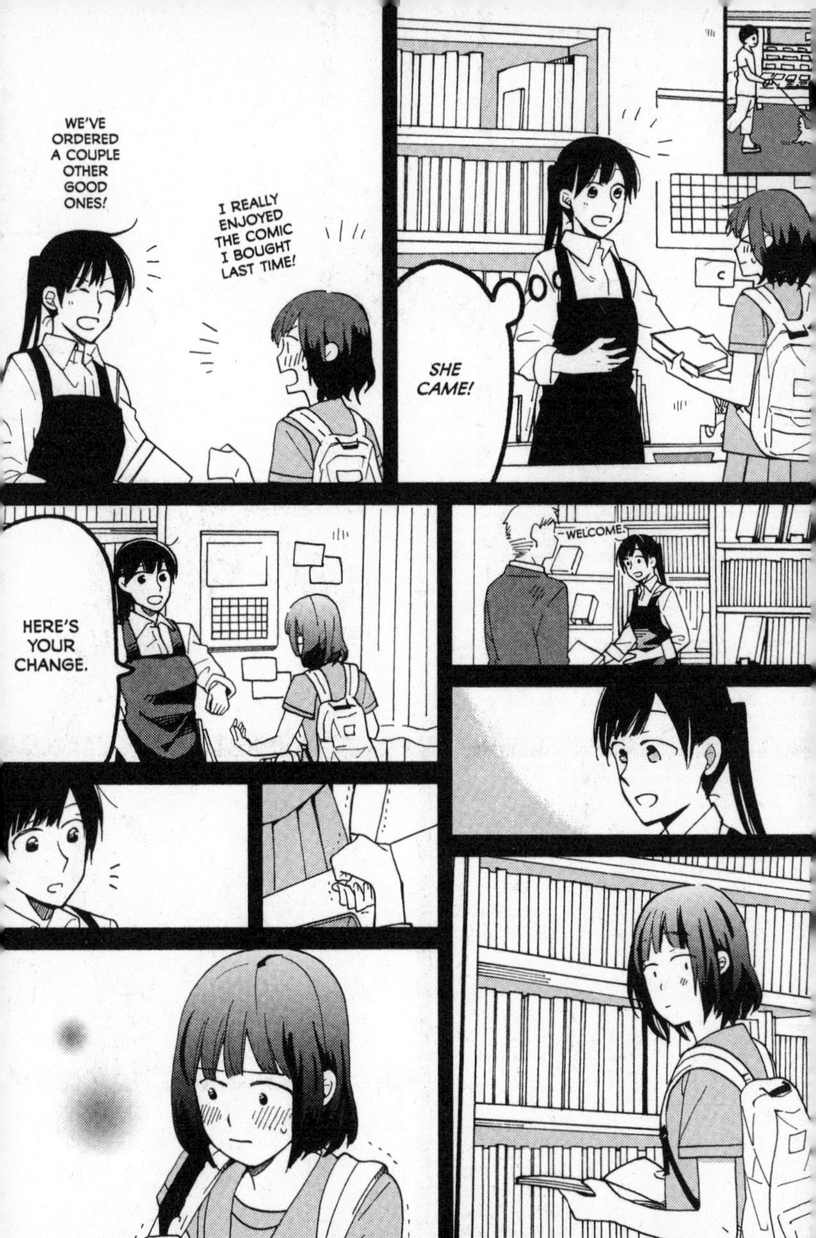
SHE CAME!
I REALLY ENJOYED THE COMIC I BOUGHT LAST TIME!
WE'VE ORDERED A COUPLE OTHER GOOD ONES!
WELCOME.
HERE'S YOUR CHANGE.

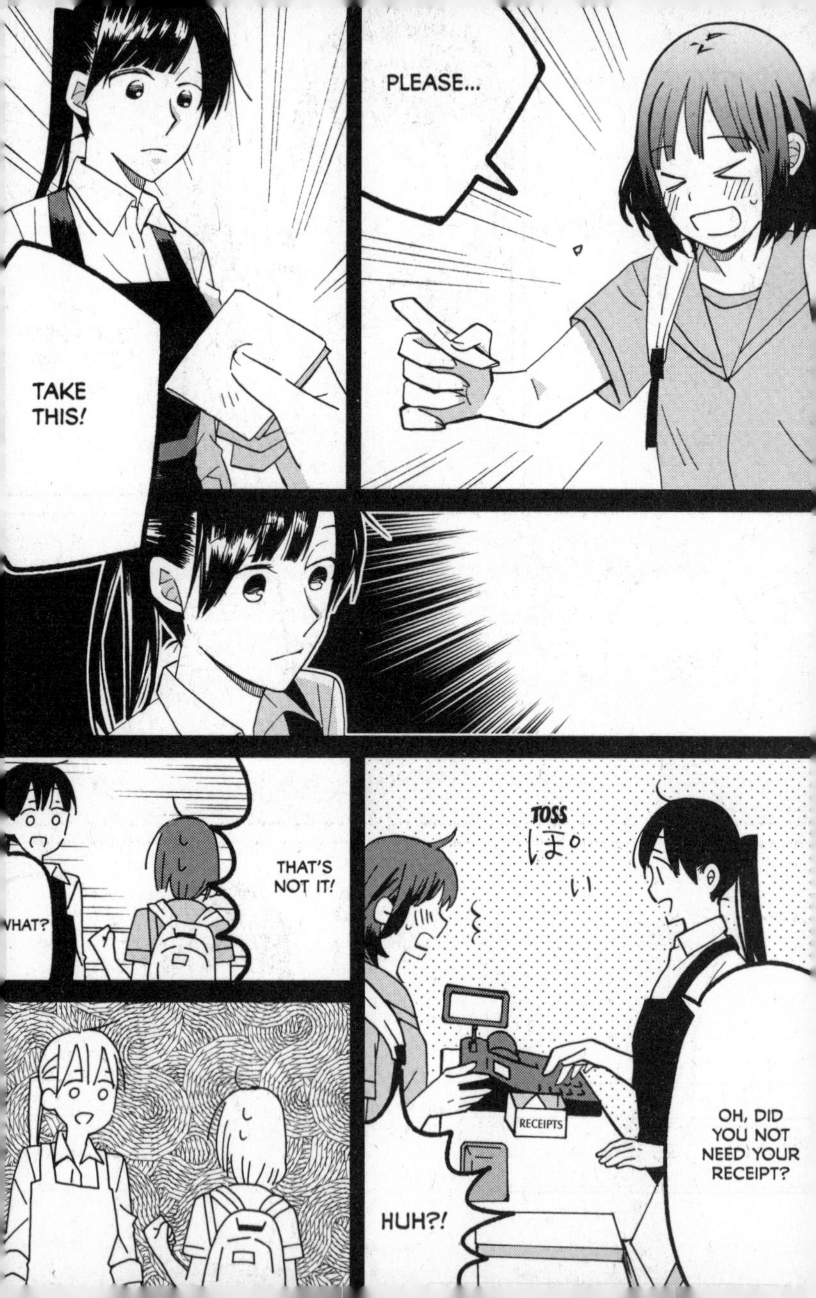
PLEASE...
TAKE THIS!
TOSS
ぽい
OH, DID YOU NOT NEED YOUR RECEIPT?
RECEIPTS
HUH?!
THAT'S NOT IT!
WHAT?

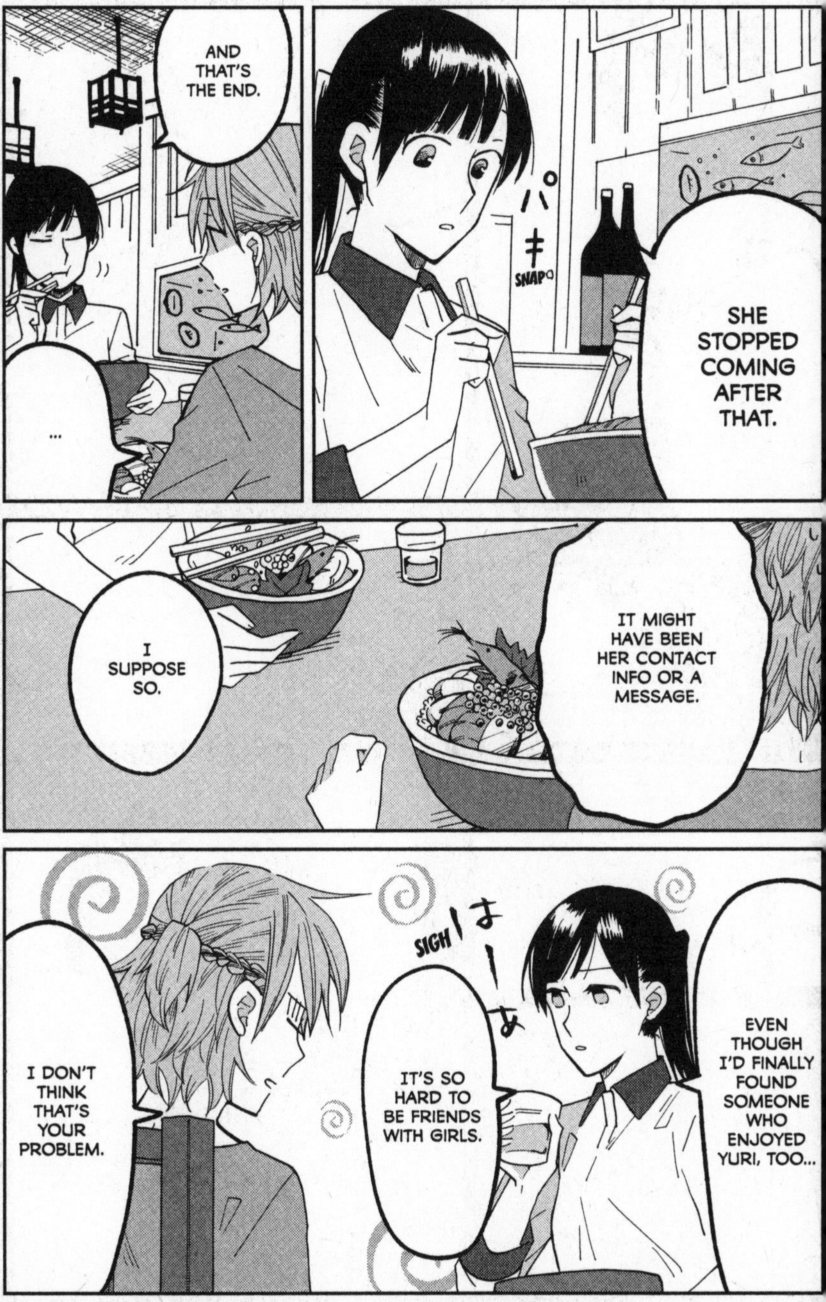
SHE STOPPED COMING AFTER THAT.
パキ
SNAP
AND THAT'S THE END.
...
IT MIGHT HAVE BEEN HER CONTACT INFO OR A MESSAGE.
I SUPPOSE SO.
EVEN THOUGH I'D FINALLY FOUND SOMEONE WHO ENJOYED YURI, TOO...
はーぁ
SIGH
IT'S SO HARD TO BE FRIENDS WITH GIRLS.
I DON'T THINK THAT'S YOUR PROBLEM.

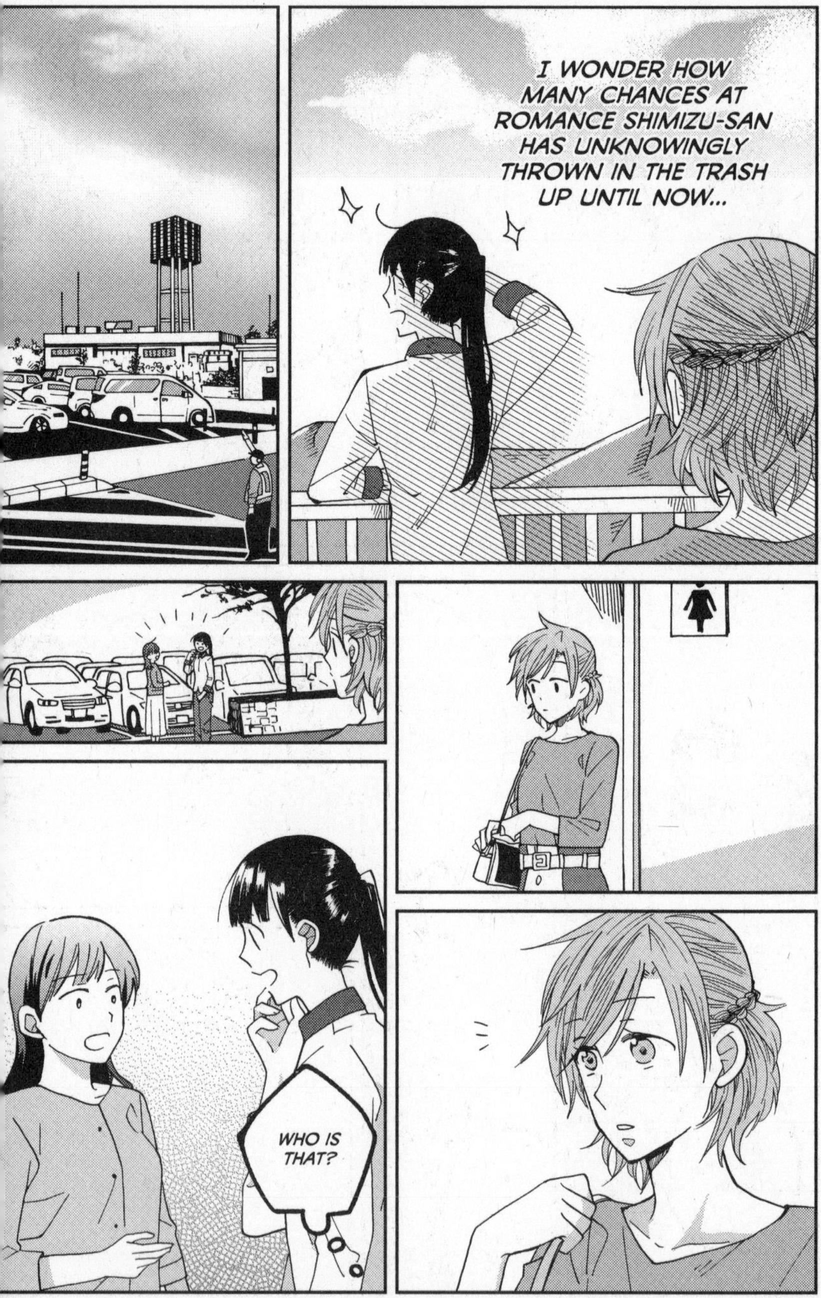
I WONDER HOW MANY CHANCES AT ROMANCE SHIMIZU-SAN HAS UNKNOWINGLY THROWN IN THE TRASH UP UNTIL NOW...
WHO IS THAT?

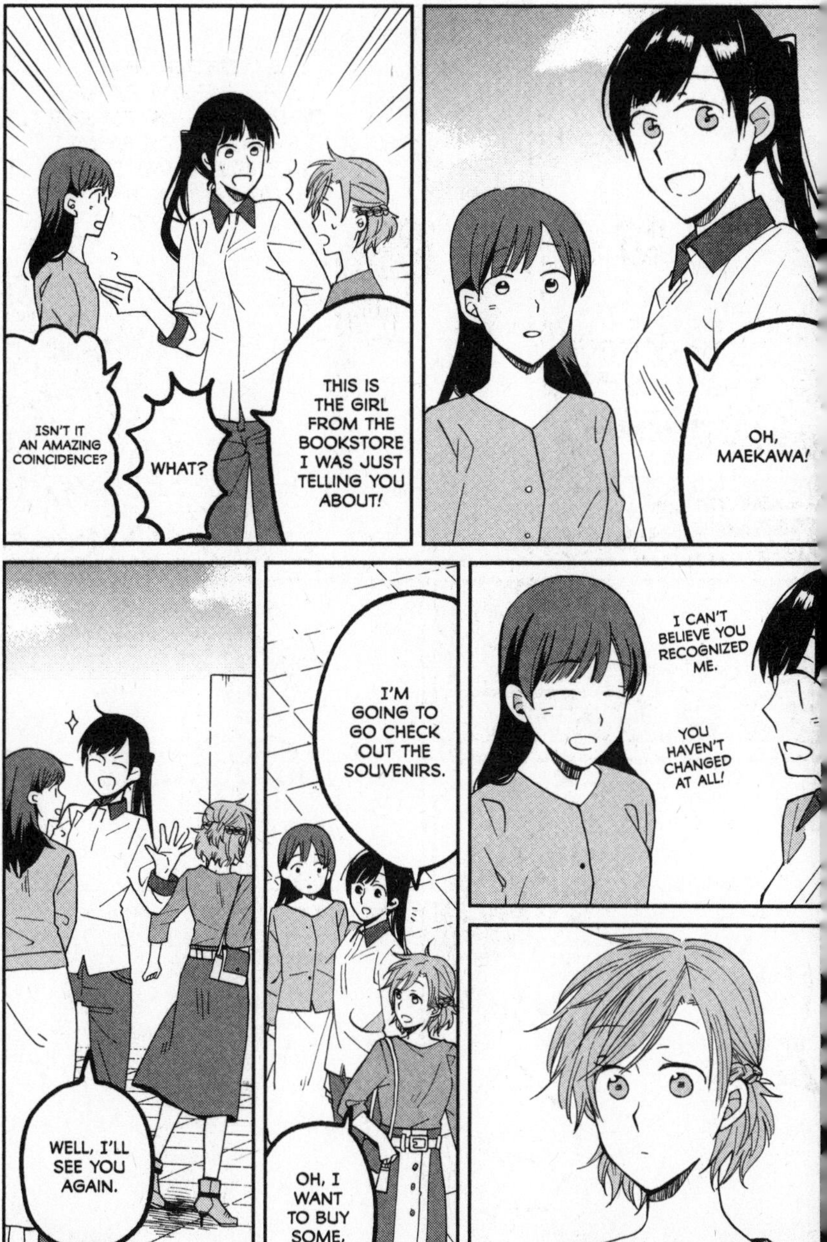
OH, MAEKAWA!
THIS IS THE GIRL FROM THE BOOKSTORE I WAS JUST TELLING YOU ABOUT!
WHAT?
ISN'T IT AN AMAZING COINCIDENCE?
I CAN'T BELIEVE YOU RECOGNIZED ME.
YOU HAVEN'T CHANGED AT ALL!
I'M GOING TO GO CHECK OUT THE SOUVENIRS.
OH, I WANT TO BUY SOME, TOO.
WELL, I'LL SEE YOU AGAIN.

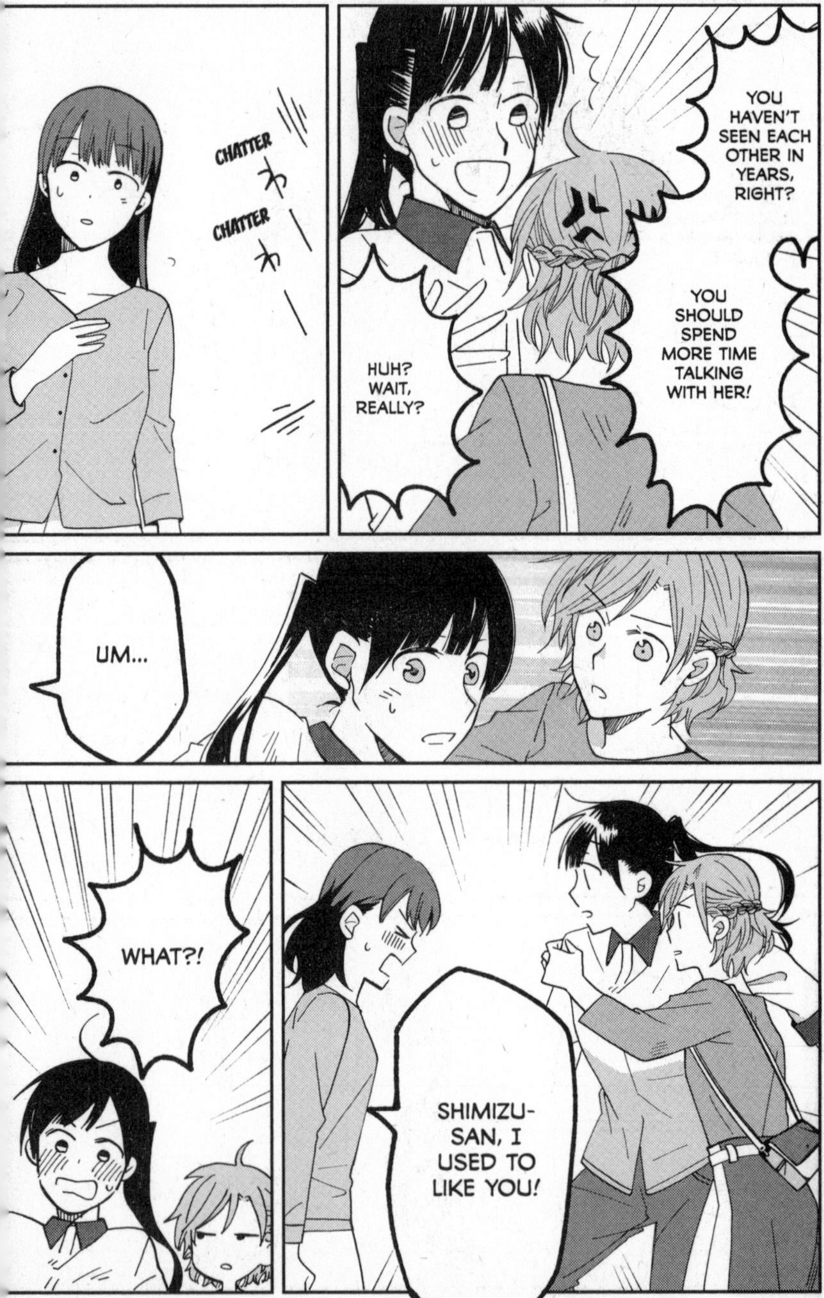
YOU HAVEN'T SEEN EACH OTHER IN YEARS, RIGHT?
YOU SHOULD SPEND MORE TIME TALKING WITH HER!
HUH? WAIT, REALLY?
CHATTER わー
CHATTER わー
UM...
SHIMIZU-SAN, I USED TO LIKE YOU!
WHAT?!

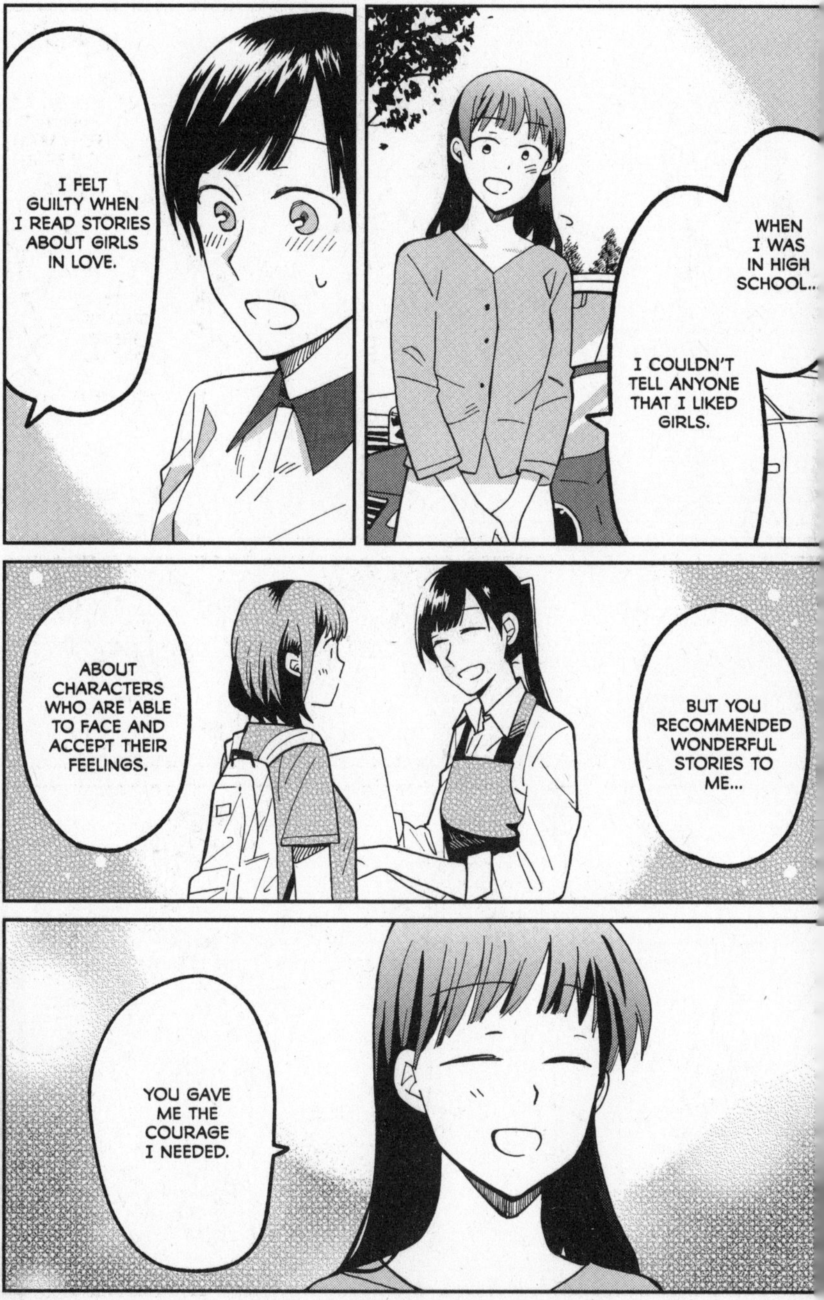
WHEN I WAS IN HIGH SCHOOL...
I COULDN'T TELL ANYONE THAT I LIKED GIRLS.
I FELT GUILTY WHEN I READ STORIES ABOUT GIRLS IN LOVE.
BUT YOU RECOMMENDED WONDERFUL STORIES TO ME...
ABOUT CHARACTERS WHO ARE ABLE TO FACE AND ACCEPT THEIR FEELINGS.
YOU GAVE ME THE COURAGE I NEEDED.

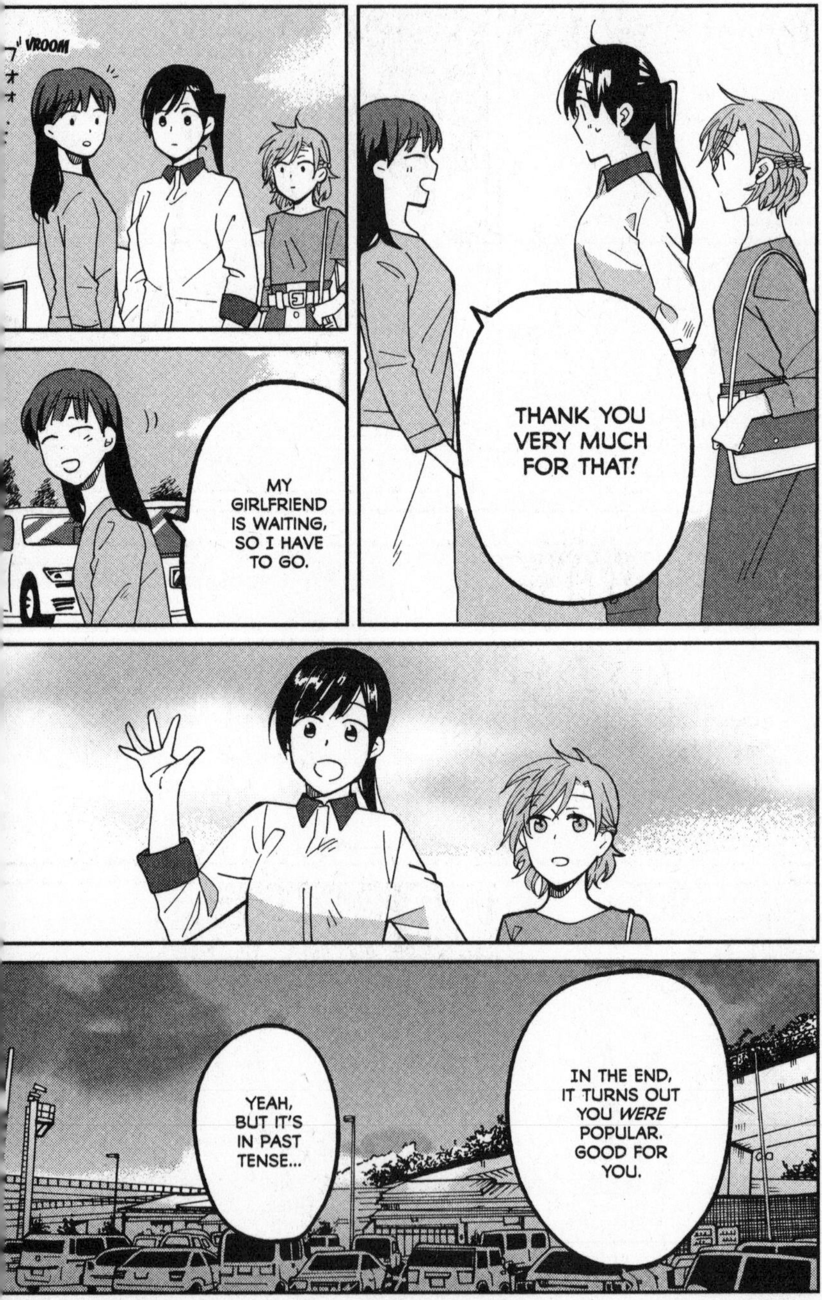
THANK YOU VERY MUCH FOR THAT!
VROOM
MY GIRLFRIEND IS WAITING, SO I HAVE TO GO.
IN THE END, IT TURNS OUT YOU *WERE* POPULAR. GOOD FOR YOU.
YEAH, BUT IT'S IN PAST TENSE...

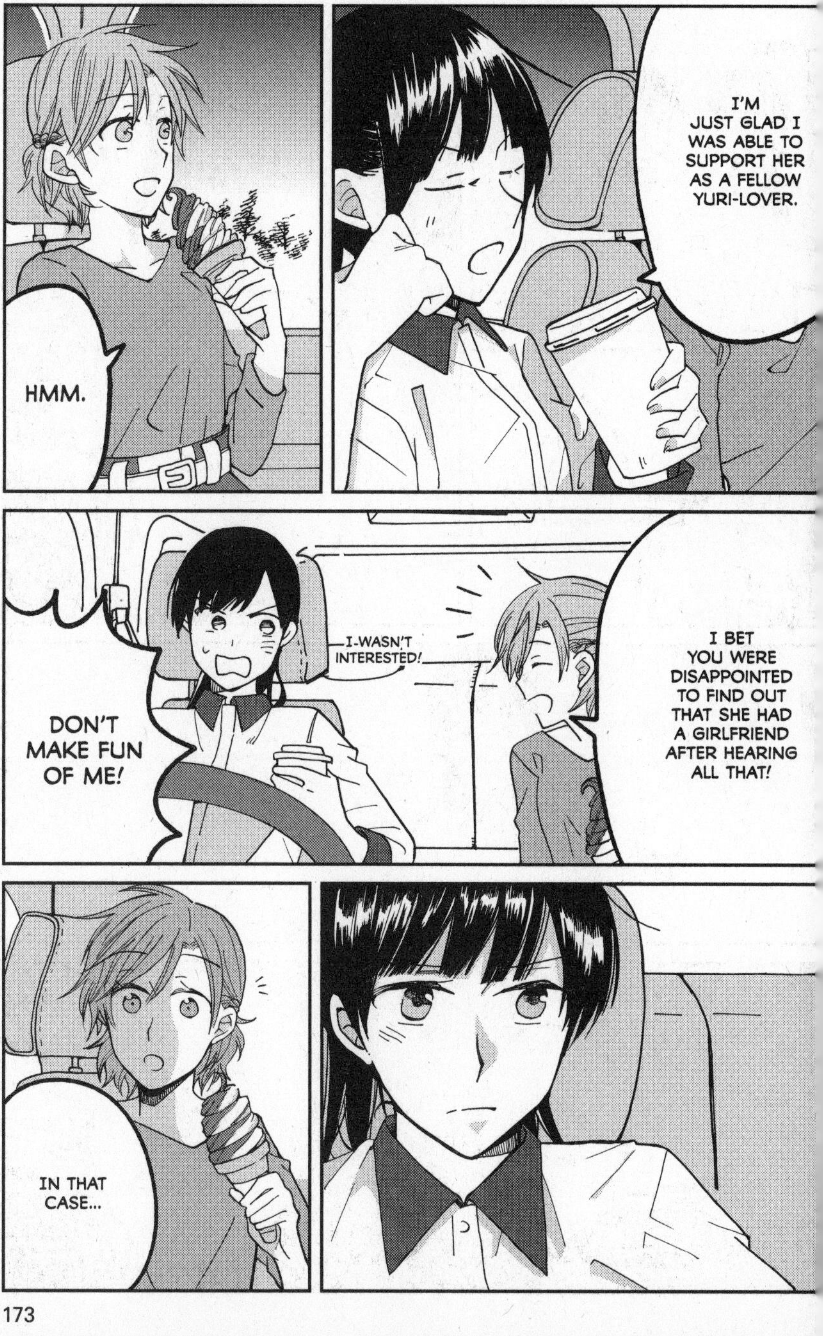
I'M JUST GLAD I WAS ABLE TO SUPPORT HER AS A FELLOW YURI-LOVER.
HMM.
I BET YOU WERE DISAPPOINTED TO FIND OUT THAT SHE HAD A GIRLFRIEND AFTER HEARING ALL THAT!
I-WASN'T INTERESTED!
DON'T MAKE FUN OF ME!
IN THAT CASE...

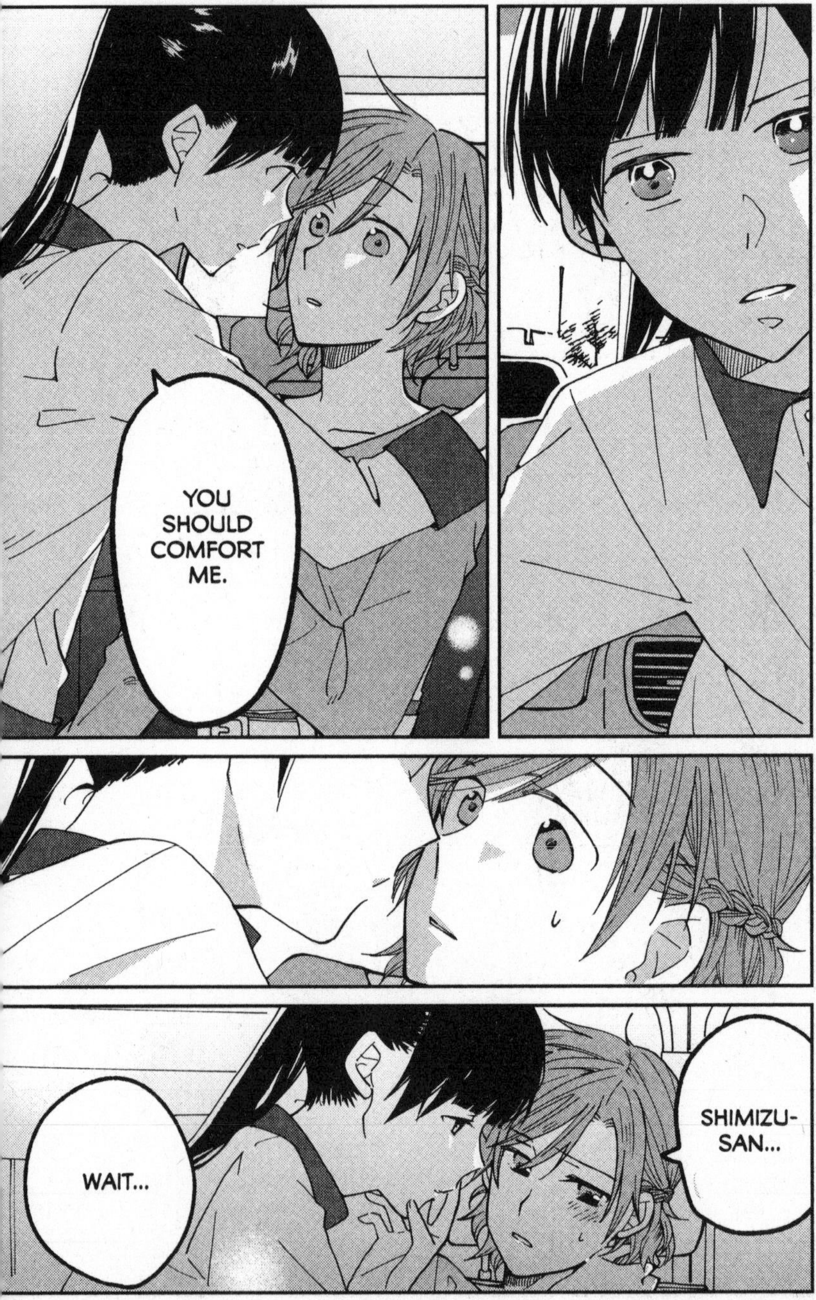
YOU SHOULD COMFORT ME.
SHIMIZU-SAN...
WAIT...

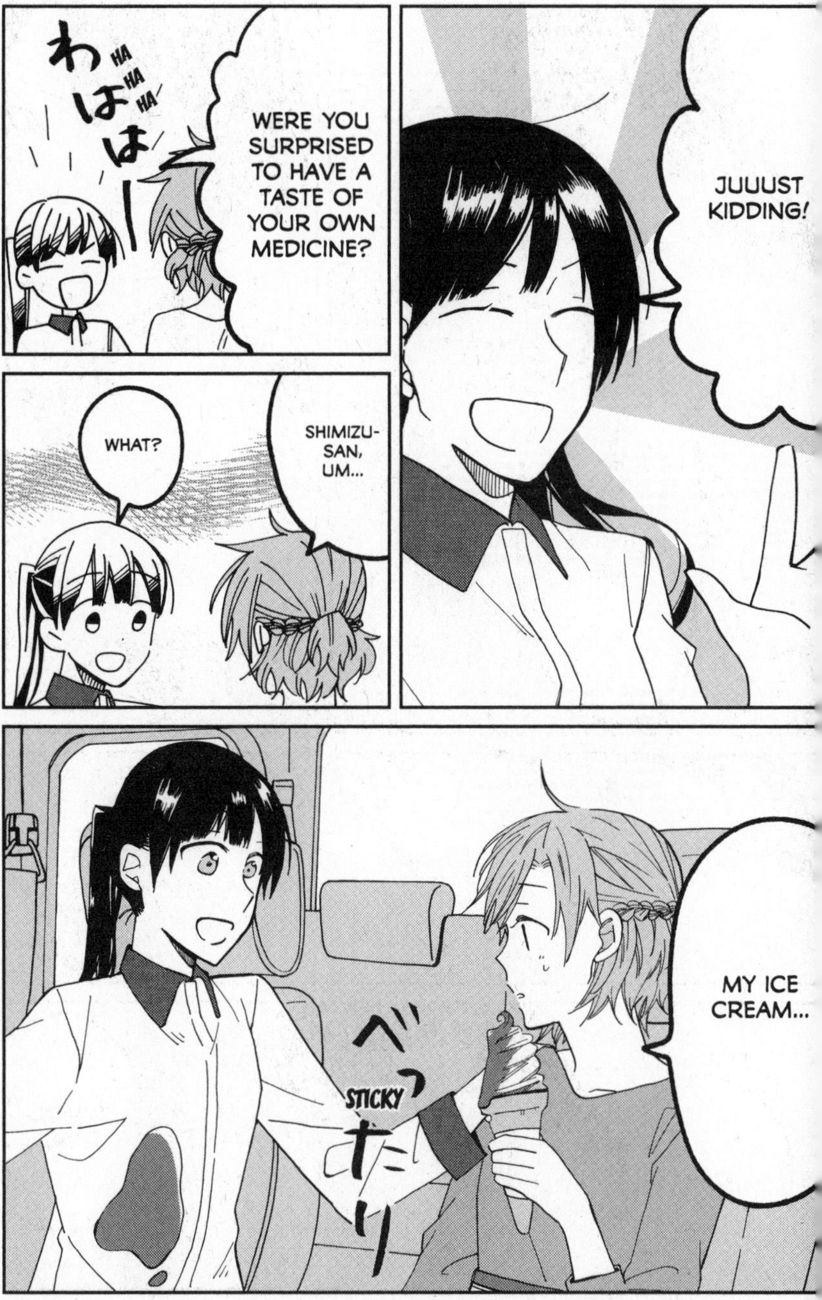
JUUUST KIDDING!
WERE YOU SURPRISED TO HAVE A TASTE OF YOUR OWN MEDICINE?
わはは－
HA HA HA
SHIMIZU-SAN, UM...
WHAT?
MY ICE CREAM...
べっ
STICKY
だー

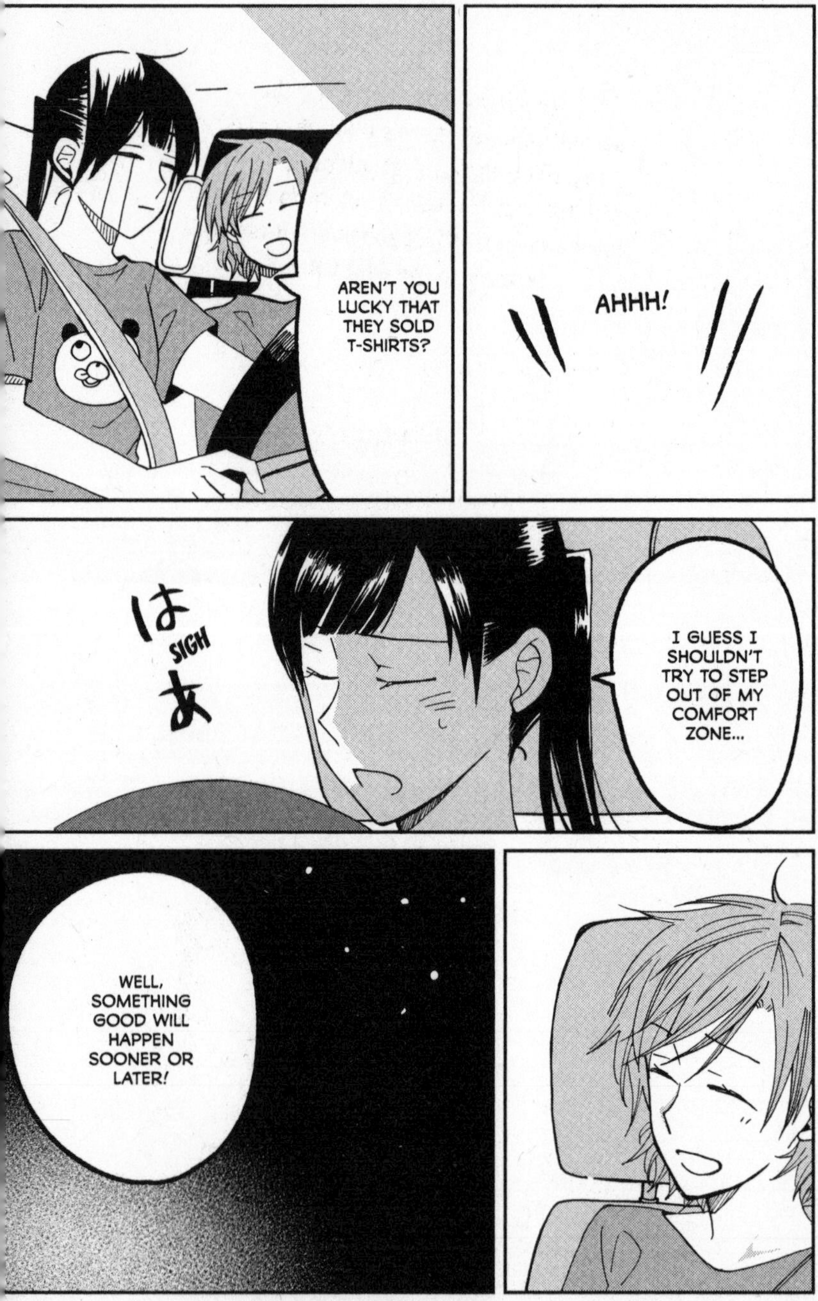
AHHH!
AREN'T YOU LUCKY THAT THEY SOLD T-SHIRTS?
I GUESS I SHOULDN'T TRY TO STEP OUT OF MY COMFORT ZONE...
はあ SIGH
WELL, SOMETHING GOOD WILL HAPPEN SOONER OR LATER!

Thank you for purchasing the second volume! There's a lot of confusion regarding the girls' relationship in this volume, but Maekawa's return to being a manga creator is just starting! Please look forward to the next volume.

Akashi

SPECIAL THANKS

I WOULD LIKE TO THANK MY READERS, EVERYONE WHO HAS SENT ME MESSAGES OF SUPPORT AND COMMENTS REGARDING THEIR OPINIONS, MY EDITOR KOKUBA-SAMA, AND EVERYONE WHO WAS INVOLVED IN THE PUBLICATION OF THIS MANGA FROM THE BOTTOM OF MY HEART!

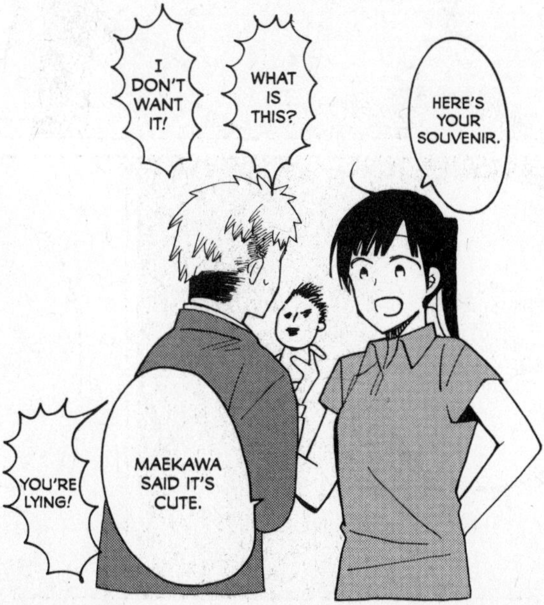

HERE'S YOUR SOUVENIR.
WHAT IS THIS?
I DON'T WANT IT!
MAEKAWA SAID IT'S CUTE.
YOU'RE LYING!

Still Sick

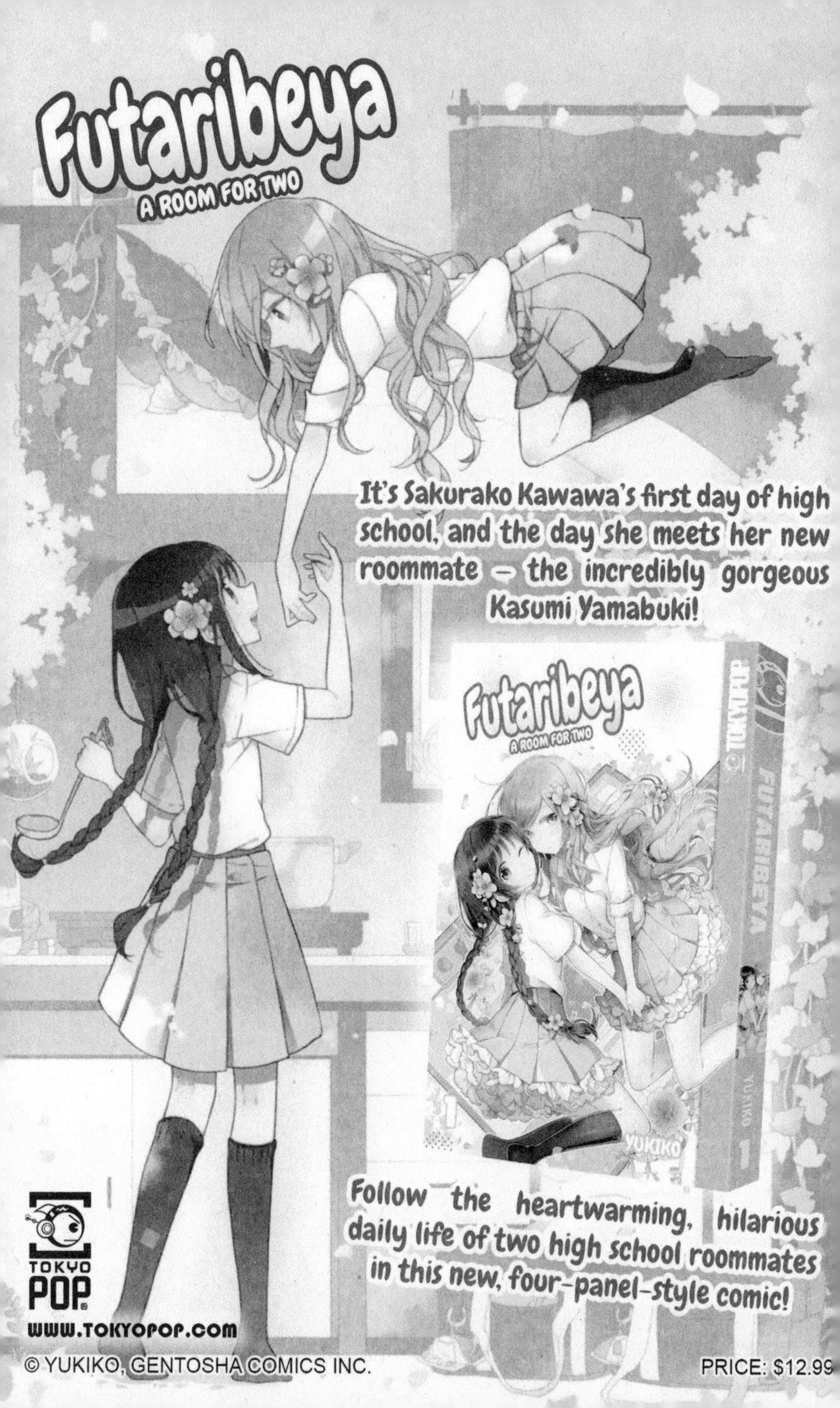
Futaribeya
A ROOM FOR TWO
It's Sakurako Kawawa's first day of high school, and the day she meets her new roommate – the incredibly gorgeous Kasumi Yamabuki!
Futaribeya
A ROOM FOR TWO
TOKYOPOP
FUTARIBEYA
1
YUKIKO
Follow the heartwarming, hilarious daily life of two high school roommates in this new, four-panel-style comic!
TOKYO POP
www.TOKYOPOP.com
© YUKIKO, GENTOSHA COMICS INC.
PRICE: $12.99

BREATH OF FLOWERS
IN THE LANGUAGE OF FLOWERS, EVERY BLOSSOM IS UNIQUE
BEING A TEEN IS HARD. IT'S EVEN HARDER WHEN YOU'RE HIDING A SECRET...
BREATH OF FLOWERS
Story and Art by CALY
1
TOKYOPOP
BREATH OF FLOWERS
CALY
1
TOKYO POP
INTERNATIONAL WOMEN of MANGA
Girls Love / LGBTQ+
© CALY, PIKA EDITION – Editions H2T

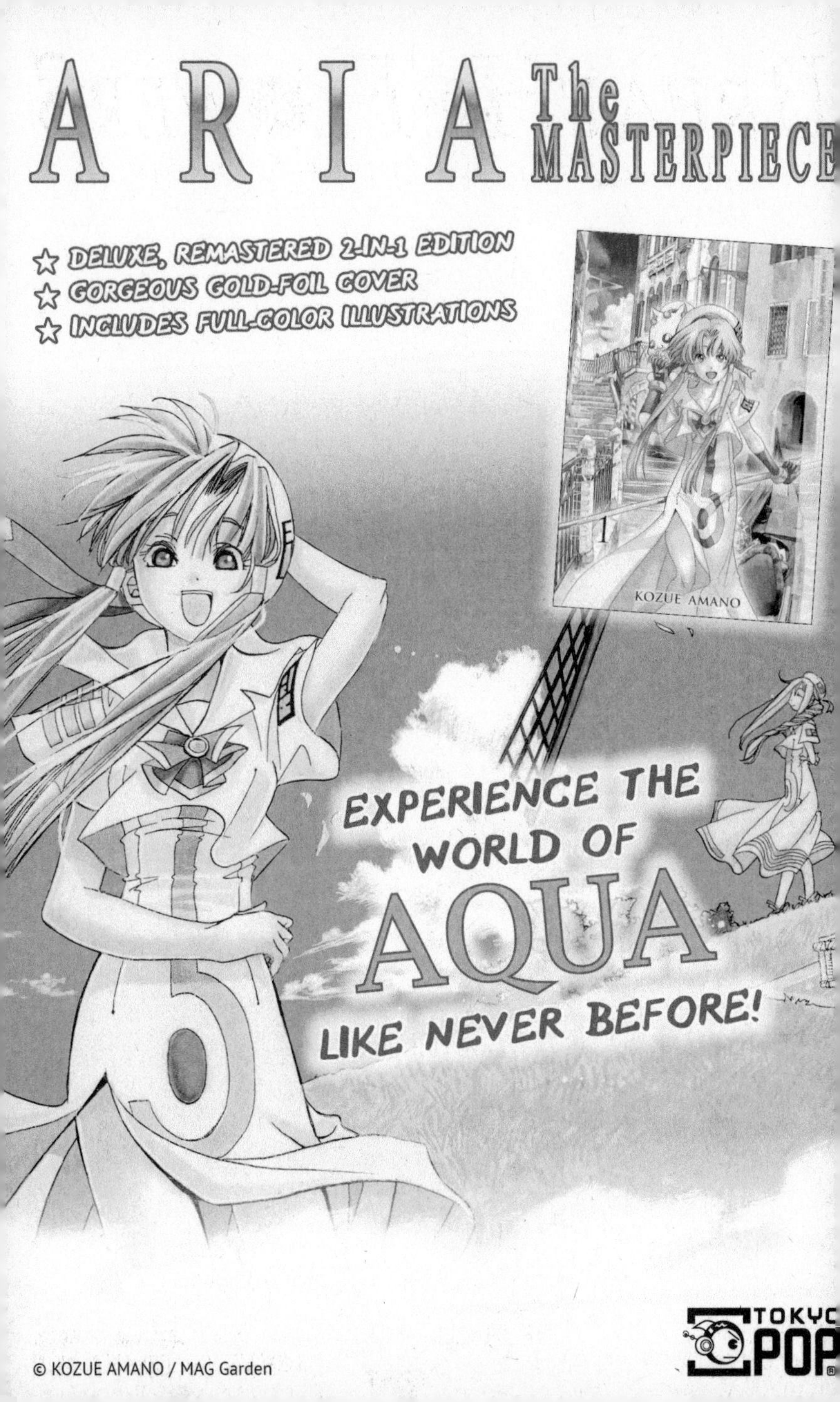
ARIA The MASTERPIECE
☆ DELUXE, REMASTERED 2-IN-1 EDITION
☆ GORGEOUS GOLD-FOIL COVER
☆ INCLUDES FULL-COLOR ILLUSTRATIONS
1
KOZUE AMANO
EXPERIENCE THE WORLD OF
AQUA
LIKE NEVER BEFORE!
© KOZUE AMANO / MAG Garden
TOKYOPOP

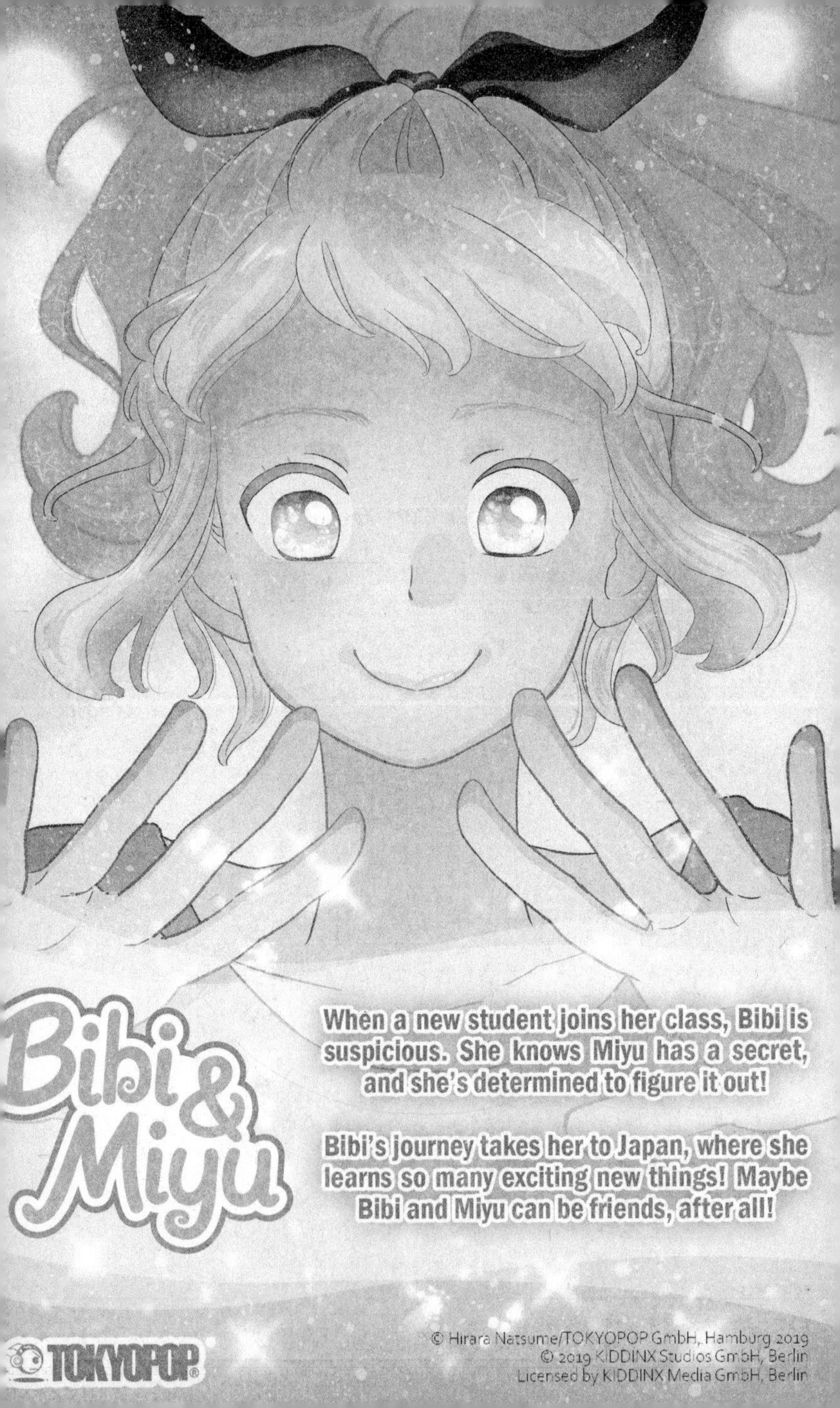
Bibi & Miyu
When a new student joins her class, Bibi is suspicious. She knows Miyu has a secret, and she's determined to figure it out!
Bibi's journey takes her to Japan, where she learns so many exciting new things! Maybe Bibi and Miyu can be friends, after all!
TOKYOPOP®
© Hirara Natsume/TOKYOPOP GmbH, Hamburg 2019
© 2019 KIDDINX Studios GmbH, Berlin
Licensed by KIDDINX Media GmbH, Berlin

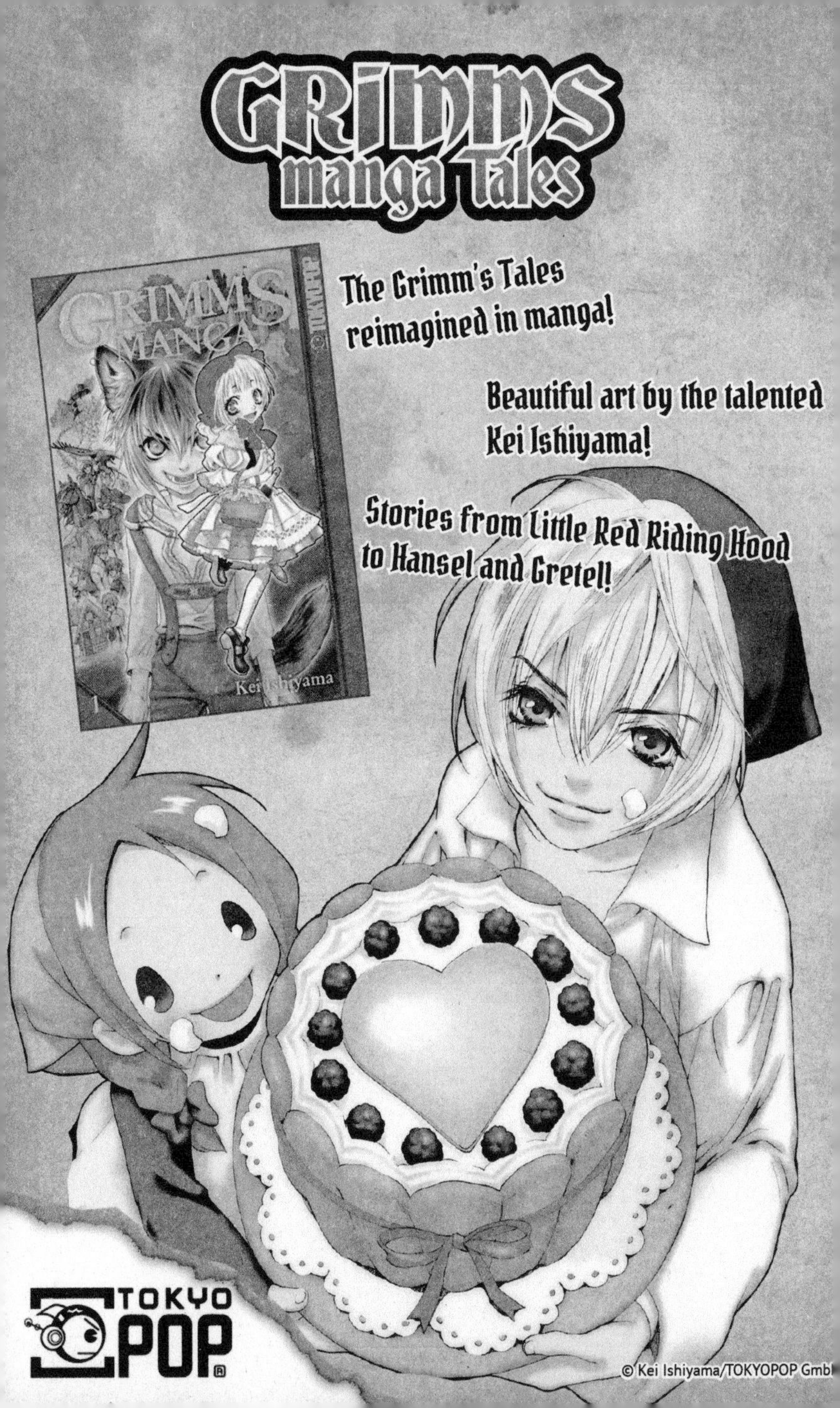
GRIMMS manga Tales
GRIMM'S MANGA
TOKYOPOP
Kei Ishiyama
1
The Grimm's Tales reimagined in manga!
Beautiful art by the talented Kei Ishiyama!
Stories from Little Red Riding Hood to Hansel and Gretel!
TOKYO POP
© Kei Ishiyama/TOKYOPOP GmbH

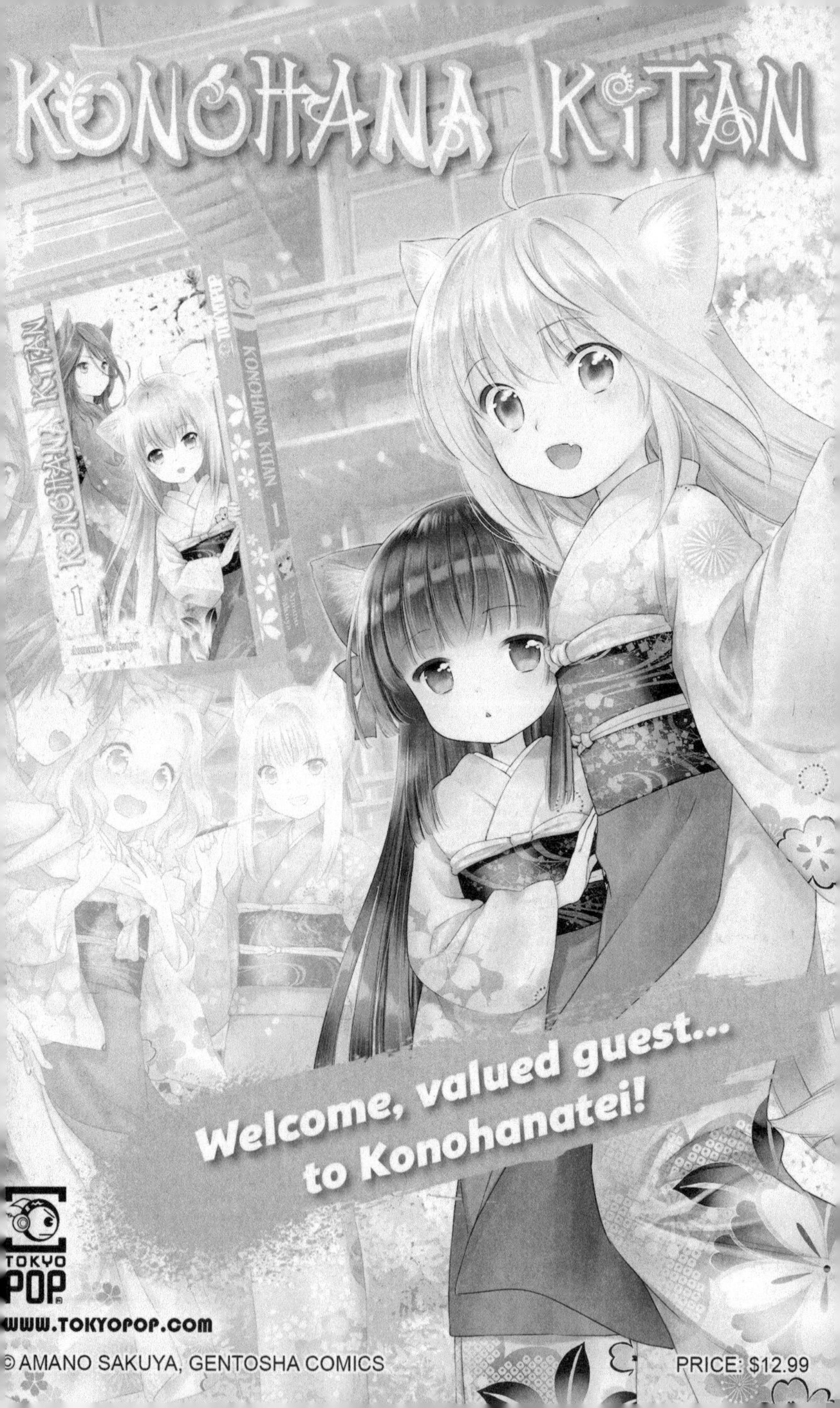
KONOHANA KITAN
KONOHANA KITAN 1
KONOHANA KITAN 1
Welcome, valued guest...
to Konohanatei!
TOKYO POP
WWW.TOKYOPOP.COM
© AMANO SAKUYA, GENTOSHA COMICS
PRICE: $12.99

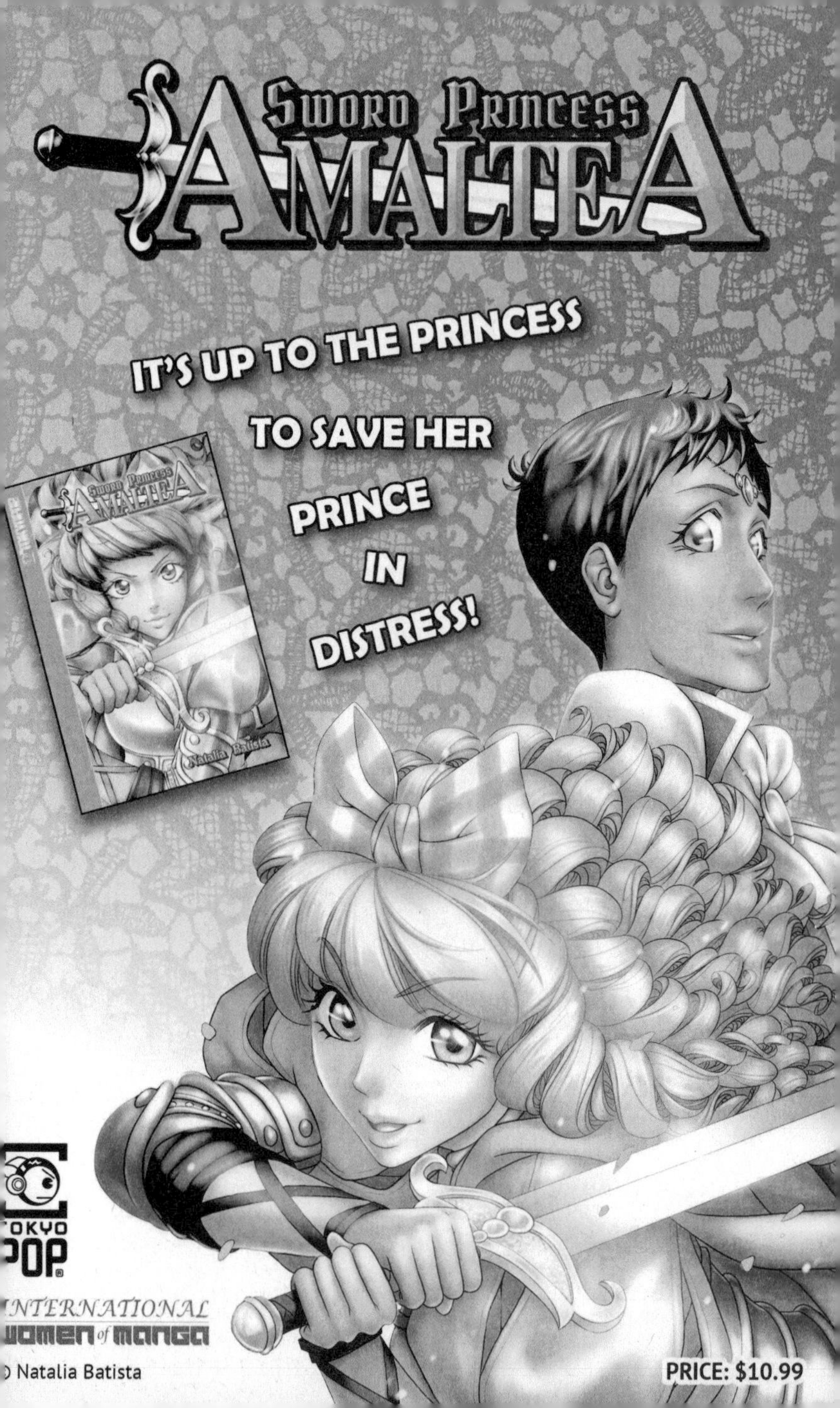

Sword Princess Amaltea
IT'S UP TO THE PRINCESS
TO SAVE HER
PRINCE
IN
DISTRESS!
Sword Princess Amaltea
Natalia Batista
TOKYOPOP
INTERNATIONAL
women of manga
© Natalia Batista
PRICE: $10.99

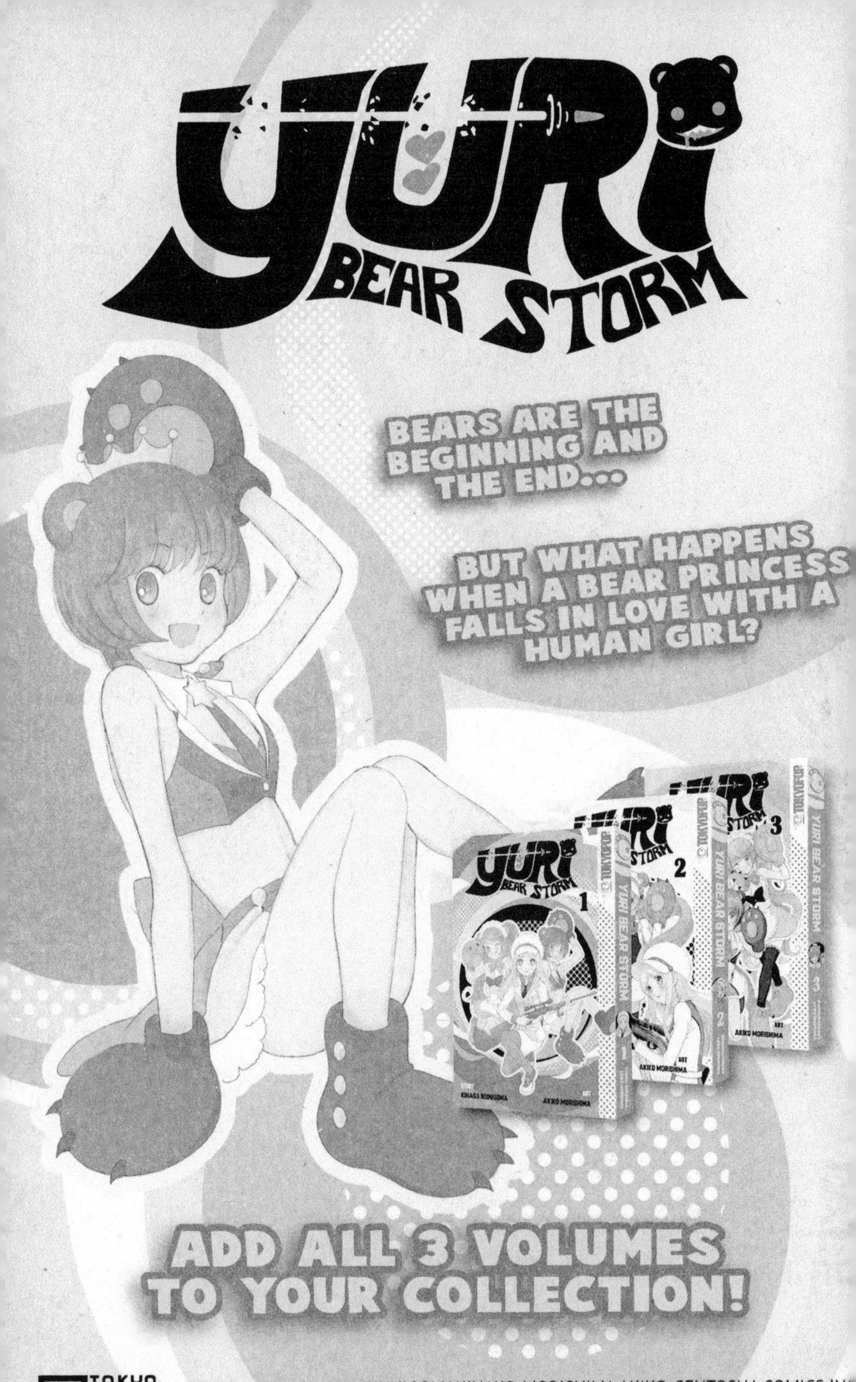
YURI BEAR STORM
BEARS ARE THE BEGINNING AND THE END...
BUT WHAT HAPPENS WHEN A BEAR PRINCESS FALLS IN LOVE WITH A HUMAN GIRL?
YURI BEAR STORM 1
YURI BEAR STORM 2
YURI BEAR STORM 3
ADD ALL 3 VOLUMES TO YOUR COLLECTION!

STAR COLLECTOR

By Anna B. & Sophie Schönhammer

A ROMANCE WRITTEN IN THE STARS!

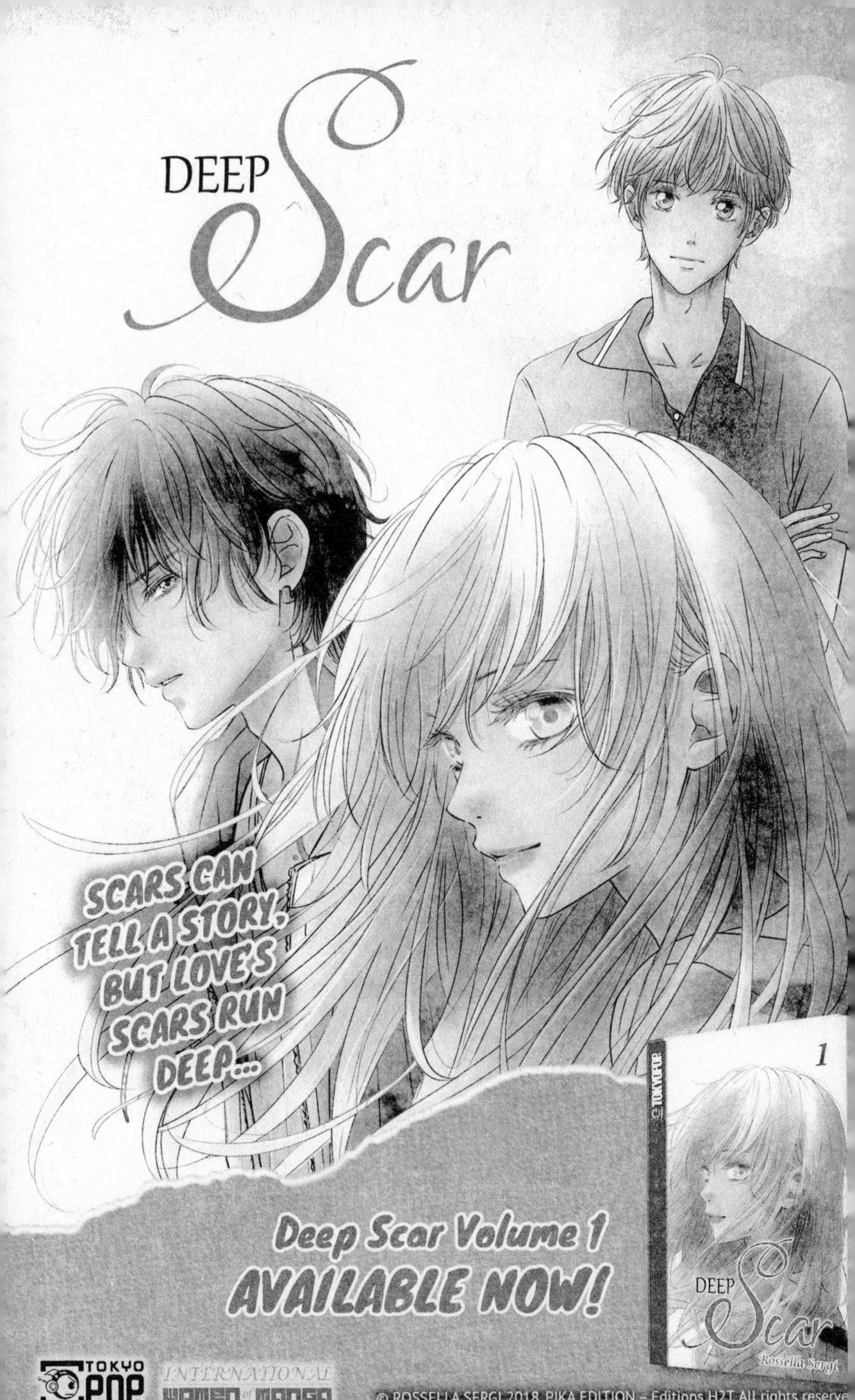
DEEP Scar
SCARS CAN TELL A STORY, BUT LOVE'S SCARS RUN DEEP...
Deep Scar Volume 1
AVAILABLE NOW!
1
TOKYOPOP
DEEP Scar
Rossella Sergi
TOKYO POP
INTERNATIONAL WOMEN of MANGA

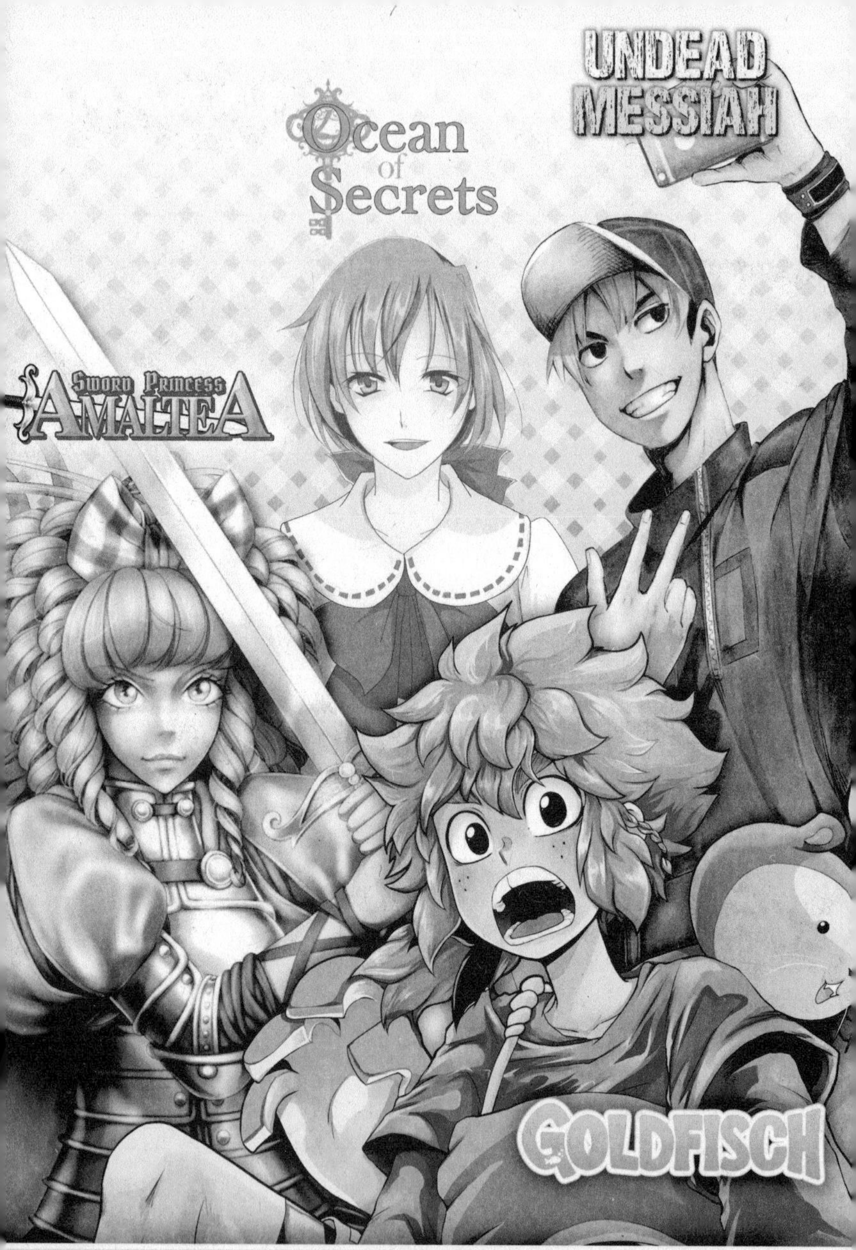
UNDEAD MESSIAH
Ocean of Secrets
SWORD PRINCESS AMALTEA
GOLDFISCH

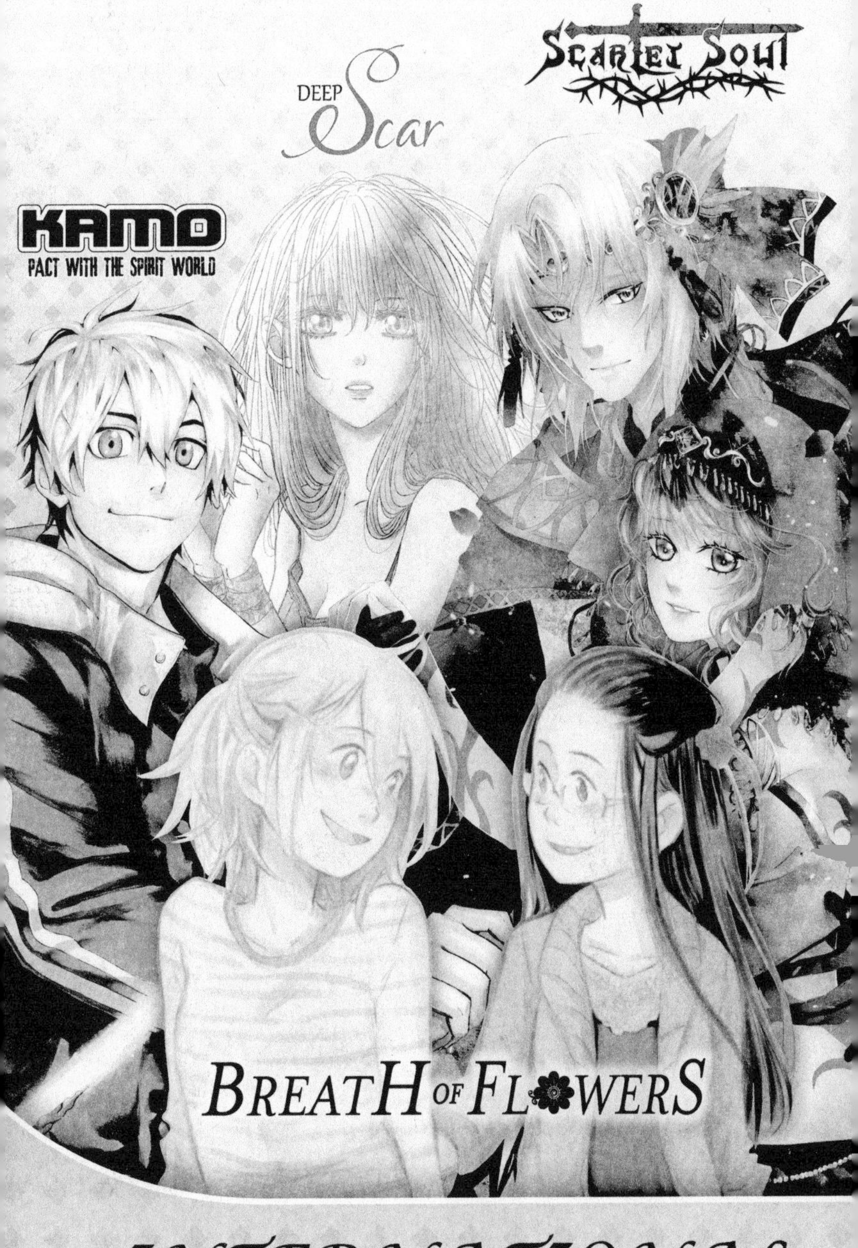
SCARLET SOUL
DEEP Scar
KAMO
PACT WITH THE SPIRIT WORLD
BREATH OF FLOWERS

INTERNATIONAL
WOMEN of MANGA

Still Sick Volume 2
Akashi

Editor - Lena Atanassova
Marketing Associate - Kae Winters
Technology and Digital Media Assistant - Phillip Hong
Translator - Katie Kimura
Copy Editor - Massiel Gutierrez
QC - Daichi Nemoto
Graphic Designer - Phillip Hong
Retouching and Lettering - Vibrraant Publishing Studio
Editor-in-Chief & Publisher - Stu Levy

A **TOKYOPOP**® Manga

TOKYOPOP and 🔘 are trademarks or registered trademarks of TOKYOPOP Inc.

TOKYOPOP
5200 W Century Blvd
Suite 705
Los Angeles, CA 90045 USA

E-mail: info@TOKYOPOP.com
Come visit us online at www.TOKYOPOP.com

f www.facebook.com/TOKYOPOP
🐦 www.twitter.com/TOKYOPOP
📌 www.pinterest.com/TOKYOPOP
📷 www.instagram.com/TOKYOPOP

ISBN: 978-1-4278-6235-8
First TOKYOPOP Printing: March 2020
10 9 8 7 6 5 4 3 2 1
Printed in CANADA

ST...

THIS IS THE BACK OF THE BOOK!

How do you read manga-style? It's simple! Let's practice -- just start in the top right panel and follow the numbers below!

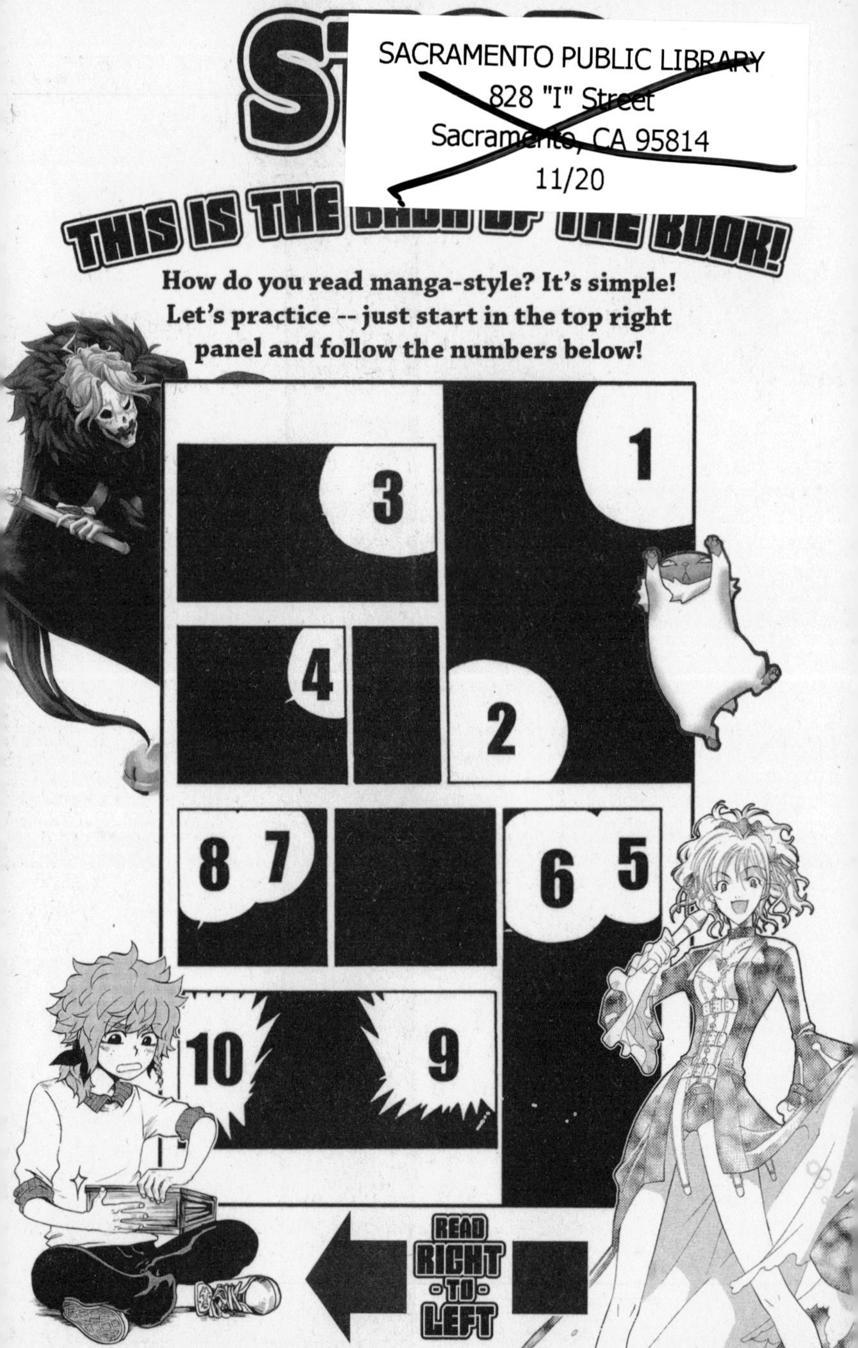
1
2
3
4
5
6
7
8
9
10
READ
RIGHT
-TO-
LEFT

Crimson from ***Kamo*** / Fairy Cat from ***Grimms Manga Tales***
Morrey from ***Goldfisch*** / Princess Ai from ***Princess Ai***